EMINENT
OUTLAWS

EMINENT OUTLAWS

OUTLAWS

THE GAY WRITERS
WHO CHANGED AMERICA

CHRISTOPHER BRAM

TWELVE

NEW YORK   BOSTON

Twelve
Hachette Book Group
237 Park Avenue
New York, NY 10017

www.HachetteBookGroup.com

Twelve is an imprint of Grand Central Publishing.
The Twelve name and logo are trademarks of Hachette Book Group, Inc.

The Hachette Speakers Bureau provides a wide range of authors for speaking events.
To find out more, go to www.hachettespeakersbureau.com
or call (866) 376-6591.

The publisher is not responsible for websites (or their content) that
are not owned by the publisher.

Printed in the United States of America

First Edition: February 2012
10 9 8 7 6 5 4 3 2 1

Library of Congress Cataloging-in-Publication Data

Bram, Christopher.
Eminent outlaws : the gay writers who changed America / Christopher Bram. — 1st ed.
    p. cm.
  ISBN 978-0-446-56313-0
  1. Gays' writings, American—History and criticism.   2. Authors, American—20th
century.   3. Gay authors—United States.   I. Title.
  PS153.G38B73 2012
  810.9'9206640904—dc23
                                                                      2011029910

To Draper

Contents

Part V: The Nineties and After

Introduction

The gay revolution began as a literary revolution.

Before World War II, homosexuality was a dirty secret that was almost never written about and rarely discussed. Suddenly, after the war, a handful of homosexual writers boldly used their personal experience in their work. They were surprisingly open at first, then grew more circumspect after being attacked by critics and journalists. But they were followed by other writers who built on what they had initiated. The world was changing and the new authors could be more open; their openness produced further change. A third set of writers took even greater liberties, treating their sexuality as equal to straight sexuality, no better and no worse.

This book is the history of fifty years of change shaped by a relay race of novelists, playwrights, and poets—men who were first treated as outlaws but are now seen as pioneers and even founding fathers. Their writing was the catalyst for a social shift as deep and unexpected as what was achieved by the civil rights and women's movements.

Beginning with figures as different as Gore Vidal, Allen Ginsberg, and James Baldwin, these men are wonderful characters in their own right: smart, articulate, energetic, ambitious, stubborn, and even brave. They were often brilliantly funny. They were never boring. They could also be competitive, combative, self-destructive, and confused. Their lives were not always exemplary. A career in the arts can make anyone crazy ("We Poets in our youth begin in gladness," wrote William Wordsworth, "But thereof come in the end despondency and madness"), but to tell gay stories in the Fifties and Sixties (and later, too) guaranteed further hardship. Not only was it difficult just to get published or produced, but success often led to literary attacks that ran from brutal insult to icy condescension.

This is a collection of war stories, but it's also a collection of love stories.

There are intense friendships between the writers themselves. There is also a wide variety of sex and romance. These were passionate men who used desire in different ways, ranging from the fiercely unromantic to the affectionate and vulnerable. Almost all lived in couples at one time or another, but only a few were monogamous. Gay couples often do openly what many straight couples do in secret. Or, as social critic Michael Bronski puts it, "Gay people are just like straight people. But straight people lie about who they really are."

This book is about gay male writers and not lesbian writers. I chose this focus reluctantly, but I needed to simplify an already complicated story. Also, lesbian literature has its own dynamic and history. It needs its own historian.

The story of these men has never been told as a single narrative before, which is surprising. Contemporary critics often complain that literature is no longer culturally important, yet it played a huge role in the making of modern gay life. Teachers used to tell us that only bad art is political ("Thou shalt not...commit/A social science," wrote W. H. Auden), but I believe that good art can lay the groundwork for social change. Ernest Hemingway, of all people, indicated why when he said a writer must learn to recognize "what you really felt, rather than what you were supposed to feel, and had been taught to feel." Which is what all gay people, not just writers, must learn before they can create their own lives. This book is about a few authors who decided to write about what they really felt, even when it made their working life more difficult.

A few words about words: I sometimes use *gay* to describe books and people in times when the word was not yet fully in use. It was preferable to the words that were common then, such as *pervert, homo, pansy,* and *faggot.* People might argue that a man who called himself a pansy in 1950 had a different identity from one who called himself queer in 1995. But gay people today, no matter what they call themselves, occupy a very broad spectrum of desires, personas, and self-definitions. The names are only approximations, anyway.

I am primarily a novelist, a gay novelist, but I deliberately left myself out of this story. It would've been impossible to talk about my own work without sounding self-serving. However, my own books can't help casting a shadow. I won't pretend to be objective here: work that I admire is often work that influenced me or that I feel a kinship with.

This is not an all-inclusive, definitive literary history. I do not include everyone of value or importance. Nor am I putting together a canon of must-read writers. I am writing a large-scale cultural narrative, and I include chiefly those authors who help me tell that story—and who offer the liveliest tales.

My models were literary histories that mix criticism with biography, social history, good gossip, and a strong point of view. My favorite works in this line include *Patriotic Gore* by Edmund Wilson, *Exile's Return* by Malcolm Cowley, and *The Great War and Modern Memory* by Paul Fussell. Enjoyable in themselves, these books always leave me eager to read or reread a half-dozen other books when I am done. I hope this history has the same effect on its readers.

I

Into the Fifties

America when will you be angelic?
When will you take off your clothes?
—Allen Ginsberg

1. Innocence

—␣vw—␣

The second atom bomb fell on Nagasaki, the war ended, and nineteen-year-old Eugene Gore Vidal came home to New York. The boyish prep school graduate had served as a warrant officer on an army ship in the Aleutians, a sort of seagoing sergeant. He was now stationed out on Long Island before being discharged. He brought with him a manuscript he had begun writing in training camp, a Hemingway-like novel titled *Williwaw* about shipboard life.

He spent his weekends in the city, staying in the back bedroom of his father and stepmother's huge apartment on Fifth Avenue, working on the novel during the day and visiting Times Square at night. There he met other men in uniform in the male-only half of the busy bar at the Astor Hotel or in the movie theaters crowded along Forty-second Street. He would take his new acquaintances to a nearby bathhouse or hotel for sex. Young Vidal assumed he would eventually marry, but now he only wanted to make up for all the fun he had missed in boarding school and the army. He was not interested in love. He would later insist that the only man he ever loved was a classmate at St. Albans, Jimmie Trimble, who died on Iwo Jima.

His blind grandfather, Senator T. P. Gore of Oklahoma, spoke of setting him up in New Mexico after college in a political career. The grandson wasn't particularly interested in college, however, and thought there'd be plenty of time for politics later. His father, Eugene Vidal Sr., an airline pioneer who had been on the cover of *Time*, did not push him in any particular direction. The son soon dropped his first name to avoid being confused with his father.

He sold his novel to Dutton before the end of 1945. The editorial staff liked the personable, confident fellow and made him a part-time editor. He started work on a new novel and began ballet lessons to remedy the rheumatoid arthritis developed after frostbite in the Aleutians. He prowled the city for literary events as well as for sex. Meeting the scholar/translator Kimon Friar at the Astor Hotel Bar, he decided Friar wasn't his type but went to hear him lecture at the Poetry Center of the 92nd Street Y. There he met an exotic woman with a foreign accent, an Elizabethan hat, and an opera cape: Anaïs Nin. She was already famous for the diaries that she showed friends and hoped to publish one day. She had left Paris with her husband, Hugo, at the start of the war and had recently broken with her lover, Henry Miller, deciding he was too old. Nin herself was forty-two.

Vidal visited her regularly at her fifth-floor walk-up on West Thirteenth Street in Greenwich Village, across the street from the Food Trades Vocational High School, a building that forty years later housed the Lesbian and Gay Community Services Center. The apartment was an old-fashioned studio with a skylight an artist friend painted with the signs of the zodiac. Nin surrounded herself with young male artists, including poet Robert Duncan, already author of "The Homosexual in Society" published in 1944 in *Politics* magazine, and a poetry-writing undergraduate from Amherst, James Merrill (who was briefly Kimon Friar's boyfriend). She loved their attention, but her real love was for her career. She coaxed Vidal into getting her a two-book contract at Dutton. When her next book, *Ladders to Fire*, received a bad review in the *New York Times*, Vidal and Merrill wrote letters to the editor protesting its unfairness. (Both letters appear to have been written on the same typewriter—Nin's.) Nin was a little in love with Vidal, or rather, she loved the idea of Vidal being in love with her. They seem to have gone to bed together, but it's unclear if they actually had sex.

It was at a Nin party that Vidal first met a petite, effeminate Southerner with the voice of a strangled child. "How does it feel to be an infant terrible?" asked Truman Capote, badly mangling the French phrase. He looked as if he were twelve, but he was actually a year older than Vidal. He had spent part of his childhood in Alabama before joining his mother in Westchester and attending high school there. He was briefly a copy boy at the *New Yorker*. He had begun to publish short stories in magazines like *Mademoiselle*, starting with an elegantly written ghost story, "Miriam." He had just signed a book contract with Random House. (Nin in her diary describes Capote at this time as "painfully timid…he seemed fragile and easily wounded." It's hardly the image of him we have now, but perhaps Nin saw something invisible to others.) Vidal and Capote had much in common: Southern roots, no college, and impossible mothers both named Nina. But Capote made Vidal uneasy. Despite ballet class, Vidal was a stiff, somewhat patrician fellow who could drop an occasional camp phrase only among friends. He found Capote much too flamboyant, too bent on using homosexuality to draw attention to himself. And he recognized a rival. Nevertheless, the two young men were friendly enough during the first year they knew each other, Vidal going so far as to take Capote with him to the Everard Baths. It's amusing to picture the pair wandering the mildewed corridors with towels around their waists, Capote talking incessantly. He loved to tell stories about himself and others, and he didn't care if the stories were true or not. He was never very interested in sex with strangers. He was delighted that night to meet a Southern friend who'd seen the out-of-town tryouts of *Private Lives* with Tallulah Bankhead. Vidal happily ditched the two and went off to get laid.

The following summer, while at Yaddo, Capote met his first real love, Newton Arvin, a short, bald English professor from Smith College. Arvin wasn't anyone's physical ideal, but he adored Capote, read his prose, recommended books to him, and encouraged his writing. The two men were devoted to each other—for a while.

One afternoon in the oak-paneled Gramercy Park Tavern near the Dutton offices, Vidal began to tell a fellow editor about the homosexual men he had been "noticing" in New York. The editor, who knew nothing about Vidal's private life, suggested he write about this strange new world in his next book.

Vidal worked quickly in his early years, even though he wrote in longhand in pencil. He felt distracted in New York, however, and moved down to Guatemala for a few months in 1947. He finished his new novel, *The City and the Pillar*, before his second book, *In a Yellow Wood*, had come out. He showed the manuscript to Nin when she visited Guatemala. She hated it. She said she disapproved of its flat style but she could not have been happy with the character named Maria Verlaine, an exotic woman with a foreign accent who surrounds herself with homosexual men and seduces the gay hero. "I think you are everything, man, woman, and child," says Maria. "'I could kiss you,' he said, and he did. He kissed the Death Goddess."

Vidal dedicated the book to "J.T."—Jimmie Trimble.

In June, *Life* magazine ran a photo spread, "Young U.S. Writers." A smallish photo of Vidal accompanied smallish photos of Jean Stafford and others, but the front photo, four times as big as the rest, was of a debonair Capote, who had not yet published his first book.

Dutton was both nervous and excited about Vidal's new novel. They didn't want to publish it too close to his second book, for fear they'd glut the market with Vidal. The author was nervous, too, but his chief worry was that other writers would scoop him on this subject. Sure enough, that fall 1947, *The Gallery* by John Horne Burns was published with its strong chapter about a gay bar in Naples, followed by *End as a Man* by Calder Willingham, about sadosexual doings in a Southern military academy like the Citadel. The topic was in the postwar air.

In the first week of January 1948, a curious medical book appeared in stores, *Sexual Behavior in the Human Male* by Alfred Kinsey, Clyde Martin, and Wardell Pomeroy. Soon known as simply "the Kinsey Report," the volume was mostly charts and tables representing a ten-year-long survey. Yet the book instantly attracted attention with its evidence of how much sex and how many different kinds were actually taking place in the United States. It sold 225,000 copies by the end of the year, almost as many as *Crusade in Europe* by Dwight D. Eisenhower.

A few days after the Kinsey Report appeared, *The City and the Pillar* by Gore Vidal came out. One week after that saw the publication of *Other Voices, Other Rooms* by Truman Capote.

A new age seemed to have begun.

The two novels could not have been more different. *The City and the Pillar* is written in a direct, sometimes pulpy prose that Vidal later claimed was modeled on James T. Farrell but is actually closer to the drugstore paperbacks of the era. Seventeen years later Vidal revised the book, changing the language a little and the ending a lot and making the overall meaning clearer. *City* tells the tale of Jim Willard, a teenager who has sex with his best friend, Bob Ford, on a campout after graduation from high school. Jim journeys through life, meeting other men and having sex with them but remaining in love with Bob. He meets a heartless writer like an early version of Vidal and a woman like Nin and goes with them to Guatemala. Then the war comes and Jim joins the merchant marine. After the war Jim meets Bob again, but Bob angrily rejects him. "'You're a queer,' he said, 'you're nothing but a damned queer!'" In a fit of rage Jim murders Bob. The ending is as purple as the Biblical title (which refers to Lot's wife becoming a pillar of salt when she looks back at the city of Sodom). Yet the rest of the novel is often tartly matter-of-fact, offering sharp snapshots of American gay life in Hollywood and New York in the 1940s.

The prose of *Other Voices* is very different, colorful yet precise, a high Southern rhetoric that's been trimmed and tamed. It can be florid in patches, especially in the last chapters where it turns hallucinogenic, yet it's always fresh and readable. For example, here's the boy protagonist, Joel, riding in a mule-drawn wagon late at night, the driver fast asleep:

> He listened content and untroubled to the remote, singing-saw noise of night insects.
>
> Then presently the music of a childish duet came carrying over the sounds of the lonesome countryside: "What then does the robin do, poor thing…" Like specters he saw them hurrying in the moonshine along the road's weedy edge. Two girls. One walked with easy grace, but the other moved as jerky and quick as a boy…

Soon the girls are walking alongside the wagon, a pair of twins named Idabel and Florabel. The three children sing together: "their voices pealed clear and sweet, for all three were sopranos….Then a cloud crossed over the moon and in the black the singing ended."

This is the story of Joel Knox, a precocious child of thirteen who, after the death of his mother, is sent to live with the father he's never met in Skully's Landing, a small hamlet in Alabama. Not much happens there, but the mood and sense of place and lovely prose are enough to carry the reader. The book suggests a children's story at first, a fairy tale set in a realistic 1930s South. But this rural life is hardly pastoral or wholesome. The father is crippled and silent. Joel's only companions are the black servants, Jesus Fever and his daughter Zoo, the twins Idabel and Florabel, a spooky stepmother, Miss Amy, and the effete yet genial Cousin Randolph. The fairy tale grows darker and more sinister as it progresses—as do the longer tales of Hans Christian Andersen. Randolph tells Joel the story of Joel's mother and father and Randolph's love for a Mexican boxer. When relatives from New Orleans come to fetch Joel, Miss Amy sends them away without letting Joel know they've been there. The boy is left exiled in the dream world of Skully's Landing.

The book was dedicated to Newton Arvin.

Readers nowadays find *Other Voices* elusive and mysterious, but when it was published people projected one particular meaning onto the mystery, chiefly because of the jacket photo of the author. This is the famous Harold Halma shot of young Capote supine on a sofa, facing the camera with his baby bangs and seductive gaze. "Honey...*you* stay away from *him*," a young wife was overheard telling her husband in a coffee shop in Cambridge. The photo made some readers think this novel could only be about one subject: its author's homosexuality. A magazine editor told friends the book was "the faggots' *Huckleberry Finn*."

Reviewers who ignored the sexual implications tended to give the book good reviews. "A short novel which is as dazzling a phenomenon as has burst on the literary scene in the last ten years," said the *Chicago Tribune*. The sexual critics almost all leaped to negative conclusions. "The book is immature and its theme is calculated to make the flesh crawl," said *Time* magazine. "The distasteful trappings of its homosexual theme overhang it like Spanish moss." Carlos Baker, future biographer of Hemingway, said in the *New York Times Book Review*, "The story of Joel Knox did not need to be told except to get it out of the author's system." Diana Trilling in the *Nation* began by praising the book but claimed it was an apology for homosexuality, that it argued that men became gay only because of their early experiences. In a loony leap of logic, she indignantly asked, "Is no member of society, then, to be held accountable for himself, not even Hitler?" (Trilling was fascinated with the subject at this time, reviewing almost every gay novel that came along, in contrast to her husband, Lionel, who rarely mentioned homosexuality. Even in his review of the Kinsey Report, he had much to say about premature ejaculation but little about Topic H.)

The reviews of *City and the Pillar* were equally blunt and dismissive, and without the sugar of Capote's many good notices. The *Times Book Review* said, "Presented as the case history of a standard homosexual, his novel adds little that is new to a groaning shelf." As early as 1948, the mainstream nervously dismissed the subject as old hat. Other reviewers called the book "disgusting," "sterile," and "gauche." The two or three good reviews were couched in sociological terms. "Essentially it's an attempt to clarify the inner stresses of our time, of which the increase in homosexuality and divorce are symptoms," wrote Charles Rolo in the *Atlantic*. "It should be added that Mr. Vidal has not neglected to provide an entertaining story."

One of the unkindest pieces was in the first issue of the *Hudson Review*, which was managed by a close female friend. Vidal hoped to publish there himself. Someone writing under the pseudonym J. S. Shrike (the cynical editor in *Miss Lonelyhearts* by Nathanael West), discussed *City* and *Other Voices* and *Sexual Behavior in the Human Male* together under the heading "Recent Phenomena." (Novels were reviewed under "Recent Fiction.") "Aside from its sociological demonstrations, Mr. Vidal's book is undistinguished. It is humorless, and most of its scenes are faked, as are the house interiors, the natural landscapes, and all the characters." (How can a writer do anything *but* "fake" a house interior?) It's a shrilly moralistic review, dressing its disgust in social-worker jargon, reading old clichés into Kinsey and the two novelists. Shrike says that, "Mr. Vidal's hero is irrevocably corrupted by his initial adolescent experience; Mr. Capote creates suspense by threatening the seduction of a thirteen year old boy." (It's bizarre how many of these reviewers assume that Randolph, the lover of a Mexican boxer, is plotting to seduce an androgynous little boy.) Shrike prefers Capote's prose to Vidal's yet does not like him much, either. "It is obvious that Mr. Capote has talent, but it is not a promising talent; it is a ruined one."

Vidal later said that the review that hurt most was one that wasn't written: Orville Prescott, critic for the daily *Times*, had praised *Williwaw*, but reportedly told friends that Vidal's new book disgusted him so much he would never read or review Vidal again. For the rest of his life, Vidal used this unwritten review as evidence of how antigay critics had blocked his career. Yet Prescott reviewed Capote in the *Times*, a mixed review but one that closed with "Many a first novel is sounder, better balanced, more reasonable than *Other Voices*. But few are more artistically exciting, more positive proof of the arrival of a new writer of substantial talent." Whatever put Prescott off *City and the Pillar*, it was not just its subject.

City ended up selling 30,000 copies in hardcover. *Other Voices* sold 26,000. (One needed to sell fewer books to be a best seller in the 1940s, and both books spent several weeks on best-seller lists.) These were not the only novels with gay content to appear that year. There was also *The Welcome* by Hubert Creekmore, about two men in love in a small Southern town. (It's striking how much gay fiction of this period is set in Dixie, as if the rest of the country could think about perversion only when it spoke with a funny accent.) *The Naked and the Dead* by Norman Mailer came out that summer, with a homosexual villain, General Cummings, the army commander. The June issue of *Partisan Review* contained "Come Back to the Raft Ag'in, Huck, Honey" by Leslie Fiedler, the notorious essay where Fiedler first argued that homosexual race-mixing was a major theme in American literature, with white heroes fleeing to the wilderness "in the arms of their dusky lovers": Huck and Jim, Ishmael and Queequeg, Natty Bumppo and Chingachgook. The essay included brief discussions of Vidal and Capote. Fiedler argued that this emphasis on homosexuality was a failing in American books, yet he discussed it with mischievous calm and no hysterical righteousness.

Years later Vidal would talk as if *City* had destroyed his career. It didn't. His next four novels sold 10,000 copies each, not bad for the hardcover book slump of the early Fifties—a temporary side effect of the flood of new, twenty-five-cent paperbacks. He said he wasn't reviewed again in the daily *New York Times* for the next fifteen years—and he wasn't, but his work was regularly covered in the *Times Book Review,* and he was the subject of feature stories in the daily *Times.* He turned to writing for TV and then to theater and the movies not because publishing was closed to him, but because the other fields paid so much better. Also his fiction now required more time and effort. He came to dislike the quick, gray style of the first books and took more pains with his language. I believe he was emulating Capote. He could never admit it, of course, but Capote wrote better prose and Vidal resented him for it. The closest he came to admitting as much was in a letter to his British editor, John Lehman: "Most people seem to be born knowing their way through literature, the young lions at least, like Truman," said Vidal, adding that he had spent the last four years working on his own style.

But the reception of *City and the Pillar* left him badly shaken. In an earlier letter to Lehman, a year after the book appeared, he said, "I am back amongst my people ready to lead them to the new Sodom, out of this pillar-marked wilderness," but he was only joking. He was more careful in the future, more cagey. He would not write at length about gay life again for another twenty years, when he returned to it in *Myra Breckinridge,* his wonderfully mad fantasy about camp, gender, and the movies.

There is no denying that *City and the Pillar* changed his career. Yet the older Vidal often contradicts himself in how he talks about the experience. The mature man of letters, the unflappable Mr. Know-it-all of interviews and essays, speaks as if he were born wise. In his autobiography, *Palimpsest,* he insists that he knew exactly what was at stake when he published *City*: he was saying good-bye to politics and probably hurting his future as a novelist. But how many twenty-two-year-olds have that kind of foresight? Fiction writers, even those who work autobiographically, often assume readers will think they are making things up. For legal reasons, reviewers could not accuse Vidal of being homosexual yet they certainly implied it. The reaction to *City* caught the young novelist completely off guard. He hadn't guessed he would out himself so nakedly. His journal for this period is the one piece of writing he refused to show his biographer, Fred Kaplan. His blind grandfather, the Senator, didn't read the novel, of course. Vidal says neither of his parents finished it. One suspects his father's reaction must have stung as much as the reviews. (Vidal was already at war with his mother, and his sexuality gave her new ammunition.) Whatever the exact cause of his hurt, the experience stamped Vidal for the rest of his life, affecting him more personally than he could admit. He protected himself by insisting the book was better than it was, then going back and revising it in 1965. He was a much better writer in 1965 than he'd been in 1948, yet he revised the book in the voice of his younger, more callow, pulpier self.

Capote, too, was disappointed with the reception of his book, but he'd been hoping for success along the lines of *Gone with the Wind*. No matter what an author gets, he or she wants more. Capote moved on and did not look back, but he did not write directly about homosexuality again for almost thirty years. He was silent about it in print, neither professing nor denying his own sexuality when he used himself as a character. He let his very public persona fill in the blank for readers.

Vidal and Capote do not appear to have ever compared notes or commiserated with each other over their early treatment by critics. It's a weakness to confess an injury, and one can never admit hurt to a competitor, even when he has suffered something similar.

Of course there were gay men and women in the United States before the Second World War. There was even some fiction with gay characters before 1947. But none of the great gay American writers—Henry James, Willa Cather, Hart Crane, Thornton Wilder—ever wrote directly about gay life. Walt Whitman celebrated the love of comrades, but later denied he meant anything sexual. Gertrude Stein touched on same-sex love in *Tender Buttons*, but in obscure, experimental prose. A few young writers published books with avant-garde presses, such as *Better Angel* by Forman Brown (1933), but the rest was silence. The truth of the matter is such books were often banned and seized. It was hard enough to print the truth about heterosexual love.

But the war changed things. First of all, national mobilization threw together millions of Americans from different parts of the country. Men who liked men and women who liked women learned that they were far from alone. When they returned home, if they returned (many moved to cities), they no longer thought of themselves as solitary freaks. Straight people too discovered there were more homosexuals in the world than they'd ever guessed. It was probably most surprising to middle-class and college-educated straight men whose lives were more sheltered than the poor and working class. We have no figures, of course, on how many straight readers purchased the new novels by Vidal and Capote compared to the number of gay readers. I presume the readership was predominantly gay. But the publishing world and the critical establishment were still straight and they were curious about this sexual underworld.

The war also began the slow change of what could be printed. The very literary, very hetero *Memoirs of Hecate County* by Edmund Wilson was banned in New York State after it became a best seller in 1946. The case made its way through the court system until it reached the U.S. Supreme Court, producing a 4–4 tie sustaining the ban. (Justice Felix Frankfurter abstained because he knew Wilson personally.) The book would be out of print for the next thirteen years. Complicating matters was the fact that standards changed from state to state, city to city. "Banned in Boston" was not just a catchphrase. Philadelphia in 1946 briefly blocked the sales of older novels by William Faulkner and James T. Farrell. But military service had accustomed middle-class men to words and names more expressive than what they'd grown up with. When the publisher of *The Naked and the Dead* insisted Mailer change *fuck* to *fug* to get past the censors—"What the fug you mean?"—everyone knew how silly it sounded.

But for a few years after the war, people were suddenly talking about homosexuality. They talked about it enough that it became demonized all over again and silence returned. Nevertheless, once you spill mercury from a bottle, you can never brush it all back in.

Vidal sailed for Naples in the middle of February 1948, happy to escape his notoriety and spend his hard-earned money in Europe, now open to travel and wonderfully cheap after the war. Capote left New York on May 14, on his own trip, going first to Paris. There the two writers met up with each other, wary yet amiable. Both struck up friendships with a third gay American writer also visiting Europe, a highly successful older playwright, thirty-seven-year-old Tennessee Williams. Williams would remain the admired friend of both men in the years ahead, even after they stopped talking to each other and communicated only through their lawyers.

2. The Kindness of Strangers

—〰—

He was born Thomas Lanier Williams in 1911 in Columbus, Mississippi, the son of a woman who was the pampered only child of an Episcopal minister, and a businessman who then worked for the telephone company. He didn't become Tennessee until he was twenty-seven, a name he chose for himself when he applied for a grant from the famous Group Theatre. The grant was for young playwrights, which meant twenty-five and under. He knocked three years off his age and took a new first name so the judges wouldn't connect him to the Thomas Lanier whose poems and stories were sometimes mentioned in St. Louis newspapers.

Williams was a compulsive writer from an early age. He needed to write in much the same way smokers need to smoke or alcoholics need to drink. (He would pursue sex in a similar fashion.) His friend Donald Windham initially admired his singlemindedness, saying, "He did something I longed to do but I didn't have the courage to. He put writing before knowing where he was going to sleep or where his next meal was coming from." Gore Vidal suggests something less admirable in his account of watching Williams take up a short story he had just published in a magazine and rewrite it into his typewriter, simply because he had nothing else to work on. He rewrote plays into stories and stories into plays. He also wrote poems and reams of letters, many of which were never sent if he didn't have a stamp or address handy. Expressing himself mattered more to him than actual communication.

He changed more than just his name and age in 1938. "Tom" had been a shy, outwardly conventional fellow, a frat man in college, a regular guy at the shoe factory where he briefly worked. The stories and plays he produced were fairly conventional, too, a tale of ancient Egypt ("The Vengeance of Nitocris" published in *Weird Tales*), a screwball comedy about high society marriage (*The Fat Man's Wife*) and a social drama about prison (*Not about Nightingales*). And he pretended to be conventional sexually, claiming to love women, yet he was a virgin with both genders. But around the time he applied to the Group Theatre, he moved to New Orleans hoping to write for the WPA. The minister's grandson found himself living contentedly among prostitutes, gamblers, drug addicts, and homosexuals; he went to bed with his first man, fell in love with a friend, discovered alcohol (it began with brandy alexanders), went to bed with another man, and another, and soon learned he was happiest when he had sex every night. He later described himself as "a rebellious Puritan," but the rebellion was never complete. The conforming, conventional "Tom" remained hidden inside "Tennessee" to the end of his life.

He continued to write every day in New Orleans, but his stories, plays, and poems were no longer stiff and secondhand; they were more alive, more emotional. He didn't write autobiographically—not directly, anyway. He wrote about what he *felt* rather than what he knew or understood. He had very strong emotions about the people he imagined. As his friend Windham puts it, "The richness of words in Tennessee's stories and plays of the 1940s isn't a richness of vocabulary. It is a richness of verbal texture.... There are a good many metaphors and similes; but they are always, even when physically descriptive, used to reveal an inner state. They are used to draw the reader or listener into the author's emotions."

He won the Group Theatre grant and used his new name when he spoke to a literary agent, Audrey Wood, who wanted to see more of his work. She represented him for the next thirty-two years.

The 1940s was a rollercoaster decade for Williams. Plays were rejected or almost produced or produced only to flop. Between productions, he took a variety of jobs, including elevator operator, movie usher, and poetry-reciting waiter at the Beggar's Bar in Greenwich Village. Using New York as his base, he traveled constantly, going to Mexico and Los Angeles and returning to New Orleans. He spent six months in Hollywood working under contract at MGM. He briefly lived with Windham and Windham's lover, but he was the world's worst roommate, filling his room with dirty clothes and empty cigarette packs, playing his old-fashioned wind-up Victrola while he hammered away at his typewriter and another coffeepot melted on the stove. He collaborated with Windham on a play, *You Touched Me*, based on a short story by D. H. Lawrence. Williams loved and drew inspiration from a handful of authors: Lawrence, Anton Chekhov, and, most important, Hart Crane. He carried a volume of Crane's word-drunk poems wherever he went.

Then, in 1944, he revised one more time a play inspired by his family, *The Gentleman Caller*, and sent it to Audrey Wood. After a few conferences and a change of title, *The Glass Menagerie* found a producer and a leading lady, Laurette Taylor. It opened in wartime Chicago in December and suffered a shaky first week before two local critics discovered and praised it. The play moved to Broadway three months later and was a huge success. (It isn't really a memory play, as Williams claimed. Among other changes, he wishfully imagined his disapproving father falling "in love with long distances" and abandoning the family.) Meanwhile another work-in-progress, *The Moth*, became *Blanche's Chair in the Moon*, then *The Poker Night*, and finally *A Streetcar Named Desire*. Directed by Elia Kazan and starring Jessica Tandy and a young new actor, Marlon Brando, it opened on Broadway at the end of 1947. It was an even bigger artistic and commercial triumph than *Menagerie*.

In three short years, this man who'd worked alone in a private fever dream of words found himself flung into the world of money, fame, and public admiration—what Williams later called "the catastrophe of success." People did not discuss his sexuality yet—that would come later—but as Wilfrid Sheed wrote, "Clearly, he wasn't the Elks Club Father of the Year." Homosexuality is present in his first two hits for anyone who cares to look—hinted at in Tom's offstage life in *Menagerie*, confessed in Blanche's sad story about her husband's suicide in *Streetcar*—but it was not yet the problem it became for the playwright and his public.

Success made Williams as restless as failure had. He continued to travel, visiting New Mexico, Nantucket, and Provincetown, returning to New Orleans and St. Louis. Soon after the opening of *Streetcar*, he left for his first adult visit to Europe—he had gone as a teenager with his grandfather on a six-week church tour.

He arrived in Rome in February 1948, where he took an apartment and bought a used army jeep. He met Gore Vidal at a party at the American Academy. The two men immediately hit it off. They took a trip down the coast to Naples and Amalfi in the jeep, passing Ravello, Vidal's future home. Williams drove on that twisty road high above the Mediterranean, a reckless yet lucky driver. The two new friends next took the dangerous step of reading each other's prose. Vidal read a new story by Williams and told him it didn't work. "So fix it," said Williams. Vidal actually wrote a new draft, but Williams hated his changes. "What you have done is removed my *style*, which is all I have." Meanwhile Williams read *The City and the Pillar*. "You know, you spoiled it with that ending. You didn't know what a good book you had."

These are very intimate, difficult moments for any writer, yet the two remained friends. It's hard to say what drew them together. It wasn't sexual attraction. Once when they went out cruising together, they returned empty-handed. "That leaves only us," said Williams. "Don't be macabre," Vidal replied. Williams was far more famous, yet the competitive novelist did not resent his older peer. Vidal recognized early that he was smarter than Williams, more logical and literate. Yet he never denied Williams's poetic gifts and power. Usually so proud and guarded, Vidal later wrote about Williams in essays with genuine affection, showing a tenderness that rarely appears in his work. But the respect was not entirely mutual. The playwright described his first meetings with Vidal in a letter to Windham: "I liked him but only through the strenuous effort it took to overlook his conceit. He has studied ballet and is constantly doing pirouettes and flexing his legs, and the rest of the time he is comparing himself and Truman Capote (his professional rival and Nemesis) to such figures as Dostoyevsky and Balzac."

Williams went off to London for the rehearsal of John Gielgud's production of *Menagerie* starring Helen Hayes, then came to Paris where he met up again with Vidal. He brought Vidal along as translator when he met with Jean Cocteau to discuss a French production of *Streetcar* to star Cocteau's boyfriend, Jean Marais. Vidal gives a witty account of the meeting: "Between Tennessee's solemn analyses of the play and Cocteau's rhetoric about the theater (the long arms flailed like semaphores denoting some dangerous last junction) nobody made any sense at all until Marais broke his long silence to ask, apropos his character Stanley Kowalski, 'Will I have to use a Polish accent?'"

Then Truman Capote arrived in Paris. Vidal's distrust had been building since Capote upstaged everyone in the photo pages of *Life*, but he introduced his rival to Williams. Always anxious to entertain, Capote worked harder than ever to impress the famous playwright. He told Williams and Vidal tales of Hollywood movie deals, meetings with starlets, and his own romantic encounters with André Gide, Errol Flynn, and Albert Camus—encounters that have never been verified. Williams was wary and uncertain. Later, when he grew fond of Capote, he would say he was "full of fantasies and mischief." Vidal would call him an outright liar. The three went to a Paris nightclub one night, and Capote attempted to get Vidal out on the dance floor for the latest song from America, "Bongo, bongo, bongo, I don't want to leave the Congo." Vidal refused.

October found all three men back in New York, photographed together at a party with drinks and grins, looking like good buddies at a college mixer. Yet Vidal's dislike of Capote was already so strong he found it difficult to be in the same room or even the same city with him. Colleagues began to make jokes about his rivalry, one man telling the tale of a cross-country trip where they stopped at every public library so Vidal could see if his books were checked out as often as Capote's. Vidal later wrote, "It's not enough to succeed, our friends must fail." One assumes he had a particular "friend" in mind.

Williams had returned to New York for the rehearsals of *Summer and Smoke.* This is a surprisingly quiet play for him, a period piece mixing comedy and melancholy set in the golden age before the First World War, the tale of two friends, a man and a woman, who almost become lovers. It received bad reviews and closed early. Williams was devastated. *Summer and Smoke* didn't find success until its revival in 1952.

He published a novel, *The Roman Spring of Mrs. Stone,* in 1950, and won a Tony for his next play, *The Rose Tattoo,* in 1951. And he met Frank Merlo, a short, dark, handsome young man with Sicilian roots and lots of practicality. Williams nicknamed him "Little Horse." Merlo provided an anchor for the playwright in the coming years, an anchor Williams didn't always want. They took a house in Key West, where Williams's grandfather frequently stayed with them. Williams spent his mornings writing, his afternoons swimming, and his evenings drinking, but he couldn't meet new men at night while he lived with Frank. He grew restless again.

He followed *Rose Tattoo* with a curious experiment, *Camino Real,* a dream play in ten scenes that explores the conflict of romance and realism using a cast of characters that range from Don Quixote to Casanova to the American Everyman, Kilroy (as in the G.I. graffiti, "Kilroy was here"). One scene features the Baron de Charlus, Marcel Proust's remarkable creation, the first great gay character in literature. The play was a complete failure, rejected by both critics and the public, but not because of Charlus. Some have speculated it was perceived as anti-American, but it's too elusive to be perceived as anything. It's loose, scattered, and cerebral, Williams's least emotional work. As Windham and others have said, his writing is emotional or it is nothing.

A writer's unconscious is difficult to read, but the imagination is rooted in the unconscious. Williams had run out of imaginative energy. I believe he was now trying, consciously or not, to find a way to use his sexuality in his work. Eroticism is an important part of most artists' creativity. A gay writer can produce a book or two while ignoring his or her sexuality and still do good work. Innocence helps for a spell. Yet it's difficult to keep one's real sexuality buried for too long without the work suffering. Windham called *Mrs. Stone* the first of his friend's "fictional self-portraits after his success," but giving your promiscuity to a fifty-something widow doesn't let you express your full body and soul. *Rose Tattoo* was a heterosexual love story about yet another widow, Serafina, and an Italian fisherman, Alvaro, using pieces of Williams and Merlo, but the disguise smothered any self-expression. With Charlus in *Camino Real,* Williams let the cat out of the bag, so to speak, but it wasn't enough. The need was still there, stronger than ever, and it fed his next play, *Cat on a Hot Tin Roof.*

Gay sexuality was in a tricky position in American theater after the war, even more vulnerable than it was in the book trade. Then as now, the theater was full of gay people and more accepting of homosexuality than the rest of the country. Yet producers not only worried about how audiences would respond to gay matter, they worried about the police. Still on the books was a 1927 law—Section 1140-A of New York City's Criminal Code, known as the Wales Padlock Law. A theater found guilty of showing "an immoral play"—which included any presentation of homosexuality, good or bad—could be shut down for a year. The law was rarely used but had been invoked to close Dorothy Baker's *Trio* in 1945. Producers cited it whenever they wanted to cut a gay character or adjust a story line. Nevertheless, Danny Kaye was free to play a flamboyant fashion photographer in the musical *Lady in the Dark* in 1944 and John Huston was able to stage

Jean-Paul Sartre's *No Exit* in 1946 despite its predatory lesbian. There was even a play version of Calder Willingham's *End as a Man* in 1952, with the homosexual sadist identified as only a sadist.

So homosexuality was not completely forbidden, but it was in a tight spot. One solution was to tell stories that weren't about real homosexuality but about false accusations of it. In the Fifties we get a string of plays with this device: *Tea and Sympathy* by Robert Anderson (1953), *The View from the Bridge* by Arthur Miller (1955), and the 1952 revival of *The Children's Hour* by Lillian Hellman (where the accusation turns out to be true, but not until the last scene). The theater strived to have it both ways, which had a strong effect on the writing and rewriting of *Cat*.

It began as a short story, "Three Players of a Summer Game," about a game of croquet in the 1920s played by a former athlete, Brick Pollitt, a local widow, and the widow's little girl. The story is told by a small boy who doesn't fully understand what he sees. We hear about Brick's wife, Margaret, whose coldness has driven Brick to drink and into the arms of the widow. In the end the widow is defeated and Margaret recaptures Brick—we're not sure exactly how. The story is all summer mood and grown-up mystery.

Williams turned it into a play and it became an entirely new animal. We see how radically he rethought and reinvented old material when he rewrote. He shifts the story from the past to the present. A game of croquet is still taking place outside, but we're in the house now, alone with Brick and Margaret. Brick is still a former athlete and he still drinks. But cold, bossy Margaret has become Maggie the Cat, a spirited, immensely likable woman who loves her husband and wants to save their marriage. The widow, daughter, and child narrator are gone, replaced with Brick's brother and sister-in-law and their five "no-neck monsters." And dominating all is Brick's boisterous, cancer-haunted father, Big Daddy.

It is a mad, brilliant mess of a play, half soap opera, half comedy, with some of the funniest dialogue Williams ever wrote. The airy vagueness of *Camino Real* is gone. Big Daddy was based on Williams's own father, yet any autobiographical elements are split and distorted and reconfigured in the funhouse mirror of the author's imagination. Williams liked to say that he was all his characters; here different pieces of Williams argue and woo and bond with each other. Maggie burns to win Brick back, like an ex-spouse in a screwball comedy, the genre philosopher Stanley Cavell called "the comedy of remarriage." Why doesn't Brick love her anymore? Williams's imagination drew upon the subject he itched to use: homosexuality. But then the artist—or his unconscious—changed his/its mind about how far to go. Brick had been close to a fellow athlete, Skipper, now dead. Had the two men loved each other? Or had Skipper loved Brick without being loved back? Or did Brick only imagine their friendship was impure because other people thought so? Williams kept shifting back and forth and the subject became messier and messier. When Brick and Big Daddy throw the word *mendacity* at each other, one can't help hearing Williams cast a similar charge of lying against himself.

He wanted Elia Kazan to direct the play, thinking only Kazan could give him another commercial success like *Streetcar*. He badly needed a hit, not so much for the money as for his own mental well-being. Kazan asked for more rewrites before he finally agreed to direct. Then he asked for a new third act, which Williams gave him. Then Kazan barred Williams from rehearsals.

Cat on a Hot Tin Roof opened in March 1955, starring Ben Gazzara, Barbara Bel Geddes, and Burl Ives. It was a huge success, praised by the critics and loved by audiences, and it eventually won the Pulitzer. But Williams wasn't sure what it meant anymore. When he published the play in book form, he included *both* third acts, even though they're not very different: each ends with Maggie winning Brick. The new version includes a thunderstorm and Big Daddy returns for the finale, as Kazan requested, but Williams never satisfied Kazan's other request, which was that Brick respond to Big Daddy's second-act charge that he drank because he had been in love with Skipper. Despite this silence, several reviewers wondered about Brick's sexuality. Walter Kerr compared the accusation in *Cat* to the one in *The Children's Hour*, implying it was true. (Reviewers were often very polite in the 1950s.) Williams went into a panic. He wanted his play to be understood, but he didn't want it understood too well. He wrote a response to Kerr, but didn't send it. He added a long stage direction to the book edition trying to explain Brick's sexuality but only confused things further.

The experience left him completely exhausted. He achieved his success, but it did not make him feel better. He now suffered a major case of writer's block. And writer's block for a man who writes every day can be as frightening as an inability to breathe. All he could do was drink, like Brick, which only made the problem worse.

Alcohol will be a recurring subject in this book, as important as sex and love and success for these artists. Gay men are hardly alone here. Booze affected the lives of many twentieth-century American authors. Tom Dardis in *The Thirsty Muse* identifies two traditions of writers, those who drank—Eugene O'Neill, F. Scott Fitzgerald, Ernest Hemingway, William Faulkner—and those who didn't—Edith Wharton, Willa Cather, T. S. Eliot, Wallace Stevens. Alcohol and drugs deeply stamped the careers of more than one figure in our story.

Drinking only deepened problems that were already present, in much the same way that Williams's mixed feelings about his sexuality only fed his paralysis. It's hard to distinguish between cause and effect here. Williams eventually took up an old play, *Battle of Angels*, and rewrote it into *Orpheus Descending*. It opened to the worst reviews he had yet received. He became so unhappy that he did what friends had been suggesting for years: he began to see a psychiatrist. And the man he chose was Dr. Lawrence S. Kubie.

Kubie was a famous figure with a lot of experience treating writers with sexual issues, including William Inge, Charles Jackson (author of *The Lost Weekend*), and Moss Hart. He insisted patients see him three to four times a week. One would love to know what the Williams sessions were like, but Kubie ordered his records destroyed after his death. Williams told his mother, "He said I wrote cheap melodramas and nothing else." In his *Memoirs* he says Kubie wanted him to give up not only sex with men but writing, too. What he wrote to Kazan shortly after ending treatment is probably closer to the truth: "He said I was overworked and must quit and 'lie fallow,' as he put it, for a year or so, and then resume work in what he declared would be a great new tide of creative power, which he apparently thought would come out of my analysis with him." Williams stopped seeing Kubie after eight months.

Analysis does not seem to have done him much good. He continued to drink and soon added barbiturates *and* amphetamines to his routine. But the psychiatric experience strongly influenced his next play, *Suddenly Last Summer*, an extended one-act written while he was still seeing Kubie. Some people love it; I don't. A mad, gothic-fever dream of a play, it succeeds best as the tale of a young woman hospitalized after being exploited by her rich gay cousin and the cousin's mother. But it's also an attack on Williams's own sexual appetite. The author ends the play by giving his gay predator a cannibal death that might seem racist and offensive if it weren't so preposterous. (It is so absurd that I want to think Williams was laughing off his own fantasy.) Nevertheless, Kubie admired the work, singling out for special praise the sensitive portrait of the doctor.

Psychiatry in later decades might have helped Williams, but the profession in the 1950s could do little for him.

Meanwhile Capote and Vidal had crossed into playwriting themselves, Capote adapting his novel *The Grass Harp* for the stage in 1952, and Vidal coming to theater by way of television, expanding a TV drama into a satirical play, *Visit to a Small Planet,* in 1957. His friend, novelist Dawn Powell, ran into Vidal in the lobby on opening night and teased him. "How could you give up *The Novel*? Give up the security! The security of knowing that every two years there will be—like clockwork—*that five-hundred-dollar advance!*"

Williams never felt threatened or competitive over his friends' entry into his realm, partly because their success never came close to his, but also because other people were never as important to Tennessee as he sometimes was to them.

3. Howl

—⟋⟋—

Plays are more public than novels, and novels more public than short stories. Tennessee Williams wrote and published several gay short stories at this time, including "One Arm" and "Desire and the Black Masseur," without attracting too much attention. (Nor was he able to express this side of himself fully enough that he could let go of it.) But the least public genre of all, the most private, is poetry. The privacy consists in how few people read it, and how discreet and even obscure a poem can be and still succeed.

Nevertheless, the next important work in our story is a long poem by Allen Ginsberg, which was anything but discreet. The poem and its publisher ended up in court in San Francisco, and in newspapers across the country.

American poetry before World War II was dominated by straight men: Robert Frost, T. S. Eliot, E. E. Cummings, Wallace Stevens, and William Carlos Williams. The only major woman was Marianne Moore. The late Hart Crane was known to have been gay, but he was read only by avant-garde readers like Tennessee Williams. Walt Whitman radiated homosexuality, but the New Critics didn't trust Whitman: he was too sloppy, too vulgar. (The critics were silent about his love of men, but Whitman himself was evasive about it in his last years. It didn't stop the next generations of gay readers from using him as a hero and an example.)

After the war, a handful of gay poets began to use their sexuality in their work in a quiet, matter-of-fact manner that didn't proclaim their difference but didn't hide it, either. Their gayness was an open secret, which meant gay readers could see themselves in the work while straight readers could still play dumb.

W. H. Auden came to America just before the war. He was very sociable and soon known in the gay literary circles of New York. His sexuality did not appear directly in his work, but by deft use of the second person ("Lay your sleeping head my love/Human on my faithless arm") and double meanings (an exclamation like "O God!" could be both religion and camp), he showed how gay experience could be incorporated into poetry without lying. Within a few years, a young art lover, Frank O'Hara, who worked in the bookstore of the Museum of Modern Art, was writing free and easy poems to his friends. (But the poems he printed only hinted at the life he led. His carefree evocation of a pack of pals going out dancing, "At the Old Place"—"Wrapped in Ashes' arms I glide./(It's heaven!) Button lindys with me. (It's/heaven!)"—was written in 1955, but not published until 1969, the year of Stonewall.) Other young gay poets—James Schuyler, James Merrill, Richard Howard, and John Ashbery—were also appearing in print, but the gay takeover of New York poetry took place in secret, between the lines. The public eruption happened elsewhere, with a poem that some considered too raw to be called poetry from a poet many still believe to be more a genius of publicity than one of verse.

Yet Allen Ginsberg grew up in poetry. Born in 1926, he was the son of a poet, Louis Ginsberg, a high school and college teacher whose work appeared in several major anthologies. Young Ginsberg grew up on the site of a poem, Paterson, New Jersey, the factory town that's the subject of the sprawling Whitmanesque epic by William Carlos Williams. Allen's older brother, Eugene, also wrote poetry. Their mother, Naomi, however, had a more fragile, cracked imagination. She suffered a psychotic break when Allen was ten and spent the next years in and out of sanitariums as her paranoid delusions worsened.

In 1943, Allen crossed the Hudson River to attend Columbia University as a scholarship student. He was only seventeen, but his knowledge of poetry, especially William Blake and Percy Shelley, immediately caught the attention of professors there, including Lionel Trilling. During his freshman year he met many of the people who'd be important to him for the rest of his life: Jack Kerouac, a craggily handsome football player with whom he fell in love; William Burroughs, a boyish would-be writer of thirty with an independent income (he already dressed like a middle-aged gentleman, a look he soon grew into); and Lucian Carr, a precocious blond beauty from St. Louis who loved art and music. The summer after freshman year, Carr confronted an obsessed older man who'd followed him from St. Louis; he stabbed the man to death with a Boy Scout knife. Ginsberg's only connection with the murder was that he and other friends convinced Carr to turn himself over to the police, but the university began to watch Ginsberg more closely. Two months into his sophomore year, the cleaning lady reported obscene graffiti written in the dirt on his dorm window, and he was expelled.

He used his new freedom to experiment with his writing, and with drugs (mostly Benzedrine at first), and with sex. He was a skinny Jewish kid with horn-rimmed glasses, big ears, and full lips. Photos of him in this period suggest a young Sal Mineo with a wider mouth. He tended to fall in love with men who were straight-identified if not entirely straight. They might go to bed with him, but the emphasis was on their pleasure, not his. He blew them or they fucked him, and afterward he listened to their girlfriend problems. This began with Kerouac, who was reluctant to have sex with men. He was more successful with Neal Cassady, who was happy to have sex with anyone, male or female. Ginsberg fell into an intense two-month affair with Cassady. This was before Kerouac joined Cassady for the cross-country trips he would immortalize in *On the Road*.

Ginsberg reenrolled at Columbia, then dropped out again. He would continue this pattern until he finally graduated. He spent one summer at the National Maritime Academy and another sailing to Africa on a merchant ship. He added new drugs to his repertory, including marijuana and heroin. He hung out with a thief and addict, Herbert Huncke, and Huncke's friends Jack Melody and Vicki Russell. He told himself he was getting closer to real life by knowing criminals. One night in the spring of 1949, he was riding in a stolen car with Melody and Russell in Queens when they turned the wrong way on a one-way street. A police car began to pursue them. Melody tried to escape, crashing the car and flipping it over. Nobody was hurt but all were arrested for car theft, drug possession, and possession of stolen goods. Trilling and two other professors, Mark Van Doren and Jacques Barzun, testified in support of Ginsberg—they feared jail would destroy their former student's mental health. Ginsberg was advised to plead insanity, which he did. Proving his insanity were the facts that his mother was in a mental hospital and he was having sex with men. He was sent to the Columbia Presbyterian Psychiatric Institute on West 168th Street.

Ginsberg never spoke or wrote in full detail about his eight long months in a mental hospital. This was in the age before drugs like Thorazine rendered inmates numb and docile, the era of *The Snake Pit*. He was not given electroshock, but he did see psychiatrists three times a week and was asked endless questions about his family, his beliefs, and his sexuality.

Early on he met another inmate, Carl Solomon, a younger but tougher, self-educated man. At their first meeting Ginsberg said, "I'm Myshkin"—the saintly hero of Dostoyevsky's *The Idiot*. Solomon replied, "I'm Kirilov"—the brutal nihilist in *The Possessed*. Solomon had been to Paris and knew the work of Artaud and the surrealists. His mind fizzed with too many thoughts; he didn't want to live, but he wanted a lobotomy rather than suicide. He called Ginsberg "the dopey daffodil." Yet his friendship sustained the college boy during his time at Columbia Presbyterian. They saw each other daily, talked books, spoke French, and played Monopoly. Ginsberg wrote regularly to friends and even finished a book of poems, which he submitted to a young editor, Robert Giroux (who rejected it). The doctors decided Ginsberg was only "a standard neurotic," but convinced him he wouldn't be able to function unless he lived a more normal life, which meant giving up his homosexuality.

When he was released in February 1950, he decided to put his old life behind him. He lived at home with his father and new stepmother, Edith. (His father divorced the institutionalized Naomi yet remained close to her.) Allen took a job at a ribbon factory. He had a prolonged affair with one woman, then another. He stayed in touch with his old friends, however, and continued to write poems. One month after his release, he attended a reading by William Carlos Williams, then sent a fan letter and nine poems to the former physician. Williams was unimpressed by the poems, but he met with his admirer. Ginsberg continued to send him work, disappointing the good doctor until one week, as an experiment, he sent a batch of isolated lines from his journals. Williams encouraged him to go further in *that* direction.

In 1952 Ginsberg wrote a short autobiographical sketch titled "A Novel," that closes with:

At 26, I am shy, go out with girls, I write poetry, I am a
freelance literary agent and a registered democrat; I
want to find a job. Who cares?

While Ginsberg grew more practical and even conventional, his friends grew stranger. After Kerouac published his first novel, *The Town and the City*, he wrote a wild, new, exciting book, *On the Road*, that no publisher wanted. Ginsberg took over as his agent, but he couldn't find a home for it, either. Kerouac grew irritable, resenting Ginsberg, resenting other novelists, even resenting their friend William Burroughs when Ginsberg helped sell *his* book.

Burroughs had married a woman, Joan Vollmer, and left New York, going first to Louisiana, then to Mexico. He had become a heroin addict, but he kicked his addiction and wrote a memoir, *Junky*. Ginsberg sold the book for him to Ace Books, a small paperback house owned by Carl Solomon's uncle. Solomon now worked there as an editor. Life was looking good for Burroughs, but at a party one night in Mexico City in 1951, playing a drunken game of William Tell with a pistol, he accidentally shot and killed Joan. He was devastated. The Mexican court didn't charge him with homicide, but he fled the country, afraid the court would change its mind. He returned to New York and stayed with Ginsberg.

Ginsberg had his own life now with a girlfriend and a nine-to-five job. Nevertheless, he often joined his friends at the San Remo, a dark, smoky bar at the corner of MacDougal and Bleecker. Joe LeSueur, in his wonderful book *Digressions on Some Poems by Frank O'Hara*, describes the San Remo as "a semi-gay place" with an espresso machine, a loud jukebox, and fifteen-cent beer. O'Hara and his friends hung out there, as did Auden's boyfriend, Chester Kallman. Kallman horrified O'Hara and LeSueur one night with an elaborate account of fellating a pick-up in one room while talking between strokes to a half-awake Auden in the next room. Afterward LeSueur told O'Hara, "If you ever catch me talking the way Chester did tonight, get a gun and shoot me."

Ginsberg wasn't at the San Remo on the hot August night in 1953 when Burroughs and Kerouac met Gore Vidal.

The author of *The City and the Pillar* now lived outside the city in an old villa, Edgewater, on the Hudson River that he purchased cheap and was renovating with his partner, Howard Austen. Vidal had found a solution to his very contradictory feelings about sex and intimacy: he and Austen went to bed with other men but never each other. They were never physical lovers, not even when they first met—at the baths in 1950. But they enjoyed each other's company and shared support and advice, and apparently that was enough.

Burroughs admired Vidal. Kerouac hated him, partly for his prose style but chiefly for his success. He didn't know how much trouble Vidal was having with his own career at the time. Vidal had met Kerouac briefly, at the Metropolitan Opera of all places, and he recognized him at the San Remo and came over to the table. Before Burroughs could tell Vidal how much he liked his work, Kerouac jumped in and began to compliment Vidal, extravagantly, mockingly. He began to flirt. Vidal flirted back. Eventually the three men left to go barhopping. Burroughs soon dropped out, understanding there was no place for him here. Kerouac proposed to Vidal they get a room. When they checked in at the Chelsea Hotel on West Twenty-third Street, Vidal laughingly insisted they register under their real names, saying the guest book would be famous one day. Upstairs, the two men undressed and took showers—it was a hot night. Vidal has written or talked about this encounter several times and says Kerouac couldn't get an erection. Whatever was going on here, it wasn't primarily about sex.

When Kerouac saw Ginsberg the next day, he proudly told him how he had blown Gore Vidal. Ginsberg never mentioned his own reaction when telling this story, but he must have recognized the malice here. Kerouac was angrily striking out at the gay men around him: at Vidal for being famous, at Burroughs for selling a book, and at Ginsberg for failing to help him enough—he gave a more successful writer what he had refused to give his best friend years ago. Somewhere in there, of course, is Kerouac's own confused sexuality, which he couldn't release except in drunkenness or anger. (Later Norman Mailer would claim Vidal had fucked Kerouac in the ass that night and destroyed his masculinity and made him an alcoholic. But anal sex was the heterosexual Mailer's obsession and fear.)

Life in New York was becoming too close and familiar for Ginsberg. He and Burroughs briefly became lovers, even though Ginsberg was still seeing a woman, the men weren't sexually compatible, and Ginsberg found Burroughs too emotionally demanding. Ginsberg finally said, "I don't want your ugly old cock."

He left for Mexico at the beginning of 1954. But Mexico was too alien and lonely, and a little scary with the new drugs he was trying. So he went up to

San Jose, California, to visit his old friend, Neal Cassady. Cassady was married but had given up sex, claiming his turn to Buddhism required celibacy. It was already an uncomfortable visit when Carolyn Cassady opened a bedroom door one afternoon and found their guest making love to her husband with his mouth. Cassady promptly left for work, leaving his wife and his friend to confront each other. A few days later Carolyn drove Ginsberg up to San Francisco, three hours away, the two still apologizing for what had happened and what had been said. She dropped him off and returned to San Jose.

This is the first appearance of a city that will play a major role in this history. San Francisco in 1954 was a small but busy seaport in one of the most beautiful landscapes on the planet. The neighborhood of North Beach was home to a bohemian community dating back to the First World War. The city hosted a lively art scene, with poets like Kenneth Rexroth, Kenneth Patchen, and Robert Duncan (Anaïs Nin's old friend), and cultural institutions like the Purple Onion, a folk club, and City Lights Bookshop, owned by a tall, married, clean-shaven poet with a receding hairline, Lawrence Ferlinghetti.

One night soon after he arrived, Ginsberg took the last of the peyote from Mexico, looked out his window, and saw the Sir Francis Drake Hotel across the park turn into Moloch, the huge machine god who devours workers in Fritz Lang's silent classic, *Metropolis*.

Nevertheless, he decided to stay. He took a full-time job as a market researcher and moved in with yet another woman, a copywriter and sometime jazz singer with a four-year-old son. Their relationship was good until he told her about his history with Neal Cassady; she asked him to move out. A few days later, a painter, Robert LaVigne, showed Ginsberg nude portraits of a tall, beautiful, yellow-haired man. Then the man himself walked into the room, Peter Orlovsky, and Ginsberg fell in love. Orlovsky was basically straight, but he responded to Ginsberg both sexually and emotionally. The men saw each other steadily for several months, then Ginsberg drew back, afraid there was no future here. He was in therapy again, seeing a dollar-a-session analyst, Dr. Philip Hicks, at the Langley Porter Clinic in Berkeley. He told Hicks that he felt he should live as a heterosexual. When Hicks asked what he really wanted, he admitted he wanted to live with Orlovsky. "So why don't you do that?" Ginsberg said he didn't think it would last and he was afraid of growing old. "Oh, you're a nice person," replied Hicks. "There's always people who will like you." (One can't help wondering what would have happened if a doctor had given Tennessee Williams such practical advice.)

Ginsberg and Orlovsky moved in together in February 1955, swearing to "an exchange of souls & bodies." Orlovsky was free to have sex with women so long as he also had sex with Ginsberg.

That summer Orlovsky left to hitchhike cross-country to visit his family in New York. Alone again, Ginsberg resumed work on his poetry. He had been away from it for a while, although he continued to scribble ideas and phrases in his journal. One afternoon in August, he sat down at his typewriter to expand a promising line he'd written about his friend Carl Solomon, who he'd heard was back in a mental hospital. In one furious, inspired sitting, he typed out what became the long first section of "Howl."

> I saw the best minds of my generation destroyed by
> madness, starving hysterical naked...

It was and still is an amazing piece of writing, a sermonlike march of words that carries a remarkable load of raw emotion. It's the kind of poem that often only pretends to have been written all at once, yet here a lifetime of experience and craft actually poured forth in a sustained explosion of images. There are good accounts elsewhere of the writing of the rest of the poem, clear biographical readings of individual lines, and smart analyses showing the influence of William Carlos Williams, Kerouac, even *The Waste Land*. What I want to emphasize here is what Ginsberg and others have said: this was a coming-out poem. There is nothing coy about the homosexual imagery. It is so coolly matter-of-fact that it can disappear for many readers when they now read about men:

> who let themselves be fucked in the ass by saintly
> motorcyclists, and screamed with joy,
> who blew and were blown by those human seraphim,
> the sailors, caresses of Atlantic and Caribbean
> love,
> who balled in the mornings in the evenings in rose-
> gardens and the grass of public parks and
> cemeteries scattering their semen freely to
> whomever come who may...

Yet it was highly visible to early readers. It can still be startling for a young gay person first encountering the poem. The sexuality is both shocking and liberating. It was certainly liberating for Ginsberg. He had never addressed his sex life so openly in his poetry, and it freed him to talk about everything else.

The poem quickly works through the initial shock and makes homosexuality the emblem of all sexuality, which in turn evokes the bodies and minds crushed by society. The second section of the poem uses Moloch as the killer god of modern society. The third section mourns the victims of Moloch as represented by Carl Solomon, now held in Rockland Psychiatric Center in upstate New York:

> I'm with you in Rockland
>> where we hug and kiss the United States under
>> our bedsheets the United States that coughs all
>> night and won't let us sleep...

"Howl" works more from sound and energy than it does from sense or logic. Most of the energy is sexual. After years of hiding, sexual honesty was now very important to Ginsberg. His favorite expression of honesty was nakedness. "The poet stands naked before the world," he said, and it was not just a metaphor. He once faced down a heckler at a reading in Los Angeles by stripping naked and demanding the man do the same.

Writing the first section of "Howl" unlocked Ginsberg. He wrote the rest of the poem in the next few weeks, then quickly followed it with other great works: "Sunflower Sutra," "A Supermarket in California," and "America," with its grand closing line:

> America I am putting my queer shoulder to the wheel.

The first public reading of "Howl" took place at the Six Gallery, a converted garage, on Friday night, October 7, 1955, when Ginsberg read with five other poets. Ginsberg read only the first section, but the poem immediately attracted attention. Ferlinghetti wanted to publish it in his new City Lights Pocket Poets series. Ginsberg sent a mimeograph of the completed poem to his father. Louis Ginsberg's response was both perceptive and prescient:

My expression, at first blush, is that it is a weird, volcanic, troubled, extravagant, turbulent, boisterous, unbridled outpouring, intermingling genius and flashes of picturesque insight with slag and debris of scoriac matter. It has violence; it has life; it has *vitality*. In my opinion it is a one-sided, neurotic view of life; it has not enough glad Whitmanian affirmations. (The fact that you write in such an energetic glow of poetry is one affirmation.) The poem should attract attention and perhaps be a sensation; one will hear defenders and detractors. But it should give you a name.

Ginsberg even sent a copy to his mother in her sanitarium. She wrote back that she found the wording "hard" and wondered what his father thought. She closed by saying she hoped he wasn't using drugs, as implied by his poems. "Don't go in for ridiculous things." There is no date on the letter, but it's postmarked two days after her death from a cerebral hemorrhage. Someone must have found it by her bed and mailed it. Ginsberg could not return east for the funeral. He was saddened to hear that kaddish, the Jewish prayer for the dead, was not read for his mother. He resolved that he would one day write his own kaddish for her.

Howl and Other Poems appeared in September 1956 from City Lights Books with an introduction by William Carlos Williams. It was dedicated to Jack Kerouac, William Burroughs, Neal Cassady, and Lucian Carr. The first printing was a thousand copies. The booklet was fifty-seven pages and cost seventy-five cents.

Richard Eberhart almost immediately discussed the title poem in the *New York Times Book Review* in an article about the new California poets. "Its positive force and energy come from a redemptive quality of love." After that, however, reviews trickled in slowly. John Hollander in *Partisan Review* found the book "a dreadful little volume." James Dickey, who later made anal rape the sin of sins in his novel *Deliverance*, dismissed the poem in the *Sewanee Review* as a meaningless diatribe "really not worth examining." Ginsberg heard that his old teacher, Trilling, found it dull and that Ezra Pound disliked it. (Williams had sent Pound a copy, and Pound wrote back that he shouldn't waste people's time by making them read "wot they dont know"—his gnarled way of saying that he didn't want to read about homosexuals. He wrote from his cell at St. Elizabeths Hospital where he had been incarcerated since being declared insane for his fascist radio broadcasts during the war. More than one poet went to the madhouse in the 1950s.) Norman Podhoretz in the *New Republic* used the poem to attack the Beat Generation for using "homosexuality, jazz, dope-addiction and vagrancy" to rebel for no purpose except to rebel. But the gay material did not elicit the overt disgust it had nine years earlier in novels by Vidal and Capote. Perhaps readers of poetry were more sophisticated, or maybe they were simply less honest: many critics called the poem boring.

Yet the little book continued to sell and gather attention during its first year after publication. It attracted interest not only for itself, but also as a part of a wider social phenomena: the arrival of the Beats. *On the Road* was finally published in September 1957, with a glowing review in the *New York Times*. A few weeks earlier, making the poem more visible than ever, *Howl and Other Poems* went on trial in San Francisco for obscenity.

The first signs of legal trouble appeared back in March, when U.S. Customs seized 520 copies of the second printing. Ferlinghetti was having the book produced in Britain. The customs agents found objectionable not just the use of words like *cock* and *balls* but the phrase "who let themselves be ...... in the ... by saintly motorcyclists." At the insistence of their British printer, Ferlinghetti and Ginsberg put the poem's most provocative line into what looked like Morse code—and it still offended people.

Ferlinghetti outmaneuvered customs by having the next printing of 2,500 copies done in the United States. The San Francisco newspapers supported Ferlinghetti and found the authorities absurd. At the end of May, the seized books were released when the U.S. attorney general decided not to press charges. But a few days later, two San Francisco detectives from the Juvenile Bureau walked into City Lights Bookshop, bought a copy of *Howl*, departed, read it, then returned and arrested the store clerk, Shigeyoshi Murao, for selling lewd and obscene material. Ferlinghetti was out of town, but surrendered to the police when he returned.

The author himself was not charged. Besides, he was on the other side of the Atlantic. Like every other American writer of the twentieth century, Ginsberg had gone abroad. He and Orlovsky left in April, never dreaming that events would take such a wild turn. He stayed in touch with Ferlinghetti as well as he could, first from Morocco, then from Italy.

The trial began August 16, presided over by Judge Clayton Horn. The defense attorney, Jake Erlich, supported by two lawyers from the ACLU, decided to waive trial by jury and present the case solely to a judge, even though this judge taught Sunday school and had recently sentenced five shoplifters to watch Cecil B. DeMille's new Biblical epic, *The Ten Commandments.*

From the start, the trial was followed closely by the press and attended by a capacity crowd. The *San Francisco Chronicle* reported an audience wearing a "fantastic collection of beards, turtlenecked shirts and Italian hairdos." Judge Horn laid down strict ground rules: the defense and prosecution could discuss the value of the book but not if it were obscene or not. That would be *his* determination. He also said no witnesses would be allowed to speculate on what the author meant to put in the sets of Morse code dots.

The charge against Murao, the salesclerk, was quickly dropped. Only Ferlinghetti was on trial, but he was not called to testify. Instead the defense brought forward experts. Critic and teacher Mark Schorer testified that the poem, "like any work of literature, attempts and intends to make a significant comment on or interpretation of human experience" and that "the language of the street" was "essential to the aesthetic purpose of the work." (He also claimed that the poet uses homosexuality as evidence of how corrupt the world had become.) Walter Van Tilburg Clark, author of *The Ox-Bow Incident,* called "Howl" "the work of a thoroughly honest poet," and Kenneth Rexroth said it "is probably the most remarkable single poem, published by a young man since the second war." The only experts the prosecution offered were David Kirk, a professor who said the poem was worthless because it imitated Whitman, and Gail Potter, a teacher who had rewritten *Faust* and found reading Ginsberg's figures of speech was like "going through the gutter." The prosecutor, deputy district attorney Ralph McIntosh, focused his effort on his closing statements where he argued that literary merit was irrelevant if a book were obscene. He compared the poem to modern painting, which he found ridiculous, and said it must be judged by how it was perceived by "the average man," not "the modern man." This might have worked with a jury, but there was no jury.

It was a very unusual, very artistic trial. Not only was there talk of Dada and surrealism, there were extensive quotations from the Book of Job, Christopher Marlowe, Samuel Johnson, and Ginsberg's own "Go fuck yourself with your atom bomb."

Judge Horn deliberated for two weeks, using the time to read *Ulysses* as well as Judge John Woolsey's 1933 judgment freeing the James Joyce novel for publication. Horn gave his decision on October 3. The first half is a clear, cool description of the poem and its themes—a very smart piece of literary criticism, not at all what one expects from a federal judge. The second half builds to twelve rules on what makes a book obscene or not. Horn drew upon the Supreme Court's recent *Roth v. United States* decision, but added his own touches. The first rule is that material with any redeeming social importance is *not* obscene. The fourth is that a book must be judged by its effect as a whole on the average adult reader. The twelfth is that one should never charge a book with being obscene without consideration of one's own point of view: *"Honi soit qui mal y pense."* (Evil to him who thinks evil.) He closed with, "Therefore, I conclude the book *Howl and Other Poems* does have some redeeming social importance, and I find the book is not obscene. The defendant is found not guilty."

The trial was reported in several national newspapers, *Life* magazine, and *Saturday Review*. Articles in *Time* and *Esquire* followed. Sales of *Howl* skyrocketed. No other first book of poems has ever received this kind of national attention. Before the end of the year, 10,000 copies were sold. The court case would be cited later when commercial houses decided to publish *Lady Chatterley's Lover*, *Lolita*, and William Burroughs's *Naked Lunch*.

Ginsberg was in Venice when the trial began. He alternated between hope and fear, worrying Ferlinghetti would lose money if they lost, then in his next letter asking if Ferlinghetti could reinstate the missing words if they won. He went down to Rome for a magazine interview and continued south to meet W. H. Auden. He joined the older man and his friends at an outdoor café on the island of Ischia. Auden talked about *Howl*, which he had read and disliked, then about Shelley and Whitman, whom he didn't like either. Ginsberg wrote about the meeting in a letter to his father:

> I quoted the first line of Whitman, "I celebrate myself," and Auden said, "O but my dear, that's so wrong and so shameless; it's an utterly bad line—when I hear that I feel I must say please *don't* include me"...I tackled the whole table on the Whitman issue & wound up tipsy calling them a bunch of shits—Auden seems to have a long-winded rationalistic approach to his opinions—I doubt he respects his own feelings anymore—I think his long sexual history has been

relatively unfortunate and made him very orthodox and conservative and merciless in an offhand way—he sounds like an intelligent *Time* magazine talking.

Auden was a man of many moods, and it's a pity Ginsberg didn't meet him in a more generous one. In his next letter to his father, Ginsberg enclosed a sprig of clover plucked from Shelley's grave in Rome.

He was in Amsterdam when he finally heard that they had won the case. "Natch was glad and thankful," he wrote Ferlinghetti. He hoped they could continue the battle and free the work of Henry Miller, Jean Genet, and others for publication. And then, like any nice person, he asked, "Is there anyone I should write thank you notes to??"

The missing *fucked* and *ass* were reinstated in the seventh printing in 1959.

Fifty years later, it's remarkable how the gayness of both the poem and Ginsberg himself are often downplayed by admirers. Just as there are now books titled *Queer Forster* and *Queer Burroughs*, we need one called *Queer Ginsberg* to reconstitute the man in his full homosexual nakedness. A fiftieth anniversary collection of essays about *Howl* included only one gay male contributor, Mark Doty. Neither of Ginsberg's major biographies mentions his visit to the Stonewall Inn after the 1969 riots, as if afraid to tie him to anything as narrow as gay liberation. The literary mainstream prefers to see homosexual artists as isolated rebels or criminals, not as members of another tribe.

Yet after *Howl*, Ginsberg never denied the importance of his gay self. When people at readings asked why there were so many references to homosexuality in the poem, he blithely told them, "Because I am a homosexual." In his *Who's Who* entry in 1963, he insisted on being described as "married" to Peter Orlovsky. Nor did he deny his bond with other gay artists. It's at the core of his famous "whisperered transmission." He had slept with Neal Cassady who had slept with Gavin Arthur who had slept with Edward Carpenter who had slept with Walt Whitman—the gay equivalent to the lists of *begat*s in the Bible.

In Gordon Ball's famous 1991 photo of cadets at the Virginia Military Institute reading *Howl and Other Poems*, crewcut young men in gray uniforms frown into uniform copies of the black-and-white City Lights edition. What do they see there? What are they thinking? Is it just madhouse gibberish for them? Or does the sexuality tap into the wound-up energy buried in their stiff-backed bodies? Or are they worrying about those "saintly motorcyclists"?

4. Soul Kiss

—∞—

Years later, in the new medium of television that would change so much about American culture, James Baldwin was asked by a British journalist how it felt starting as a writer when he was black, impoverished, and homosexual. "You must've thought to yourself, 'Gee, how disadvantaged can I get?'" Baldwin smiled. "No, I thought I'd hit the jackpot." It was not just a smart joke, it was a brilliant judo move: he treated obstacles as golden opportunities. Yet those obstacles were also duties, a crushing set of obligations. Baldwin was often able to outplay them in his long career, but not always.

He began his professional life by trying to escape the expectation that a minority writer must use his art for politics. One of his first major essays, "Everybody's Protest Novel," was an attack on the very idea that great literature should be political. In his "Autobiographical Notes" to *Notes of a Native Son*, he argued: "I have not written about being a Negro at such length because I expect that to be my only subject, but only because it was the gate I had to unlock before I could hope to write about anything else." But the gate never stayed unlocked for long, and he needed to unlock other gates as well.

Critics often speak of Baldwin as a black writer who never lived up to the promise of his first novel, *Go Tell It on the Mountain*. Yet the shape of his career looks very different when we speak of him as a gay writer.

He was born in Harlem Hospital on August 2, 1924, James Arthur Jones, the illegitimate son of Emma Jones, a single woman who had just come north from Maryland. He never knew who his father was. His mother soon met and married a much older man, David Baldwin, a lay preacher and factory worker who gave the boy a new name. Seven more children followed.

"As they were born, I took them over with one hand and held a book in the other," Baldwin later wrote. "The children probably suffered, though they have been kind enough to deny it, and in this way I read *Uncle Tom's Cabin* and *A Tale of Two Cities* over and over and over again." His brothers and sisters would be important to him for the rest of his life.

He was a remarkable-looking creature from an early age. Because of his wide mouth and enormous, heavy-lidded eyes, he was sometimes called "sandwich mouth" and "frog-eyes," as was his mother—as are the mother and son in *Go Tell It on the Mountain*. But it was his intelligence that attracted the attention of his teachers. They encouraged him to attend school outside Harlem, and he commuted up to DeWitt High in the Bronx, one of the best schools in the city. There he worked on the literary magazine with future editor Sol Stein and future photographer Richard Avedon. Back home in Harlem he became a boy preacher at the local storefront church, following in his stepfather's footsteps even as he fought and competed with that difficult, unhappy man. He continued to preach until he finished high school.

Yet he was already exploring the rest of life: movies, jazz, art, and sex. New York City jumped with fresh opportunities during World War II. Baldwin met the painter Beauford Delaney, who was black and gay and lived downtown in Greenwich Village. Baldwin later described him as "a cross between Brer Rabbit and St. Francis." Delaney played records by Louis Armstrong and Bessie Smith for the former boy preacher while he painted pictures of him, including a nude oil and an idealized portrait in pastels—the latter done to show a mutual acquaintance that Baldwin was beautiful if looked at in the right way. The forty-something Delaney was in love with the teenager, but the feeling was not reciprocated. Nevertheless, the two remained friends for the next thirty-some years. Young Baldwin was going to bed with both men and women, but he thought of himself as homosexual by the time he was twenty.

He also thought of himself as a writer. He wrote poems and stories and began novels and plays. There was no money for college and he supported himself with a variety of jobs, including work at a defense plant in New Jersey where he was humiliated and driven away for being black. Meanwhile his aging stepfather deteriorated mentally and physically. The old man died in 1943, and his funeral was held on the day of a major race riot in Harlem. Shortly afterward, Baldwin began a novel about his family, *In My Father's House*. He showed early chapters first to Delaney, who thought they were wonderful, and then to Richard Wright. There had been black novelists before Wright—Charles Chestnutt, Nella Larson, Jean Toomer—but none had received half the attention Wright did for his raw racial thriller, *Native Son*. The novel was published in 1941 and adapted into a Broadway play the following year. Wright read the young man's chapters and recommended him for a literary grant. Baldwin was awarded five hundred dollars. He wrote more of the novel, now retitled *Crying Holy*, but was unable to sell it.

He continued to work sweeping floors, operating elevators, and waiting tables, helping to support his mother and siblings as well as support himself. He lived in Greenwich Village, which wasn't always easy. A white friend would sign a lease and Baldwin would move in; he was sometimes evicted when the switch was discovered. "There were very few black people in the Village in those years, and of that handful, I was decidedly the most improbable," he wrote toward the end of his life. "But the queer—not yet gay—world was an even more intimidating area of this hall of mirrors. I knew that I was in the hall and present at this company—but the mirrors threw back only brief and distorted fragments of myself." He found that guys who called him "faggot" when they were with their buddies on the street could be friendly and sweet when they encountered Baldwin alone. "I was far too terrified to accept their propositions, which could only result, it seemed to me, in making myself a candidate for gang rape. At the same time, I was moved by their loneliness, their halting, nearly speechless need."

He put his fiction aside and began a new career writing book reviews for various literary magazines. His first pieces showed a cool, bitter authority and were always critical. It didn't matter if Baldwin were reviewing a white or black author—he even attacked the wife of W. E. B. DuBois—he found fault in everyone he read. There was a lot of anger in these early reviews, but Baldwin had much to be angry about.

He burned to escape the United States after the war. When he won another grant, he used half the money to fly straight to Paris, a twelve-hour flight by plane in that pre-jet era, though it would've been much cheaper to travel by boat. He arrived in November 1948, a few months after Vidal, Capote, and Williams had departed. He brought the manuscript of *Crying Holy* with him, intending to finish it while he paid his way writing non-fiction for *Partisan Review*.

On his first day in Paris he went to the famous literary café, Deux

Magots, and met with Richard Wright, who had moved to France the previous year. Sitting with Wright was Themistocles Hoetis, a Greek-American novelist from Detroit who was starting a new magazine, *Zero*. He asked Baldwin to contribute.

The first issue of *Zero* appeared that spring and included a short story by Wright and Baldwin's essay "Everybody's Protest Novel." This fierce attack on politics in fiction uses *Uncle Tom's Cabin* as the prime example of how political righteousness reduces literature to one-note banalities. It's hard to say what turned Baldwin against a book he once loved. He never really describes it—one wonders if he had a copy with him in Paris. He attacks the idea of the book, not the book itself, but the Harriet Beecher Stowe novel is richer and more complex than its reputation. Stranger still, Baldwin closes the essay with a jab at *Native Son*, treating his benefactor's book as a sensational variation on Stowe's sentimental theme. Wright confronted Baldwin about the essay at their next meeting. Baldwin insisted he wasn't really attacking him and sat down and wrote a new piece, "Many Thousands Gone," a long, cold, detailed criticism of *Native Son* that ended their friendship for good.

This strange episode is difficult to interpret. Despite what Baldwin said, both essays are clearly attacks. He was trying to clear a space for himself as a writer, of course, but he was fiercely, crazily, biting the hand that had fed him. Most writers are competitive, and minority writers can be even more combative—there is less pie to share and more grievances at work. Yet Baldwin was fighting not only Wright, he was fighting himself. When he attacks Wright for being too angry to capture the black experience, he does it so angrily that one suspects he's attacking his own anger, too.

Virginia Woolf writes in *A Room of One's Own* that too much anger is bad for literature. Baldwin's early essays often bear her out. We forget the angry Baldwin because he was later attacked for not being angry enough. Joe LeSueur tells how the black playwright LeRoi Jones was often chided in the 1950s for being too nice. "Why isn't he more like Jimmy Baldwin?" a white friend asked. Jones later changed his name to Amiri Baraka and outdid Baldwin in righteous rage. Baldwin was friendly and garrulous in public, but the act of writing can tap into anger in the same way that alcohol can. Baldwin could be a charming drinker, but he could also be an angry one. His first essays explore different ways to write with and sometimes around anger. He felt many other emotions, too: tenderness, humor, sorrow, and joy. He himself once referred to "all these strangers called Jimmy Baldwin."

Later in 1949 he published another essay in *Zero*, a companion to "Everybody's Protest Novel" titled "Preservation of Innocence." The subject is "the problem of the homosexual." The piece wasn't included in his first book of essays or even the collected essays, *Price of the Ticket*, published in 1985. It didn't appear in book form until Toni Morrison included it in the Library of America volume of *Collected Essays*. It's a curious polemic that addresses sexuality in dry, impersonal terms—one would never guess the speaker was gay. It says smart things about relations between men and women (Baldwin always wrote about women with sympathy and intelligence), but doesn't fully come to life until it explores the absence of love in recent fiction, first in the heterosexual pulp of Raymond Chandler and James Cain, then in recent books with gay story lines, including *The City and the Pillar*. Baldwin argues that such books aren't about homosexual love, but only about the fear of sex between men. Here too he is trying to clear a space for himself, but he closes with a wise statement that could serve as the motto for his future fiction: "A novel insistently demands the presence and passion of human beings, who cannot ever be labeled."

Baldwin lived hand to mouth during his first years in Paris, borrowing money, selling articles, owing rent, and drinking and hanging out with other Americans, including Otto Friedrich and Mary Painter. Talking about writing is often more fun than sitting down and doing it, and Baldwin was a glorious talker. A new acquaintance moved in with him at one point, bringing his own bed linen. The police showed up a few nights later and arrested both men for possessing stolen sheets from a hotel. Baldwin spent eight nights in jail, wondering if he would ever get out. He might be more accepted as a black man in Paris than he was in America, but he was still a foreigner. Shortly after his release, he visited a favorite bar, the Reine Blanche, and met a tall, lean, dark-haired, seventeen-year-old Swiss boy with a receding hairline that made him look much older than he was, Lucien Happersberger. A runaway from Lausanne, Happersberger loved Paris, good times, and sex—with both men and women. He and Baldwin didn't live together, but they saw each other daily and saw other lovers, too.

Happersberger spoke little English and Baldwin's French was still pretty basic, but their relationship was not about conversation. Baldwin would fall in and out of love with Happersberger over the years, yet their friendship endured.

His unfinished novel still ate at Baldwin and, in the winter of 1951, Happersberger arranged for them to spend three months in the family cottage in a Swiss village in the mountains so his pal could write one more draft. The village had never seen a black man or a typewriter. During the day Baldwin hammered out fresh chapters while Bessie Smith sang on his portable Victrola, then he read the new pages each night to Happersberger, who could appreciate the sound of the prose if not always the sense. Baldwin later described this winter in one of his finest essays, "A Stranger in the Village," but without mentioning the novel in his typewriter or friend in his bed. He hit upon a new title for the book: *Go Tell It on the Mountain*.

When they returned to Paris, Baldwin mailed the manuscript to New York. While he waited to hear back, Happersberger's girlfriend announced she was pregnant. Baldwin encouraged the boy to marry her, insisting it was the right thing to do. When Knopf expressed interest in his novel, Baldwin borrowed money from a visiting American acquaintance, Marlon Brando (they had met when he briefly studied acting), and took a boat home. He talked with the editors and revised the book, incorporating some but not all their ideas. He stayed in New York long enough to be best man at his brother David's wedding and sailed back to Europe. He was in Paris when the book was published in May 1953.

Go Tell It on the Mountain is a remarkable novel, beautifully written and richly observed. The structure is deceptively simple: twenty-four hours in the life of the Grimes family in Harlem in 1935. It opens and closes with the eldest son, fourteen-year-old John, who hates his stepfather and has not yet found God. But most of the novel takes place inside the minds of his stepfather, mother, and aunt during a Saturday night prayer meeting. This extended sequence is a literary tour de force worthy of Virginia Woolf, although rawer, more emotional, and physical. Baldwin shifts back and forth in time, presenting the pasts of the three adults, their sins and sorrows. Not only did they suffer the restrictions of white America, they suffered their own inner wars between religious belief and sexual desire. In their community, heterosexuality is only slightly less sinful than homosexuality.

We return to the outer world of the prayer meeting when John falls into a swoon and suffers a series of hallucinations. "Then John saw the Lord— for a moment only; and the darkness for a moment only, was filled with a light he could not bear.... Then he cried, 'Oh, blessed Jesus! Oh Lord Jesus! Take me through!'" The presence of an older teenager in the congregation, a saved boy named Elisha, is as important to him as God. "'Oh yes!' cried the voice of Elisha. 'Bless our God forever.' And a sweetness filled John as he heard this voice." When he comes to, he finds himself surrounded by the congregation, all glad he has found God.

It's daylight now and everyone walks home through the empty Sunday morning streets. The adults confront each other over past crimes, but the most moving encounter is between John and Elisha. John thanks the older boy for praying him through and asks Elisha to continue to pray for him. "'For me,' persisted John, his tears falling. 'For *me*.'" He wants not just Elisha's Christian love, but his personal love. Elisha says good-bye by planting a "soul kiss" on the younger boy's forehead. John can't help smiling at his stepfather afterward, suddenly able to love the man—yet his stepfather won't smile back.

It is a phenomenal first novel, not just deeply felt but expertly crafted. Baldwin worked on it off and on for nine years, but it is all of a piece. People often call it Baldwin's best novel, but that's not quite true. It might be consistently better written—its prose a hybrid of King James Bible and Henry James—but it's not always a better novel than his other books. The war between the three grown-ups is sometimes muddled; long sections of the middle run out of steam; there is often more flash than sense in John's hallucinations. One can't help suspecting that mainstream critics prefer this novel simply because there are fewer gay elements. But Baldwin's later accounts of gay desire are no more lurid than the accounts here of straight desire. And John's love for Elisha is one of the book's most human and touching parts.

An equally memorable scene comes in the opening. John goes to the movies on Forty-second Street—his stepfather forbids both movies and jazz—and sees *Of Human Bondage* with Bette Davis. Sitting in the exciting hell of a crowded theater, John knows the nasty woman on the screen is damned, and he loves her for it. Baldwin himself adored Davis. Gore Vidal later described Baldwin as a cross between Bette Davis and Martin Luther King, but he wasn't the only person to see the electric actress in the electric writer. In *The Devil Finds Work*, his later book about Hollywood, Baldwin tells how he was transfixed from an early age by Davis: "the tense intelligence of the forehead, the disaster of the lips: and when she moved, she moved just like a nigger." He describes her as if he were describing himself, and the words aren't always pretty.

The new novel was reviewed widely and well. Baldwin did not want to be treated as "a Negro novelist," but he inevitably was. He was often compared to Ralph Ellison, who had published *Invisible Man* only the year before. Our old acquaintance Orville Prescott praised *Go Tell It on the Mountain* in the daily *New York Times*, but he also called it "an odd and special book" whose "story seems almost as remote as a historical novel about Hebrew patriarchs and prophets." (It doesn't seem so remote in our current age of evangelical Christianity.) Sales figures were good if not great. Baldwin was able to pay back some of the people he owed money to, including his agent and editor. Knopf immediately pressed him for a new book.

He had a hard time starting it. First he wrote a play, *The Amen Corner*, a companion piece to *Go Tell It* about a religious family where the wife was the preacher. But Knopf didn't want a play, they wanted another novel. Eventually he began work on a story set in the American colony in Paris that would address both race and love. He soon dropped race from the project. He warned his editor and agent that the new novel was a love story between two white people. He did not tell them that they were both men.

The novel was *Giovanni's Room*, and it's difficult to say when its love story became a gay love story. At one point it was about a divorced woman and a younger man, an actor. Baldwin had several reasons for writing a novel with all-white characters. He wanted to escape the label of "Negro novelist," which was not only artistically limiting, it was commercially restrictive. Two other African-American novelists, Frank Yerby and Willard Motley, had produced best sellers with white protagonists. Changing the race also enabled Baldwin to put distance between himself and his story: he wasn't writing about *his* life, he was writing about other lives. It gave his imagination more breathing room. In addition, there must have been bitter pleasure in putting himself inside a privileged white skin.

He had made a solid start on the new novel when he left Paris for New York in 1954. Lucien Happersberger followed him a few months later after leaving his wife and his child. Baldwin began to think they might become a couple. He was more in love with Happersberger now than when they had first known each other. But nothing went according to plan in America.

The details are sketchy about what happened between the two men. They were together, apart, then together again. Baldwin worked steadily on the new novel while staying with friends in New York and at the MacDowell colony in New Hampshire. He finished the book that spring and showed it to Helen Strauss, his agent at William Morris. She did not like what she read. Years later Baldwin reported, "My agent told me to *burn* it." Strauss denied she said such a thing: "I just thought he could do better." Nevertheless, she submitted the manuscript to Knopf, and after much in-house discussion Knopf rejected it. They claimed they were doing Baldwin a favor, that the book would ruin his career. Their chief argument among themselves was that they could be prosecuted for obscenity. It was only an excuse, of course—there's nothing obscene in *Giovanni's Room*.

The cold fact is that the big houses almost completely stopped publishing gay fiction in the years after *City and the Pillar* and *Other Voices*. It wasn't because of money—those books had done well. It wasn't because of censorship, either—the patchwork of state and local obscenity laws didn't prevent the distribution of adult novels by John O'Hara or James Jones. No, the change was due to the return of old attitudes about homosexuality. It was no longer exotic, it was just nasty. The numbers in the Kinsey Report made homosexuality seem both common and dangerous. Dr. Kinsey himself was under attack after 1950 and needed to struggle for funds in the years before his premature death in 1956. The gay scapegoating of the McCarthy years infected editorial offices, too, and genteel editors kept their distance from fiction with story lines about forbidden love.

There was now a readership for such books, however—a gay readership. The vacuum in the market was filled by small houses like Greenberg Press, which put out *Quatrefoil* by James Barr (1950) and *The Homosexual in America* by Donald Webster Cory (1951), or the growing paperback trade, which specialized in racy work with racy covers sold in drugstores. The paperback houses found a goldmine in lesbian titles like *Beebo Brinker* or *Odd Girl Out* by Ann Bannon and occasional gay male titles. (Marijane Meeker, who wrote both lesbian and gay pulp under various pseudonyms, reports that her publisher let her write almost anything so long as there was no graphic sex and the story ended unhappily—to make it "moral.") But these books were rarely promoted and never reviewed. Serious attention was given only to work published by mainstream houses like Knopf and Dutton. Gay fiction in effect went underground in these years. That underground was enlarged in 1953 by the appearence of two small gay magazines, *ONE* and *Mattachine Review*, but their circulation remained limited.

Baldwin was hurt and angered by Knopf's rejection. He had worked hard to get through the publishing door, but now the door was slammed shut again. He remained scalded by the experience for the rest of his life.

Luckily he had another project to work on. Sol Stein, his old friend from high school, had been at MacDowell with him the previous fall. Stein was an editor at Beacon Press, where he pioneered a new line of "library-size" quality paperbacks—what was later known as trade paper. He thought a collection of Baldwin's essays and reviews would make a good book for Beacon. The two friends discussed what to include and Baldwin wrote two new essays, "Equal in Paris," about his eight nights in jail, and "Notes of a Native Son," which became the title of the book. It was a provocative title, usurping Richard Wright's most famous work, but the piece itself might be the best single essay Baldwin ever wrote. This is his account of the summer of 1943, when he was humiliated for his race in New Jersey, his stepfather died, and Harlem erupted in riot. He found a way to use his anger here, giving it to an "I," then stepping back and watching from a slight distance. The anger is powerfully present, but does not take over the essay. The young man's private fury with his family is juxtaposed with his anger at white society; the narrator offers no resolution for either. (Baldwin's anger is different from Ginsberg's. Ginsberg's anger is quicker, more immediate, more temporary. One feels Baldwin's anger can fill his entire emotional life, and understandably so.)

Stein also read Baldwin's rejected novel, praised it and gave him detailed notes. Stein had no difficulty with the gay content. The same year he published *Notes of a Native Son*, he published *An End to Innocence* by Leslie Fiedler, with Fiedler's notorious 1948 essay, "Come Back to the Raft Ag'in, Huck Honey." But unfortunately Beacon did not publish fiction.

Baldwin's year in America ended. Happersberger returned to his wife and child, and Baldwin returned to Paris with a new lover, a black musician known to biographers only as "Arnold." Soon after his return, Baldwin read the rejected novel aloud to friends in Beauford Delaney's hotel room—Delaney had moved to Paris a few years before. The reading lasted all night and the guests left at dawn, exhausted but impressed.

Notes of a Native Son was published at the end of 1955. It was reviewed in the *New York Times Book Review* by Langston Hughes, who admired the prose—"The thought becomes poetry and the poetry illuminates the thought"—but felt Baldwin would not become a major writer until he wrote as a man rather than as a black man. Other reviewers were more complimentary, but the book didn't find a readership until years later.

Nowadays it's commonplace to praise Baldwin's essays at the expense of his fiction. But I prefer the fiction. He wrote several great essays, yet many start strongly only to fall apart. The authority of his voice can't disguise the mess of emotion and ideas he is unable to work out. The same contradictions, however, often produce life and drama in his novels.

(When the *Times Book Review* asked Baldwin to review Hughes's *Selected Poems* in 1959, Baldwin repaid Hughes for his criticism. The opening sentence reads: "Every time I read Langston Hughes I am amazed all over again by his genuine gifts—and depressed that he has done so little with them.")

Meanwhile, on his own, Baldwin found a home for *Giovanni's Room* with an English publisher, Michael Joseph. This forced his agent, Helen Strauss, to resume submitting the book in the States, until it was taken by a young editor, Jim Silberman, at a new publishing house, Dial Press. Dial remained Baldwin's fiction publisher for the rest of his career. He dropped Strauss, however, as soon as the contract was signed, refusing to work with her again.

Giovanni's Room was published in October 1956, with only minor changes, none of them sexual. Despite the fears of Knopf and Strauss, there was no prosecution for obscenity. The reviews were excellent. Granville Hicks in the *Times Book Review* warned that the characters were "as grotesque and repulsive as any that can be found in Proust's *Cities of the Plain*," but argued, "Mr. Baldwin writes of these matters with an unusual degree of candor and yet with such dignity and intensity that he is saved from sensationalism." Mark Schorer, a year before he testified at the trial for *Howl*, called the book "nearly heroic." In the *Nation* Nelson Algren wrote, "This novel is more than just another report on homosexuality"—as if the market were flooded—but accurately added, "It is a story of a man who could not make up his mind, who could not say yes to life." The book sold well, going into a second printing after six weeks. It's safe to assume that it was primarily gay men who bought it.

Unlike *Go Tell It on the Mountain*, Baldwin's second novel is not overtly autobiographical, yet there is autobiography present. This book about a white bisexual "who could not make up his mind" is dedicated "to Lucien." Yet the protagonist also contains pieces of Baldwin: his intelligence and self-awareness.

It's a miraculously concise novel. The narrator, David (we never learn his last name), spends a long night alone in a rented house in the south of France, getting drunk and remembering the past year. In Paris, while his girlfriend Hella toured Spain, David met and became involved with an Italian bartender named Giovanni. The two men lived together in a small room for several months until Hella returned and David needed to choose between his loves. He chose Hella and handled it badly. Giovanni fell apart, giving himself first to a man he didn't love, then to a hated boss who humiliated him. Giovanni murdered the boss. He is sentenced to die on the morning after the night we spend with David.

Giovanni's Room is as neatly constructed as a great film noir, a tight little machine intended simply to thrill us and break our hearts. But the eloquent prose and complex emotions lift the story past the mechanical. Now and then there's a slightly clunky phrase, such as Hella telling David, "If I stay here much longer...I'll forget what it's like to be a woman," but we can look past the period cliché to what she and Baldwin mean. There's also the wonderfully elastic metaphor of the room itself. The shabby ground-floor chamber the two men share can be read as shelter or prison, closet or home. The sex that happens here is never described—the book's only sex scene is between David and a female friend on the eve of Hella's return—yet the descriptions of the room with its low ceiling, whited-out windows, its printed wallpaper with faded eighteenth-century lovers, have a haunting, erotic melancholy. Only a handful of pages deal with the room, no more than deal with the river in *The Adventures of Huckleberry Finn*, yet room and river are equally resonant.

This is *the* classic coming-out novel—made more powerful by the fact that David fails to come out. The plot has not become dated, sad to say, which is why the novel is still powerful for readers fifty years later. The closet is still with us, which is why so many people, gay and straight, could respond to the 2005 movie of *Brokeback Mountain*. Our poisonous fear of what other people think of us remains strong. Baldwin goes beyond the fear of others and accuses David of being afraid of love itself. The fear of love will become his chief subject in his later fiction.

Despite the initial praise of *Giovanni's Room*, a curious backlash set in over the years from straight readers and critics. They grew to distrust and dislike the book—perhaps because gay readers liked it so much. Baldwin's friend, Otto Friedrich, in his otherwise perceptive profile of the young novelist in Paris, dismissed it as "an unpleasant attempt to write about white homosexuals"—as if a black gay man could never understand white ones. Baldwin's own biographer, James Campbell, expresses surprise over the book's popularity, since it has no sex scenes and is just "a short novel with many flaws." More recently, Claudia Roth Pierpont in a long essay in the *New Yorker* claims it is "marred by a portentous tone that at times feels cheaply secondhand—more *Bonjour Tristesse* than Genet or Gide," which is high-sounding nonsense. Her larger complaints are that Baldwin wasn't writing about the new civil rights movement and that his second novel isn't as strong as *Go Tell It on the Mountain*. Maybe it's just me reading as a gay man, but, good as *Go Tell It* is, it's not nearly as intimate or as real as *Giovanni's Room*. The three portraits of adults in the middle of the first novel are beautifully executed, yet they are people seen from a distance, in long shot. We are not inside their hearts as we are in John's heart in *Go Tell It*, or in David's culpable, conflicted heart.

The attacks disguised as second thoughts started early. The most famous came from Baldwin's friend Norman Mailer. The men had met in Paris in 1955 and liked each other. Then in 1959 Mailer published a wild book of previously printed odds and ends, *Advertisements for Myself*. The title says it all—the book marks the rise of the novelist as celebrity rather than storyteller—and it included a new essay, "Evaluations—Quick and Expensive Comments on the Talent in the Room," where Mailer judges his contemporaries. He trashes them all: William Styron, James Jones, Jack Kerouac, and Saul Bellow. He has a few nice words for Truman Capote ("a ballsy little guy" who is "the most perfect writer of my generation"), but dismisses his stories as saccharine. His words about Baldwin are almost all ugly and wrong: "James Baldwin is too charming a writer to be major…Baldwin seems incapable of saying 'F—— you' to the reader." (They still couldn't print *fuck* in 1959.) "If he ever climbs the mountain and really tells it all, we will have a testament and not a noble toilet water. Until then he is doomed to be minor." His one bit of praise is when he calls *Giovanni's Room*, "A bad book but mostly a brave one," but he never says why it's bad.

Mailer was straight, of course (he spent his career striving to out-butch Hemingway), but he was fascinated by homosexuality. He discussed it endlessly and fearlessly. He actually treated gay people fairly in a short essay, "The Homosexual Villain," apologizing for his evil gay characters and calling for equality. But he backtracked when he printed the piece in *Advertisements*, mocking the gay editor at *ONE* magazine who commissioned it and calling it the "squarest" thing he ever wrote. His allusions to Baldwin's sexuality in "Evaluations" are all indirect: in addition to "noble toilet water," there's repeated mention of perfume, first for Baldwin's prose, then "the perfumed dome of his ego."

Baldwin had attacked other writers himself, fairly and otherwise, and he did not act hurt and indignant. He resisted the urge to send Mailer a telegram that said simply "F—— you," but remained friendly. He waited two years to respond. Published in *Esquire* in 1961, "The Black Boy Looks at the White Boy" is a cool, tough, sly piece of work, a history of their friendship that shows more understanding of Mailer than Mailer ever showed him. Baldwin alternates praise with merciless put-downs, pointing out that this tough guy is a nice middle-class boy who went to Harvard. He says the black jazz musicians whom Mailer worshiped never took Mailer seriously: "They thought he was a real sweet ofay cat, but a little frantic." He nakedly reveals much of himself, talking about his own fears and career insecurity when he describes the dangers of the writing life. The essay closes on a warm, friendly, damning note. Baldwin has learned Mailer is running for mayor of New York City, which he thinks is a terrible idea. He believes Mailer is a great writer who has it in him to write a great novel. A writer's duty is to write and not get lost in politics or public life. "His work, after all, is all that will be left when the newspapers are yellowed, all the gossip columnists silenced, and all the cocktail parties over, and when Norman and you and I are dead. I know that this point of view is not terribly fashionable these days, but I think we do have a responsibility, not only to ourselves and our own time, but to those who are coming after us. (I refuse to believe that no one is coming after us.)"

It was a remarkably prescient warning, not only about the future of Mailer but the future of American literature as it moved from a world of print into a world of celebrity and television. A writer's public image could become more important than his books or writing. And as with his remarks about Richard Wright, James Baldwin was talking not just to Mailer, he was talking to himself.

5. Going Hollywood

—ᘯᘯ—

Gore Vidal came to Los Angeles to work for MGM in July 1955. Like many other novelists, he was in Hollywood chiefly for the money, but Vidal and the movies were made for each other.

He needed money badly. He had bought Edgewater, his villa on the Hudson, for only $16,000 in 1950, but it was a white elephant that required endless repairs and renovation. The rundown 1820 structure sat between the river and the New York Central railroad tracks—it shook every half hour or so when a train thundered by. The Greek revival facade with white columns suggested a bigger, fancier place than it actually was. Vidal and his partner Howard Austen camped out in half-furnished rooms during their first years there. Austen had an advertising job in the city, which he hated, but he came up every weekend to cook and entertain. Vidal tried to increase their income by writing genre fiction under various pseudonymns, including a series of clever murder mysteries set in the ballet world, yet they didn't pay enough, either. He complained nobody read novels anymore, not even trashy ones. But then he discovered television.

Many of the early TV studios were in New York City and they devoured material. A half-hour script earned from $500 to $1,200; an hour script earned as much as $2,500, roughly what Vidal made from his last novel, *Judgment of Paris*, which had taken two years to write. He began with an episode of *Janet Dean, Registered Nurse*, written for an actress friend, Ella Raines. This led to an original melodrama, *Dark Possession*, done for CBS's *Studio One*, about a murderess with a split personality: her good half squeals on her evil half. Adaptations of William Faulkner, Henry James, and John P. Marquand followed. Soon so much TV work was coming in that Austen was able to quit his job and act as Vidal's secretary and manager. The two men moved back and forth between Edgewater and an apartment in New York.

Vidal had a new idea for an original teleplay, a satirical comedy about an alien who tries to trick the Earth into destroying itself with a nuclear war. CBS turned down *Visit to a Small Planet* as too grim, but it was picked up by NBC's *Philco-Goodyear Playhouse*. Broadcast in May 1955, it was a huge success. MGM signed him at $2,000 a week to adapt a teleplay by another TV writer, *A Catered Affair* by Paddy Chayevsky. Vidal had no more movie experience than Chayevsky, but MGM didn't care. He moved into the Chateau Marmont, across Sunset Boulevard from the giant rotating statue of a painted cowgirl that would later appear on the cover of *Myra Breckinridge*. Austen remained in New York, taking care of Edgewater, but occasionally flying out to the Coast.

Vidal enjoyed California. The weather was soft and golden, friends from New York were often in town—including Joanne Woodward and Paul Newman—and hustlers were plentiful. Arthur Laurents later claimed Vidal was delighted to learn the young men on Santa Monica Boulevard charged only ten dollars before six o'clock, which was when Vidal preferred sex anyway. (Vidal jokes in his memoirs that he was unexciting in bed—he didn't even kiss—and thought it only fair he pay for sex. In another self-deprecating moment, he said a woman once told him he made love like Picasso. "Oh, I'm a genius, too?" he asked. "Yes, and a very bad lover. Just in and out and back to work.")

At the MGM commissary, he ate lunch with a pack of jaded screenwriters whom he later celebrated in his essays about the movie industry. More important, his office was next door to the office of a fellow novelist, Christopher Isherwood.

Vidal already knew and respected the older man. Isherwood was fifty-one in 1955, a short, ruggedly handsome, blue-eyed Englishman with the build of a bantam boxer and a surprisingly thin, reedy voice. He had been in Hollywood since 1939.

One afternoon while they walked around the MGM lot, he confided in Vidal: "'Don't,' he said with great intensity,... 'become a hack like me.'" Vidal thought he was only playacting. He didn't know that the author of *The Berlin Stories* really did feel like a failure. Despite his craft and talent and decades of accomplishment, Isherwood had not yet fully expressed himself as a writer. His breakthrough was still several years away.

Christopher Isherwood spent much of his life as an exile. He was, among other things, a citizen of love without a country.

He began as the son of English landed gentry, with a career army officer father who died in the First World War. He did not get along with his mother or their class. He wasn't happy until he left England and visited Berlin for the first time when he was twenty-five, invited there by his school friend and occasional bedmate, W. H. Auden. Berlin was a revelation. He found working-class Germans far sexier than he'd ever found any Englishman. He lived in Berlin off and on over the next four years, pursuing young men until he found his first real love in sixteen-year-old Heinz Neddermeyer. When Hitler came to power in 1933, Isherwood left Germany and took Neddermeyer with him. The pair wandered Europe in a traveling limbo of rented rooms and temporary visas.

Meanwhile he was writing—he was always writing. He published two lean, elegant novels in his twenties and collaborated with Auden on several plays. He now began a long, sprawling novel about his time in Berlin with the working title of *The Lost*. When the manuscript proved too unwieldy, he mined it first for a shortish novel, *Mr. Norris Changes Trains*, then for a linked set of stories and vignettes, *Goodbye to Berlin*. Both were told by a first-person narrator too busy describing the world around him to tell us much about himself. "I am a camera," the narrator famously declares. In the novel he is called Bradshaw, an Isherwood family name. In the stories even that pretense is dropped and he becomes just "Christopher," "Chris," and "Herr Issywoo."

Isherwood had hit upon an ingenious solution to the gay writer's problem of how to write about his life when so much of that life is despised or illegal: he did it indirectly, by writing about *other* people's lives. He lived for love, but he could not yet write about his kind of love. He never lied, never invented heterosexual love stories to hide the truth. He simply left sexual matters blank. We can go back now and fill in those blanks with his gay experience and the stories make perfect sense. The most famous story in *Goodbye*, "Sally Bowles," is the tale of a friendship between a gay man and a straight Englishwoman, a tough little cocotte who occasionally sings at the Lady Windemere Club. Christopher's lack of romantic or sexual interest in her is presented without explanation or apology, yet it could not read more clearly to a gay reader.

Mr. Norris was published in 1935; *Goodbye to Berlin* didn't appear until 1939. (The two were published together as *The Berlin Stories* in 1945.) The novel is good, but the book of linked stories is extraordinary. The prose has a hard, dry, quick poetry; the snapshots of people and places are unforgettable. Fraulein Schroeder's rented rooms on Nollendorfstrasse place the book in the rich tradition of boarding-house novels, looking back to *Père Goriot* by Balzac and forward to *Tales of the City* by Armistead Maupin. We also see other sides of Berlin: the cramped rooms of the working-class Nowak family; the spooky, unearthly mansion of the wealthy Jewish Landauers. Expanded further with diary chapters, the book gives us a very full picture of German life during the rise of Hitler.

Goodbye to Berlin appeared in pieces before the war and was broken up into new pieces afterward: a play, a bad movie, a musical, and a great movie. However, it deserves to be read and appreciated by itself, without the distractions of *Mr. Norris* or Liza Minnelli.

Isherwood and Neddermeyer continued to shift from country to country. When British officials refused to let the German refugee enter England on his second visit, Isherwood stood by helplessly while his lover was sent back to the Continent. They were apart when Neddermeyer was arrested in Paris in 1937 without his identity papers. He was deported to Germany, charged with draft-dodging, and sentenced to six months of prison and two years in the army.

Isherwood was shattered. He did what he could to help his lover from England, but it wasn't much. He eventually resumed life without him. Nevertheless, he seemed to suffer a crisis of faith over the next few years. It's hard to know how else to explain his restless, busy discontent. Isherwood no longer knew what he wanted or what he believed in—not his antifascist politics, not even his writing.

He visited China with Auden to collaborate on a book about the war there. Crossing the United States on their way home, he fell in love with the new continent—and with "Vernon," a savvy seventeen-year-old he met in New York. He thought he might find meaning in America. By early 1939, he was living in Hollywood with Vernon and studying pacifism and Eastern religion. He was a pacifist now, fearing and hating violence, not only the violence of fascism and possible war in Europe, but the violence he sensed in himself. He began to meditate. He studied yoga, but only briefly—he later found the breathing routines excellent for dealing with hangovers. Soon he met Swami Prabhavananda, a humorous, chain-smoking priest from Bengal who practiced Vedanta, one of six orthodox systems of Hindu philosophy. Vedanta promises inner peace through the contemplation of the oneness of existence and the rejection of the false self. This appealed to Isherwood, even though the false self includes the body and renouncing the body meant renouncing sex. After he and Vernon amicably separated (Vernon, who studied Vedanta, too, was always more friend than lover), he tried celibacy, with mixed results. He funded his spiritual quests by doing screenwriting work for another refugee, Bertold Viertel. Hollywood was full of German Jewish artists, and Isherwood was often reminded of Berlin.

So there he was: the worldly spiritualist, the angry pacifist, the ascetic sybarite. Isherwood was full of contradictions yet somehow managed to sustain his fundamental sanity and decency. The tensions of his contradictions seemed to hold him together.

Then Hitler invaded Poland in September 1939 and war was declared. People still debate Isherwood's decision to stay in the United States, but at the time nobody expected him to return to England. He wrote to the British consulate and offered himself for noncombatant work; they said it wasn't necessary. Nevertheless, he and Auden were attacked in the British press as deserters. He explored his reaction in his diary (he was an inveterate diary keeper; it was like a meditation exercise in prose):

> I'll try to be absolutely honest about this. Am I a coward, a deserter? Not according to my standards...Am I afraid of being bombed? Of course. Everybody is...No, it isn't that....If I fear anything, I fear the atmosphere of the war, the power which it gives to the things I hate—the newspapers, the politicians, the puritans, the scoutmasters, the middle-aged merciless spinsters. I fear the way I might behave, if I were exposed to this atmosphere. I shrink from the duty of opposition. I am afraid I should be reduced to a chattering, enraged monkey, screaming back hate at their hate.

He grew more alienated than ever from his homeland. He became an American citizen after the war in 1946.

In the meantime, he did war work with the Quakers in a refugee camp in Pennsylvania, then registered for the U.S. draft as a conscientious objector.

He moved into the Vedanta Center in Los Angeles in 1944 with the intention of becoming a monk. He translated Hindu scripture for Prabhavananda, filling his head with Indian gods and goddesses. Auden, who had settled in New York, thought he was making a big mistake getting involved in this "mumbo jumbo," but Auden was drifting back to the High Anglican beliefs of his childhood. Isherwood continued to live at the Vedanta Center even after he took a writing job at MGM. Then he fell in love with a blond ex-soldier. Nothing came of the blond, but Isherwood gave up the idea of celibate monkhood. The war ended, and he left the center and made up for lost time by throwing himself into sex and alcohol. He met Bill Caskey, a heavy-drinking, twenty-four-year-old photographer who was smart and funny, but who also brought out Isherwood's dark side. The two fought regularly, breaking up and getting back together, again and again over the next six years.

Isherwood was traveling with Caskey in South America when he was sent the galleys of a new novel for a quote. It was titled *The City and the Pillar*, and he didn't like it at first. But on second thought he decided to blurb it. (It was a very careful blurb: "One of the best novels of its kind...") He then wrote a long, frank letter to its author explaining his reservations, especially about Jim's murder of Bob:

> Dramatically and psychologically, I find it entirely plausible. It could have happened, and it gives the story a climax. (I wasn't absolutely convinced that Jim cared for Bob that much—but let that pass.) What I do question is the moral the reader will draw. This is what homosexuality brings you to, he will say: tragedy, death and defeat... Now it is quite true that many homosexuals are unhappy; and not merely because of the social pressures under which they live. It is quite true that they are often unfaithful, unstable, unreliable. They are vain and predatory, and they chatter. But there is another side to the picture, which you (and Proust) don't show. Homosexual relationships can be and frequently are happy. Many men live together for years and make homes and share their lives and their work, just as heterosexuals do. This truth is peculiarly disturbing and shocking even to "liberal" people, because it cuts across the romantic, tragic notion of a homosexual's fate....I am really lecturing myself,

because I, too, have been guilty of subscribing to the Tragic Homo-sexual myth in the past, and I am ashamed of it.

As early as 1948 Isherwood addressed the difficulty of serving both art and gay politics, and how a good story isn't always good politics. He was struggling with similar issues himself in his current work-in-progress, a long novel loaded with everything he'd learned in America, a book that eventually became *The World in the Evening*. The narrator was straight, but the novel included a shocking surprise: a subplot where two gay men live together *without* tragedy.

Isherwood met Vidal that summer in Paris. Isherwood was there with Caskey. Vidal introduced himself one afternoon at the inevitable Deux Magots café. The next day Isherwood visited Vidal in his hotel room. A trick had just left, fleeing when he heard Vidal's *ami* was coming. Vidal remained in bed in his underwear, chatting, flirting, while the two con-sidered each other sexually. They decided against it and never considered it again. They spent the next few days together. Isherwood wrote up a por-trait of Vidal in his diary:

> He is a big husky boy with fair wavy hair and a funny, rather attrac-tive face—sometimes he reminds me of a teddy bear, sometimes of a duck. Caskey says he's typical American prep school. His conver-sation is all about love, which he doesn't believe in—or rather, he believes it's Tragic....He is very jealous of Truman [Capote], but determined not to quarrel with him because he feels that when a group of writers sticks together it's better business for all of them.... What I respect about him is his courage. I do think he has that—though it is mingled, as in many much greater heroes, with a desire for self-advertisement.

A month later, Isherwood was in London and saw Tennessee Williams, whom he'd met during the playwright's brief gig at MGM. ("He's a strange boy, small, plump, and muscular, with a slight cast in one eye; full of amused malice.") Isherwood and Caskey shared a cab with Williams one night, rid-ing in a classic London fog. "We are the dreaded fog queens," declared Wil-liams and cackled loudly. They improvised a fairy tale about the fog queens, who roam the streets whenever a fog rolls in, and the townspeople close their shutters, afraid to look. Then one day a small boy opened a window and saw them. "But they're beautiful!" he said, and begged them to take him away. He was never seen again.

Back in California, Isherwood broke up with Caskey for good and met a new boyfriend. Don Bachardy was eighteen but looked much younger. "Christopher has with him the youngest boy ever," wrote magazine editor Leo Lehrman in his diary when the two visited New York. "'Twelve!' says Lincoln [Kirstein] with that wonder and delight at the naughtiness of the world." Isherwood was following his old pattern: he fell in love with a teenager, but stayed in love as the young man grew older. Bachardy sometimes reminded Isherwood of Neddermeyer, but he saw that Bachardy was brighter and more independent, which Isherwood preferred. His life settled down enough for him to finally finish *The World in the Evening* after working on it for seven years. The novel was published in 1954 to mostly bad reviews.

And it is a mess, a loose, talky jumble. The narrator, Stephen Monk, does not hold it together the way that "Christopher" holds together the other books. He is straight and married (with a gay affair in his past) and spends most of the novel stranded in bed with a broken hip. He talks endlessly about himself without becoming fully convincing. Yet this failed novel contains two remarkable things. The first is a playful discussion of camp sensibility written ten years before Susan Sontag's "Notes on Camp." The other is the presence of that untragic gay couple, Charles and Bob. Charles is a doctor; Bob is an artist serving in the navy. They visit Stephen only now and then, like guest stars on a TV show. But what a refreshing surprise for the modern reader: two gay lovers who aren't doomed, who care and worry and joke about each other like a real couple, who even argue like a real couple.

Reviewers didn't know what to make of them. Isherwood's own editor found Bob "much too hearty." Angus Wilson, gay himself and author of the bitchy *Hemlock and After*, complained that Isherwood confused "'goodness' and 'cosiness.'" Yet gay readers were delighted by the portrayal. Isherwood wrote a friend, "I have received lots and lots of fan-mail of the type you can guess.... Actually, it's heart breaking, the sense you get of all these island existences, dotted like stars and nebulae, all over the great black middle west." A young English poet, Thom Gunn, praised the book in a review for *London Magazine* and shortly afterward met Isherwood while passing through Los Angeles. Isherwood naturally put the twenty-five-year-old admirer into his diary: "He has pockmarks and a vertically lined face like a convict's, and his nose and chin are both too big—yet he's quite attractive, with his bright brown eyes. He likes America, especially California. I warm to all Britishers who do that."

Gunn, too, wrote about this first meeting, but many years later. He was quite taken with Isherwood: "He was tanned and youthful-looking, the famous bright eyes alert and observant; he perfectly adapted himself to the listener; his conversation was enthusiastic, lively, funny; and I said to myself, *this* is the way I want to age."

Gunn eventually settled in California as well, but he chose San Francisco as his home.

Gore Vidal came to work at MGM a few weeks after Gunn's visit. The two novelists immediately reconnected. Isherwood enjoyed the younger man's wisecracks and energy; Vidal admired his elder's intellect and dry wit. Isherwood had just finished rewrites on *Diane*, a sixteenth-century costume drama starring Lana Turner as Diane de Poitiers. ("Lana can do it," he told Vidal with a straight face.) Next he wrote a screenplay about the Buddha, *The Wayfarer*. Hollywood in the 1950s didn't know what they *or* their audiences wanted anymore. After Vidal finished *A Catered Affair*, his contract was extended for him to write a script about the trial of Alfred Dreyfus. Neither the Buddha nor the Dreyfus movie was ever made.

We don't know if the two talked about Isherwood's *City and the Pillar* letter or if they discussed the difficulties of writing about gay life. Isherwood was having enormous trouble with his fiction that summer. He really was, as he told Vidal, feeling like "a hack." After the failure of *World in the Evening*, he wanted to return to telling stories in his own voice, as with *Goodbye to Berlin* and *Prater Violet*, the gem-like short novel he had published in 1945. But stories told in his own voice would inevitably draw on his own experience, and the experience that now mattered to him most was love. He feared he couldn't write about that and still be published.

Perhaps I'll never write another novel, or anything invented, except, of course, for money.

Write, live what happens; Life is too sacred for invention—
though we may lie about it sometimes, to heighten it.

Oh, if I could have the wisdom to spend these last twenty years
in some better way—not messing with this crap.

Vidal, on the other hand, was not thinking about fiction at all. He was
busy with screenplays and with adapting *Visit to a Small Planet* for Broadway.
But he enjoyed working with invented stories—he preferred it, in fact.

Howard Austen came out for a long visit, and he and Vidal saw a lot of
Isherwood and Bachardy. They preferred the gentle Bachardy to the unpredictable Caskey. Isherwood liked Austen and took to calling him "Tinker"
in his diary—Vidal's nickname for him, short for Tinkerbelle. Isherwood
assumed Vidal and Austen were exactly like him and Bachardy, despite
Vidal's dismissive talk regarding love.

But as the months passed, toes were stepped on. Vidal gave Isherwood
his new novel to read, *Messiah*; Isherwood didn't know how to tell Vidal
that he found it dull and couldn't finish it. Vidal pestered Isherwood with
endless questions about his diary keeping, telling him about Anaïs Nin's
diaries and his fear of how she was portraying him. Isherwood wrote about
it in *his* diary: "I believe he really thinks about 'posterity' and its verdict—
just like a nineteenth century writer! And I don't know whether to admire
this or feel touched by it, or just regard him as a conceited idiot." But it's
hard to imagine Isherwood didn't have similar concerns himself, despite
the selfless ideals of Vedanta. The chief topics in his diary at this time were
life with Bachardy (there were quarrels and sulks as well as happiness), the
mescaline he had procured through his friend Aldous Huxley (he was looking for the best moment to take it), and his fears that he was writing only
for money and would never do good work again. He was in a very fragile
mood that fall.

Two days ago, for example, I was quite blue....I walked around
some movie sets with Gore, who looked at the books to see if any
were by him. Being with Gore really depresses me, unless I'm feeling
absolutely up to the mark, because Gore really exudes despair and
cynical misery and a grudge against society which is really based on
his own lack of talent and creative joy.

But as Vidal's biographer points out, Vidal was in good spirits that year; Isherwood was projecting his own bad mood here. He needed to get away from Hollywood, which he intended to do with a long trip to Europe.

He and Bachardy attended a preview of *Diane* in October before they left. ("General opinion—it's too long, Lana's a bore.") They were away for five months. In Tangiers they did hashish with Paul Bowles, which bonded the couple closer together after Bachardy went into a panic and Isherwood tenderly looked after him. In France they visited elderly Somerset Maugham, who cattily told Bachardy, "You must remember, Don—anything that's very beautiful only lasts a very short time." In England Isherwood made a kind of peace with his homeland and his mother, and he finally did his mescaline—in London, of all places, on a cold day in February. (Westminster Abbey "was very funny—a charmingly absurd little antique shop, full of ridiculous statues....No God there. No life at all—") But the most important development was that he had a new idea for a novel, a modern-day version of Dante's *Inferno* set in Mexico. It would be told by another first-person narrator, a straight man named William, and include people Isherwood had known over the years. He had a good title: *Down There on a Visit.*

It's often said that writers sometimes need to go around the block a few times to get where they're going. Isherwood was still circling his destination.

By the time he and Bachardy returned to California, Vidal was back at Edgewater on the Hudson, working on another TV play and pressing his producer to stage *Visit to a Small Planet* on Broadway. The two writers stayed in touch by mail. They remained respectful, admiring friends in the years ahead, despite the occasional exasperation.

One subject that Isherwood and Vidal did not agree on was Truman Capote. Isherwood didn't always like Capote's writing, but he adored the man. He remained friendly with him to the end. "There was one wonderful thing about Truman," began Isherwood at Capote's memorial service. "He could always make me laugh." And he laughed for a moment, then sat down again.

Capote had been busy since *Other Voices, Other Rooms* in 1948. He wrote more short stories and another novel, *The Grass Harp,* but he avoided anything overtly gay after the storm over *Other Voices.* He returned to ghost stories and fairy tales; the new work was well-crafted, well-written and well-received (*The Grass Harp* was actually praised for steering clear of homosexuality), but emotionally thin. Yet, like Vidal, Capote found that fiction didn't pay the bills. Traveling in Europe, he stumbled into movie work, rewriting the dreary *Indiscretions of an American Wife* for David Selznick in Rome and the wonderfully goofy *Beat the Devil* for John Huston on the Amalfi coast (where Vidal would later live). He turned *The Grass Harp* into a play, hoping to have some of the same success that Carson McCullers achieved when she adapted *The Member of the Wedding* to the stage. Walter Kerr compared Capote's play to an album full of dried flowers: "The flowers have been pressed into attractive patterns, but they are quite dead." The play closed after thirty-six performances. The same producer then paid Capote to turn "House of Flowers," a fairy tale/ghost story set in a bordello in Haiti, into a musical. With songs by Harold Arlen, direction by Peter Brook, and a cast that included Pearl Bailey and Diahann Carroll, *House of Flowers* opened in December 1954 to raves for Arlen's songs and bad reviews for Capote's book. The show lasted five months.

Capote's romantic life went through a major change as well. After amicably parting with Newton Arvin, he fell in love with Jack Dunphy, an ex-dancer and ex-husband of musical comedy star Joan McCracken (who later married Bob Fosse). The thirty-four-year-old redhead was now writing novels. The still-boyish Capote pursued, wooed, and won the older man. Dunphy was an unsociable, often prickly fellow who preferred to stay home while Capote grew more fiercely sociable, already befriending the high society wives he called "the swans." Dunphy wrote plays as well as novels, but never had a quarter of the success of his partner. The two men spent much time apart, yet Dunphy was the base that Capote always returned to.

Only now did Capote discover journalism. And it changed his career completely.

He accepted an offer to write about the 1955 tour of *Porgy and Bess* in the Soviet Union for the *New Yorker.* His experience in theater made him a natural for backstage stories. More important, real life was good for his prose. His beautiful sentences could turn precious and pretty without strong emotion to anchor them; reality kept his invention focused. Later published as a book, *The Muses Are Heard* is a drily funny account of a black American opera company visiting Leningrad during the Cold War. Capote's amused eye is color blind and he casts it on everyone: performers, bureaucrats, spies, fellow journalists, and a drunken Russian who can't stop singing "St. Louis Woman." Capote next wrote his notorious 1957 *New Yorker* profile of Marlon Brando, "The Duke in His Domain," the extended account of a long evening in Kyoto with the frustrated, self-absorbed star of *A Streetcar Named Desire*. People still argue over how much Capote remembered and how much he invented for his journalism, done in an age before portable tape recorders. But when Brando complained about the profile, he never accused Capote of making anything up, only of tricking him into talking about his love and sorrow for his mother. But those are the very passages where Brando stops sounding like an actor and becomes likable and human.

Capote had not completely given up fiction but worked intermittently on a short novel about a young woman in New York during World War II. He returned to it after his Russia book, using the first-person voice of his journalism to make himself a character in the story. He said little about his life except that he was a writer. The piece became a fictional memoir of his neighbor, Holiday (Holly) Golightly, a funny, smart-mouthed, independent girl of questionable means who hangs out at El Morocco and the Stork Club. Capote called it *Breakfast at Tiffany's*. Donald Windham, who was a good friend of Capote as well as of Tennessee Williams, had hoped to use the title himself for a book about encounters between servicemen and civilians. He didn't mind losing it too much, since he couldn't finish his book and he had taken the title from Lincoln Kirstein. Kirstein liked to tell a story of how he picked up a Marine one night and offered to take the man someplace fancy for breakfast. The only fancy place the Marine knew in New York was Tiffany's.

The short novel was published in November 1958 in *Esquire* and simultaneously in a book from Random House with three short stories. It was reviewed well but not ecstatically. (William Goyen in the *Times Book Review* was full of backhanded compliments: "There is in this work the quality of doll-like glee; of creating and dwelling in a doily story-world entirely of the author's own tatting"—while gay writers used code for their sexuality, reviewers did the same for their fag-baiting.) The book was on the bestseller list for ten weeks. It only slowly became a classic and it's hard to say why. Holly Golightly's speech, her American slang sprinkled with oddball French, is wonderful; the glimpses of 1940s New York are highly evocative.

(Two of America's favorite novels, *Breakfast at Tiffany's* and *Catcher in the Rye*, are both set in New York in the 1940s, a fact we often forget.) Yet none of this explains why people fell in love with it as the ultimate "coming to New York" fairy tale, even before the 1961 movie with Audrey Hepburn. I suspect that much of its charm comes from something left half-said: it's the story of a romantic friendship between a straight woman and a gay man. Since their affection cannot end in sex or marriage, the two must explore other, less obvious ways to be intimate. They can have romance but must remain pure, the modern equivalent of courtly love. This is not our last encounter with this electric situation.

Gore Vidal accused Capote of stealing his book from Christopher Isherwood: Holly Golightly is nothing but Sally Bowles transplanted to America. Many reviewers saw echoes, but Vidal said it more harshly. He was never objective about Capote, of course, but I believe he hit upon a truth here. Influence is difficult to discuss without making it sound like theft, but all writers learn from each other. *Breakfast at Tiffany's* is very different from the short story "Sally Bowles," yet there are striking similarities. Both feature the actual author as narrator. Both are about a friendship between a gay man and a straight woman without saying so openly. (Capote didn't need to say it; even the reviewer at the *Times* acknowledged why the two friends did not become lovers.) Both stories end with the woman disappearing and the narrator not knowing what's become of her. Yet two very different characters are put into these similar boxes. Sally is cruder and meaner than Holly; Holly is more innocent—more American, if you will. She is that curious paradox, the not-so-bad bad girl, an American type dating back to Henry James's Daisy Miller.

The women are different, but the approaches are so similar that it's hard to believe Capote didn't learn from Isherwood, consciously or unconsciously, taking structure and strategies from the older writer. Capote read widely and well. "Sally Bowles" had been around for almost twenty years in 1958. Influence is hardly a crime, but in the competitive world of postwar fiction, Capote could not admit being anything but original.

Isherwood never accused or even suggested that Capote stole from him. He included Capote in his 1961 UCLA lecture series on new voices in the novel. But he didn't correct Vidal when he started making accusations.

Capote and Isherwood had similar yet different experiences when their books were made into movies. In *Breakfast* with Audrey Hepburn, the

Capote character is played by butch George Peppard and a tale of friendship becomes a heterosexual love story. The same thing happened with *I Am a Camera*, the 1951 play that John van Druten made from *Goodbye to Berlin*, built around the story "Sally Bowles": Herr Issyvoo is straight and tries to save Sally from her aimless life with an offer of marriage. This solution was kept for *Cabaret*, the stage musical made from the play in 1966. But the musical became a movie in 1972 and screenwriter Jay Presson Allen and director Bob Fosse turned the Isherwood character gay again. Times had changed and the filmmakers could go even further than Isherwood had in his book. In fact, I think their solution—Christopher *almost* marries Sally—is more dramatic and interesting than what's half-hidden in the original. The movie was able to finish in 1972 what Isherwood began in 1939.

Gore Vidal continued to go back and forth between Hollywood and New York until the end of the decade, writing movie scripts and stage plays, wishing he had time to write fiction again. He agreed to work on the screenplay of the ponderous epic, *Ben-Hur* so that he could finish his MGM contract and be free again.

Vidal has told his *Ben-Hur* story many times, his role growing in importance with each telling. The most trustworthy version is the first in his excellent essay, "Who Makes the Movies?" When Vidal rewrote the front half of the movie (English dramatist Christopher Fry rewrote the second half), he needed to find motivation for Messala (Stephen Boyd) wanting to destroy his friend Ben-Hur (Charlton Heston) and his family. Vidal had an idea which he shared with director William Wyler:

> "As boys they were lovers. Now Messala wants to continue the affair. Ben-Hur rejects him. Messala is furious. *Chagrin d'amour*, the classic motivation for murder."
>
> Wyler looked at me as if I'd gone mad.

Vidal said he'd put it between the lines and only people who cared about motive would even notice. Wyler agreed to try it, but insisted, "Don't ever tell Chuck what it's all about or he'll fall apart." Not everyone is convinced by the story. Ben-Hur himself, Charlton Heston, says he remembers reading new lines for the encounter and they didn't work. He also points out that "Don't ever tell Chuck" sounds suspiciously like the punchline of a tale about Laurence Olivier wanting to play Iago as gay to Ralph Richardson's Othello. The director said go ahead, "but for God's sake don't tell Ralph." Heston thought both tales were apocryphal. Nevertheless, in the scene in the finished film, Boyd gazes at Heston like a famished wolf.

Vidal wanted to write his own novel set in ancient Rome, one about the last pagan emperor, Julian the Apostate. But as soon as he escaped MGM, he was hired by Sam Spiegel to adapt *Suddenly Last Summer* at the insistence of Tennessee Williams. He did what he could to circumvent the censors, making Sebastian's sins vague and mysterious. Afterward, he had a new idea for a play about politics. Instead of going back to Julian, he wrote *The Best Man*. He wrote it quickly—plays can be written faster than novels—but it whetted his appetite for a brand-new career. Isherwood announced the change in his diary when Vidal next visited California in 1960.

> Gore is running for Congress and full of politics, which, he rather hints, is his alternative to writing. (As a matter of fact, his play, *The Best Man*, is probably the best thing he's done...) He is sure Jack Kennedy will win, and he expresses enormous admiration for Kennedy, as the happy-go-lucky kid who turned tough and ambitious. "Russell" in his play is obviously part Kennedy, part Gore.
>
> What one feels and rather loves in Gore is his courage. He's most definitely not a crybaby. He has a great good-humored brazen air of playing the game—constantly using the latest fashionable expressions, such as "grimsville" and "closetwise."

Gore Vidal was a sexually active gay man who lived with another man, yet he was not afraid to run for Congress—and as a Democrat in Republican Dutchess County. There was a half-hearted whispering campaign about his sexual preferences, but the press described him as only a bachelor who knew many movie stars. He won more votes than any other Democratic candidate ever had in his district, but he still lost the election.

It was not cowardice but raw practicality that led so many gay authors to write about other things besides their sexuality in the 1950s. A knowing silence was a good strategy for the time being. But homosexuality was so despised in some circles that even silence could be seen as a threat.

II
The Sixties

6. The Great Homosexual Theater Scare

—꿍—

In 1958, while working on the screenplay of *Suddenly Last Summer*, Gore Vidal took Tennessee Williams to Palm Beach to meet Senator John F. Kennedy and his wife, Jackie. Vidal knew Jackie because they shared the same stepfather, the much married, much divorced Hugh Auchincloss. Williams had no idea who the Kennedys were, but the young couple were certainly familiar with the famous playwright. The four drank cocktails and did a little skeet shooting—Williams was a better shot than the senator from Massachusetts. When Kennedy stepped forward to take aim, Williams whispered to Vidal, "Get that ass!" Vidal told Williams he shouldn't cruise our next president, then repeated the remark to Kennedy. "Now, that's *very* exciting!" said Kennedy with a grin. Williams later told Vidal, "They'll never elect those two. They are much too attractive for the American people."

Williams returned to Key West and Vidal to Edgewater. Two years later Kennedy was elected president, and the Sixties began.

Tennessee Williams was now very famous and very rich. His work was regularly produced on Broadway; Hollywood bought up all his plays, even quieter ones like *Summer and Smoke*. It was the height of what he later called "the catastrophe of success." He did not live extravagantly, but wealth added to the unreality of his life. He could have fallen apart without fame and money, yet they definitely accelerated the process.

He was still with Frank Merlo, "Little Horse," moving back and forth between their modest three-bedroom house in Key West and various apartments in New York. The handsome, black-haired Merlo was his majordomo as well as his boyfriend, looking after their homes, arranging schedules, paying bills. Merlo loved Williams more than Williams loved him; the imbalance produced guilt and paranoia in the playwright. He often avoided returning to Key West when Merlo was there alone. At times he even believed Merlo hated him and wanted him to die. Donald Windham once saw Williams take a drink Merlo had mixed for him and pour it down the sink. "Poison," he muttered to himself, thinking nobody else was present.

Williams was becoming more and more unhinged. He still drank heavily; his use of barbiturates *and* amphetamines produced extreme mood swings. His hypochondria worsened, and he was certain each play would be his last. Of course, his writing suffered. The emotion that powered his best work grew wilder, sloppier, and more baroque. He followed *Suddenly Last Summer*, his post-therapy play, with *Sweet Bird of Youth*, a masochistic extravaganza about a gigolo, Chance Wayne, who returns to his hometown on Easter weekend and is castrated by his ex-girlfriend's vengeful father; Chance is accompanied by a mad, pill-popping actress, Alexandra del Lago, aka the Princess Kosmonopolis, often read as a self-portrait of the author. Next came *Period of Adjustment*, a domestic comedy of sorts that might be called a Tennessee Williams Christmas play, if one can imagine such a thing. Afterward, hunting for a new project, Williams took out an old short story, "Night of the Iguana," and ran it through his typewriter again, first as a one-act, then as a full-length play. It would be his last commercially successful production, and perhaps his last artistic success as well.

A comic, sometimes poetic drama about lost souls grabbing at last chances in a small hotel in Mexico, *Night of the Iguana* is also full of autobiographical fragments, but they are quieter, less shrill. One nice touch is Miss Jelkes's elderly grandfather being called Nonno, which was Merlo's Italian nickname for Williams's grandfather, Reverend Dakin, when he lived with them in Key West. There is nothing overtly or even covertly gay in the play, yet the emotional drama never feels forced or stifled.

Williams went to New York in October 1961 to supervise rehearsals. Miss Jelkes was played by Margaret Leighton and Maxine, the foul-mouthed owner of the hotel, was played by Bette Davis. True to her own form, Davis fought with Williams, with director Frank Corsaro, and with her costars, whom she accused of upstaging her and sabotaging her performance. (She dropped out early in the run and was replaced by Shelley Winters.)

Before the company left for out-of-town tryouts, Williams did an interview for the Sunday *New York Times* Arts and Leisure section to promote the new work. The piece ran on November 5, 1961. As usual, he moaned about his life, saying he was exhausted and ill and this was probably his last play. Next to the profile, however, was something unusual, a think piece from the new drama critic, Howard Taubman, "Not What It Seems." The opening line declared: "It is time to speak openly and candidly about the increasing incidence and influence of homosexuality on New York's stage." Taubman, whose background was in music, worried that there were too many gay playwrights and they only wrote about gay men disguised as straight men and women. "Characters represent something different from what they purport to be. It's no wonder they seem sicker than necessary." He named no names (it would've been libelous in 1961), but the interview with Williams stood directly beside it.

There is no record of how Williams responded—or if he even saw the article. But Taubman's piece was the first shot in the prolonged, incessant bombardment of a charge that became an obsession with mainstream critics during the next few years.

Night of the Iguana opened in December to rave reviews. The play had a long, successful run and won the New York Drama Critics Circle Award. *Time* magazine put Williams on its cover in March 1962. Nobody said anything about gay disguises in this play or any other—for the time being.

A few months later, on October 13, 1962, a startling new drama by a new playwright opened on Broadway: *Who's Afraid of Virginia Woolf?* by Edward Albee.

Albee had already received attention for several short plays produced downtown. *Virginia Woolf* was his first full-length work, but he did not come out of nowhere. He had a long apprenticeship before his so-called overnight success.

The adopted only child of a wealthy couple on Long Island, he had attended Lawrenceville prep school with James Merrill, another son of money, before his family sent him first to a military academy, then to Choate. He was at Trinity College in Hartford for three semesters before he was expelled for skipping classes. In 1949, when he was nineteen, he got into a bitter quarrel with his parents one morning, phoned for a cab, and left home, breaking with his family for good and moving to Greenwich Village.

He had known he was gay since puberty—"I took to it, as they say, as a duck to water." In New York, he found first one boyfriend, then another—William Flanagan, a composer who was only five years older but became his artistic mentor. Flanagan was smart, witty, original, and malicious. His music was respected by his teachers, Aaron Copland and David Diamond, but his career never took off. He and Albee shared a weakness for alcohol and melancholy; they were known in the downtown gay bar circuit as the Sisters Grimm. Albee later said he never smiled in the old days only because his teeth were uneven. Nevertheless, he maintained the straight, thin-lipped frown like a cut made by a scalpel long after his teeth were fixed. The Sisters Grimm were regulars at the San Remo, at Julius's on West Tenth Street and at the College of Complexes (later called the Ninth Circle), also on West Tenth Street, where the mirror behind the bar was covered with clever graffiti written in soap by patrons. It was there that Albee saw the phrase, "Who's afraid of Virginia Woolf?"

He supported himself with various jobs, including delivering telegrams for Western Union. After he turned twenty-one, he received twenty-five dollars a week from a trust fund set up by his grandmother. He was already writing, but slyly, almost secretly. He tried poetry, novels, then a verse play, and finally prose plays. A one-act titled *Ye Watchers and Ye Lonely Ones* juxtaposed scenes of two boys in love with scenes of two grown gay men. One man asks the other, "Why do homosexuals always write rotten love poetry to each other?" The other replies, "Because homosexual love is rotten, too." Albee showed his work to Flanagan but almost nobody else.

The 1950s saw the rise in New York of what became known as off-Broadway. The Provincetown Playhouse had been around since the First World War, but it was now joined by the Living Theatre, Circle in the Square, Café La MaMa, and Caffe Cino. Albee and Flanagan went to these theaters often, seeing revivals of O'Neill and Williams, and imported work by Eugene Ionesco and Jean Genet. Here is where Albee learned what a play could be, not in the commercial houses of Midtown.

A few weeks before he turned thirty, Albee had a new idea for a piece, a dialogue between two men on a bench in Central Park. He wrote it slowly and steadily over the next two and a half weeks, then revised it and finished just before his birthday. The first person to read *The Zoo Story* was Flanagan, who was knocked out by it. He immediately showed it to their friends and acquaintances—Copland, Thornton Wilder, Richard Howard, William Inge—whose responses ranged from mild amusement to wild approval. But one-act plays were hard sells, even downtown, and nobody knew what to do with it. Flanagan's former teacher, David Diamond, sent the play to friends in Germany, who loved it, translated it into German, and gave the one-act its world premiere at the Berlin Festival of 1959—on a double bill with *Krapp's Last Tape* by Samuel Beckett. Albee was present for the performance, witnessing the first staging of his work in a language he didn't understand.

This foreignness feels perfectly appropriate. *Zoo Story* belonged to a new kind of playwriting: spare, abstract, minimal. Critics were trying out the term "Theater of the Absurd" for this new antirealism, yet there is realism, too, as there was in the work of his contemporary Harold Pinter. Albee's play is an exchange between two strangers, unhappy loner Jerry taunting married middle-class Peter into intimacy—Jerry ultimately achieves intimacy in suicide. We now think of this as Albee's "gay play." And there *is* a sexual edge to the situation, which resembles a pick-up, but it's addressed in only one line, when Jerry confesses that for eleven days, when he was fifteen, he was "a h-o-m-o-s-e-x-u-a-l."

The first English-language performance was a reading at the Actors Studio, which was considering a production. "That's the best fucking one-act play I've ever seen," said Norman Mailer afterward, but the Studio didn't know what to make of it.

A New York production was eventually put together elsewhere, the play paired again with *Krapp's Last Tape*. It opened at the Provincetown Playhouse in January 1960. The program received respectful but mixed reviews from Brooks Atkinson in the *Times* and Walter Kerr in the *New York Herald Tribune* (they were disturbed by the nihilism of both plays, not by the sexual undercurrents in Albee). But an absolute rave in the *New York Post* by Richard Watts turned the play into a hit. This was an age when New York theater was not driven by just one newspaper. The play found an audience and Albee became a star in the downtown art scene.

More work followed, all short plays: *The Death of Bessie Smith*, *The Sandbox* (with music by Flanagan), and *The American Dream*. *Zoo Story* continued to make its way in the world, first in a national tour, then in regional productions and in foreign translations. It even went to Argentina as part of the cultural exchange program.

Meanwhile Albee and Flanagan had broken up. They parted on the eve of the success of *Zoo Story*, but remained friends. Flanagan would interview his ex for *Paris Review* in 1966. Sex and alcohol had created enormous problems for them as a couple—they were famous for their fights. Each soon found new boyfriends: Albee began to see a college student from Texas named Terrence McNally, who later became a playwright himself; Flanagan fell in love with Sanford Friedman, the partner of their friend Richard Howard. Couples often mix with other couples, break up and come back together in new combinations. Gay couples tend to do it more visibly and remain friends more often afterward. Yet such messy, open relationships occur in any life, gay or straight. Years later, Richard Howard could hear echoes of evenings with Albee and Flanagan in *Who's Afraid of Virginia Woolf?* but so did their married pal, composer Charles Strouse. "It's like all of us talking," Strouse told his wife. People at Wagner College on Staten Island, where Albee briefly taught, would argue that George and Martha were based on a married couple there—only they couldn't agree on which couple.

Albee began work on his first full-length play in 1960. Originally titled *The Exorcism: or Who's Afraid of Virginia Woolf?* it was initially about a husband and wife who cure themselves of their belief in a fictional lost child. But the emotional truths and role-playing that Albee added as the two-act play became a three-act play overshadowed the original concept. George and Martha fight endlessly, brilliantly, with an intimacy that turns their quarrels into a kind of lovemaking. They play games with each other and with the younger couple they invite home for a nightcap, Nick and Honey. The games have become famous: Get the Guests, Hump the Hostess, Humiliate the Host. But it's the language that's the real strength of the play, raucous and electric, in rapid-fire exchanges and extended monologues. The rhythm of George and Martha's drunken exchanges is exhilarating.

> Martha: Hey, put some more ice in my drink, will you? You never put any ice in my drink. Why is that, hunh?
> George: (Takes her drink) I always put ice in your drink. You eat it, that's all. It's that habit you have...chewing your ice cubes...like a cocker spaniel. You'll crack your big teeth.
> Martha: THEY'RE MY BIG TEETH!
> George: Some of them...some of them.
> Martha: I've got more teeth than you've got.
> George: Two more.
> Martha: Well, two more's a lot more.

These zigzag rhythms carry the play forward for three and a half hours, taking it from domestic comedy to black comedy to raw confrontation to an exhaustion that resembles peace. Under the brilliant verbal fireworks are two unhappy, three-dimensional people who are bound together in love. Love does not soften or sweeten their arguments, it only adds to their pain.

Albee's producers, Richard Barr and Clinton Wilder, were very excited by the new play and thought it would work on Broadway. They raised $75,000, but the production ended up costing only $47,000. Money was saved with such shortcuts as singing the title not to "Who's Afraid of the Big Bad Wolf," which was a Disney tune, but to "Here We Go Round the Mulberry Bush," which was in public domain. The director was Alan Schneider, who specialized in Beckett and Ionesco. The play was cast with Uta Hagen as Martha, Arthur Hill as George, George Grizzard as Nick, and Melinda Dillon as Honey.

The play opened on a Saturday, which meant there were no reviews until Monday. The first notices were bad. "A sick play for sick people," said the *Daily Mirror*. But then the good reviews started to come in, raves with reservations (the chief reservation was about the fictional child) and total raves. More than one reviewer compared the play to the best of Eugene O'Neill. People began to line up to buy tickets. Tennessee Williams attended opening night, and liked it so much he returned repeatedly the following week.

Nobody said a word about Albee's sexuality. Howard Taubman, in fact, despite his fear of homosexual influence, praised *Virginia Woolf* to the skies. "Like Strindberg, Mr. Albee treats his women remorselessly, but he is not much gentler with his men. If he grieves for the human predicament, he does not spare those lost in its psychological and emotional mazes.... It marks a further gain for a young writer becoming a major figure of our stage."

Virginia Woolf ran for two years. It was promptly translated into other languages: Ingmar Bergman directed a production in Sweden and another was done in Prague where it was retitled *Who's Afraid of Franz Kafka?* The play spoke to people everywhere. The verbal and emotional energy were only part of the appeal. The real secret of the play's success was its subject: marriage.

The start of the Sixties marked a new age of truth telling about married life. The old myths of domestic bliss and normalcy were now seen to be make-believe; people wanted to know how other couples actually lived.

John Cheever and John Updike wrote about troubled marriage in the *New Yorker*; Richard Yates wrote about it in his ferocious 1961 novel, *Revolutionary Road*. The sophisticated team of Mike Nichols and Elaine May began to explore the rhythms of domestic spats in their comedy routines. Couples attending *Virginia Woolf* were fascinated to learn that their own quarrels might not be as perverse as they feared, that arguments might even be healthy, and that at least one marriage was worse than their own.

Virginia Woolf won the Tony and the New York Drama Critics Circle Award for best play of 1963. The judges for the Pulitzer awarded the drama prize to Albee, too, but the Pulitzer board, comprised of newspaper editors from different parts of the country, overruled them. There was no Pulitzer for drama that year. Newspaper editors might have disliked the play, but theatergoers and critics loved it.

Then the critics began to turn against *Woolf*. It happened slowly, imperceptibly: a growing unease with both the play and Albee. A trickle of critical remarks became a mudslide, falling not just on Albee but on all gay playwrights. Within a few years it became commonplace to dismiss *Virginia Woolf* as a gay play in drag.

What happened to produce the change? At some point theater writers must have heard that Albee was gay. It's hard to guess what was said in private based on what was published. The earliest sexual attack in print appears to have been in the spring of 1963 in the *Tulane Drama Review*, a prominent theater quarterly. Editor Richard Schechner wrote an editorial that appeared in the front of the issue: "The American theater, our theater, is so hungry, so voracious, so corrupt, so morally blind, so perverse that *Virginia Woolf* is a success.... I'm tired of morbidity and sexual perversity which are there only to titillate an impotent and homosexual theater and audience. I'm tired of Albee."

Albee followed *Virginia Woolf* with an adaptation of *Ballad of the Sad Café* by Carson McCullers. It was well received but seen as more McCullers than Albee. His next original work didn't open until December 1964. *Tiny Alice* is a very different animal from *Virginia Woolf*, a surrealistic comedy closer to Ionesco than to O'Neill. It's a playful dream play about faith, religion, and theater. A Catholic lay brother is sent to the mansion of a wealthy woman, Miss Alice, and eventually marries her only to learn she is merely the symbol of the real Alice, a tiny Alice who lives in the perfect scale model of the mansion standing onstage. Julian is killed by a lawyer so he can join his real bride inside the model. Critics were respectful but baffled. Taubman gave it a good review, but admitted he was puzzled. Even John Gielgud, who played Julian, confessed he didn't have a clue what it meant. Nevertheless, the play found an audience, who seemed to enjoy the giddy vertigo of confusion.

One critic, however, wasn't confused in the least. A young novelist, Philip Roth, reviewed the play two months into its run in a new publication, the *New York Review of Books*. Under the title "The Play That Dare Not Speak Its Name," the future author of *Portnoy's Complaint* and *My Life as a Man* called *Tiny Alice* "a homosexual daydream." He attacked it for "its gratuitous and easy symbolizing, its ghastly pansy rhetoric and repartee." Nobody reading the play today will find much "pansy rhetoric," ghastly or otherwise, nor did the other reviewers. Roth barely describes the play itself and says nothing about the actors or the production. The closest he comes to explaining why he found it gay is to say that like *Virginia Woolf*, it showed a woman defeating a man. Presumably a straight man could never imagine such a thing. Roth concluded the review by demanding, "How long before a play is produced on Broadway in which the homosexual hero is presented as a homosexual, and not disguised as an angst-ridden priest, or an angry Negro, or an aging actress; or worst of all, Everyman?" (Fifty years later, Roth himself wrote a novel titled *Everyman* about a dying, sex-obsessed Jewish heterosexual male, which presumably does qualify for universality.)

This was only Roth's second theater review. Nine months earlier he gave a bad review to *Blues for Mr. Charlie* by James Baldwin, which he found a poor imitation of a better play, *The Zoo Story*. He gave no hint that he even suspected Baldwin or Albee were gay. Somebody must've tipped him off in the meantime. I also believe he must have read a new essay by a woman that broke the code of this secret homosexuality. More about that in a moment.

Roth's attack opened the door for new attacks. Wilfrid Sheed, reviewing a batch of plays in *Commentary* in May 1965 (including the first play by Terrence McNally), wanted to see "the homosexual sensibility asserted openly in one play rather than sneaked into twenty. It would, if nothing else, leave a cleaner smell." In the summer of 1965, the *Tulane Drama Review* ran a thirty-page critique of *Virginia Woolf* by a psychiatrist, Donald Kaplan, using it as a prime example of the infantile sexuality of "homosexual theater." In November 1965, Martin Gottfried in *Women's Wear Daily* defended homosexual theater, sort of ("The fact is that without the homosexual American creative art would be in an even sorrier state than it is now"), then called *Who's Afraid of Virginia Woolf?* "perhaps the most successful homosexual play ever produced on Broadway. If its sexual core had been evident to more people it probably never would have run—even though it is perfectly exciting theater."

By January 1966, when Stanley Kauffmann, the new lead drama critic at the *Times*, wrote his now famous piece, "Homosexual Drama and Its Disguises," the subject was getting pretty old. He admitted as much: "The principal charge against homosexual dramatists is well known. Because three of the most successful playwrights of the last twenty years are (reputed) homosexuals and because their plays often treat of women and marriage, therefore, it is said, postwar American drama presents a badly distorted picture of American women, marriage and society in general." Kauffmann couldn't name names, but he meant Williams, Albee, and William Inge, author of *Bus Stop* and *Picnic* (and another patient of psychiatrist Lawrence Kubie). Inge's work is good, juicy, old-fashioned melodrama with no gay indicators, so it's hard to say why he's here, unless Kauffmann simply heard that Inge was wrestling with repressed homosexuality.

Because Kauffmann never gives names or discusses specific plays, the piece reads like the literary equivalent of a poison pen letter. And it really is poisonous. "We have all had much more than enough of the materials presented by these three writers in question: the viciousness toward women, the lurid violence that seems a sublimation of social hatreds, the transvestite sexual exhibitionism that has the same sneering exploitation of its audience that every club stripper has behind her smile." He trots out the now old argument that gay playwrights should be able to write about themselves—"The homosexual dramatist must be free to write truthfully of what he knows"—and not confuse matters with their masquerade. Even so, he thinks badly of gay people no matter what they do. "Homosexuals with writing ability are likely to go on being drawn to theater. It is quite the logical consequence of the defiant and/or protective histrionism they must employ in their daily lives.... But how can we blame these people? Conventions and puritanism in the Western world have forced them to wear masks for generations, to hate themselves and thus to hate those who have made them hate themselves. Now that they have a certain relative freedom, they vent their feelings in camouflaged forms."

The ponderous prose doesn't hide the old-style bigotry about "these people." There is so much nonsense in the specific charges that one doesn't know where to begin. What is vicious about Williams's portraits of Blanche and Maggie or Inge's picture of Cherie in *Bus Stop* or even Albee's presentation of Martha? And exactly how much time did this scholarly critic spend at strip clubs studying those "sneering" dancers? Who's the one with misogynistic fantasies?

During the same week as the Kauffmann article, *Time* magazine ran a one-page essay titled "The Homosexual in America." As was standard with the magazine in this period, there is no byline. The essay is a stunning concentration of liberal platitudes and ugly stereotypes. "[T]he great artists so often cited as evidence of the homosexual's creativity—the Leonardos and Michelangelos—are probably the exceptions of genius. For the most part…homosexuals are failed artists and their special creative gift a myth." Yet weak as homosexual art is, it's still seen as a terrible threat. "Homosexual ethics and aesthetics are staging a vengeful, derisive counterattack on what deviates call the 'straight' world. This is evident…in the 'camp' movement, which pretends that the ugly and banal are fun."

What was going on here? What did this eruption of homosexual culture panic mean and what triggered it?

The meaning is too large and various to explore fully in a short space. Let's just say that no sooner was Albee elevated to the pantheon of great American playwrights with Tennessee Williams and Arthur Miller, than critics noticed that Miller was the only straight man in the bunch. It made them nervous. Miller's best plays, *Death of a Salesman* (1949) and *The Crucible* (1953), are the antithesis of Williams and Albee: solemn, gray, sincere, and direct. But his last play, *After the Fall* (1964), an autobiographical memory play with episodes from both the House Un-American Activities Committee hearings and his marriage to Marilyn Monroe, had been a critical disappointment. Albee was the first major new playwright to appear in a long, long time. It suggested that the homosexuals were taking over. The fear spread to other arts. Music was already considered a lost cause.

One of the triggers for these attacks was an essay mentioned earlier, a surprising source that I've never seen fully discussed.

As said before, it's hard to know what writers were saying to each other in private. The New York intellectual scene of these years was very small and very parochial. These men and women were not as worldly as they pretended. They had little contact with the gay world or even with theater. But in 1964 an essay was published that told them things they didn't know. The connection is circumstantial, but the timing is undeniable. This essay didn't create the wave of culture panic, but I believe it was an important catalyst.

"Notes on Camp" by Susan Sontag first appeared in *Partisan Review* that fall. Not many people saw it there, although it would've been read by literary intellectuals. Then *Time* magazine gave it five paragraphs in December 1964, the same month that *Tiny Alice* opened. The complaints in the later *Time* essay about the "'camp' movement" did not come out of nowhere. "Notes on Camp" was reprinted in Sontag's first collection, *Against Interpretation*, which appeared in early 1966, in time to influence the Kauffmann essay.

Sontag was lesbian herself, but she spent her life being coy about it. Not until she died and her son published her diaries did we learn she had always loved women. Her essay is awfully coy, too, taking forever to admit that camp is special to homosexuals and talking about gay people as if they were a lost tribe and she were only an anthropologist. "Notes on Camp" never makes clear that there are (at least) two different meanings of the word. On the one hand, *camp* identifies a deliberate style of gay behavior, the nelly variations of talk and movement that include female pronouns and limp wrists: "Don't camp, darling." On the other hand, the word identifies an approach to art best summed up in the phrase "So bad it's good." We can acknowledge that a movie or play or painting is terrible but still enjoy its energy or silliness or absurdity. This simple concept opens the door to complicated ideas about beauty and pleasure, success and failure, in the production of art as well as its appreciation. Gay men may have named this attitude, but it is universal. Anyone can enjoy the diverse pleasures of camp in material that ranges from Busby Berkeley dance spectacles to anthologies of bad poetry to Henri Rousseau paintings to Japanese monster movies.

Sontag's intentions were good: she wanted to publicize the gay presence in the arts in a positive way. "The two pioneering forces of modern sensibility are Jewish moral seriousness and homosexual aestheticism and irony." Her taxonomy is so thorough, however, that she sucks the subject dry. Also she mistakes anything that gives pleasure for camp (including Mozart and Henry James), so the term becomes meaningless. More important, many straight readers came away thinking of camp as a secret gay language, an

elaborate set of inside jokes at the expense of heterosexual sincerity. I suspect this was why Philip Roth read the playful mystery of *Tiny Alice* as one
big pansy joke. An awareness of camp now caused people to read *Who's
Afraid of Virginia Woolf?* as a gay play in disguise: after all, it begins with
a husband and wife arguing about a Bette Davis movie. (They somehow
forgot that Bette Davis was not just an icon for gay men but an icon for
straight women who loved her toughness, as well as an icon for any admirer
of serious acting. They even forgot that heterosexual couples often enjoy
old movies.)

So began the myth that *Virginia Woolf* was about a quartet of gay men.
Straight people who loved the play for telling the truth about marriage were
confused to learn it wasn't about them after all. Critics had second thoughts.
Walter Kerr pruned his praise when he reprinted his review in book form:
"brilliant" became "admirable."

It needs to be said here that, yes, Albee drew upon gay married life for
Virginia Woolf. It enabled him to say valid things about *all* married life. As he
later pointed out, "There's not that much difference between straight and
gay couples in their fights." He and Williams both responded to the attacks,
but not immediately. Albee told his biographer, "I know I did not write the
play about two male couples." Williams told an interviewer in 1970, "If I
am writing a female character, goddamnit, I'm going to write a female character, I'm not gonna write a drag queen. If I wanna write a drag queen, I'll
write a drag queen."

Most of the critics insisted they had no problem with homosexuals,
only with homosexual characters disguised as straight ones. It was a standard line in their attacks. If gay writers could write real gay characters, they
claimed, they'd be satisfied. Ten and twenty years later, however, when gay
playwrights did write openly gay characters, none of these men ever said
one good word about this work—not Taubman, not Kauffmann, not Roth.

Gay writers could not win for losing. If they wrote about gay life, they
weren't universal. But if they wrote about straight life, they were distorting what they despised or didn't understand. Yet to quote Michael Bronski
again: "Gay people are just like straight people. But straight people lie about
who they really are."

In June 1966, six months after the Kauffmann and *Time* pieces, the movie
of *Who's Afraid of Virginia Woolf?* opened, directed by Mike Nichols and

starring Elizabeth Taylor and Richard Burton. It was a huge success. The review in the *New York Times* was by none other than Stanley Kauffmann (he'd been demoted from the theater pages), who said nothing about the original being a gay show in drag, only that it was "the play of the decade." None of the major reviews of the film said a word about gay subtext. In fact, the movie appears to have stopped all such talk in the mainstream press. After hearing those powerhouse lines belted out by Taylor and Burton, the most famous heterosexual couple in the world, critics couldn't claim that George and Martha were gay men in disguise without sounding like idiots. Taylor was already a gay icon, of course, but she wasn't a drag queen—not yet. The general attack of culture panic began to subside by the end of 1966. Perhaps it had simply run its course, but I believe the movie helped: killing the charge against Albee, it killed the chief cause for alarm.

Critics stopped looking so feverishly for hidden homosexuals—chiefly because they didn't like talking about homosexuality to begin with. But the gay masquerade cliché about Williams and Albee did not completely go away. In 1969 William Goldman wrote a book about Broadway, *The Season*, where he went on and on about homos taking over the theater. It was stale stuff by then, his only fresh touches his repeated use of the word *fag* and his praise of a new play, *The Boys in the Band*, which he did only to slam Albee. ("Yes, those first two acts of *Virginia Woolf* are marvelous bitch dialogue— not as good as Mart Crowley's bitch dialogue in the *Boys in the Band*—but still marvelous.") But that takes us ahead of our story. The damage to Albee was already done. After being damned and torn apart for having the gall to write about straight people, it's no wonder he resisted writing an actual play about gay men. The best portrait came thirty years later in *Three Tall Women* (1994), with the son, a preppy young man who is talked about and talked to, but who never speaks himself.

Meanwhile, the career of Tennessee Williams followed its own curious course. After being on the cover of *Time* in 1962, he wrote a new play, *The Milk Train Doesn't Stop Here Anymore*, featuring yet another self-portrait in the guise of a prima donna, Mrs. Goforth. He broke off with Frank Merlo but continued to live with him. He found a new friend, a young poet named Frederick Nicklaus, and brought him into their household. Then Merlo fell ill. He stayed in Key West when Williams went to New York for the *Milk Train* rehearsals, but the two exes remained in constant contact by phone.

Williams grew anxious and distracted. *Milk Train* opened in January 1963 to the worst reviews of his career. "Mistuh Williams, He Dead," was the title of a piece by Richard Gilman. That month Merlo was diagnosed with lung cancer.

Merlo flew up to New York and eventually went into the hospital, where Williams visited him daily. Williams found it easier to love Merlo in sickness than he had in health. He forgot his fears of being poisoned. Hoping to lose himself in work, Williams revised *Milk Train*, determined to fix it. His director, Frank Corsaro, later said, "With Frank ill, Tennessee just couldn't cope for himself with the details of real life. Of course he told me, 'Baby, it's my last play.'" His producer, Cheryl Crawford, said, "Frankie was the only one who really understood him, really knew how to deal with him and help him. When Frankie was dying, there was a new form of grief, and maybe a new form of guilt for Tennessee to deal with, and I think it just broke him."

Williams visited Merlo in the hospital on the evening of September 21, 1963. Merlo looked tired and Williams offered to go. Merlo asked him to remain but not admit anyone else. "I've grown used to *you*," he told Williams. Years later the playwright explained in his *Memoirs* with elegant formality, "The statement of habituation was hard to interpret as an admission of love, but love was never a thing that Frankie had been able to declare to me except over a long-distance telephone." Williams waited until Merlo fell asleep and left to meet friends at a bar. He returned to the apartment around midnight, where he received word that Merlo had died at eleven. "They say he just gasped and lay back on the pillow and was gone," Williams wrote two days later to his friend, Maria St. Just. "I am just beginning, now, to feel the desolation of losing my dear little Horse."

7. The Medium Is the Message

—ᴍ—

*Never pass up the opportunity to have sex
or appear on television.*
—Gore Vidal

Mass media strongly influenced how people responded to these books and plays, and the mass media was changing. The weekly newsmagazines, *Time* and *Newsweek*, were major powers in American culture in 1960. It's funny now to read John Cheever's letters and find him worrying about his reviews in *Time*. The *New Yorker* was losing its reputation for blandness and taking more risks, especially in its nonfiction. There were new weekly newspapers, too, such as the *Village Voice*, which first published in 1955. There were even a few gay magazines.

ONE began in Los Angeles in 1953 (its all-caps name is from a quote by Thomas Carlyle: "A mystic bond of brotherhood makes all men ONE") and was more interested in legal and political matters than in the arts. The typical article had a title like "New Deal for Deviants" or "Successful Homosexuals." However, the magazine ran Norman Mailer's surprisingly forward essay, "The Homosexual Villain," and, in the 1960s, began to review novels. The *Mattachine Review*, a publication of the first national gay rights organization, the Mattachine Society, was founded in 1955 and occasionally printed poems, such as "The Green Automobile" by Allen Ginsberg, but was even less interested in cultural matters than *ONE*. They ran an occasional piece about Plato or Whitman, but nothing about Albee, Williams, or camp. The publishing schedule was erratic and subscribers were few. In the Sixties *ONE* sold roughly 2,300 copies per issue.

The vast majority of gay readers continued to hear about gay books and plays through mainstream publications. *ONE*'s most important achievement was to work its way through the court system as an "obscene publication" until the U.S. Supreme Court reversed the lower courts and freed the magazine to be sent through the mail. (The high court didn't hear the case but made their decision based entirely on *Roth v. United States*, the same case cited in the trial of *Howl*.)

Surprisingly, the most important change in media for gay people happened not in print but on television. Dramas and sitcoms remained closed to homosexuals—as they were to blacks until halfway through the decade. No, the venue where gay figures could shine was the late night talk show.

The 1960s was a golden age of the public intellectual; almost all of the major literary figures appeared on TV. It was a golden age of pretension, when people wanted to appear smarter than they were, unlike our current age when even politicians strive to seem average. But a pretense to intellect can often produce real intelligence. *Time* and *Newsweek* competed with each other in putting major writers on their covers. The *New Yorker*'s standing as a status symbol enabled it to run long, serious, book-length pieces without losing readers. An actual book publisher, Bennett Cerf of Random House, was a regular on a TV game show, *What's My Line?* And late night talk show hosts from David Susskind and Jack Paar to David Frost and Dick Cavett enjoyed bringing important authors on their shows.

A few of these writers were gay. They couldn't talk about it on the air, of course, but some didn't need to say it in words.

Truman Capote came to television relatively late in his career. He was beaten to it by Gore Vidal, who first went on TV in 1957 to publicize *Visit to a Small Planet* on Broadway. Vidal's handsome looks and smooth, patrician voice worked well in the cool medium. He seemed so respectable that he could get away with saying disrespectful things. He became a regular on Jack Paar's *The Tonight Show* and sometimes appeared on the *Today* show with Dave Garroway and J. Fred Muggs, a chimpanzee.

Capote had no television experience when he was invited to be on David Susskind's show, *Open End*, in January 1959. *Breakfast at Tiffany's* had been published two months earlier and he was there to promote it. He was between projects, a vulnerable time for any writer, but it's safe to assume that part of him was thinking: *If Gore can do this, so can I.*

He worried aloud on the ride to the TV studio in Newark in a limo shared with Norman Mailer and Mailer's wife, Adele. He insisted he was there only because his publisher, Bennett Cerf, thought TV was the future of books.

Norman Mailer wrote about the evening in a long, strange, brilliant essay, "Of a Small and Modest Malignancy." (The title refers not to Capote but to television.) For all his macho windbagging, Mailer could be oddly likable, self-deprecatory as well as self-pitying, generous as well as competitive. He was fascinated by gay men and not afraid to speak his mind, for good *and* ill.

The Mailers and Capote arrived at the studio and joined Susskind and his third guest, Dorothy Parker. The writers sat down, the show began—it was broadcast live—and Mailer immediately took over, holding forth on politics. After an hour of monopolizing conversation, he sensed Susskind turning against him, so he shut up, wanting to punish Susskind, thinking the show would die without him. He let Capote talk.

The subject of the Beats came up. Mailer had mixed feelings about Jack Kerouac, but Capote despised his work. "It is not writing. It is only typing," Capote said. Dorothy Parker agreed.

The show ended. On their way out they stopped to look at the kinescope playback. Parker hated seeing herself and hurried off, but Mailer and Capote lingered to watch. Capote thought Mailer looked great, but that he looked terrible.

They returned to Manhattan for drinks and dinner at El Morocco, where Capote knew all the waiters. Mailer and his wife assured him that he had been fine.

The next morning Mailer's friends began to call to say how much they'd enjoyed the show, especially for Capote. They kept quoting his line, "It's not writing; it's only typing." Some went so far as to say that Capote had walked all over Mailer, but even those who complimented Mailer wanted to hear more about the other writer. Capote himself called Mailer that afternoon and said he was surprised by all the praise he was getting.

Furious about being upstaged, and baffled, Mailer returned to the TV studio a few days later and asked to see the kinescope. He discovered that Capote had gotten far more close-ups than he had; he felt the show had been tilted against him. (He never acknowledges that his endless monologue may have put off viewers.) But he also saw that Capote had earned those close-ups:

> Capote did not look small on the show but large! His face, in fact, was extraordinary, that young-old face, still pretty and with such promise of oncoming ugliness; that voice, so full of snide rustlings and unforgiving nasalities; it was a voice to knock New York on its ear. The voice had survived; it spoke of horrors seen and passed over; it told of judgments that would be merciless.

Where other people heard only a freak or a fag, Mailer heard the mystic androgyny of a new Tiresias. It's a generous, imaginative leap, and it captures the appeal of Capote's otherness. The next time Mailer encountered Capote in person, he found him changed, with "a new assurance to put on top of the old one."

Many Middle Americans in years to come would roll their eyes and sigh whenever the little man with the androgynous voice appeared on TV. But others—men and women, gay and straight—would be transfixed. Capote discovered that the fame of writing books, even best sellers, was nothing compared to the fame of appearing regularly on television.

He finally began work on a new project, a *New Yorker* piece about life in Moscow like a follow-up to *The Muses Are Heard*. But it wasn't clicking. He spent his time instead with his "swans," rich lady friends like Babe Paley and Slim Keith. Then, on the morning of November 16, 1959, he read a short piece in the inside pages of the *New York Times* about a brutal murder in Kansas. A family of four, the Clutters, had been bound, gagged, and shot in an isolated farmhouse; nobody knew who did it. Capote asked William Shawn, his editor at the *New Yorker*, if he could drop the Moscow project to explore the Kansas story. Shawn said yes. Originally it was to be the portrait of small-town America stunned by modern violence, a mood piece with an unsolved mystery at the center. But while Capote was in Garden City, Kansas, interviewing neighbors with the help of his childhood friend, Harper Lee, a pair of ex-cons were arrested and charged with the murders. Capote recognized he had a full-scale book on his hands.

He spent the first two weeks of January 1960 visiting the jail and talking with the accused, Perry Smith and Dick Hickock. He then went back to New York and didn't return until the trial in March. It's startling to realize how quickly everything happened during the first stage of the story. The trial lasted only a week. Smith and Hickock were convicted and sentenced to be hanged on May 13. Capote immediately left for New York to write his book. He found he couldn't work in the city so he took his boxes of notes and crossed the ocean to Spain with Jack Dunphy and isolated himself in a fishing village on the Mediterranean.

Only then, when Capote was living with Smith and Hickock on a daily basis in his imagination, did he become truly intimate with the two men, especially Smith. Smith was shorter and more soulful than Hickock—more like Capote, in fact, easier to identify with. A written man is more porous and accessible than a live one. Capote was not allowed to correspond with Smith and Hickock—that would come later—but he wrote constantly to Alvin Dewey of the Kansas Bureau of Investigation, checking on details and clarifying points and learning new developments. He was relieved when the Kansas Supreme Court issued a stay of execution to hear an appeal for a new trial.

He worked slowly and steadily on the book, writing it out in pencil on yellow legal pads, re-creating scenes, building up portraits of the murdered family, the townspeople, the police, and the killers. It was an epic with a huge cast of characters. Capote decided that a true-crime story could be as well-written as a fine novel. He took enormous pains with the prose, and it shows.

> The village of Holcomb stands on the high wheat plains of western Kansas, a lonesome area that other Kansans call "out there."...
> The land is flat and the views are awesomely extensive; horses, herds of cattle, a white cluster of grain elevators rising as gracefully as Greek temples are visible long before a traveler reaches them.

In Cold Blood has had many imitators, but it remains fresh and powerful decades later. Nobody has matched its lean, elegant prose, its emotional richness, or its solid architecture. Capote made two brilliant technical decisions early on. First, in the opening pages, he built up to the murder, crosscutting between the Clutters and the killers; then he jumped over the killing and left it blank until after the arrest, when Smith and Hickock confess to the police. Second, he left himself entirely out of the story. He was not just an onlooker, as he was in *The Muses Are Heard* or *Breakfast at Tiffany's*; he was completely invisible. Yet his presence haunts the book, like the Invisible Man whose faint outline appears only in the rain. (His secret presence is so tantalizing that, forty years later, *two* different movies—*Capote* and *Infamous*—retold the story simply by editing Capote back into his book.)

It took Capote a little over three years to write *In Cold Blood*—everything except the ending. He and Dunphy stayed in Europe almost the entire time. Through lawyers and Dewey, he heard about the appeals and stays of execution that kept Smith and Hickock alive on Death Row. Not until he returned to the States in June 1963 did Capote get permission to write to the convicted killers. Suddenly two men who had become characters in his imagination were sending him letters. He visited them in prison and mailed them books: Thoreau and dictionaries and his own work for Smith, Harold Robbins novels and girlie magazines for Hickock. He impatiently waited for the court system to decide what would happen so he could write his final pages. His letters to Smith and Hickock are full of grave concern for their future while those to other people express frustration over the delays. I assume that both sets of feelings were perfectly sincere.

Finally the last appeal was denied; the execution was set for April 14, 1965. Capote flew out to Kansas with his Random House editor, Joe Fox. At the motel he changed his mind and decided he didn't want to see the men. He told Smith over the phone that the officials wouldn't let him visit. Then at the last minute he changed his mind again and drove out to the prison with Fox, arriving in time to exchange a few last words with Smith and Hickock. Fox remained outside while Capote joined twenty other men, including Detective Dewey, in the warehouse with the gallows.

First Dick Hickock was hanged, then, a half hour later, Perry Smith. In *In Cold Blood*, Capote never mentioned his own presence in the warehouse but described the death of Smith entirely from Dewey's point of view:

Steps, noose, mask; but before the mask was adjusted, the prisoner spat out his chewing gum into the chaplain's outstretched palm. Dewey shut his eyes; he kept them shut until he heard the thud-snap that announces a rope-broken neck.... He remembered his first meeting with Perry in the interrogation room at the Police

Headquarters in Las Vegas—the dwarfish boy-man seated in the metal chair, his small booted feet not quite brushing the floor. And when Dewey now opened his eyes, that is what he saw: the same childish feet, tilted, dangling.

A few hours later, Capote flew back to New York with Fox, clutching his editor's hand and crying for the entire flight.

He finished writing the final pages by the middle of June. *In Cold Blood* was published in four installments in four consecutive issues of the *New Yorker* at the end of 1965. It came out as a book in January 1966, dedicated to Jack Dunphy and Harper Lee. It was praised to the skies. Capote claimed to have invented a new genre, the "nonfiction novel," which the smarter critics knew not to believe, but it didn't matter. The book sold like no literary book had sold before. It was on the *New York Times* best-seller list for thirty-seven weeks, twelve weeks as number one. The author was on magazine covers, TV talk shows, and the radio. NBC News filmed a half-hour special, *Capote Returns to Kansas*, that April. He had left himself out of his book, but he seemed to be everywhere else, the effeminate little man who wrote a best seller about two hardened killers.

The book appeared the same month as the *Time* magazine essay about homosexuality and Stanley Kauffmann's attack on gays in the theater. One would expect this antigay mood to splash Capote. Kauffmann, in fact, reviewed *In Cold Blood* in the *New Republic*, giving the book one of its few bad notices. This time, he did his name-calling in code: "Are we so bankrupt, so avid for novelty that merely because a famous writer produces an amplified magazine crime-feature, the result is automatically elevated to serious literature just as Andy Warhol, by painting a soup-carton, has allegedly elevated it to art?" Many people knew about Andy Warhol. But strangely enough, nobody else called Capote on his sexuality, not in code or otherwise. The homosexual panic in the lively arts did not affect the reception of *In Cold Blood*. It was as if books existed in an entirely different dimension. Maybe book reviewers were too polite to mention it. Or perhaps *In Cold Blood* was too straight for Middle America to read homosexuality into it. They never suspected that gay men know more about the rough trade world of Smith and Hickock than most family men do. There is a gay story line in *In Cold Blood*, but it remained hidden until those two movies were made.

One other bad review stung Capote deeply. Kenneth Tynan in the *Observer* in Britain accused him of letting Smith and Hickock die in order to give his book a stronger ending: "For the first time an influential writer in the front rank has been placed in a privileged intimacy with criminals about to die and, in my view, done less than he might have to save them.... No piece of prose, however deathless, is worth a human life." It's an accusation that persists to this day. But the appeals process went on for five long years. The case was heard in many courts and presented by different teams of experienced lawyers. It's hard to know what Capote could have done that wasn't done already. Yet the charge stuck in his craw for years to come.

Making the charge more damning is the belief that Capote was in love with Smith: he let his beloved die for the sake of a best seller, and then paid for it for the rest of his life. Well, it makes a great story. But one does not need to fall in love with a man to become emotionally connected with him. Donald Windham makes some wise comments about Capote's friendship with Smith and Hickock: "For although the word 'friends' should be put into quotation marks, he had become closely involved with the two criminals, especially Perry Smith, as closely involved as a soldier with two prisoners trapped in a no-man's-land in a battle might be, on opposite sides but inexorably bound together." In his book Capote identifies as much with the victims as he does with the killers, and it creates a powerful tension for the reader. I assume a similar tension existed in the author, an intense knot of fear, righteousness, pity, and survivor's guilt. No wonder Capote's drinking grew worse and new nervous tics appeared while he waited for the execution.

Afterward he insisted his conscience was clear and claimed he had done all that he could for Smith and Hickock. And he threw himself a party.

He rented the grand ballroom at the Plaza Hotel for a masked ball to be held on November 28, 1966, ostensibly in honor of his friend, Katherine Graham, publisher of the *Washington Post*. He invited every famous person he had met or wanted to meet. He even invited a few unknown friends, including Alvin and Marie Dewey. (Jack Dunphy was invited, of course, and he actually attended, much to everyone's surprise. He and Capote were still a couple, but Dunphy grew more withdrawn as he grew older, avoiding Capote's society friends, which meant seeing less of Capote. Capote bought them two "his and his" cottages in the Hamptons, then spent more time at

Dunphy's than his own because Dunphy's place was homier and Dunphy was usually home. They were a curious couple.)

George Plimpton provides a wonderful account of the Black and White Ball in his oral biography, *Truman Capote*, by letting two dozen participants share their conflicting stories. Some describe it as an overblown prom for grown-ups. Others imbue it with the magic of a grand ball in Proust. Jerome Robbins danced with Lauren Bacall. Harold Prince and his wife left after a half hour. Norman Mailer got into an argument with McGeorge Bundy from the White House about Vietnam. Knowing what had been and what would be for Capote, one can't help but think of the party as an elaborate defense mechanism against guilt and unease. Yet for twelve hours, from ten at night to ten the next morning, famous names in tuxedos, evening gowns, and masks poured in and out of the bright hotel overlooking Central Park, and success looked very much like what a small, precocious boy in Alabama might imagine it to be.

Fifteen blocks downtown from the Plaza Hotel, a black jazz musician named Rufus Scott leaves a shabby Forty-second Street movie theater around midnight. Heartbroken and broke, crazy with guilt, he roams Times Square in the bitter cold.

> A hotel's enormous neon name challenged the starless sky. So did the names of movie stars and people currently appearing or scheduled to appear on Broadway, along with the mile-high names of the vehicles which would carry them into immortality. The great buildings, unlit, blunt like the phallus or sharp like the spear, guarded the city which never slept.
>
> Beneath them Rufus walked, one of the fallen—for the weight of this city was murderous—one of those who had been crushed on the day, which was every day, these towers fell. Entirely alone and dying of it, he was part of an unprecedented multitude.

We have stepped from fact to fiction, to the opening chapter of *Another Country* by James Baldwin, published four years earlier, in 1962. The novel's first eighty pages are extraordinary, a powerful flow of city scenes and flashbacks that carry Rufus through his last night on earth to his suicide leap off the George Washington Bridge. According to received opinion, the book falls apart afterward, but it isn't true. There are things wrong with

Another Country, but, as Randall Jarrell said in italics of the faults in a Walt Whitman poem, "they *do not matter.*"

Baldwin began work on the novel before the publication of *Giovanni's Room* in 1956. The country of the title is love. But where *Giovanni's Room* is about the fear and defeat of love, the new novel is about love's triumph, which is much harder to write about. Adding to the challenge, he included race this time. His characters strive to cross the great divide between whites and blacks in uneasy friendships and heated love affairs. Complicating matters further, Baldwin put in gay men who sleep with women and straight men who sleep with men.

Rufus, a young drummer, becomes involved with a circle of white artists in Greenwich Village; he is loved by both men and women. Scalded and scarred by racism, his paranoia turns his love of Leona, a white girl from the South, into something poisonous and ugly. Leona ends up in a mental hospital, which leads to Rufus's nervous breakdown. After his suicide, Rufus's younger sister, Ida, joins the circle of white friends. A rising blues singer, Ida is ambitious, angry, and unpredictable. The white friends fall in love with her just as they did with her brother. Then Eric, a gay actor from Alabama, returns from Paris, where he has fallen in love with a French street boy named Yves. While waiting for Yves to join him in New York, he begins an affair with Cass, the wife of a successful novelist.

There is an element of soap opera in this crisscross of plots, but soap opera has its own emotional truth. One wishes more soaps had some of the dangerous power that Baldwin achieves here. He covers a remarkable range of life, from nights in New York jazz clubs to a gay white childhood in the South to a pot party on a Greenwich Village rooftop to violent marital quarrels to a straight man and a gay man talking about their lovers—and then having sex with each other just to clear the air. This novel about pain and forgiveness is scored to multiple recordings of Bessie Smith.

It was a complex project that needed peace and concentration, but Baldwin's life was anything but peaceful. He divided his time between Paris and New York, taking an apartment at 81 Horatio Street in Greenwich Village. He remained friendly with Lucien Happersberger (there's a lot of Happersberger in the character of Yves), but he had a new friend in his life, a Turkish actor named Engin Cezzar. Cezzar studied at Yale Drama School, and they met when Cezzar was cast as Giovanni in an Actors Studio production of *Giovanni's Room*. In effect, Baldwin was bonding with one of his characters.

Cezzar later wrote in a memoir that he saved Baldwin from his "incessant homosexuality" by showing him the value of pure masculine friendship. Cezzar soon married, and Baldwin became good friends with his wife. In an odd essay about André Gide written at this time, "The Male Prison," Baldwin complains about "the phenomena of present-day homosexuality… where it is impossible to have a lover or friend, where the possibility of genuine human involvement has altogether ceased." He admires Gide for staying married, as if a double life gives a man the stability he could never find in gay life. Baldwin's feelings about gay love were more conflicted than one might imagine from his fiction. Whatever the truth about his feelings for Cezzar, he visited him in Turkey and began to use Istanbul as a second home, in much the same way he had used Paris.

His personal life was placid compared to what was happening in the United States. The political climate was changing radically, and Baldwin's career changed with it. The paperback of *Notes of a Native Son* had begun to sell with the success of *Giovanni's Room* in 1956, but it fully took off with the rise of the civil rights movement. White readers wanted to understand the world of race, and Baldwin wrote about it clearly and passionately. *Esquire* and *Harper's* commissioned articles from him. His next book of essays, *Nobody Knows My Name*, appeared to high praise in 1961 and was a best seller. Baldwin became involved in the movement himself, speaking at rallies and conferences and appearing on television—people found his clarinet-toned voice and beautifully odd face as fascinating as they found the voice and face of Truman Capote. It's a wonder he was able to finish his novel at all, which he managed to do in Istanbul.

He was invited to a dinner at the White House honoring Nobel Prize winners in April 1962. He was delighted to meet Jackie Kennedy, but spent more time with Katherine Anne Porter.

Another Country was published that June. People who admired the essayist of race were startled to be reminded that he was also a novelist who wrote about gay sex. The novel received a contradictory mix of reviews, ranging from praise by Lionel Trilling to being called pornography by Stanley Edgar Hyman to being dismissed in the *Times Book Review* by Paul Goodman, who called the book "mediocre" but didn't bother to describe the plot or name any characters. (Goodman was famously bisexual, but fiercely competitive with all other writers.)

The novel was a best seller in hardcover and a huge best seller in paperback the following year, second in sales only to *Lord of the Flies*. It appeared only a few months before *Who's Afraid of Virginia Woolf?* opened on Broadway. Baldwin and Albee both used anger and obscenity to dig into the darker side of love—*Another Country* is full of words that were banned from print a year or two earlier: *fuck, cunt, cocksucker,* and *motherfucker.* People were excited by the adult rawness of the language and the emotions.

The book had many gay readers, but not all of them liked it. Forty-four-year-old Donald Vining, who worked in the offices of Columbia University, kept a copious diary from 1933 to 1975, which he later published as *A Gay Diary* in four useful volumes. Vining preferred plays to novels, but he did read Baldwin.

> I read late last night...*Another Country*, which I didn't like a bit. Baldwin can certainly write but his sex scenes are much too explicit and since his characters' sex tastes are by no means mine, it's rather revolting. They seem to share an author's taste for sweaty bodies, which I find extremely repulsive, and there is always so much crying, gasping, panting, etc.

Sweat aside (much of the novel takes place in the summer), Vining has a point. The sex scenes are written in the language of pulp fiction, and there's lots of throbbing and thrashing, especially in the straight couplings. *Another Country* went through many drafts, but the book could have used one more revision to smooth out purple patches and remove repetitions. (Every ten pages or so somebody throws his or her head back and laughs.) But ultimately it doesn't matter. The chaos of Baldwin's life probably fed the energy of the book, and that energy and electricity carry the reader through to the end. Even Vining stayed up late to finish it.

But the world did not have much time to digest his novel before Baldwin hit them with something entirely new: a long essay about race published in, of all places, the 1962 Thanksgiving issue of the *New Yorker.* The original title was "Letter from a Region in My Mind." A year later it was reprinted as a book, *The Fire Next Time.*

Ostensibly Baldwin's account of his dinner with Elijah Muhammad, founder of the Black Muslims, it's a long, eloquent monologue about the cost of racism in America. Written in the cadences of a sermon, it is built out of extended perorations and the music of words. Like many sermons, it works more from sound than from argument or narrative. It is better written than any of Baldwin's novels, yet not nearly as expressive or involving. The beautiful phrasing creates a kind of trance music, and there are more generalizations than specifics. Now and then a memorable idea comes out of these lovely clouds, but much of the piece evaporates after it's read. The strongest idea is the threat of violence promised in the book's title, which is addressed only in the closing sentences, when he insists that the conscious whites and conscious blacks must, "like lovers," do everything they can to raise the consciousness of others and "end the racial nightmare."

> If we do not now dare everything, the fulfillment of that prophecy, re-created from the Bible in song by a slave, is upon us: *God gave Noah the rainbow sign, No more water, the fire next time!*

The race riots that did not begin until two years later made this threat seem like the most important part of the essay. Starting in 1965, not a year passed without another inner city erupting in violence: Los Angeles, Detroit, Newark, Chicago, even Washington, D.C. Baldwin looked like a prophet.

A reader in 2010 can't help being struck by other details, such as Baldwin's skepticism about "Bobby Kennedy's assurance that a Negro can become President in forty years." (He was off by only six years.) A gay reader can't help noticing some of his own experience echoed in Baldwin's black experience: "Ask any Negro what he knows about the white people with whom he works. And then ask the white people with whom he works what they know about *him*." But the essay is not nearly as valuable now as when it was first published. Its fine phrases and lovely cadences provided educated white readers with a safe place where they could think about the damage of three centuries of racial oppression. It was far harder even to begin to think about such things in 1962 than it is now.

The Fire Next Time came out as a short book in January 1963. Over the next few months, Baldwin's accelerating career picked up even more speed and shifted into a new direction. Martin Luther King, who met Baldwin in 1957 after the Montgomery bus boycott, organized a prolonged campaign against segregation ordinances in Birmingham, Alabama. Weeks of demonstrations and arrests reached their climax on May 2 when the white cops attacked a march by black schoolchildren with fire hoses and police dogs. TV cameras were present, and the brutality was seen that night on *The Huntley-Brinkley Report*. The nation was appalled. Two weeks later, *Time* magazine put Baldwin on their cover as the literary voice of civil rights. The article inside emphasized his essays over his fiction and said nothing about his sexuality—this is the same magazine that three years later attacked homosexuals for poisoning American culture. People forgot Baldwin's sex life—for now, anyway—while they spoke about black civil rights. Baldwin himself kept it out of his speeches and articles, understandably so. A person can fight only one war at a time.

Within days of appearing on the cover of *Time*, Baldwin received a phone call from Robert Kennedy, who was now attorney general. A mutual friend, Dick Gregory, had suggested Kennedy talk to Baldwin about what could be done to end the strife in the South. Baldwin visited the Kennedy home in Virginia for breakfast, then arranged a meeting in New York the next day for Kennedy with a few figures whom he thought would help him see the light: singers Harry Belafonte and Lena Horne, playwright Lorraine Hansberry, sociologist Kenneth Clark, actor Rip Torn, and veteran activist Jerome Smith. The meeting did not go well. Tempers were lost; Hansberry walked out, disgusted to be in the room with a powerful man who just didn't get it. Baldwin and Clark went to a TV studio soon afterward and filmed a conversation that can be seen on YouTube: Clark is calm and collected, but Baldwin, beneath his precise diction and eloquent sarcasm, is still furious. Kennedy finished the meeting angry himself, but later said his anger helped him see the other point of view and committed him more deeply to civil rights.

Events moved still faster. Baldwin traveled all over the country, giving speeches, appearing on television, expressing doubt about the power of black nonviolence against the violence of the Southern whites. He attended the March on Washington and heard King declare, "I have a dream," but didn't speak himself. A month later, a black church in Birmingham was firebombed by white supremacists and four little girls were killed. It was another violent turning point. Baldwin appeared on a Sunday morning talk show in New York with the German-born theologian Reinhold Niebuhr. The two men shared their moral shock over the crime. Then Baldwin said that Negroes are "the only hope this country has." Most Americans "don't have any longer a real sense of what they live by. I really think it may be Coca-Cola."

John F. Kennedy was assassinated in November and Lyndon Johnson became president. Baldwin continued to make speeches and write articles, but he also finished a play, *Blues for Mr. Charlie.*

Inevitably, a backlash set in, from blacks as well as whites. Black critics found him too white-identified, while white critics found him too political. *Freedomways* magazine criticized *Another Country* because one did not feel his "love of his people in his writing"—the same criticism that Philip Roth got from fellow Jews for *Goodbye, Columbus.* But when *Blues for Mr. Charlie* opened on Broadway in April 1964, starring Diana Sands and Rip Torn, Philip Roth attacked it in the *New York Review of Books* for being too righteous: "If there is ever a Black Muslim nation, and if there is a television in that nation, then something like Acts Two and Three of *Blues for Mr. Charlie* will probably be the kind of thing the housewives will watch on afternoon TV." It was hard to make literature in the 1960s without somebody jumping on you, including fellow artists. A few months later Roth attacked *Tiny Alice.*

That summer President Johnson succeeded in driving the Civil Rights Act of 1964 through Congress. He then ran for president against Barry Goldwater. On Labor Day, his campaign broadcast the famous "daisy" commercial: a little girl with a flower is juxtaposed with a nuclear explosion and Johnson drawls in voiceover: "We must either love each other or we must die." One of his speechwriters obviously knew W. H. Auden's "September 1, 1939" with its famous line, "We must love one another or die." (Auden complained to a friend, "One cannot let one's name be associated with shits," and rashly removed the poem from his *Collected Shorter Poems* the following year.)

Baldwin was in England in February 1965, invited to Cambridge University to debate the question: "Has the American dream been achieved at the expense of the American Negro?" Arguing in the negative was another American, William F. Buckley, publisher/editor of a new conservative magazine, the *National Review.* The gray-on-gray television footage of the debate shows Baldwin at his most eloquent, especially in his quiet, damning description of the daily experience of being black in America.

> By the time you are thirty, you have been through a kind of mill. And the most serious effect of the mill you've been through is not the catalogue of disasters—the policeman, the taxi drivers, the waiters, the

landlady, the *landlord*, the banks, the insurance companies, the millions of details twenty-four hours of every day which spell out to you that you are a worthless human being. It is not that. It is that by that time you've begun to see it happening in your daughter or your son or your niece or your nephew.

His bitter emphasis of the words *landlady* and *landlord* is electric, enabling us to see real people; his focus on daily humiliations rather than on horrors makes the experience easier for whites to enter imaginatively. Buckley could offer little in response except flick his tongue and murmur a few words about not being too quick to judge America negatively simply because its black population was treated unfairly.

Baldwin was still in England when Malcolm X was assassinated in a mosque in Harlem. Baldwin was called upon to share still more words and more thoughts. He returned to the United States to join King's protest march from Selma to Montgomery for voter registration. He was photographed walking with Joan Baez.

Meanwhile, Lucien Happersberger had come back into his life, leaving his wife, Suzy, and moving to America. Baldwin fell in love all over again. With Baldwin and his brother David, Happersberger set up a movie company to film *Blues for Mr. Charlie*. David Leeming, a young Englishman who had met Baldwin in Istanbul, joined them and became Baldwin's assistant.

In August 1965, the Los Angeles neighborhood of Watts erupted in six days of the worst race riots since World War II. More people read *The Fire Next Time*, treating it as prophetic. Baldwin found himself in still greater demand for speaking engagements, TV, and interviews. But he was exhausted. He was worn out.

Then Happersberger married Diana Sands—Yves from *Another Country* had fallen in love with Juanita, the heroine of *Blues for Mr. Charlie*. Baldwin was devastated. He broke off with Happersberger yet again, dissolved the film company and decided to give up New York for Istanbul. The betrayal by Happersberger was only the last straw. He explained his decision in a letter to Leeming, saying he had been living too selflessly and did not want to live like a Henry James character. He asked Leeming to come with him. Leeming later said, "He needed me in his arms as well as his office." Baldwin expected Leeming to replace Happersberger as his lover. Leeming said no to that, but agreed to come to Istanbul as a secretary. (Leeming can only paraphrase this important letter in his biography, even though it was written to him. The Baldwin estate, which currently means his sister Gloria, refuses to allow his letters to be published or even quoted, since they weren't intended for the public. As a result, not only is there no edition of Baldwin letters, his biographers must leave out his gritty, living words whenever they use his correspondence.)

Baldwin returned to his small apartment near Istanbul's busy Taksim Square, but eventually moved to a house on a hill, a nineteenth-century building known as the Pasha's Library, looking over the Bosphorus. He now followed the civil rights movement from a distance. He published little in 1966, but resumed work on a new novel, *Tell Me How Long the Train's Been Gone,* the first-person life story of a black actor/director recovering from a heart attack.

And so, in November 1966, while Truman Capote threw his glamorous masked ball in New York City, James Baldwin lived a surprisingly orderly life outside Istanbul, writing during the day and drinking only at night, playing host to visiting family and friends, including Beauford Delaney. He deepened his friendship with Engin Cezzar, working with him on screenplays and theater productions. He went for walks in the city, visiting markets and cafés, and he was certainly noticed, but there were no TV cameras.

Baldwin said he loved Istanbul because he did not feel "black" there and his homosexuality did not matter as much as it did in the United States. He said he loved the Turkish people. But in ten years of living off and on in Turkey, he never bothered to learn the language. His own other country was one of badly needed silence.

8. Love and Sex and *A Single Man*

—⚹—

From the worlds of television and politics, Christopher Isherwood was still writing, still quietly mining his realm in private. He worked steadily on *Down There on a Visit*, the Mexican novel conceived on his 1956 trip to England, while he supported himself and his young lover, Don Bachardy, with occasional movie work. Life with Bachardy was usually good, although the younger man was often frustrated and depressed. It wasn't easy being the boyfriend of an older, recognized artist. Bachardy depended on Isherwood not only for financial and emotional support, but for whole pieces of his identity. Within a year of moving in together, the nineteen-year-old American spoke with an English accent. Encouraged by Isherwood, Bachardy began to study art himself, taking classes in drawing at the Chouinard Art Institute. He had an excellent eye and a real gift for portraiture. His personal style of detailed textures and simplified wholes was present from the start. He drew endless pictures of his partner, who was always available as a model, then did a portrait of their friend Gerald Heard, the English guru. It was promptly purchased by Igor Stravinsky. Bachardy had found his vocation.

But Isherwood was having trouble with his Mexican novel. He worked on it for nearly three years without it fully coming to life. He had good secondary characters taken from his own history, but the straight narrator eluded him, as it had in *World in the Evening*. He put the novel aside in 1959 to discuss plans for a possible musical derived from *I Am a Camera*, the John van Druten play based on *Goodbye to Berlin*. A young writer named Victor Chapin had sent him a script. Isherwood found it too fragmentary, too faithful to his book. He began to make notes and became excited by the project. He asked advice from Auden, who liked the idea and said the show should be "as brutal as *Pal Joey*"; he thought the German singer Lotte Lenya might be good as Fraulein Schroeder, the landlady. Isherwood produced an outline and discussed possible composers with Auden and Chester Kallman, who had collaborated on several operas. But nothing came of the project.

However, the detour produced a breakthrough for Isherwood with his Mexican novel. He recognized that the new novel was actually about his post-Berlin expatriate life. He didn't need Mexico or a fictional narrator. He could use the voice of *Goodbye to Berlin* for a new set of linked stories. The facts of his life were subtler and truer than anything he'd been inventing. A passage in his notebook for March 17, 1959, announces the discovery:

> At last!
> I almost dare to say I think I see how this can be done.
> Very simply. Without any fantasy construction.
> Just three unrelated character-studies, which nevertheless are related, through the character of the narrator to each other.
> Mr. Lancaster. Ambrose. Paul.

Which is what *Down There on a Visit* became, with the addition of a fourth study, a fictional version of his German boyfriend, Heinz Neddermeyer, renamed Waldemar. Mr. Lancaster was based on a stuffy older cousin, Basil Fry; Ambrose represents Isherwood's friend, the saintly aesthete, Francis Turville-Petre; Paul was the notorious Denham Fouts, a debauched beauty from Florida who briefly joined Isherwood in a search for God through Vedanta. Other real-life portraits included Gerald Heard disguised as Augustus Parr. Just as Bachardy had sketched Heard in pencil, Isherwood now rendered him in words.

Isherwood narrates as himself, as he did in *Goodbye to Berlin* and *Prater Violet*, in four travel episodes that cover his life from a trip to Bremen in 1929 to a sojourn on a Greek island in 1934 to London during the 1938 Munich Crisis to his years in California.

People often praise his next novel, *A Single Man*, as his masterpiece, but *Down There on a Visit* is richer, more varied and ambitious. It might be my favorite Isherwood book. The prose is clear, lively, and quick, able to express a great deal in a short space, as in this verbal snapshot of Berlin after the war:

There were businessmen with flesh-roll necks and gross cigars, and women deep in make-up and heavy with jewelry, and pageboys darting back and forth like nervous fish; and it seemed to me as if they were all muttering auto-suggestively to themselves, "nothing has happened—nothing has happened—this is where nothing whatever has happened!"

The book can also be very funny:

I see my twenty-three-year-old face...so touchingly pretty that it might have been photographed and blown up for a poster appealing on behalf of the World's Young: 'The Old hate us because we're so cute. Won't *you* help?'

The voice is self-critical without being self-absorbed, alert to both the outside world and interior life. Isherwood captures the intense sense of place that one gets in a foreign country, and the intense sense of other people met there. The book is an intimate epic with a large cast. Isherwood's use of the first person is pitch-perfect, not just in his own voice but in the many little narratives told by other characters.

Isherwood wondered what the novel meant as a whole, but it's too rich to be reduced to a single idea. *Down There* gives us twenty-five years of expatriate life in the shadow of war. Five male and two female characters struggle to give meaning to their lives in exile through sex, money, drugs, and politics; art, religion, and love. The first four devices are discarded. Only the last three offer any hope.

Future readers would criticize Isherwood for not being entirely frank about his sexuality: Chris in the novel is Waldemar's friend, not his lover. Isherwood plays a tricky game with his own sex life, saying nothing about it for a long time, then referring to bed partners by their initials without giving their gender. He makes his lovers unimportant, claiming he was only an observer and not involved with anyone. Paul attacks Chris at the end of the book for being detached: "You know, you really are a tourist, to your bones. I bet you're always sending postcards with 'down there on a visit' on them." Yet Paul has become an opium addict and is not the best judge of character. And the real Isherwood was often *too* involved with his lovers. The novel is both an accurate mirror of his experience and a funhouse mirror. In place of the truth he couldn't tell yet, he tells a different story that is also valid. But as in *Goodbye to Berlin*, he doesn't lie. We can now go back to *Down There* and fill in the blanks and transform the book into a gay novel.

Isherwood worked on it steadily, submitting the different sections as long short stories to various magazines. *Down There* was published as a book by Simon and Schuster in 1962, and was dedicated to Don Bachardy. There were some good reviews. Dorothy Parker praised it in *Esquire*. But despite the "just visiting" strategy, most critics were put off by the number of gay characters. "World Is Just One Big Sodom to Him" was the headline for a bad review in the *Miami News*. "This One's Not for Aunt Minnie," declared the headline in the *Detroit Free Press*. "It is a measure of Mr. Isherwood's brilliance as a writer, of his remarkable skill in presenting people, places, and moods," said the *Oxford Times*, "that one continues to read despite a growing aversion, despite the increasingly nauseating reek of homosexuality." Herbert Mitgang in the *New York Times* snidely asked, "It's saying a great deal about Isherwood's ability as a novelist that perhaps he meant the reader to be repulsed—and succeeded?" Several reviewers wished the author of *Goodbye to Berlin* had given them another Sally Bowles instead.

The book was not the success Isherwood had hoped for. He swore to himself that he would not make the same mistake with his next novel, but would write only about heterosexuals. As was still the case with Isherwood himself, the new book would go around the block a few times to get where it needed to go.

Meanwhile, the musical based on *Goodbye to Berlin* had taken on a life without Isherwood. There was a question about who owned the performing rights after the Van Druten play. Sandy Wilson, author of the charming 1920s parody *The Boyfriend*, was hired by a producer to create a new show, *Welcome to Berlin*, to star Julie Andrews as Sally Bowles. (Her agent wouldn't even let Andrews read the script, steering her instead to *Mary Poppins*.) A young producer named Hal Prince was also pursuing the project, but with another writer, Joe Masteroff. It was Prince who first proposed using an M.C. at the Lady Windemere Club—soon renamed the Kit Kat Club—to set the tone. There is no such character in the stories. After he secured the performing rights, Prince heard the Sandy Wilson songs but decided they were much too sunny for Weimar Berlin. He brought in another composer and lyricist, John Kander and Fred Ebb. Masteroff hit upon a new title: *Cabaret*. But the project was still years from being finished.

Bachardy had gone to London in 1961 to study art at the Slade. He enjoyed his six months of independence and had a hard time reacclimating to life with his lover when he returned to California. He was twenty-seven; he and Isherwood had been together for nearly ten years. He was no longer the boy-next-door with a crew cut and jeans. Because Isherwood kept a diary, we have a detailed record of their fights and sulks and grievances—perhaps too detailed. Most diary keepers use their journals as wailing walls, going to them only in times of anger. We can get a distorted picture of their married life. Yet Isherwood was too honest a writer, even in his diary, not to include other notes. One day he bitterly complains about Bachardy:

> Right now he is nerve-strung almost to screaming point and it is misery to be with him. I'm sure he hates me and I rather hate him, I mean on the surface. Underneath things are more or less as they've been for years.

That "on the surface" speaks volumes. Anyone who has been in a long-term relationship will recognize the feeling. But the two lovers were going through a very rough patch.

Both were seeing other men. They had agreed from the start on an open relationship, but the rules changed depending on their states of mind and the seriousness of the outside affair.

This is a good place to say a few words about the absence of monogamy in many of the relationships in this book. Since gay couples needed to invent their own rules anyway, they often chose rules that were more flexible and realistic than those handed down by centuries of heterosexual marriage. They were never part of a tradition where the husband had all the legal rights and the wife had none. Nor did they have to worry about illegitimate children and family bloodlines. They also knew that, for men at least, sex is often just sex and has nothing to do with love. Many couples decided to let each other play outside the home. Gore Vidal and Howard Austen are the most extreme only in that they never had sex with each other. Such open agreements should be eminently practicable, except for the fact that gay men can get envious as well as jealous over whom their lovers are sleeping with. And people sometimes fall in love with their sex partners.

Isherwood and Bachardy could both be terribly jealous. "When I suffer, I suffer like a dumb animal," Isherwood wrote in his diary. But extramarital sex was also an expression of larger dissatisfactions in their life. Bachardy's painting was going badly—he was confident about his drawing but not his painting; he blamed his partner when he couldn't work. And Isherwood's writing was going badly, too. After the disappointment of *Down There*, he decided to disguise his experience in *The Englishwoman*, the story of an English war bride living unhappily in California and wanting to return to England. But the bit of secret autobiography—he didn't know if he and Bachardy would stay together—wasn't enough to bring the book to life. He felt himself floundering again.

Like many quarreling couples, they remained each other's best confidant, even when the problem being discussed was the listener. One day at the beach Isherwood complained to Bachardy that the new book was slipping away. Bachardy asked what he really wanted it to be about. Isherwood told him. "And in no time at all the blindingly simple truth was revealed that the book isn't about the Englishwoman but about the Englishman— me," Isherwood recorded in his diary. Bachardy suggested he give this woman's problems to someone more like himself, a middle-aged gay man. Isherwood did not hesitate, despite his experience with *Down There on a Visit*. He immediately went back to his manuscript, retitled it *The Englishman*, and began again. Indirection hadn't protected him on the last book: he might as well go all the way. He must tell the truth or be silent.

He did not write as first-person "Chris" this time, but in the third person. Fifty-eight-year-old George (with no last name) is and isn't Isherwood. He lives in the same house and neighborhood of Santa Monica where Isherwood and Bachardy lived. Like Isherwood, he occasionally teaches literature at a state college. But a huge difference is that George is alone. He is a gay man whose lover has recently died. It was both a painful fantasy for the author and a quiet act of revenge.

Life with Bachardy remained difficult while Isherwood worked on the new book. The painter had two serious affairs at this time—one with a man named George. Isherwood's fear of losing Bachardy enabled him to imagine the loneliness that drives the book. But it was Bachardy who suggested a new title: *A Single Man*.

The lean, precise novel, broken into short, unnumbered chapters, follows a single day in the life of one individual. While *Down There on a*

Visit covered twenty-five years, *A Single Man* doesn't quite fill twenty-four hours. It's written in present tense, the tense of screenplays, and begins in detached, distant strangeness, as if narrated by God. A consciousness comes to life, George comes into focus, then his middle-aged body and his snug little house. Then comes the memory of Jim, his deceased lover. Enough time has passed for death to register more as physical absence than as emotional pain.

In his neighbors' eyes, George is just a crabby old bachelor. But Isherwood quickly climbs behind that facade and gives us George's thoughts, which are often the author's thoughts, a headful of private satires about American life in 1962, short personal essays about freeways, college culture, computer punch cards, the recently ended Cuban missile crisis, the gym, the supermarket. *A Single Man* is like a smaller, more human version of James Joyce's *Ulysses*, the ultimate day-in-the-life novel; George is Leopold Bloom in Los Angeles. His sexuality is only one part of his life, dispersed through a hundred other parts, yet it is a key part of George's sense of being. The mere sight of two shirtless tennis players in tight white shorts can break through his melancholy and give life meaning for him.

The hour-by-hour structure enables Isherwood to be loose and inclusive, but the book doesn't feel shapeless. It addresses a lot through the grab bag of George's thoughts. George's anger with the heterosexual majority erupts in comic fantasies of vengeance on his drive to the college. His class in English literature is full of minorities: female, black, Asian, Jewish, elderly, and one gay boy. They discuss *After Many a Summer Dies the Swan* by Aldous Huxley. An older Jewish refugee asks if Huxley were anti-Semitic based on a line in the novel. George says no, Huxley was not anti-Semitic, then jumps ahead in an argument he's been having with himself: George declares that minorities *are* different from each other and the liberal idea that all people are brothers and sisters under the skin is a lie.

> And I'll tell you something else. A minority has its own kind of aggression. It absolutely dares the majority to hate it. It hates the majority—not without a cause, I grant you. It even hates the other minorities, because all minorities are in competition: each one proclaims that its sufferings are the worst and its wrongs are the blackest. And the more they all hate, and the more they're all persecuted, the nastier they become. Do you think it makes people nastier to be

loved? You know it doesn't. Then why should it make them nice to be loathed? While you're being persecuted you hate what's happening to you, you hate the people who're making it happen; you're in a world of hate. Why, you wouldn't recognize love if you met it. You'd suspect love. You'd think there was something behind it—some motive—some trick.

George knows firsthand how persecution makes a person angry and crazy. If oppression produced saints, we'd want everyone to be oppressed. And George sees homosexuals as a minority like blacks, Jews, and Asians— he is years ahead of his time in seeing the similarities *and* the conflicts. His students don't know he is speaking of himself here; we wait for somebody to misunderstand and be offended. But in a cruel but believable twist, the class is nearly over, and they are too concerned about the bell to pay full attention.

It's a startling scene. James Baldwin never addressed the issue more directly and realistically. Isherwood does it through a character who cannot make himself fully understood. (But the author might not have made himself clear, either. Few critics have given this scene the attention it deserves. Only recently, when Isherwood's journals began to appear and we learned about his obsession/fascination with Jews, did people talk about this scene, but as an example of anti-Semitism, not recognizing that George is talking about his own anger and nastiness as a gay man.)

We follow George through the rest of his day. He visits Doris, a woman dying of cancer in the hospital, who once had an affair with his dead lover, Jim. He sits with her, holding her hand, sorry he can't hate her anymore. "As long as one precious drop of hate remained, George could still find something in her of Jim. For he hated Jim too, nearly as much as her, while they were away together in Mexico. That has been the bond between him and Doris. And now it is broken. And one more bit of Jim is lost to him forever."

He escapes the shadow of death to visit the gym, not a shiny industrial gym of our time but a shabby place where two other men and a twelve-year-old boy amiably lift weights together. He has dinner with his friend Charlotte, the Englishwoman of the original novel. They drink too much and talk about their lost partners—Charlotte's husband left her for a younger woman—and compare memories of England. Afterward, instead of going home, George goes down to a bar by the ocean, where he finds Kenny Potter, a tall, skinny student from his literature class. Kenny has had a fight with his girlfriend. The two get drunk together and Kenny suggests they go back to George's place. We—and George—think we know where this is going, especially when professor and student share a drunken nude swim in the ocean. But the novel takes a more interesting, devious twist before it ends with George at home in bed alone.

> George smiles to himself, with entire self-satisfaction. Yes, I am crazy, he thinks. That is my secret, my strength.

And he falls asleep. The God-like narrator returns to ask and answer questions about the future, much like the Q. and A. chapter near the end of *Ulysses*. The narrator steps back further to compare individuals to rock pools of consciousness beside a vast ocean. Then the narrator closes by imagining George's death. He might die in his sleep from a heart attack. The narrator gives a few clinical details.

> Then one by one the lights go out and there is total blackness. And if some part of the nonentity we called George has indeed been absent at this moment of terminal shock, away out there on the deep waters, then it will return home to find itself homeless. For it can associate no longer with what lies here, unsnoring, on the bed. This is now cousin to the garbage in the container on the back porch. Both will have to be carted away and disposed of, before too long.

The lessons of Vedanta, soul, and death are translated into the homeliest metaphor imaginable. It's shocking in its matter-of-factness, and liberating, too.

Isherwood gives the world a fully realized gay man and makes him ordinary by submerging his sexuality in the universal buzz of metaphysical being. And he makes homosexuality more acceptable by making George single. The narrator even bitterly jokes about the tactic: "Let us even go so far as to say that this kind of relationship can sometimes be almost beautiful—particularly if one of the parties is already dead, or, better yet, both."

This is also a novel about grief, yet it's not overtly sad. George successfully navigates his sadness, even floats in it, with surprising seren-ity. Jim is everywhere in George's consciousness. He died in a car wreck while visiting his family in Ohio, and George did not go out for the funeral. George tells acquaintances only that Jim has gone away, not that he's dead. He saves that brutal fact for close friends. George's seeming serenity looks like denial in our current age of therapy, but George carries Jim's memory with a kind of grace that feels neither hysterical nor repressed.

Isherwood's American and British publishers accepted the novel without difficulty, although Simon and Schuster asked him to remove a sentence about George wiping off with a handkerchief after he masturbates. Isher-wood sent the book to the *New Yorker* for possible serialization, but Roger Angell rejected it, claiming, "While I can believe this novel, I don't find it particularly interesting." The *New Yorker* was now publishing highly origi-nal nonfiction, but its fiction remained narrow and predictable.

A Single Man was published in August 1964. The reviews were an amaz-ing mix of progressive intelligence and old-fashioned bigotry. Alan Pryce-Jones in the *New York Herald Tribune* called it "a small masterpiece." The incoherent review in the *Los Angeles Times* was headlined "Disjointed Limp Wrist Saga." Both the *Catholic Standard* and *Daily Worker* disliked the novel, but Graham Greene in, of all places, the *Catholic Herald*, said it was one of the best books of the year. Other reviews made clear the world was chang-ing but had a long way to go. The *Nashville Tennessean* observed of Isher-wood, "By making his leading character a sex deviate, he has provided a sharp contrast with the normal man and yet he has been able to show that all people experience the same emotions and face similar crises, no matter how they differ in normality and perspective." But in New York literary circles, little had changed. Elizabeth Hardwick in the *New York Review of Books* was so full of sneers and condescension ("Poor Corydon is now in California, driving the freeways with a daydreaming ardor, attacking the ants with Flit, and mourning among the hibiscus") that it's a surprise to come to the end of her review and learn she liked the book, sort of. (Hard-wick praises Isherwood for understanding that gay life isn't amusing but is a "trap.") And everybody's favorite homosexual expert, Stanley Kauffmann, wrote in the *New Republic*: "The book holds us because it runs parallel with the truth of our lives, but like any parallel it keeps a certain distance." We wouldn't want to get too close.

Luckily the small but struggling gay media came through on this novel. Novelist James Colton (aka Joseph Hansen) wrote in *ONE*, "The most honest book ever written about a homosexual...about life, death, love, sex...it would be difficult to overpraise it." Not many readers read *ONE*, but the paperback publisher quoted Colton on the jacket, perhaps the first time a gay magazine was used to promote a novel. Publishers were finally acknowledging there was a gay readership for their books.

Isherwood left for India as soon as he completed the book. He was there for two months with his guru, Prabhavananda, researching a biography, *Ramakrishna and His Disciples*, and giving talks in Calcutta and surrounding towns. But he felt trapped and dishonest in his role as a spokesman. "As long as I quite unashamedly get drunk, have promiscuous sex, and write books like *A Single Man*, I simply cannot appear before people as a sort of lay monk. Whenever I do, my life becomes divided and untruthful—or rather, the only truth left is my drunkenness, my sex, and my art." He decided it was time to break with Vedanta.

When he returned to Los Angeles, he discovered Bachardy's most recent affair was over. He made his peace with Bachardy, and with himself as well. As always he wrote about it in his diary:

> When Don isn't here, my life simply isn't very interesting. He creates disturbance, anxiety, tension, and sometimes jealousy and rage; but never for a moment do I feel our relationship is unimportant. Let me just recognize this fact, and not bother making good resolutions. He will behave badly; I shall behave badly. That's par for the course.

They continued to see other men—Bachardy more than Isherwood, but Isherwood was hardly monogamous. They continued to get frustrated about their work and blame each other and forgive each other and resume working. They sustained their life together.

Cabaret finally opened in New York in November 1966 to rave reviews. Lotte Lenya played the landlady. Isherwood refused to see the show but sent Bachardy, who disliked it and reported back that Isherwood would hate it. Hal Prince and Joe Masteroff had added a moralistic love story where the

Isherwood character, now American, tries and fails to save Sally Bowles from her decadent lifestyle with marriage. Kander and Ebb had suggested Sally be played by Liza Minnelli—the star of their last show, *Flora the Red Menace*—but Prince killed the idea, saying she was much too strong a performer. From the start, people insisted that Sally be mediocre—if she were any good she'd be singing in a nicer club. Even Isherwood repeated this line when Minnelli was later cast in the movie. I've never understood it myself. Who wants to see a musical about a singer who can't sing? And do we really believe the world is so fair and just that people with talent inevitably rise to the top?

For all its faults, *Cabaret* helped to keep Isherwood's name alive until the world had changed enough that it was ready for the real Isherwood. A novel is such a small thing, but *A Single Man* has endured, like an early mammal surrounded by dinosaurs.

9. The Whole World Is Watching

—ɷ—

Isherwood dedicated *A Single Man* to Gore Vidal. Vidal was honored and later dedicated his most notorious novel to Isherwood. But in the meantime he paid his friend the higher compliment of competing with him. Shortly after *A Single Man* appeared, Vidal went back to his old novel, *The City and the Pillar*, and revised and reissued it, as if to establish his position as the *first* chronicler of American gay life. The new *City and the Pillar* was published in 1965, a year after *A Single Man*. It included an afterword where Vidal explained why he wrote the novel and offered his strongest statement to date about sexuality:

> I decided to examine the homosexual underworld (which I knew rather less well than I pretended), and in the process show the "naturalness" of homosexual relations, as well as making the point that there was no such thing as a homosexual. Despite the current usage, the word is an adjective describing a sexual action, not a noun describing a recognizable type. All human beings are bisexual.

Declaring the categories null and void was an ingenious move. It suggested a whole new approach to sexual tolerance, and it put Vidal himself above the name-calling of the mid-Sixties. He couldn't be called a homosexual: there was no such animal. Yet the position left him standing outside when the ground shifted in the next decade.

Gore Vidal remained a man of many hats and enormous energy. He wrote plays and screenplays; he appeared on television; he ran for Congress. He was also making a name for himself as a major essayist. His early pieces were occasional prose on topics that happened to interest him, exercises in excess intellect. But he wrote more regularly and his essays became more accomplished. The form played to his strengths: his wit, his curiosity, his knowledge, and his ego. His editor, Jason Epstein, later said that Vidal "had too much ego to be a writer of fiction because he couldn't subordinate himself to other people.... It was always him wearing different costumes." The essays are Vidal playing Vidal, and he did it beautifully. He had a fluent first-person voice and a wide range of interests: literature, history, culture, and politics. He became a regular contributor to the *Nation* and *Esquire* and, after 1964, the *New York Review of Books*.

But what Vidal most wanted to do was write fiction. He had two works in progress on his desk: his novel about ancient Rome and a novel about Washington, D.C. But fiction requires time, and Vidal needed to make money. He bought himself some time when he adapted his political play, *The Best Man*, for the screen in 1963. Tired of Edgewater and New York, he and Howard Austen moved to Rome for six months. There Vidal finished *Julian*, his best novel to date.

The last pagan emperor, known to Christians as Julian the Apostate, is the subject of four fascinating chapters in Edward Gibbon's *The History of the Decline and Fall of the Roman Empire*. Expanding on the first-person examples of *I, Claudius* by Robert Graves and *Memoirs of Hadrian* by Marguerite Yourcenar, Vidal told the tale through multiple narrators, a device that enabled him to use pieces of the voice developed in his essays. He was better at telling than showing anyway, and first-person narrative is all telling—storytelling. The book came out in 1964 to excellent reviews and was a surprise best seller.

He returned to Edgewater, wrote more essays, more political journalism, and worked on other screenplays before he returned to Rome to finish his Washington novel. The succinctly named *Washington, D.C.* is a family saga about political life from the New Deal to the McCarthy era. Published in early 1967, it was a step backward, a surprisingly clunky novel written mostly in expository dialogue. ("Then Enid was right. You do love Clay. And you are mad.") There's a promising subplot in the homoerotic bond between a newspaper publisher and his son-in-law, a young politician, but Vidal was limited by the conventions of third-person fiction and his tendency to express strong emotion in the language of trashy melodrama. The book received mixed reviews, but it too was a best seller, doing even better than *Julian*. Many people thought it was a roman à clef about the Kennedys.

He wrote far better about politics as an essayist. He also spoke about it well. During this time he not only covered the 1964 political conventions for *Esquire*, he was a regular guest on the Jack Paar and David Susskind shows. "My entire life is now devoted to appearing on television: a pleasant alternative to real life," he wrote to friends. He found a new vocation as an articulate political insider, even though his only real political experience had been to run for office and lose. But Vidal was rare in literary circles in being fascinated with the dirt of party politics. He claimed to have picked up his cynical wisdom from his mother's family, in particular his grandfather, Senator T. P. Gore, but I suspect he learned more from his father, Eugene, who'd been badly burned by the government in his work with the airline industry. Vidal picked up much more political experience later when he lived intimately with Aaron Burr and Abraham Lincoln while writing fiction about them.

The question of homosexuality almost never came up on TV. However, in March 1967, a news special was broadcast, *CBS Reports: The Homosexuals*. Hosted by Mike Wallace, it featured talking heads in silhouette discussing their unhappiness, and several pontificating psychiatrists, including fiercely antigay Charles Socarides. Gore Vidal appeared not as a homosexual but as a cultural expert to debate with Albert Goldman. Goldman, who later wrote a positive biography of Lenny Bruce and negative biographies of Elvis Presley and John Lennon, argued that homosexuality was one of the "things tending toward the final erosion of our cultural values." Vidal replied, "I think the so-called breaking of the moral fiber of this country is one of the healthiest things that's begun to happen."

Vidal and Austen returned to Rome in May 1967 to live in a rooftop apartment near the Piazza Navona with a large sunlit terrace. Both men loved the city for many reasons, including the availability of young men for sex. Austen could be quite friendly with his Italian visitors, while Vidal's relationships remained strictly professional. Rome was an excellent place to write, and he concentrated on his work.

Kenneth Tynan had asked for an erotic sketch for a show he was putting together, *Oh! Calcutta!* One morning on the terrace, while exploring a possible orgy scene, Vidal hit upon a line: "I am Myra Breckinridge whom no man will ever possess." His imagination took off in a new direction and he followed it, forgetting Tynan and starting a novel. He wrote the first draft of *Myra Breckinridge* in a monthlong burst of creativity.

A wildly inventive comic fantasy about a movie scholar who changes his sex and goes to Hollywood, *Myra Breckinridge* is half parody, half lyric celebration. It suggests an American *Orlando*, but where Virginia Woolf's cross-gendered fantasy is soaked in British literature, Vidal's is soaked in American cinema. There are witty descriptions of old movies, prose poems about studio backlots, and comic homages to eccentric gay film critic Parker Tyler (who was still alive at the time). The book takes the form of Myra's first-person journal, which enables Vidal to mix narrative, social analysis, movie lore, and blatant erotica. There is not only an orgy but *two* extended scenes where Myra literally plays doctor with straight blond stud Rusty Godowsky, and sodomizes him with a dildo. The literate voice of the essays is pushed into the absurd, but it's serious as well as playful. "The novel being dead, there is no point to writing made-up stories. Look at the French who will not and the Americans who cannot. Look at me who ought not, if only because I exist entirely outside the usual human experience." The book is more about voice than story, and it doesn't entirely live up to the promise of its voice. But the same has been said about *Orlando*.

This was the book Vidal dedicated to Christopher Isherwood. "I AM HONORED AND DELIGHTED TO HAVE ANY BOOK OF YOURS DEDICATED TO ME," Isherwood telegraphed in reply.

Myra Breckinridge was published in February 1968 with no advance copies being sent to reviewers. Little, Brown wanted to keep Myra's transsexual identity a secret (it's difficult to imagine a time when people didn't already know) and present the book as a classy underground novel in the tradition of *Lolita* and *Candy*. The cover featured a photo of the cowgirl statue Vidal had seen from his room at Chateau Marmont when he first arrived in Hollywood. The initial printing was 55,000 copies, and the book was an instant best seller. Reviewers slowly caught up with it. "A funny novel, but it requires an iron stomach," said Eliot Fremont-Smith in the daily *New York Times*. The *Times Book Review* was terribly coy in describing the book's probable audience: "the pokerfaced jacket art manages to be both sexy and epicene; even the dedication will be a tip-off to the In-group." It's safe to assume gay readers made up a large proportion of the first buyers, but the book soon crossed over and remained on best-seller lists for thirty weeks. The other literary best seller that year was John Updike's hotly heterosexual novel, *Couples*. Writers needed to offer something new and outrageous to hold their own with what was happening in the outside world in 1968.

It was a year of politics and violence. The country was torn apart by Vietnam and race. Lyndon Johnson declared on March 31 that he would not seek the nomination for president, leaving the upcoming election wide open. On the night of April 4, Martin Luther King was murdered by a sniper in Memphis. Riots broke out in black neighborhoods across the country. In June Robert Kennedy was murdered in Los Angeles immediately after winning the California primary. Then, at the end of August, the Democrats met in Chicago.

CBS and NBC provided full coverage of both the Republican and Democratic conventions, but ABC decided to give only evening wrap-ups. They hired Gore Vidal to deliver fifteen minutes of commentary each night. Appearing with Vidal to offer the conservative point of view was William F. Buckley.

The editor and founder of the *National Review* had fully established himself as *the* spokesman of American conservativism. Author of *God and Man at Yale* and other books, he also had a syndicated newspaper column, "On the Right," and a TV show, *Firing Line*. Erudite, witty, and unearthly, he was famous for his elaborate sentences, breathy delivery, manic eyebrows, and reptilian tongue. He is now remembered as a representative of an age when conservatives could be civilized and reasonable. But Buckley was ahead of his time in many ways.

His exchanges with Vidal during the Republican convention in Miami were testy but without serious mishap. TV journalist Howard K. Smith served as moderator. Buckley supported the war in Vietnam, Vidal opposed it, but neither man liked the Republican nominee, Richard Nixon. Buckley was more excited by the governor of California, Ronald Reagan.

But the Democratic convention in Chicago was different. The situation was far more tense. The Democrats were bitterly divided over the war, with pro-war delegates supporting Vice President Hubert Humphrey and peace delegates supporting Senator Eugene McCarthy. The division was echoed outside the convention hall in the streets, where anti-war demonstrators—National Mobilization Against the War (MOBE), Yippies

(Youth International Party) and others—faced Mayor Richard Daley's army of police. Allen Ginsberg came to town, not to read poetry but to chant for peace. The author of "Howl" had become less literary and more spiritual in recent years, going deep into Eastern thought. He still wore a necktie but let his bushy hair and beard grow out. In Chicago he saw his old friend William Burroughs and the French gay writer Jean Genet. Burroughs and Genet were covering the convention for *Esquire*. Norman Mailer was there, too, covering the convention for *Harper's*. Mailer had published an odd novel the year before, *Why Are We in Vietnam?* about two boys on a hunting trip in Alaska who love each other as friends, but each is afraid to show his love for fear his pal will then sodomize him. Mailer continued to have weird issues about homosexuality, but he remained alert and curious about gay writers.

Vidal and Buckley had their first TV exchange on Sunday, and it went badly. Sometime during the two weeks since Miami, Buckley had read *Myra Breckinridge*. He hated it. He attacked Vidal for being no better than a pornographer. A pornographer, he said, had no business calling the Republican Party immoral. Vidal was amused, but their conversations remained on edge.

During the day Vidal visited the convention floor as both a journalist and a McCarthy supporter. It was the familiar world of his play, *The Best Man*. But he also visited the new world of student protesters several miles away in Lincoln Park on the lake. The police cleared the park each night so nobody could sleep there, using billy clubs and tear gas. Mayor Daley hated the protesters and encouraged his cops to do whatever they wanted. Mailer visited the park, too, and in his excellent book *Miami and the Siege of Chicago*, describes meeting Ginsberg and his friends there on Monday evening: he thought they looked like infantrymen, but Genet reminded him of Mickey Rooney. Late Monday night the police attacked the park again and Ginsberg was badly gassed. For the rest of the week his voice was hoarse from tear gas and chanting.

On Tuesday night, the police came through the park one more time. The students resisted and threw rocks; the police became angrier. The students fled south and regrouped in Grant Park, which was closer to the convention and the hotels where the delegates stayed. It was also closer to the TV news crews. There were no live video feeds on the street, only 16mm movie cameras whose footage needed to be rushed to TV stations and developed before it could be broadcast. The Chicago police were more restrained, for a while.

The climax came on Wednesday, August 28. In the convention hall that afternoon, the anti-war Democrats attempted to get a peace plank into the party platform. They failed. Up in Grant Park, there was a major disturbance when somebody climbed a flagpole to take down the American flag and raise another—some said a Vietcong or Vietnamese Liberation Front flag, others a red scarf. A couple of cops tried to stop it and rocks were thrown. The police then formed a wedge and attacked the crowd, indiscriminately slamming people with nightsticks. Camera crews raced behind the wall of helmeted cops, capturing the mayhem in broad daylight.

In another corner of the park, Ginsberg calmed a group of protesters by teaching them how to chant "om."

As the hot summer afternoon turned into evening, protesters crowded out of Grant Park and moved toward Michigan Avenue. They hoped to march down Michigan to the convention. But at the intersection of Balbo Avenue, outside the Hilton hotel, they were blocked by the police. Boxed in on three sides, the protesters were unable to move. Everybody waited—for thirty minutes. Then, at 7:57 p.m., as if on command, the police charged into the crowd. Columns of cops tore through the massed bodies, swinging clubs and fists, stampeding people left and right, knocking down individuals and dragging them across the pavement to paddy wagons while still beating them. They went after journalists, too, spraying them with mace or smashing their equipment. But the TV cameras on the canopy of the hotel were out of reach and continued filming. Recognizing what the cameras meant, protesters began to chant, "The whole world is watching, the whole world is watching."

Within an hour, the film was processed and broadcast raw with minimal commentary, seventeen minutes of police violence. People across the country saw cops brutally beating up unarmed students. It was as shocking as seeing Alabama cops attack civil rights marchers with dogs and fire hoses. This time the faces were white, but some became black with blood on black-and-white TV sets.

In the ABC studio that night, Howard K. Smith opened the broadcast with clips of the police attack in Grant Park. Buckley defended the police and blamed the demonstrators, saying they were breaking the law. Vidal defended the demonstrators, saying they were practicing their constitutional right to assemble. The exchange became more heated and incoherent. Buckley cited Oliver Wendell Holmes—"whom you must despise." Vidal cited the Constitution. Buckley interrupted:

Buckley: And some people were pro-Nazi.
Vidal: Shut up a minute.
Buckley: No, I won't. Some people were pro-Nazi and the answer is that they were well-treated by the people who ostracized them, and I'm for ostracizing people who egg on other people to shoot American Marines and American soldiers. I know you don't care—
Vidal: As far as I'm concerned, the only pro or crypto Nazi I can think of is yourself. Failing that—
Howard K. Smith: Let's not call names.

And Buckley delivered the insult heard around the world.

Buckley: Now listen, you queer. Stop calling me a crypto Nazi or I'll sock you in the goddamn face.
Howard K. Smith: Let's stop calling names!
Buckley: And you'll stay plastered. Let Myra Breckinridge go back to his pornography and stop making any allusions of Nazism. I was in the infantry in the last war!
Vidal: You were not in the infantry. As a matter of fact, you didn't fight in the war.
Buckley: I was in the infantry.
Vidal: You were not. You're distorting your own military record.

The two men sat side by side, half turned toward each other, Buckley in a gray suit, Vidal in a dark one. Both remained seated the entire time. Buckley had a finger pressed to one ear, presumably to keep his earpiece in place so he could hear how he sounded. Vidal broke into a smile when Buckley called him a queer, an oddly gleeful, boyish smile. Then he understood how angry Buckley was and his smile wavered. Buckley bared his teeth and leaned forward as if to hit Vidal, but his finger remained stuck in his ear.

A sixteen-year-old boy in Virginia watched the exchange with his mouth wide open. I was home from a summer at Boy Scout camp and I was amazed that two grown men could attack each other like angry adolescents. I suspected Buckley meant *queer* in the nastiest sexual way and wondered if it were true. I was impressed by how cool and unflustered Vidal remained.

"What happened at Sharon—," Vidal began before Smith cut him off. Smith proposed that the protesters may have provoked the violence by raising a Vietcong flag, as if that justified all the beatings that followed. Vidal insisted that even a Vietcong flag was an act of speech. "We are guaranteed freedom of speech. We've just listened to a grotesque example of it." The session ended with Smith declaring that Buckley and Vidal had given "a little more heat and a little less light than usual," but it had still been interesting.

Newspapers discussed the exchange the next day, but could only refer to "the disgraceful language"; they couldn't quote it. Besides, there were more important things to talk about. Nobody had been killed on Michigan Avenue, but many were injured and hundreds were arrested. A shouting match had broken out at the convention when Abe Ribicoff of New York condemned Mayor Daley for "gestapo tactics in the streets of Chicago." Americans were disgusted by the violence, but many blamed the protesters, not the police. This was an age when the country still trusted its police. In the middle of this chaos, Hubert Humphrey was nominated as candidate for president.

Vidal and Buckley appeared again on the last night of the convention and were subdued, professional, and dull. In November they were called back for postmortems on the election. Nixon won, in part because the Democratic convention had been so disorderly; Nixon represented law and order. Yet the third-party segregationist candidate, George Wallace, attracted many white conservatives, and the election was surprisingly close. Buckley insisted a screen separate him and Vidal so he wouldn't have to look at his antagonist while they spoke.

That should have been the end of it, but Buckley continued to brood about Vidal. After their last TV exchange, he contacted *Esquire* magazine and said he wanted to write about the televised fight. He told them he needed to be able to call Vidal a homosexual in print. *Esquire* enjoyed controversy and, after discussing it with their lawyers, they accepted but insisted Vidal be allowed to respond. Buckley agreed. Vidal hesitated—he had never acknowledged he was a homosexual (after all, there was no such thing)—but eventually he agreed, too. Each man wrote his article and drafts were exchanged. Lawyers were consulted and the articles were rewritten. Then, after both sides agreed on what could be printed, three months before either piece ran, Buckley sent a telegram to twenty magazines and newspapers declaring that Vidal had libeled him on TV and now wanted to libel him with an article in *Esquire*. He didn't mention his own article. Two days later he sued Vidal for libel. He still expected *Esquire* to publish his piece but threatened to sue them as well if they published Vidal's.

One cannot read about Buckley's actions without feeling one is dealing with a crazy person. But the very idea of homosexuality can turn some people temporarily insane.

Buckley's piece ran in August 1969. "On Experiencing Gore Vidal" appears with a subhead, "Can there be any justification in calling a man a queer before ten million people on television?" Which is what part of the essay is about—the part that makes sense, anyway. It's a long, obsessive, tedious piece. It's difficult to understand why *Esquire* went ahead and printed it—it's clearly not what they hoped for. It's even harder to figure out what Buckley hoped to prove. He begins by quoting an old article in the *East Village Other* that attacked him for practicing "faggot logic." He complains that other people can call him names, and protesters can call Lyndon Johnson names, so why can't he call Vidal a queer? He quotes his TV exchanges with Vidal in great detail. He talks about Vidal's writing and his "almost obsession with homosexuality," which is as close as he comes to actually saying that Vidal is a homosexual. The lawyers must have made him remove anything more direct. Buckley seemed to think that if he could identify Vidal as an actual pervert then he would prove that he himself was more moral and would win the argument. He closes with a strange paragraph on how "faggotry is countenanced, but the imputation of it—even to faggots—is not.... But the imputation of it in anger is not justified, which is why I herewith apologize to Gore Vidal."

Vidal's piece ran in September: "A Distasteful Encounter with William F. Buckley, Jr." The subheading was: "Can there be any justification in calling a man a pro crypto Nazi before ten million people on television?" The cover displayed the title, "The Kids vs. the Pigs" and a photo of a college boy going face-to-face with a real pig.

The essay is clear, coherent, and merciless. Vidal's account of what happened in Chicago, on the streets and in the TV studio, is more cogent than Buckley's woolly rambling. But more damning is his look at the past of Buckley and his family. Vidal opens and closes with the ugly story of how the Buckley children in 1944 vandalized an Episcopal church in Sharon, Connecticut—*Sharon* was the cryptic word Vidal delivered after Buckley lost his temper. The Buckleys, who were famously Catholic, hated the local Episcopal minister for selling a home to Jews. Vidal quotes local newspapers and court records about the crime, but never specifies that Buckley himself was not involved, only his three sisters. He repeatedly makes the point that this is the family Buckley came from. It's a painful story and is perhaps what angered Buckley so much that he sued Vidal for writing an article he had forced him to write in the first place. Far more damaging, however, is Vidal's encyclopedia of racist remarks made by Buckley over the years. Vidal offered his own apology of sorts, saying he was sorry to suggest that Buckley had associated with Hitler. He meant to call him a fascist.

Buckley took Vidal to court when he couldn't defeat him on the printed page. His own essay is a big floppy pillow compared to Vidal's well-aimed baseball bat. One can't help picturing a furious Elmer Fudd being clobbered by Bugs Bunny. But Buckley could have stopped the whole affair if he'd simply withdrawn his essay and let the matter drop. However, his pride and his moral righteousness were involved, and he could not let go.

When *Esquire* printed Vidal's essay, Buckley sued *Esquire*, too. The case went back and forth between lawyers and judges for three years. There were countersuits and dismissals, depositions and subpoenas. Legal costs mounted. Finally, in August 1972, *Esquire* settled with Buckley out of court, agreeing to pay his legal fees and declare in their pages that they didn't agree with Vidal's accusations if Buckley dropped his suit. Buckley then dropped his suit against Vidal as well. Buckley next issued a press release claiming that he had won. The *Times* reported the settlement, again without mentioning Buckley's original piece, making it look as if Vidal had started the whole thing.

A few years later in his novel *Burr,* Vidal included a thoroughly unpleasant character named William de la Touche Clancey, an Irish Catholic sodomite who puts on airs and is despised by everyone. It is a not-so-private joke, yet no lawsuit was ever threatened, perhaps because it would have been preposterous to suggest that William F. Buckley could be a sodomite—and after all, there was no such thing.

But Gore Vidal was not the only political writer attacked for being gay in 1968. And one did not need to be white, wealthy, and Harvard-educated to sound crazy when denouncing a queer.

James Baldwin was back in the United States after his sojourns in Istanbul. He appeared frequently on television, always as a black spokesman, never as a gay one. He restricted his sexuality to his fiction. He spent time with the political organizers around Martin Luther King. He also spent time with the new black radicals who offered a militant alternative to King's pacifism, Huey Newton and the Black Panthers. His pleasure in their company is caught in a description of their followers in his next novel:

> They were younger than they thought they were, much: they might arrive in their Castro berets, their parkas and hoods and sweaters and thin jeans or corduroys and heavy boots, and with their beautiful black kinky hair spinning around their heads like fire and prophecy... but they were goggle-eyed just the same, and so far from being incapable of trusting, they had perpetually to fight the impulse to trust, overwhelmed, like all kids, by meeting a Great Man.

The "Great Man" in the novel, *Tell Me How Long the Train's Been Gone*, is Leo Proudhammer, a black actor, but it was also Baldwin, now a major public figure in the civil rights movement.

The Minister of Information for the Panthers was an older man, a thirty-three-year-old ex-con named Eldridge Cleaver. In March 1968, he published a collection of essays, *Soul on Ice*, which included strong pieces about life in Folsom Prison, where he served time for rape, and a long essay on Baldwin, "Notes on a Native Son." After declaring first love of his writing, then unease, Cleaver abruptly announces that Baldwin's work contains "the most grueling, agonizing total hatred of the blacks, particularly of himself, and the most shameful, fanatical, fawning, sycophantic love of the whites... of any black American writer of note of our time." When he finally gets to specifics, Cleaver attacks Baldwin for having qualms about African nationalism in his essay "Princes and Powers," and for mocking Norman

Mailer's essay "The White Negro." Cleaver treats Mailer as *the* authority on black male experience, shamelessly fawning over the white novelist.

Then he gets on the subject of homosexuality and goes completely bonkers: "It seems that many Negro homosexuals...are outraged and frustrated because in their sickness they are unable to have a baby by the white man." He claims that this is why they are so eager to bend over for white lovers. He builds to his famous declaration: "I, for one, do not think that homosexuality is the latest advance over heterosexuality on the scale of human evolution. Homosexuality is a sickness, just as are baby-rape and wanting to become the head of General Motors." This is a kind of joke, of course, but where exactly does it land? He closes by quoting Murray Kempton out of context in order to dismiss Baldwin as the new Stepin Fetchit, the shuffling, slow-talking black comedian of the 1930s and 1940s.

Cleaver's remarks about black women ("the silent ally, indirectly but effectively, of the white man") and his political explanation of the rape of white women are even more appalling. The book had its critics, but it's shocking how many people praised it in 1968. The *Times Book Review* included it in their ten best books of the year. Sympathy for the oppressed blocked out the sad truth that Christopher Isherwood identified in *A Single Man*: oppression can make people crazy and hateful.

Needless to say, Baldwin did not like Cleaver's essay. He told a friend, "All that toy soldier has done is call me gay. I thought we'd gone through all that with the [Black] Muslims and were past it. All he wants is a gunfight at the OK Corral." But Baldwin wrote some strange things about Cleaver in his next nonfiction book, the journal-like memoir, *No Name in the Street*:

> I thought I could see why he felt impelled to issue what was, in fact, a warning: he was being a zealous watchman on the city wall, and I do not say that with a sneer....I felt that he used my public reputation against me both naively and unjustly, and I also felt that I was confused in his mind with the unutterable debasement of the male—with all those faggots, punks, and sissies, the sight and sound of whom, in prison, must have made him vomit more than once.

Baldwin goes on to say that both he and Cleaver are "odd and disreputable" and that "the odd and disreputable revolutionary" and "the odd and disreputable artist" have much to learn from each other. Yet there's a masochistic note in Baldwin's response that's unsettling. It's as if part of him thought he deserved to be abused as a faggot, punk, and sissy. Cleaver wasn't the only activist slamming Baldwin for being gay. In political circles he was sometimes known as Martin Luther Queen.

Baldwin may have responded directly if other, more public events hadn't intervened. A few weeks after *Soul on Ice* was published, the police raided a Black Panther office in Oakland, California. There was a real gunfight and Cleaver was wounded and arrested; another Panther, Bobby Hutton, was killed. That was on April 6. More important, two days before, on April 4, when Baldwin was in Palm Springs working on a screenplay about Malcolm X, a friend telephoned from Memphis to say that Martin Luther King had been shot. Baldwin was devastated. Many friends said he was never the same afterward. He wrote about it himself: "Since Martin's death in Memphis...something has altered in me, something has gone away. Perhaps even more than the death itself, the manner of his death has forced me into a judgment concerning human life and human beings which I have always been reluctant to make."

Baldwin grew more bleak and bitter in interviews on TV and in magazines, talking about white reactionaries, black genocide, and the death of hope. He didn't bother to look at the page proofs of *Tell Me How Long the Train's Been Gone* before it was published in June. He was too depressed by politics, but he also must have known that the book was a failure.

A first-person narrator, a black actor, Leo Proudhammer, tells the story of his life while he recovers from a heart attack. He grew up in Harlem, rose to fame, had affairs with women and men, and is now involved with a young black radical. Leo should provide Baldwin with the opportunity for a deeply personal, autobiographical novel, but it is a flat, impersonal book, with only a few good firsthand moments such as that description of young radicals. The strong emotion that carried *Another Country*, despite its huge cast and uneven prose, is gone. His emotions were all engaged elsewhere— first in politics, then in grief—or numbed by alcohol. The heavy drinking that had helped Baldwin live with his demons of love and anger was catching up with him.

The reviews were bad. Some quoted Cleaver's charge that there was no politics, economics, or social referents in Baldwin's fiction and it was only about sex. People began to make the soon-to-be familiar argument that the essay and not the novel was his domain. As I said before, I disagree.

Baldwin's best novels are better than his essays. I suspect people often prefer the essays simply because there's no sex in them (which with Baldwin usually means gay sex). But while the first-person essay helped Gore Vidal find his strengths as a fiction writer, the form may have hurt Baldwin. The loose, rambling, hit-or-miss qualities of his essays led to a similar rambling quality when he used the first person for his later novels.

By the end of the summer Baldwin had left the United States, going first to Paris, then to Istanbul. He was out of the country at the time of the Chicago riots. A year later in Istanbul, he directed a Turkish production of *Fortune and Men's Eyes* for his friend Engin Cezzar. This is the John Herbert play about prison life and rape, the world of "faggots, punks, and sissies" that Baldwin said he could almost understand Eldridge Cleaver for hating.

Cleaver meanwhile jumped bail and fled to Algeria, where he lived for six years. He returned to America in 1975 and was convicted of assault but sentenced only to probation. He soon renounced Marx, became a Mormon, and eventually joined the Republican Party.

Truman Capote was also unraveling at this time, not from politics but from fame. He was high on it, intoxicated. A year after the masked ball at the Plaza, a movie was made from *In Cold Blood* and the media revisited him and his book. He returned to the TV circuit, speaking as an advocate against the death penalty. Also shown on TV in 1967 was a film of his story "A Christmas Memory," with Capote narrating. His voice became more famous than ever.

The politics that meant so much to Vidal and Baldwin barely touched Capote. When he talked about Vietnam or black power in his 1968 *Playboy* interview, his ideas sounded only glib and secondhand. ("I think both sides, Hanoi and Washington, are terribly, tragically wrong. And the mistakes of statesmen are always written in young men's blood.") Even his comments about capital punishment—the death penalty would be good if it were used quickly and consistently; life sentences should mean life without parole—had a thoughtless, mechanical quality. He was busy working on his next project—or said he was busy. By 1968 *Answered Prayers* was already the world's most famous unwritten novel. He told *Playboy* that it was "a roman à clef, drawn from life yet suffused with fictional elements and partaking of both my reportorial abilities and imaginative gifts." He told friends it would be twice as long as *Remembrance of Things Past*. But when Donald

Windham spent a month with him in a rented house in Palm Springs, he found that Capote did not sit down to write until after lunch and he always took a bottle of wine to his workroom, where he could be heard talking on the telephone.

The drinking that had escalated while he finished *In Cold Blood* now became epic. Windham noticed his routine during their time together: "a bloody mary before lunch, followed by three or four large vodkas, then wine. Before dinner a bottle of white wine (instead of 'early drinks'), then four or five vodkas at the house, and two or three more at the restaurant." It's an insane amount of alcohol to put into a five-foot-three body. Mailer in *Miami and the Siege of Chicago* described Mayor Daley as "looking suspiciously like a fat and aged version of tough Truman Capote on ugly pills." Capote was approaching that version himself, despite a facelift.

Windham made another discovery during this trip. Capote's regular TV appearances were often taped and rerun and he enjoyed watching himself. He lost his last bond to reality. "[He] began to talk to me as though I knew no more about him, and was no more to him, than another guest on one of the talk shows."

A lover might have provided some kind of anchor, but he and Jack Dunphy were spending more and more time apart. Dunphy was frustrated as a writer and worked harder at his novels and plays, becoming a hermit. Capote often didn't want to hear anything critical Dunphy had to say on the few occasions when they *were* together. He began to see other boyfriends on the side, usually married men with no interest in literature.

Capote achieved the wealth and fame he had dreamed of as a boy in Alabama. He expanded in it, like a high-altitude balloon rising toward the sun. He was a fascinating spectacle—for a while. It's a myth that success is the worst thing that can happen to an artist. Failure is far more destructive. Yet adulation can feed not only the social confidence of artists, it can turn up the volume of self-criticism and doubt. As Capote grew louder and more baroque in public, he became more silent whenever he sat alone at his typewriter.

As the Sixties came to an end, three gay writers were major spokesmen on important national issues: Vidal on party politics, Baldwin on civil rights, Capote on capital punishment. They were all dismissed at one time or another for being gay, even though their sexuality had nothing to do with what they were saying. But they were also taken seriously. The age of literary television would go on for a few more years, into a time when gay writers could talk a little about their own lives and issues. But this early gay presence, often between the lines, was excitedly noticed and seized upon by audiences of gay men and women.

A future novelist named Edmund White saw Capote on TV at this time and remembers him as being an embarrassment, little more than a literary Liberace. Yet other gay people still in college or high school found Capote exciting, even promising. Most of us were impressed by Gore Vidal, despite his cool, supercilious manner. All of us were in awe of James Baldwin, even though we didn't discover his sexuality until we read his novels. But if these three homosexuals could publish their books and be taken seriously and even appear on television, then homosexuality was not the total taboo that society claimed it to be. Maybe there was hope for us lesser mortals.

10. Riots

—⚬—

Oh, my God, it's Lily Law!
Everybody three feet apart!
—Emory, *The Boys in the Band*

In 1967 in New York City, a twenty-six-year-old former dance student, Craig Rodwell, opened a bookstore on Mercer Street on the southern edge of Greenwich Village. It was not just another bookstore, however; it was a gay bookstore, the first of its kind. Rodwell wasn't much of a reader, but he had great respect for literature. He intended to combine art and politics, using the store as a center for activism while selling books to attract visitors *and* pay the rent. Needing an identifiably homosexual name, he called it the Oscar Wilde Memorial Bookshop.

Rodwell had been active in the tiny world of gay politics since 1964, after a suicide attempt led to a stay in a mental hospital. He found strength and purpose working with the Mattachine Society. The organization's deliberately obscure name (an order of jesters in the Middle Ages) illustrates how oppressive society was in the 1950s and 1960s: a homosexual rights group could not afford to identify itself as homosexual.

Sex between consenting same-gender adults was still a crime in all fifty states except Illinois. Gay and lesbian bars were frequently raided. Men and women were regularly fired from their jobs for being gay—this included federal employees and schoolteachers. Conservatives later complained that homosexual activists publicized what should have remained private, but it was the police and the courts who made homosexuality a public matter.

To cite just one incident: on a Friday night in April 1960, in a gay bar in Miami, Florida, the "E" club, five plainclothes cops entered, ordered customers to put down their drinks, and arrested twenty-two men for "disorderly conduct." But that wasn't the end of it. On Sunday, a local tabloid, the *Miami News*, ran a story of the raid, naming those arrested with their ages, occupations, and addresses. Imagine your neighbors or even your boss reading that you were caught in a bar where, "habitués of the place were reported to embrace each other, wear tight-fitting women's pants and bleach their hair." (This is just one raid among thousands. Historians know of it chiefly because *ONE* published a detailed account.)

The federal post office still maintained a ban on what could be sent in the mail. Lives were often ruined as a result. The most famous case is that of Newton Arvin, the English professor who was Truman Capote's first lover. The Massachusetts police entered his home near Smith College in September 1960 with a search warrant because he had received beefcake magazines in the mail. They seized more magazines, pornographic photos, and, worst of all, his diaries. They arrested not just Arvin but six other men, including two junior faculty members: named by a frightened Arvin, according to one source; named in Arvin's diaries, according to another. They were charged with sodomy and distributing pornography.

Arvin signed himself into a nearby mental hospital while waiting for the trial. Capote was in Spain working on *In Cold Blood* when he heard the news. He wrote Arvin a letter of solace and advice. "It's happened to many others—who, like Gielgud, took it in stride and did not let it be the end of the world." Actor John Gielgud had been arrested for solicitation a few years earlier in London. Arvin was supported by the literary world—Lionel Trilling, Malcolm Cowley, Edmund Wilson, and others—but he still lost his job at Smith, as did the two junior faculty. In the end, the seven men were convicted, fined, and given suspended sentences.

So an organization like Mattachine was working against enormous odds. It was a brave action when, on a weekend in May 1965, ten members led by a fired government worker, Frank Kameny, picketed the White House with placards declaring "Bill of Rights for Homosexuals!" and "15,000,000 Homosexuals Ask for Equality, Opportunity, Dignity." Rodwell marched with them. He was so elated by the experience that he proposed they protest every year—on July 4 at Independence Hall in Philadelphia. Which they did. For the next four years, a band of a dozen or so impeccably dressed protesters—the men in coats and ties, the women in skirts—appeared in Philadelphia for what they called the Annual Reminder.

As often happens in minority politics, being right was more important than being effective. There were constant arguments which led to schisms in homophile organizations that were small to begin with. The Mattachine Society itself had broken up into regional divisions. Rodwell thought a bookstore might be more inclusive and inviting, but he did not have a terribly inclusive personality himself. Shortly before he opened the store, he split off from Mattachine New York to form his own group, HYMN (Homophile Youth Movement in Neighborhoods—it was a golden age of acronyms and the names didn't always make sense).

The Oscar Wilde Memorial Bookshop opened on Thanksgiving weekend with a sign outside declaring "Bookshop of the Homophile Movement" and a sign in the window saying, "Gay Is Good." On the shelves inside was a grand total of twenty-five titles. There was little available in 1967, but Rodwell reduced it further by avoiding not only pornography but most pulp fiction. However, he did stock novels by Vidal, Isherwood, and Baldwin, *City of Night* by John Rechy, *Desert of the Heart* by Jane Rule, and the historical fiction of Mary Renault. (Ever since 1956 with *Last of the Wine*, the British lesbian novelist had been publishing intelligent, well-reviewed novels about same-sex love, getting away with it chiefly because her books were set in ancient Greece and the love was literally Platonic.) There were novels in translation, too, in particular work by André Gide and Jean Genet.

Rodwell also sold political pamphlets, some more homemade than others. There were only a few magazines. After its own struggle with internal politics, *ONE* published its last issue earlier that year. (The final letters column included one from a scornful reader who questioned the attention given to literature. "Book reviews? Who reads books these days?") But that fall a new monthly newspaper appeared, the *Los Angeles Advocate*, soon to be known as simply the *Advocate*. There was also the lesbian journal, the *Ladder*, and a new male magazine, *DRUM*, but it included photos of beefcake as well as articles about politics, so Rodwell refused to carry it.

Over the next fifteen years, stores like Oscar Wilde would appear in every major American city. Their owners were less squeamish than Rodwell about using porn to pay the rent, but their real emphasis was on literature and politics. The gay and lesbian bookstore movement would play an enormous role in the social change ahead.

* * *

Early gay politics was too small and pure to accomplish much on its own. Novels were impure and more effective, but they were read in private and rarely discussed. Theater, on the other hand, was as impure as fiction and highly public. People didn't even need to see a play in order to talk about it.

Two months before Craig Rodwell opened his bookstore, thirty-three-year-old Mart Crowley arrived in New York with the manuscript of an unfinished play in his suitcase. Crowley had lived in New York before—he was originally from Mississippi—but he had been in Los Angeles trying to break into TV and movie writing.

There's a surprising number of Southerners in this history, and it's hard to say why. Crowley was born in Vicksburg, Mississippi, in 1934. He left home to study drama at Catholic University in Washington, D.C., intending to be a set designer. He first came to New York in 1957 and worked as a production assistant on several low-budget films before being hired by Elia Kazan. He became close friends with Natalie Wood during the shooting of *Splendor in the Grass*, directed by Kazan and written by William Inge. For the film's final scene, Kazan asked Crowley to put on a dress and drive the pickup truck that the actress playing Wood's best friend couldn't steer—the babyfaced Crowley was very pretty and looked ten years younger than he was. When Wood and her husband, Robert Wagner, moved out to Hollywood, Crowley moved with them.

All this time he was writing, not stage plays or screenplays, but TV plays. It was the age of *Playhouse 90* and other television showcases, but, unlike Gore Vidal, Crowley was unable to sell his work. Out in Los Angeles, he took various day jobs until he saved enough to move to Italy to write a screenplay based on Dorothy Baker's 1962 novel, *Cassandra at the Wedding*, with two roles for Natalie Wood as twin sisters: one straight, the other lesbian. (Baker was the clever, risk-taking author of *Trio*, the last play shut down by the police under the Wales Padlock Law in 1945. She also wrote *Young Man with a Horn*, a novel about jazz with a strong lesbian subplot. Baker was married, but her literature professor husband seems to have encouraged her in writing about bisexuality.) The script was highly praised and bought by 20th Century Fox, but the lesbian character—as discreetly done in the screenplay as it is in the novel—scared the studio and the movie never got made. More writing work followed, however, including a 1965 TV pilot for Bette Davis, *The Decorator*. Crowley gave her a male sidekick, to be played by Paul Lynde. He would've been the first gay man on TV, but the producers insisted a woman play the role and cast butch character actress Mary Wickes. The pilot was shot but the series was never picked up. Crowley became very depressed. His friend Wood gave him a year of therapy as a gift. (Although his love affairs were intense but brief—the longest lasting only six months—Crowley had a genius for long-term friendships with both straight and gay people.)

Every Sunday, Crowley liked to buy the *New York Times*, go to the Swiss Cafe and drink bullshots (beef bouillon and vodka), and read about life back East. One Sunday in January 1966, he opened the *Times* and saw Stanley Kauffmann's article, "Homosexual Drama and Its Disguises." Where other gay men felt insulted by the criticisms and carping tone, Crowley was struck by one particular sentence: "The homosexual dramatist must be free to write truthfully of what he knows, rather than try to transform it to a life he does not know, to the detriment of his truth and ours." Crowley liked the idea of writing the truth about gay life.

He did not have the opportunity to act on it, however, until the following year, in the summer of 1967. He was housesitting for six weeks in the Beverly Hills mansion of a female friend while he decided whether or not he should move back to New York. The staff fed and looked after him, and his duties were minimal. With time on his hands, he began to write dialogue; he soon found himself writing a play about a circle of gay friends. Initially it was set in a gay bar, but he realized a bar was too crowded with superfluous people, so he moved the play to the apartment of a figure based loosely on himself, Michael. He was far harsher with this character than he was with the others. He drew upon friends for the rest of the ensemble. Bookish Douglas Murray became the bookish, loyal Donald; the former dancer Howard Jeffrey became the darkly brilliant former skater Harold. He included pieces of himself in all the characters, not just Michael. (He gave the story of falling in love with his dentist in high school to the character of Emory.) He was surprised at how quickly the writing went. He hit a block only in the second act and needed something new, so he invented a mean party game, "Affairs of the Heart," where each man must telephone the great love of his life. The game was inspired in part by the party games promised in *Who's Afraid of Virginia Woolf?*: "Hump the Hostess" and "Get the Guests."

By the end of the summer, when Crowley left the mansion, the play was finished except for the last scene. He took the manuscript with him when he flew to New York; he finished it that fall in a borrowed house on Fire Island, writing Michael's final breakdown there. He showed it to his friend, the actor/director Robert Moore, who loved it and wanted to direct it. He showed it to an agent who hated it and wanted to throw him out of her office. But he persuaded her to send it to Richard Barr, the producer of *Virginia Woolf.* If anyone would dare touch this play, he thought Barr would. The agent gave in. She sheepishly called Crowley the next day to say that Barr had read the play as soon as he got it, loved it, and wanted to meet with Crowley that afternoon.

Barr and Edward Albee had taken a portion of the huge profits from *Virginia Woolf* and formed their own company to produce new work by new playwrights. Crowley met Barr and Albee for drinks at Barr's Greenwich Village apartment. Barr did most of the talking while Albee sat by with his usual Sister Grimm expression, looking "sphinx-like and inscrutable," saying little except to ask what Crowley thought of "Brechtian objectivism." Barr wanted to do a workshop production of the play as soon as possible.

In the years ahead, critics would claim that *Boys in the Band* was mostly a variation or even a copy of *Virginia Woolf*, yet it's hard to see that when one reads the two plays back to back. Both use profanity fearlessly, but they use it differently. The only thing they really share is the idea of a mean party game. I suspect the idea of kinship was planted in critics' minds by the fact that both playwrights were gay and both plays were produced by Richard Barr. For me, *Boys* does not echo *Virginia Woolf* as much as it echoes *The Iceman Cometh* by Eugene O'Neill: an ensemble of characters is confronted by a friend who wants to strip them of their illusions. Michael turns into a truthteller like Hickey of *Iceman* halfway through the play, but his "truths" ultimately turn against him. Albee would later attack *Boys*, claiming he had always hated it. But as Crowley now points out, if he really hated it, why did he let Barr produce it? I suspect that the later endless comparisons to *Virginia Woolf*, for good and ill, turned Albee against the play.

Things happened quickly after the first meeting. Barr and co-producer Charles Woodward hired Crowley's friend Robert Moore to direct. The play was quickly cast despite the fears of actors and (more often) their agents about playing gay characters. It was workshopped downtown at the Vandam Street Theater in January 1968, playing to packed houses for five nights. The audiences were almost entirely male. Word was already out. *Boys in the Band* opened off Broadway on April 14, 1968, at Theatre Four in midtown—ten days after the assassination of Martin Luther King.

People said many unkind things about *Boys* in the years ahead, and some of them are true, but they don't undo the power of the play. Pauline Kael complained that its homosexuals were "a forties-movie bomber-crew cast: a Catholic, a Jew, a Negro, one butch type, one nellie"—but what's wrong with that? Should they be similar? The cast has the diversity of a small Southern town transferred to a birthday party. The nine men talk about being gay, of course, but they also talk about psychiatry, jobs, money, drugs, religion. The play remains genuinely funny. Not only did Crowley create a score of memorable one-liners—"Connie Casserole," "Who do you have to fuck to get a drink around here?" "You look like you been rimming a snow man," and "Life is a goddamn laff-riot"—he put them together in such a way that they bounce and ricochet off each other. Even when the play turns serious in the second act, a funny line can still jump up and bite you on the nose. (A line about a sweater, "The one on the floor is vicuna," makes me laugh solely because of the context.) And the play has three great characters: Michael, Harold, and Emory.

Emory is the nelly queen, but nelly made electric, transcendent. He begins in stereotype yet there is nothing stock or stale about him. He is wonderfully witty, but also sweet and secretly tough. A steely defiance comes through in both the gaudy performance by Cliff Gorman recorded in the movie, and the more delicate performance by James Lecesne in the 1996 revival. Emory's friendship with Bernard, the sole black man, is poignant and disturbing, two minorities within a minority bonding through shared insults. It's a dangerous kind of bond, which the two men both acknowledge.

Harold is the birthday guest, the self-described "thirty-two-year-old, ugly, pockmarked Jew fairy." He arrives stoned at the end of Act One and stays stoned. He doesn't protect his friends when Michael attacks them—he knows he can't fight Michael directly. He can only observe and make wisecracks. Yet he is the real truth teller of the play, not Michael, when he coolly confronts their host at the end:

You are a sad and pathetic man. You're a homosexual and you don't want to be. But there is nothing you can do to change it. Not all your prayers to your God, not all the analysis you can buy in all the years you've got left to live. You may very well one day be able to know a heterosexual life if you want it desperately enough—if you pursue it with the fervor with which you annihilate—but you will always be homosexual as well. Always, Michael. Always. Until the day you die.

The actor Leonard Frey made Harold unforgettable in the play and movie, an unearthly character with frizzy hair, a dazed look, and a strangled purr. He floats above the proceedings like a stoned angel, offering bitter jokes and harsh truths. He is, as Tony Kushner wrote, "Crowley's most original creation, and he seems to come from another world—perhaps the future."

Michael, the party's host, is the most important character in the play, and the most challenging. As playwright Charles Busch later said, *Boys* isn't about a pack of self-hating gay men, it's about *one* self-hating gay man, but he runs the show. Michael requires a very strong actor to make his shift of emotion in Act Two believable, when he suddenly turns against his guests. Yet the unhappiness driving his attack is there from the start: Michael's brittle jokes, the time spent in therapy, the pain he's tried to anesthetize with alcohol, shopping, the Catholic Church, and old movies. (But not love. We hear nothing about Michael's love life.) The unexpected arrival of his straight roommate from college, Alan, plunges Michael back into his closet self and releases all his demons.

At the end, after his breakdown, Michael is talking only about himself when he talks to Donald before going to midnight mass:

Michael: If we...if we could just...not hate ourselves so much. That's it, you know. If we could just *learn* not to hate ourselves quite so much.

This is a play about a gay man arguing with his own self-hatred, and self-hatred loses in the end. Whatever pieces of Michael remained in Crowley when he began the play, they were burned away by the time he finished.

An equally important truth emerges earlier, when Harold leaves the party with his gifts, including the hustler that Emory bought him.

Harold: Oh Michael...thanks for the laughs. Call you tomorrow.

It sounds like a threat but it's also a promise. Their friendship will survive this battle. In fact, battle is part of their friendship.

Boys in the Band engages in the same kind of truth telling that straight plays of this era did, yet most reviewers forgot that and spoke as if only homosexuals were unhappy. The play also includes a long-term gay couple, Hank and Larry, who have a fight but make up. They are upstairs making love during the angry speeches at the end, in secret counterpoint. But almost nobody wanted to talk about the happy gay couple.

Gay politicals like Craig Rodwell and Frank Kameny did not like *Boys*, but political activists rarely like fiction of any kind. Literature is about ambiguity, mixed emotions, and guilty pleasures. Politics is about ideals and action. *Boys* was attacked not because it was behind the times, as some claimed, but because it reflected real life all too accurately.

Gay men flocked to the play and responded in every way imaginable. Diarist Donald Vining saw it with his partner and they loved it. "In the first act we screamed with laughter as the gay party got under way but the second act, as they got drunker and nastier, was much more sober." One friend of mine, now in his seventies, remembers the original production as "a hoot." Yes, Act Two was unhappy, but he believed that was just for the sake of drama. Another gay man, however, who has just turned sixty, was taken to the play by a straight friend who wanted to save him from his homosexuality—and briefly succeeded. This gay man got married and did not come out for another five years. Younger gay men who lived outside major cities responded more positively, not least because the play showed a party of friends. Novelist Joe Keenan, who first knew the play as a movie, could not understand why people criticized it. "A bunch of gay friends hang out and enjoy each other's jokes? It was my idea of heaven."

The fact of the matter is that readers and audiences are never blank slates: individuals see in a work whatever they need to see at that moment.

There had been a handful of gay-themed plays performed in New York, such as *The Madness of Lady Bright* by Lanford Wilson in 1964, *The Bed* by Robert Heide in 1965 and his *Moon* in 1967, all produced at Caffe Cino. But there had never been a gay play that received as much public attention as *Boys*. The *New York Times* in particular was fascinated and wrote about it endlessly. Clive Barnes gave it a surprisingly perceptive review when it opened, saying it was "one of the best acted plays of the season" and was "not a play about a homosexual but a play that takes the homosexual milieu, and the homosexual way of life, totally for granted and uses this as a valid basis of human experience." Barnes began by comparing the play to *Virginia Woolf* and closed by citing the Stanley Kauffmann article: both were already touchstones in discussing *Boys*. Barnes went back the following February when the show had a new cast and found he still liked it: "the best American play for some few seasons. But I do hope that Mr. Crowley is wrong and that all homosexuals are not as wretchedly miserable as he paints them." But as if to prove the *Times* wasn't too progressive, Walter Kerr took the play apart in a long Sunday piece, complaining that these gay men were all the same "in their amused, quick-minded, diminishing address to each other," presenting them as a pack of wisecracking zombies afraid to feel any real emotion. A year later, reviewing the movie, Vincent Canby complained that the play "sounds too often as if it had been written by someone at the party"—as close as he could come to calling Crowley a fag.

When *Boys* was recorded on a set of long-playing records, the *Times* reviewed the recording, too, as an excuse to offer yet another perspective. "How Anguished Are Homosexuals?" was the headline of the piece by Donn Teal. "Realizing that the author's attempt was not to epitomize the normal American homosexual in *The Boys* any more than Albee's was to apotheosize the average (childless) American marriage in *Virginia Woolf*, we are angry still that a misrepresentation has been broadcast by an excellent play." The tangled prose tries to defend the play as well as take issue with it, but more interesting is that Teal wrote as a gay man and used his real name. A year earlier he had written an article about gay plotlines for the *Times* under a pseudonym. The world was beginning to change.

The Teal article ran on June 1, 1969. Crowley was in the city, supervising the making of the movie of the play. There had been a bidding war by the studios hungry to film a stage hit. The old Hollywood production code, which limited representations of any kind of sexuality, was dead, nobody knew what worked anymore, and the sensationalism of the material added to its appeal. Crowley insisted on serving as producer and keeping the original cast when he sold his play. Cinema Center Films, a division of CBS, agreed to his terms. However, they wouldn't let a stage director, Robert Moore, direct the movie and insisted on someone more experienced. Crowley chose a young straight director, William Friedkin, who had just made a good movie from Harold Pinter's *The Birthday Party*. Filming began at the Hy Brown Studios on Sixth Avenue and Twenty-sixth Street. Interviewed on the set by Katie Kelly for yet another *Times* article, Crowley defended his play against gay critics. "The story is about self-destruction. I'm talking about the self-destruction angle that's in all of us.... I hope there are happy homosexuals—they just don't happen to be at this party."

Summer began quietly that year with far less drama than the summer of 1968. Little was happening politically. Judy Garland died of an accidental overdose in London on Sunday, June 22. Forty-seven years old, she had been a gay icon since the 1950s. ("What's more boring than a queen doing a Judy Garland imitation?" asks Michael in *Boys*. Donald replies, "A queen doing a Bette Davis imitation.") Her body was flown to New York and seen by thousands at the Frank E. Campbell Funeral Chapel before she was buried in Westchester on Friday, June 27. That night the police raided a gay bar on Christopher Street in Greenwich Village.

There are many different accounts of the Stonewall riots and I won't sift through them all here. People want to connect the death of Garland with the riots, but no mourners appear to have been present at Stonewall. The juxtaposition is only a symbolic coincidence (yet it's hard to say exactly what it symbolizes).

The riots began as a routine bust of the Stonewall Inn, a Mafia-run bar that had been raided earlier that week. Plainclothesmen and uniformed cops entered, asked for IDs and began to arrest people. A crowd gathered outside.

Edmund White was on the street that night. The twenty-nine-year-old writer worked at Time-Life Books, but his chief interests were sex and his own writing. He had begun as a playwright but was finishing his first novel. He actually knew Crowley from Fire Island; the two had had a brief fling, and Crowley read one of his experimental plays ("Is this supposed to be funny?" Crowley asked), but White had not seen *Boys*. He described the riot two weeks after it happened in a letter to his friends Ann and Alfred Corn.

> [A] mammoth paddy wagon as big as a school bus, pulled up to the Wall and about ten cops raided the joint. The kids were all shooed into the street; soon other gay kids and straight spectators swelled the ranks to, I'd say, about a thousand people.... As the Mafia owners

were dragged out one by one and shoved into the wagon, the crowd would let out Bronx cheers and jeers and clapping. Someone shouted "Gay Power," others took up the cry—and then it dissolved into giggles. A few more prisoners—bartenders, hatcheck boys—a few more cheers, someone starts singing, "We Shall Overcome."

It was not a political crowd. These were young people out for a good time on a Friday night. Yet they watched TV and followed the news; they had read about Black Power and the Black Panthers and had seen footage of the riots in Chicago.

The paddy wagon left, leaving cops behind in the bar. "We're the Pink Panthers!" someone cried and people attacked the bar, throwing a trash can at the plywood-covered window and then setting the wood on fire. Fire engines arrived. Police returned to free the cops trapped by the crowd. Riot police in helmets filled the street. Unlike the riots in Chicago the summer before, no TV cameras recorded the event. In fact, there is only one photo of the riot itself, showing a pack of grinning street kids framed by the shoulders of cops shoving them back. The picture was taken the first night and printed on the front page of the *Daily News* the next day.

Craig Rodwell of the Oscar Wilde Memorial Bookshop watched the beginning of the riot from the stoop of a nearby brownstone. He raced home and telephoned the newspapers. He returned the next night, when the crowd reassembled and there was a fresh confrontation with the police, larger and louder than the first night. Early Sunday morning, Rodwell typed up a flyer that called for political action. He made copies and distributed them outside the bar.

Allen Ginsberg was in town that weekend. After Chicago, he had moved to a farm in Cherry Valley in upstate New York, where he spent the winter setting William Blake's *Songs of Innocence and Experience* to music. He came down to New York to record the songs for Verve Records. He visited Christopher Street on Sunday night and saw the words "Gay Power!" chalked on the front of the building. He told a *Village Voice* reporter, "We're one of the largest minorities in the country—10 percent, you know. It's about time we did something to assert ourselves." He entered the reopened bar, and came out again, saying the patrons were "beautiful—they've lost that wounded look that fags all had ten years ago."

Mart Crowley was busy with the movie production uptown and only read about the riots in a small article in the inside pages of the *Times*. For him as for most people, gay or straight, the great public events of the summer were Woodstock and the moon landing.

The riots passed; nobody knew what they meant yet. Edmund White closed his letter to the Corns by saying, "Who knows what will happen this weekend, or this week. I'll keep you posted. Otherwise nothing much. I've been going out with a mad boy who tried to kill me last Friday. He's very cute and I'm sure it'd be a kick, but I think I'll take a rain check on the death scene."

The Stonewall riots were an expression of change, not a cause of it—not by themselves, anyway. There had already been similar protests in Los Angeles and San Francisco that are now forgotten. Stonewall might have been forgotten, too, except that a year later, in 1970, a group of activists including Craig Rodwell marked the riot with a march. Instead of doing the Annual Reminder in Philadelphia on July 4, Rodwell suggested they do it a week earlier as a protest march in New York, commemorating the street battles of last year. History is made not simply with events, but by remembering those events, a double drumbeat like a heartbeat. History can be written not only with books but with ceremonies. Yet a real event read about in a newspaper is not always more important than a fictional one in a novel or play or poem.

Two theater pieces, one a play, the other raw street theater, took place in the same city but were not directly connected. Yet both were expressions of the same social change that they augmented and continued. *Boys in the Band* would run for another year and three months, a total of a thousand and one nights. When the Katie Kelly article on the movie ran in the *Times* two weeks after Stonewall, she did not mention the riots. Nevertheless, the world was already changing. New political groups sprung up over the next months. When the movie opened in Los Angeles in March 1970, it was picketed by six members of an organization called the Gay Liberation Front. They were barely visible in the large crowd outside the theater. Crowley didn't see or hear them, although he was told afterward that one protester carried a cowbell.

The movie went on to play in every major city across the country that summer. It was like a national advertisement for homosexuality. More people heard about *Boys* than heard about Stonewall that first year. You didn't need to see the movie to know about it. The ad campaign ran in daily newspapers from Portland, Oregon, to Norfolk, Virginia, featuring a photo of Leonard Frey with the caption, "Today is Harold's birthday." Next to it was a photo of Robert La Tourneux as the hustler, Cowboy, over the caption, "And this is his present."

III

The Seventies

11. Old and Young

The next big literary change was under way, the most important shift yet. But it happened slowly at first. Time was needed for magazines to be started, for bookstores to open, and, most important, for new work to be written. Poems and even plays can sometimes happen quickly, but most literature, especially novels, require long gestations followed by months of writing and rewriting. The first major gay literary work to appear after Stonewall was an English novel that was nearly sixty years old.

E. M. Forster wrote *Maurice* in 1913 but did not want it published while his mother was still alive. She lived a very long life. He showed the manuscript to like-minded friends, including young Christopher Isherwood, who admired the book. "Does it date?" Forster asked. "Why *shouldn't* it date?" Isherwood truthfully replied. Finally the mother died, but Forster still delayed publication, fearing the novel would hurt his reputation. Unable to write what he cared about, he had written no novels since *A Passage to India* in 1924. He too lived a long life, and didn't die until 1970, when he was ninety-one. *Maurice* was published the following year under Isherwood's supervision. Forster's fears came true. A long coming-out story, the novel is rather old-fashioned in both its emotion and discretion, but many critics disliked it. They were disappointed to learn their hero was a homosexual or they used the fact to claim he'd never been a major writer anyway. "*Maurice*, bad as it is, nevertheless is Forster's only truthful book," declared Marvin Mudrick, "full of nerves, hysteria, infatuations, bitterness."

Also published posthumously in 1971 was *The Collected Poems of Frank O'Hara*. O'Hara had died after he was struck by a car one night on a beach on Fire Island in 1966. He was only forty. We will talk about him more in the next chapter, but his sexuality wasn't freely acknowledged until after his death—and after gay liberation.

Several early gay rights battles were fought in the literary pages. In September 1970, a few months after the world's first gay pride march, *Harper's* ran as a cover story, "Homo/Hetero: the Struggle for Sexual Identity," an essay by critic Joseph Epstein. At great length, Epstein carefully explored what he admitted was his unexamined fear of homosexuality, using quotes from Freud, André Gide, Gore Vidal, Norman Mailer, and "Elliott, the hairdresser of a lady friend of mine." But instead of overcoming his fear, Epstein ended by justifying it. "If I had the power to do so, I would wish homosexuality off the face of this earth." He was most worried for his four sons, declaring in conclusion, "Nothing they could ever do would make me sadder than if one of them were to become homosexual. For then I would know them condemned to a state of permanent niggerdom among men." The idea that the world could be changed so that homosexuals (as well as black people) wouldn't be oppressed never crosses Epstein's mind.

One month after his essay appeared, the Gay Activist Alliance "zapped" *Harper's*: a dozen or so gay activists in long hair and jeans entered the building and occupied the offices for the day. Among the zappers were journalist Arthur Bell, Arnie Kantrowitz, later a college professor specializing in Whitman, and Vito Russo, who later wrote the groundbreaking film study, *The Celluloid Closet*. They gave the staff coffee and doughnuts and talked to them about gay rights. *Harper's* stonefaced executive editor, Midge Decter, was not amused.

Despite Epstein's antigay credentials, or because of them, the *New York Times Book Review* chose him to review *Maurice*. Again he wrote at great length, this time struggling to separate Forster's major novels, which he loved, from the homosexual who wrote them. "The homosexual influence in Forster's other novels, if it exists at all, is so negligible as to be scarcely worthy of notice." So much for the intense male friendships in *The Longest Journey* and *A Passage to India*. Epstein found *Maurice* disappointing for literary reasons, and assumed gay readers would be disappointed by its lack of "homosexual high jinks." Yet the book was very popular and widely read by gay men. They helped to create the Forster revival of the next twenty years, one that included film adaptations as well as constant reissues of the novels.

A new generation of gay writers began to appear, and they did not always speak the same language as their elders. The older writers didn't see themselves as part of anything political; the young writers did. The established figures responded to the new gay politics in different ways. Some like Truman Capote paid no attention at all. Others like Tennessee Williams were annoyed, while Gore Vidal was coolly curious. Only Isherwood and Allen Ginsberg were completely open to the gay rights movement, but they were already open about their sexuality. Most homosexual artists spoke as if political activism were something *the other guy* did. O'Hara died before Stonewall, but his friend Joe LeSueur thought gay liberation was more Allen Ginsberg's line than O'Hara's. Another friend believed that if O'Hara had lived into the 1970s, he would've found the politics silly but he would love the GAA dances held at the Firehouse downtown.

Gay Sunshine, a literary and cultural journal, was founded in Berkeley in 1970 by Winston Leyland and began to run full-length interviews with major gay figures. The new generation interviewed their elders with admiration and respect, usually. More important, they asked questions that weren't being asked elsewhere. These long conversations with Vidal, Isherwood, Ginsberg, and others now provide us with a wealth of information about their private lives and attitudes. Ginsberg talked about having sex with Jack Kerouac; John Rechy, author of *City of Night*, the highly praised 1963 novel about hustlers, criticized gay S&M culture; Samuel Steward, creator of the erotic "Phil Andros" stories, described his different lives as a professor, a tattoo artist, a friend of Gertrude Stein, and a sex partner of Thornton Wilder; Isherwood took apart the ugly myth that the Nazis were homosexual; and Vidal discussed Howard Austen, his partner of twenty-three years, for the first time in print. (The interviewers introduced the subject by asking Vidal who would inherit his money.) These frank interviews mark the rise of a gay literary world that was parallel yet separate from the culture at large. Mainstream readers didn't visit this world, only other gay people. It was not that straight people were excluded, however; they just weren't interested.

The mainstream was more open, however, even television. In an interview with David Frost, also in 1970, Tennessee Williams replied to a pointed question about his sexuality with a big pussycat smile. "I don't want to be involved in some kind of scandal," he purred, "but I've covered the waterfront."

Williams had been living a very strange life since the death of Frank Merlo in 1963, floating in a haze of alcohol and sleeping pills. "I slept through the Sixties," he later told Gore Vidal, who assured him he hadn't missed a thing. But it was worse than that. He grew paranoid and wildly unpredictable. His friends avoided him. He hired a paid companion, who was often afraid of him. During rehearsals of a new play, *The Kingdom of Earth*, Williams laughed constantly and the actors didn't know if he were laughing at them or at his own work. *Kingdom* opened on Broadway as *The Seven Descents of Myrtle* and closed a month later. His brother Dakin convinced him to enter a hospital in 1969. Williams was put in a psychiatric ward and suffered withdrawal without his pills. He later claimed to have had two heart attacks there.

He woke up from the Sixties in time to find himself at the center of a curious war. A new play titled *Nightride* by a man writing under a pseudonym, "Lee Barton," opened at the end of 1971. It featured a confrontation between an openly gay rock star and an aging gay playwright who has written nothing of value in ten years. The play was produced off-off-Broadway, but it was widely reviewed; at least one reviewer identified the old playwright as Williams. Then "Lee Barton" wrote about Williams for the *Times*.

Who really gives a damn that Tennessee Williams has finally admitted his sexual preferences in print? He has yet to contribute any work of understanding to gay theater, and with his enormous talent one of his works would indeed be worth any amount of personal data. And several others of his generation of writers, as well as some younger ones, all of them gay, have failed to come forth with anything, under *any* name, that would make a valid case for the homosexual in society.

Williams read the piece (he even saw *Nightride*) and responded in an interview in the *Village Voice* with gay journalist Arthur Bell: "I feel sorry for the author. He makes the mistake of thinking I've concealed something in my life [but] he writes under a pseudonym. I've nothing to conceal. Homosexuality isn't the theme of my plays. They're all about human relationships. I've never faked it."

"Lee Barton" wasn't the only young gay writer attacking the man who was arguably America's greatest living playwright. Michael Silverstein in "An Open Letter to Tennessee Williams" in *Gay Sunshine* declared, "You helped me free myself but I can see that you are not free."

Williams's next work was *Small Craft Warnings*, a bar play about a crew of wounded souls, one of whom is gay. The straight men and women are just as crippled as the gay man, Quentin, a screenwriter. When the play opened in March 1972, it received better reviews than Williams had gotten in years, but most critics focused on Quentin, treating the work as Williams's own personal *Boys in the Band*. His sexuality had upstaged everything else.

Christopher Isherwood remained fully awake and engaged with the world. He was still experiencing the usual ups and downs of life with his boyfriend, Don Bachardy. (Bachardy had a new outside boyfriend while Isherwood didn't, and Bachardy's new boyfriend was an old friend of Isherwood's.) He was still writing, of course. Back in 1967 he had published *A Meeting by the River*, a very fine, concise little novel about two English brothers who meet in a Hindu monastery outside Calcutta. The younger brother has decided to become a monk. The older, more worldly brother (who has a wife *and* a boyfriend) hopes to change his younger brother's mind. The novel is written entirely in letters and journal entries (it might be *too* concise). Reviewers didn't know what to make of the book, especially its spirituality. As usual, they wished the author were still writing about Berlin.

Bachardy suggested turning the novel into a play, which the two men did together, the first of many collaborations. The play was produced in both Los Angeles and New York but was not a complete success. Several screenplays followed, however, including a TV movie, *Frankenstein: The True Story*. The pair enjoyed working together. They would discuss a project at length before putting words on paper, Isherwood dictating and Bachardy typing. They still argued about extracurricular romances, but more quietly now.

On his own, Isherwood read his parents' diaries, hoping to make peace with his recently deceased mother and to know his father, who had died when Isherwood was still a boy. The results, *Kathleen and Frank*, appeared in 1971 and it's an odd book, raw yet dry, personal yet impersonal. This upperclass Englishman and Englishwoman of another era can never be as real to us as they were to their son. But the book gave Isherwood a new device, the double persona of talking about himself in the past as "Christopher" while keeping "I" for his present-day self. He used the device again after he read his own diaries and needed to reconstruct the missing volumes for his first years in California. This diarylike memoir was too rough and libelous for him to publish at the time—it did not appear until after his death as *Lost Years: A Memoir 1945–1951*. But he was already thinking about a new project.

Then in 1972 the movie of the musical *Cabaret* opened. Isherwood's feelings about the movie were almost as mixed as his feelings about the stage musical, although he was pleased his character was played by Michael York, a handsome actor with a honeyed voice a good octave lower than his own. The character was no longer straight, but Isherwood felt his homosexuality was treated as "a ridiculous weakness...like bedwetting." For gay men of my generation, however, the movie was a revelation. In our eyes the hero was clearly a gay man who almost makes the terrible mistake of marrying his female best friend. The two friends are both sleeping with the same man, which is revealed in a famous exchange. "Screw Max!" declares York. "I do," replies Liza Minnelli. York smiles bitterly and says, "So do I." The sexual triangle was the invention of screenwriter Jay Presson Allen and might be truer to the time the movie was made than to the time of the stories. Nevertheless, the film introduced a whole new audience to Isherwood and sent many of us to his other books. A recently discharged navy officer who had served in Vietnam, Armistead Maupin, was still coming to terms with his sexuality when he first saw the movie. He was so taken by it that he hunted down every book he could find written by Isherwood.

Gore Vidal was spending less and less time in the United States. He sold Edgewater and bought La Rondinaia ("The Swallow's Nest"), a cliffside villa in Ravello, Italy, with Howard Austen in 1971. There he began work on a novel about that great sinister figure of American history, Aaron Burr. In the years ahead, he concentrated on historical fiction with almost no mention of homosexuality—it had hurt the sales of his last book, *Two Sisters*, a metafictional mix of fiction, memoir, and screenplay. Yet he was happy to talk about gay sex in his essays and interviews, including interviews with gay magazines. He spoke at length with John Mitzel and Steve Abbott for the *Fag Rag* in 1973, but afterward wrote a friend, "I never do see much point in fag-mags—at least for those of us who can write elsewhere and say the same sort of thing. It is the dream of all these papers that the L.A. Chief of Police will become addicted to their style and, finally, like St. P[aul] realize with a sudden blaze that FAGS are not only good but BETTER!"

Vidal published *Burr* in 1973, and it was a huge success with both critics and readers. I think it's his best novel. Although there's nothing gay in it (except for the sodomite based on William F. Buckley), the book plays to all of Vidal's strengths. Burr is a witty, know-it-all cynic who sees through everyone, a perfect role for Vidal, a fantasy self-portrait. "Fortunately our people have always preferred legend to reality—as I know best of all, having become one of the dark legends of the republic, and hardly real." Burr tells his life story to the other protagonist, a young journalist, Charlie Schuyler, who is writing the old man's biography—Charlie suggests a Vidal-in-training. These two first-person narratives extend and complete each other. The "present" of 1833 New York is beautifully drawn, the "past" of George Washington, Thomas Jefferson, and Alexander Hamilton is lively and prejudiced, and the book has no love stories, always a stumbling block for Vidal. *Burr* succeeds more as spectacle than as drama, but it is vivid, imaginative, intelligent, and entertaining.

In 1975 Tennessee Williams published his *Memoirs* and Vidal reviewed it in the *New York Review of Books*. "Some Memories of the Glorious Bird and an Earlier Self" is one of his best essays, a rich appreciation of both the man and his work. He genuinely likes Williams, warts and all—"the Glorious Bird" was his private nickname for Williams—and the essay shows a more human side of Vidal. It also includes a wonderfully matter-of-fact portrait of postwar gay life, with glimpses of Paul Bowles, Carson McCullers, Jean Cocteau, and a devastating cameo of Truman Capote as a pest and pathological liar. Williams wrote his sinister soul sister, Maria St. Just, "Gore has written a hilarious review of *Memoirs* which will sell many copies—it's been gradually creeping up the bestseller list!!"

Memoirs itself is a loose, genial jumble of unreliable memories and anecdotes. No matter how drunk or trashed Williams had been, he could still type out a lively sentence. The book is entertaining without being especially personal or revealing. Critics were disappointed that there was more about Williams's sex life than about his plays, but he had never been very articulate about his craft. The feelings of gay readers were more positive: they enjoyed the sexual openness and many wrote fan letters. Some who knew him only as the author of *Streetcar* even praised him as a role model.

Nineteen seventy-five was also the year that Truman Capote published in *Esquire* three chapters of his unfinished novel. He had been talking about *Answered Prayers* for ten years now; he wanted to prove to the public—and to himself—that it existed. Instead he lost friends and destroyed his literary reputation.

The most famous chapter is "La Cote Basque," a polyphonic portrait of society ladies sharing gossip in an exclusive New York restaurant. It is mean but lively. The other chapters are only mean and tedious. Narrated by P. B. Jones, a Capote-like writer who supports himself as a masseur and call boy, the book is a pornographic fantasy on literary and society life, but written by someone who's come to hate sex. It's mean, joyless porn. The longest chapter, "Unspoiled Monster," contains Capote's most overtly gay writing, but also his worst. He seems determined to compete with his gay peers, but he does it very badly. The self-mocking literary voice is a tired imitation of *Myra Breckinridge*. A long episode about Denham Fouts identifies the famous kept boy as a character in *Down There on a Visit*, as if Capote hoped to steal him from Isherwood—but Capote's Fouts is just a nasty pricktease, with none of the comedy or mystery of Paul in *Down There*. (Like Isherwood, Capote shows him dying of his cure for opium addiction, but adds the ugly touch of dying whiie sitting on a toilet.) The strangest act of one-upmanship comes when Jones goes to the Plaza to service a famous playwright called Mr. Wallace, "a chunky, paunchy, booze-puffed runt with a play mustache glued above laconic lips." He is Tennessee Williams, of course, right down to the recent bad reviews and the dead boyfriend. His hotel room stinks of dog shit. Jones must take the bulldog out for a walk before he undresses for his client. Mr. Wallace would rather talk than fuck. Capote gives a very broad caricature, but a moment of truth breaks through after a long monologue by the playwright, who says he's dying. He feels Jones is lying to himself:

> No, what I thought was: here's a dumpy little guy with a dramatic mind who, like one of his own adrift heroines, seeks attention and sympathy by serving up half-believed lies to total strangers. Strangers because he has no friends, and he has no friends because the only people he pities are his own characters and himself—everyone else is an audience.

Capote could just as easily have been talking about Capote, except he no longer had pity for his characters.

Answered Prayers is a shocking work, not for the secrets it betrays, but for how coarse and unimaginative it is. ("La Cote Basque" lost Capote the friendship of his society lady "swans," including Babe Paley, whose husband, William Paley, was rumored to be the hapless adulterer who frantically washes menstrual blood from his sheets before his wife gets home.) Now and then Capote's old rhythms show in the prose, but the writing offers few pleasures or surprises. It's hard to believe that the gifted author of *Other Voices* and *In Cold Blood* could produce something so mechanical and trashy. It's even harder to believe he spent ten years working on it, but he probably didn't. Donald Windham was housesitting in Capote's UN Plaza apartment in 1970 when he stumbled on the manuscript of "Unspoiled Monsters" in Jack Dunphy's desk. He read it, of course, and was appalled. He thought it might be a joke, a parody of Jacqueline Susann, until it appeared unaltered in *Esquire* five years later.

Capote was completely lost in his own dream world now, full of his own "half-believed lies" served to strangers. In an interview in 1975 with *Playgirl*, *Playboy*'s poor cousin, he told a false story about Gore Vidal being expelled from the White House by Bobby Kennedy and historian Arthur Schlesinger for insulting Jackie Kennedy's mother. (He claimed they "just picked Gore up and carried him to the door and threw him out into Pennsylvania Avenue.") This time Vidal did not retaliate with cutting jokes. This time he sued. He demanded a million dollars, money he knew Capote didn't have. The case went on for eight long years.

The dinosaurs were taking each other to court. Vidal himself joked that at a certain age lawsuits take the place of sex. When Donald Windham published a book of the letters Tennessee Williams had written him in the 1940s and 1950s, a collection that captures Williams at his sanest and most charming, Williams sued Windham, despite a signed agreement.

In 1976, a young gay writer, George Whitmore, interviewed Williams at the Hotel Elysée in New York for the *Gay Sunshine Journal*. Williams was quite drunk. He clung to the arms of his chair and ranted at length about the Jewish critics who tried to destroy his career. Afterward Whitmore went straight to his friend, playwright Victor Bumbalo, laughing in horror over meeting his hero. Whitmore edited out everything anti-Semitic or insane when he wrote up the interview.

Meanwhile the gay press continued to grow. In 1974 an ambitious gay businessman, David Goodstein, bought the *Advocate*, moved it from Los Angeles to San Francisco, and changed it from a newspaper to a magazine. More important, he shifted its emphasis from politics to culture, which meant sex and consumerism, but it also meant literature. Gay writers began to appear on the covers—few other public figures were willing to risk the exposure. Within two years, its annual circulation had risen to 60,000 (compared to *ONE*'s 2,300 ten years earlier). A survey in 1975 estimated that there were approximately 300 different gay publications in the United States, including skin magazines, with a total circulation of 200,000.

In 1976, a new monthly magazine started up, *Christopher Street*. Named after the main gay thoroughfare in Greenwich Village, it was based in New York but distributed nationally. It was devoted to culture and politics and hoped to become the gay *New Yorker*. The publisher and editor, Charles Ortleb, was a young copywriter from New Jersey who had gone to college in Kansas. He was helped by a handful of gay journalists and editors, including Arthur Bell, Michael Denneny, and Patrick Merla. They took over the recently vacated basement offices of the *New York Review of Books* on West Thirteenth Street and put out their first issue in July 1976—with a picture of an empty closet on the cover. Denneny, who was a book editor at St. Martin's Press, later said that they assumed gay writers would have drawers full of unpublished work. In fact, it soon became clear that most gay work wasn't written until there was a place to print it. In early issues writers wrote extra pieces under pseudonyms to suggest a bigger cast of contributors. Ortleb worked with the art director Rick Fiala to create *New Yorker*–like cartoons, and Fiala too used different pseudonyms, despite his recognizable line and eternally cheerful figures. One early Fiala cartoon showed a gay man happily telling friends, "If you ask me, I think we had more fun when it was unnatural."

The magazine was originally for both gay men and lesbians. But the women dropped out and *Christopher Street* became primarily male within two years. Something similar had happened in Boston when *Lavender Visions* divided in 1971, with the men splitting off to create *Fag Rag*. The readerships and agendas were different, but in the beginning, at least, men and women tried to work together. (The first gay male best seller of this period was the 1974 novel *The Front Runner* by Patricia Nell Warren, an editor at *Reader's Digest* who had divorced her husband and come out as a lesbian only a year before.)

At the same time the gay bookstore movement begun by Craig Rodwell was taking off. The Oscar Wilde Memorial Bookshop moved to Christopher Street in 1970, its new location only a block from the site of the Stonewall Inn. Glad Day opened in Toronto in 1971, named after the William

Blake engraving; a second Glad Day came to Boston in 1977. Giovanni's Room opened in Philadelphia in 1973, named after the Baldwin novel because the owners wanted something to signal the store was gay without being too obvious. (They thought "City of Night" sounded like an adult bookstore and "The Well of Loneliness" too depressing.) These stores were joined by Lambda Rising in 1974 in Washington, D.C., then A Brother's Touch in Minneapolis, A Different Light in San Francisco, and others.

A mix of market and community was coming together, creating an audience for the books and plays of the next thirty years. This audience was as necessary to the new work as the writers who produced it—maybe even more necessary.

The cover of the December 1976 issue of *Christopher Street* featured a picture of Christopher Isherwood drawn by Don Bachardy. Inside was an excerpt from a new book, *Christopher and His Kind.*

Reviewers who wished Isherwood were still writing about Berlin finally got their wish, only this wasn't the Berlin they had wanted. Isherwood announces on the first page that his new book is going to be "as frank and factual as I can make it." On the second page he famously declares: "For Christopher, Berlin meant Boys."

Christopher and His Kind is Isherwood's wonderfully frank, brisk, clear-eyed memoir of his life from his first visit to Berlin in 1929 to 1939, when he came to America. The book is as straightforward about art and politics as it is about sex. It is built out of memories and documents, particularly Isherwood's fiction, letters, and diaries, but also the letters and diaries of others, including his mother. The double persona of "I" and "Christopher" developed in *Kathleen and Frank* enables Isherwood to step back and forth nimbly between past and present, as well as acknowledge that a person changes with time: the self that experiences life isn't always the self that understands it.

The book contains an amazing cast of characters, a vivid collection of people observed by a man who is genuinely curious about others. The portraits include his family, famous friends (W. H. Auden, E. M. Forster, Stephen Spender), the models for his characters (Jean Ross of "Sally Bowles," Gerald Hamilton of *Mr. Norris*, Bertold and Salka Viertel of *Prater Violet*), and his three German boyfriends ("Bubi," "Otto," and most importantly, Heinz Neddermeyer). Isherwood includes himself, too, portrayed more critically than the others yet also with sympathy and humor.

The years are covered in a loose, fast-paced picaresque that builds to a major crisis. After Christopher leaves Germany with Heinz, Hitler comes to power and Heinz becomes a man without a country. Barred from England as an illegal alien, Heinz goes with Christopher first to Greece, then the Canary Islands, Portugal, Denmark, and Holland. Christopher does everything he can to get Heinz a Mexican visa. He is in England when Heinz is expelled from France. They reunite in Luxembourg, but their lawyer cannot get his visa renewed without Heinz returning to Germany. He does so and is promptly arrested for draft evasion. He is tried and sentenced to prison and military service. Christopher does what he can from England, but he is helpless. He feels totally devastated afterward. He quotes from his own diary:

At first I didn't think about Heinz at all. Or tried not to. I felt like a house in which one room, the biggest, is locked up. Then, very cautiously, I allowed myself to think of him in little doses—five minutes at a time. Then I had a good cry and felt better. But it is very hard to cry, when you know in advance that crying will do you good.

The book could have ended with the high drama of losing Heinz, but doesn't. It's not only an experiment in truth telling but an experiment in realism, without melodramatic endings. Life goes on, Isherwood goes on. He and Auden go to China, where they witness a brutal war, and then to America, where Isherwood falls in love again. The book ends with the old "I" telling young "Christopher" that this new love won't last but he will eventually meet "the ideal companion to whom you can reveal yourself totally and yet be loved for what you are, not what you pretend to be." But he won't meet him right away.

He is already living in the city where you will settle. He will be near you for many years without your meeting. But it would be no good if you did meet him now. At present, he is only four years old.

The book is dedicated to that former four-year-old.

Christopher and His Kind was reviewed warmly in the *New York Review of Books* by Isherwood's friend, Gore Vidal, in a smart, informative, generous essay. "There is no excess in an Isherwood sentence. The verbs are strong. Nouns precise. Adjectives few. The third person startles and seduces, while the first person is a good guide and never coy." Peter Stansky, a literary historian who was gay, reviewed the book more temperately in the *New York Times Book Review*, yet he too was full of praise. There were bad reviews in Britain, where Isherwood was still attacked for sitting out the war, but the American reviews were generally respectful. However, more than one critic complained that Isherwood misrepresented himself by putting too much emphasis on his homosexuality, that the book reduced him to "only" a gay man. Which is nonsense. He includes his entire life: his family, his politics, his writing. He says more about himself as a writer than he ever had before. The whole man is here, and in the right proportions.

In one of the most moving passages of the book, before he arrives in America, Christopher wrestles with the sum total of his beliefs, beginning with his pacificism:

> Suppose, Christopher now said to himself, I have a Nazi army at my mercy. I can blow it up by pressing a button. The men in that army are notorious for torturing and murdering civilians—all except for one of them, Heinz. Will I press the button? No—wait: Suppose I know that Heinz, out of cowardice or moral infection, has become as bad as they are and takes part in all their crimes? Will I press the button, even so? Christopher's answer, given without the slightest hesitation, was: Of course not....Thus Christopher was forced to recognize himself as a pacifist—although by an argument which he could only admit to with the greatest reluctance.

He goes on to examine his other principles:

> What had actually begun to surface in his muddled mind was a conflict of emotions. He felt obliged to become a pacifist, he refused to deny his homosexuality, he wanted to keep as much of his leftism as he could. All he could do for the present was to pick up his ideas one after another and reexamine them, ring them like coins, saying: This one's counterfeit; this one's genuine but I can't use it; this one I can keep, I think.

One particular coin had special meaning for gay readers. *Christopher and His Kind* tapped into a new growing readership. Sales were excellent, and

Isherwood received bags of fan mail, far more than Tennesse Williams had for *Memoirs*. There was the sexual and jokey (a fifteen-year-old English schoolboy sent his photo and wrote on the back, "My tits are on fire"), but also serious, heartfelt letters, full of gratitude for his work and his example. When Isherwood came to New York and signed books at the Oscar Wilde Bookshop, long lines formed outside on the sidewalk, on the very street where police and gay demonstrators had confronted each other a few years earlier. Later Gore Vidal teased him, "They're beginning to believe that Christopher Street is named after you."

12. Love Songs

—ⱱ—

"Perhaps it is not possible to fit into American Life," wrote art critic Harold Rosenberg. "American Life is a billboard; individual life in the U.S. includes something nameless that takes place in the weeds behind it." Rosenberg was talking about the lives of intellectuals, but he could have just as easily been talking about that of gay people. Gay life happens in those tall weeds. So does love, and so does poetry.

The most visible gay male poet of this time was Allen Ginsberg. As indicated by his last two appearances, at the Chicago riots and Stonewall riots, Ginsberg did not have the traditional career of a poet in the years after *Howl and Other Poems*. He didn't live like T. S. Eliot or even Robert Lowell (who spent more time in mental hospitals than Ginsberg did), but used his energy and talents more freely. His mother, Naomi, told him in a letter that he later incorporated into a poem, "get married Allen don't take drugs." But he did take drugs. And he went to India, three times. Like Isherwood, he studied Hindu religion, but looser, more subjective forms than Vedanta. He also explored Buddhism and politics. He became more prophet than poet.

By 1969 Ginsberg had gone from being the poster boy for the Beats to the poster boy for the hippies—he was literally on posters in college dorm rooms. He received endless fan letters asking for advice, help, manuscripts, even clippings from his beard (to be auctioned off by a high school literary magazine). He was world famous, yet people rarely quoted any of the poetry written after his first book. And they never talked about his sexuality. Jane Kramer wrote a lively profile for the *New Yorker* in 1968, later published as a book, *Allen Ginsberg in America*, full of details about his drug use but very coy about his love of men. His longtime lover, Peter Orlovsky, was described as "his roommate of the past thirteen years."

It wasn't as if Ginsberg were closeted. The mainstream simply didn't want to talk about his homosexuality. Ginsberg himself regularly mentioned his sex partners in interviews, and he wasn't shy about propositioning male fans, gay and straight. (Until recently there was a Facebook page called allen-ginsberg-hit-on-me.) When he came to William and Mary for an anti-Nixon rally in 1971, he stayed at the house of a friend of mine and took a three-hour bath with a frat-boy student-newspaper editor from another school. My friend was annoyed, but only because it was the sole bathroom in a very crowded house. Ginsberg still loved Peter Orlovsky and, as said before, the two men shared a wide-open relationship, with Orlovsky sleeping with women as well as men. (Charles Shively, who had sex with both, suspected Orlovsky only pretended to be bisexual in order to keep Ginsberg interested.) Orlovsky now wrote poetry, too. His *Clean Asshole Poems and Smiling Vegetable Songs* was published in 1977 by City Lights. Winston Leyland of *Gay Sunshine* later assembled a collection of love poems and letters from Ginsberg and Orlovsky titled *Straight Hearts' Delight* chronicling their life together. The mainstream ignored the book's existence.

Ginsberg was the favorite bohemian poet of straight college boys who wanted to transgress, and of gay college boys who were not yet ready to come out. Yet he was a poet who was no longer famous for his poems. This was just as well, since his work after *Howl and Other Poems* is wildly uneven. The strong, memorable work is rare. There is "Kaddish," of course, his amazing 1959 poem about his mother, not so much a poem as a verbal breakdown, an avalanche of words without rhythm or shape. It succeeds as a flight from sense, an escape from the pain of his mother's madness. It's powerful but it's not quotable—and poems endure by being quoted. Among my own favorites are a lovely nature lyric, "Wales Visitation," a 1967 vision of Britain that mixes Blake, Wordsworth, and LSD, and a sexy little poem about the heart as an erotic organ, "Love Replied," which uses obscene frankness to look beyond sex to love.

Why do you eat
my behind & my feet
Why do you kiss
my belly like this
Why do you go down

and suck my cock crown
when I bare you the best
that is inside my breast

The rest of his work isn't bad, but it's not very exciting. Many poems read like song lyrics written on automatic pilot. Their long-breathed lines are so relaxed and easy that they simply slide away.

Ginsberg faded as a poet at the very time that he succeeded as a public man. Maybe his life was too public and he had nothing in reserve to express in verse. Or maybe he was too happy to write memorable poetry anymore.

One of Ginsberg's best later poems is "City Midnight Junk Strains" from 1966, written to Frank O'Hara shortly after his death. It has more gritty specifics than most of Ginsberg's work, as if some of O'Hara's sand had gotten into his verse.

I stare into my head and look for your/broken roman nose
your wet mouth-smell of martinis
& a big artistic tipsy kiss.

The poem builds to a lovely yet mocking image of poets after death.

I want to be there in your garden party in the clouds
all of us naked
strumming our harps and reading each other new poetry
in the boring celestial
Friendship Committee Museum.

Frank O'Hara grew up in Massachusetts, served in the navy, and went first to Harvard and then to graduate school at the University of Michigan. (He was the best-schooled writer we have discussed so far.) But his life didn't really begin until he came to New York. He worked art-related day jobs at museums and magazines while writing poetry on the side. He seemed to toss off poems with deceptive ease, published them in small magazines and collected them in slim volumes like the evocatively titled *Lunch Poems*, put out in 1965 by City Lights in the same Pocket Poets series that began with *Howl*. He shared various apartments with his good friend Joe LeSueur (whom he occasionally slept with), while falling in love with various boyfriends. He was surrounded by artists who frequently painted or drew his portrait: Larry Rivers, Fairfield Porter, Alex Katz, and Don Bachardy. Wynn Chamberlain did a witty double group portrait of O'Hara and friends—LeSueur, Joe Brainard, Frank Lima—first in white shirts, neckties, and frowns, then nude and grinning. Ginsberg must've had the painting in mind when he mentioned the "naked garden party." Acquaintances later said O'Hara had a bitchy side, but it doesn't appear in the poetry.

The Collected Poems of Frank O'Hara, published posthumously in 1971, marks his arrival as a gay poet. For all his matter-of-factness, O'Hara's sexuality could not be freely discussed until he was dead. It was an open secret, but his gayest poems, such as "At the Old Place" or "Homosexuality" ("So we are taking off our masks, are we, and keeping/our mouths shut?") were not published while he was alive. In *Love Poems (Tentative Title)* he didn't name his beloved, dancer Vincent Warren, in the poems or dedications because Warren was afraid his mother might see the book. As Joe LeSueur wrote, "To live in fear of matriarchal disapproval, all you have to be is gay and not necessarily young and naive to boot. We all know about E. M. Forster and his mom, and then there's the more recent case of Roland Barthes, who waited until his mother's death in 1978 to make a gesture toward coming out."

Yet it was all there in O'Hara's poetry, gay sensibility *and* gay experience, casually dispersed in the dailiness of what he called his "I do this, I do that" poems. O'Hara wrote regularly about favorite gay topics: old movies, Lana Turner, James Dean, Billie Holiday, classical music. Once readers know that homosexuality is there, it's impossible to ignore. "Having a Coke with You" is the most laidback love poem ever written, and perhaps the most honest *because* it is so laidback. "Having a Coke with You / is even more fun than going to San Sebastian, Irun, Hendaye, Biarritz, Bayonne..." It's like a parody Coca-Cola ad in a magazine. One happily pictures an illustration of two grown men grinning together at a soda fountain.

Unlike Ginsberg, O'Hara's long lines are relaxed without ever becoming slack. They have the slangy rhythm of American speech and are full of surprise and wit. Ginsberg and O'Hara were good friends, and Ginsberg's example helped O'Hara escape conventional form and find his own voice. But he did something different with his freedom. To describe what he was doing, O'Hara wrote a humorous manifesto about his style, which he called "Personism."

It was founded by me after lunch with LeRoi Jones on August 27, 1959, a day in which I was in love with someone (not Roi, by the way, a blond). I went back to work and wrote a poem for this person. While I was writing it I was realizing that if I wanted to I could use the telephone instead of writing a poem, and so Personism was born.

A poem is like a phone call? No wonder O'Hara's work is so cheerful and sociable.

In contrast to the unbuttoned verse of Ginsberg and O'Hara, the poetry of James Merrill was neatly buttoned in meter and form. The man himself was well-buttoned, too, coming from money and privilege, the son of Charles Merrill, cofounder of the brokerage house Merrill Lynch. Merrill's background is sometimes held against him, as if it's easier for a rich man to write poetry. But how many wealthy men or women have used their well-financed leisure to produce first-rate works of art?

Merrill was already writing poetry by the time he attended Amherst. He published his first book at sixteen, paid for by his father. Kimon Friar, his teacher and lover, introduced him to Anaïs Nin in 1947, which is how Merrill first appeared in this story: when he and Gore Vidal wrote letters to the *New York Times* defending Nin. Merrill kept his distance from Nin—she nabbed his roommate instead—and traveled to Europe. He published his first book of poems with a major publisher in 1951.

He met and fell in love with another writer, David Jackson, who also had an independent income. Jackson wrote fiction. He published short stories but was never able to sell the three novels he wrote. The two men lived simply, teaching and traveling (mainly Greece, which was very cheap), and setting up house in the top two floors of a big, nondescript shingled building in Stonington, Connecticut, on Long Island Sound. (Truman Capote stayed in Stonington one summer, but the town was too small for him; he made too many enemies and did not return.)

Merrill was a pale, lean, aloof young man, cool and cryptic, full of courteous formality. (In some photos he looks like a suave extraterrestrial.) His poems, too, were cool, cryptic, and formal. He was a wonderful wordsmith, his taut verse full of formal devices and double and even triple puns. His work has the literate wit of Alexander Pope, W. H. Auden, and Cole Porter. It was always elegant and beautiful, but for a long time it came to life only when he wrote about childhood. It was closet poetry, as Merrill himself admitted in his autobiography: "I never doubted that almost any poem I wrote owed some of its difficulty to the need to conceal my feelings, and their objects. Genderless as a fig leaf, the pronoun 'you' served to protect the latter, but one couldn't be too careful."

Inspired by the example of the Greek poet C. P. Cavafy, whose glimpses of sensuous young men ("Days of 1896," "Days of 1908," etc.) are remarkably ahead of their time, Merrill wrote his own "Days of ___" poems, and more of his life entered his work. In new poems about his childhood, "The Broken Home" (about his parents' divorce) and "Days of 1935" (about a poor little rich boy who daydreams of being kidnapped like the Lindbergh baby), he quietly evokes a *gay* man's childhood. Then in "Matinees" he wrote about his love of opera from childhood to the present, a warm, witty, self-mocking portrait of an opera queen:

> What havoc certain Saturday afternoons
> Wrought upon a bright young person's morals
> I now leave for the public to condemn.
>
> The point thereafter was to arrange for one's
> Own chills and fever, passions and betrayals,
> Chiefly in order to make song of them.
>
> You and I, caro, seldom
> Risk the real thing anymore.
> It's all too silly or too solemn.
> Enough to know the score
>
> From records or transcriptions
> For our four hands.

His beloved "dear" is indicated by the masculine form of *cara*, yet the gay sensibility of the poem is already so strong that this subtle identification of a male lover seems almost beside the point.

It didn't take much for Merrill to give life to his enameled words. All that was needed was a little truth, a little emotion. Edmund White met Merrill in the 1970s and was present at the creation of one poem. White has written about the experience twice, first as fiction, then as nonfiction. Merrill read a new poem to him and David Kalstone. They were impressed but shyly wondered if maybe it were a little too cold. Merrill slapped his forehead and said, "Oh, God, I left out the human feeling!" He went back upstairs and returned a half hour later with a new draft that was warm and alive. People have doubted this story, wondering if White were exaggerating or if Merrill had been putting them on. But I find it perfectly plausible. Merrill's poems are ingenious assemblies of phrases and metaphors that can sometimes just hang there like pretty mobiles. But the slightest breath of emotion—it doesn't take much—can set the lines swinging and dancing.

All this time, Merrill and Jackson had been amusing themselves with an old-fashioned toy popular with children and more recently with hippies: the Ouija board. A square of wood or cardboard printed with twenty-six letters of the alphabet, ten numerals and Yes and No commands, Ouija boards had existed since 1899. Two or more participants lightly set their fingers on a sliding pointer called a planchette and let it glide over the board, seemingly on its own, moving to this or that letter, spelling out words spoken by spirits. Merrill and Jackson played with the board off and on since 1955, using a willowware teacup as their planchette, writing down their elaborate conversations with the other side. Merrill tried working the material into a novel, but he lost the manuscript. Around 1974 he decided it might work better as poetry. Other writers turned to hallucinogens or India for their metaphysical liberations. Merrill turned to old-fashioned spiritualism. The result was a long, brilliant, narrative poem, "The Book of Ephraim."

The Book of a Thousand and One Evenings Spent
With David Jackson at the Ouija Board
In Touch with Ephraim Our Familiar Spirit.

Ephraim was a Greek Jew in the court of Tiberias on Capri; he was murdered for loving Caligula. He comes to Merrill and Jackson to teach them about the unseen world, the stages of the afterlife, and the rules for reincarnation. It's not as flaky as it sounds, not yet anyway. The invented mythology suggests a more intelligent version of something like Scientology, but it's kept safely in the background. In the foreground is a dense weave of earthly life made magical by glorious writing. The poem is full of formal devices, acrostics, rhymes and half rhymes. Verse is used as fluidly as the best prose. For example, Merrill and Jackson cannot see Ephraim but he can see them in mirrors.

(Any reflecting surface worked for him.
Noons D and I might row to a sandbar
Far enough from town for swimming naked
Then pacing the glass treadmill hardly wet
That healed itself perpetually of us
Unobserved, unheard we thought, until
The night he praised our bodies and our wit,
Our blushes in a twinkling overcome.)

Merrill tells the story as if it were a joke, a stunt, a lark. The reader plays along, enjoying the game without needing to take it literally. I, for one, do not believe in either spirits or reincarnation. Halfway through the poem, however, when Merrill's father dies and Ephraim reports that he's been reborn in England and Merrill and Jackson want to find the reincarnated broker/baby, I can't help laughing and wishing it *were* true.

This ninety-page poem is also a full-scale portrait of a gay marriage, perhaps the first, complete with domestic routines, friends, living expenses, and in-laws. Merrill can talk about his and Jackson's families with Ephraim, especially dead parents and newborn nieces and nephews. And the poem provides a flattering myth for gay love: Ephraim needs the two men to be together in order to give his message to the world. "LONG B4 THE FORTUNATE CONJUNCTION," he says in his metaphysical text-speak, "ALLOWED ME TO GET THRU/MAY I SAY WEVE HAD OUR EYES ON U." It's a pretty fairy tale to think the spirits *want* you to be a couple.

This marriage plot is openly acknowledged when Merrill visits a psychiatrist and worriedly tells him about Ephraim.

> "There's a phrase
> You may have heard—what you and David do
> We call folie a deux
> Harmless; but can you find no simpler ways
>
> To sound each other's depths of spirit[?"]

The psychiatrist goes on to suggest that these ghostly beings are Merrill and Jackson's substitute for children.

It's a mad work of art, a giddy fantasy about life after death, a comedy of reincarnation. But eventually every reader has to ask: How serious was Merrill about his conversations with spirits? What exactly was happening here?

The séances actually took place. Merrill's archives contain transcription notebooks and pages of raw dictate. Merrill and Jackson's friend Alison Lurie was present for a couple of sessions. She reports how Merrill set his left hand on the teacup while he used his right hand to write it all down. Jackson had his right hand on the cup—Lurie suspects that it was Jackson who drove the cup from letter to letter. She speculates in her fascinating book, *Familiar Spirits*, that Jackson, or his unconscious, provided the raw material of the séances, which Merrill then mined and shaped for his poetry. Jackson had given up writing novels after his failure to publish; he now directed his creativity elsewhere. Just as Isherwood and Bachardy created screenplays together, Merrill and Jackson created a spirit world. Theirs was a more unconscious collaboration, but not without precedent. William Butler Yeats married late in his life a younger woman, Georgie Hyde-Lees. Afraid the famous poet was getting bored with her, Georgie "discovered" a gift for automatic writing. Soon spirits began to dictate to her images and ideas that her spouse reworked for various poems and for his fat, comprehensive tome, *A Vision*. Biographers are still trying to figure out how deliberate Mrs. Yeats's contribution was.

"The Book of Ephraim" was published with several shorter poems in 1976 as *Divine Comedies*—the title cleverly married Dante and camp. In the years ahead, Merrill would expand his spirit world, populating the ether with more spirits and friends, including Auden, who had died in 1973. He and Jackson spent even more hours together at the Ouija board, in part to compensate for the time they spent with outside boyfriends—Merrill's infatuations were more serious than Jackson's. Merrill wrote two full additional volumes: *Mirabell: Books of Number*, with a new spirit, a batlike fallen angel who becomes a peacock; and *Scripts for the Pageant*, with two angels of light, Michael and Gabriel, sharing their message. The three books were published together in 1982 with a coda as *The Changing Light at Sandover*. There are pleasures in the larger work, but many dead stretches, too many didactic lectures by metaphysical spirits and not enough life on earth. And the long-term couple at the center of the tale, the best part of the fantasy, is lost.

Divine Comedies was highly praised when it appeared and won a Pulitzer Prize. Yet we can't pretend it was widely read by gay men, except other poets. There was no equivalent among men of the lesbian feminist following that Adrienne Rich developed at this time. It was not only her poems but her essays that attracted attention, beginning with "It Is the Lesbian in Us," a speech she gave to the 1976 Modern Language Association convention: "It is the lesbian in every woman who is compelled by female energy, who gravitates toward strong women, who seeks a literature that will express that energy and strength....It is the lesbian in us who is creative." Rich would expand on these ideas in her 1980 essay, "Compulsory Heterosexuality and Lesbian Existence," with its account of what she called "the lesbian continuum," which treated female homosexuality as varying by degree rather than kind among all women. (Male sexuality is usually pictured as a set of quantum leaps—a man is either straight or gay—yet men too shift and slide along a line that can include emotional as well as sexual intimacy.) Her ideas drew more readers to her poems until her public readings began to resemble lesbian gospel meetings. "Twenty-one Love Poems" in *The Dream of a Common Language* ("The more I live the more I think/two people together is a miracle") became a touchstone for women in a way nothing by Ginsberg or O'Hara or Merrill ever was for men. The men's poetry was having its effect, poem by poem, reader by reader. But the breakthrough medium for gay men would be elsewhere: the novel.

13. Annus Mirabilis

—m—

Edmund White came to New York in 1962, intending to be a playwright, not a novelist. He was twenty-two and fresh from the University of Michigan. A play he wrote his senior year, *The Blue Boy in Black*, won a prize and got him an agent at William Morris. But he had another reason for coming to New York: he was pursuing a fellow student, a beautiful actor named Stanley Redfern. White was in love, but his love was only intermittently requited, even after the two moved in together. His emotions fully engaged with Redfern, White frequently turned to strangers for sex. It was a pattern he would repeat in later years when he fell in unrequited love with yet another actor, Keith McDermott.

White was a bit of an actor himself. He was outgoing, charming, flirtatious, and extremely adaptable. He liked to be liked. A natural courtier, he seemed to know everyone and go everywhere. We have already seen him at the Stonewall riots and in the company of Mart Crowley and James Merrill.

If the central figure for the first half of this book is Gore Vidal, an intersection where many roads meet, then the central figure for the second half could be said to be Edmund White. The two writers are quite different yet have much in common. They are both highly literary and well-read, write excellent prose, and are fiercely productive. Both lived for many years in Europe; both are fond of hustlers. Yet while Vidal writes best about power, politics, and history, White's strengths are sex, art, and—sometimes—love. Each tends to stumble when he enters the other's domain.

Edmund White was born in 1940 in Cincinnati, Ohio. After his parents' divorce when he was seven, he spent summers in Cincinnati with his Texas-born, businessman father, and the school year in Chicago with his Texas-born, psychologist mother. He came out early to his mother, who promptly sent him to a shrink. He saw psychiatrists regularly for the first half of his life, learning through them how to talk about his emotions easily, even glibly. In college he studied, of all things, Chinese. He later said he was drawn to Asia by the selflessness of Buddhism. There are frequent mentions of Buddhism in his writing, yet they always feel slightly incongruous. We don't think of White as a particularly spiritual writer.

A year after he came to New York, his play was actually produced off-Broadway. *The Blue Boy in Black* is a satiric comedy about a black servant, Joan, who works for a white writer of potboilers, becoming his amanuensis before going on to be a successful writer herself. Joan was played by Cicely Tyson, the former fashion model who was already making a name for herself on stage and in television. Howard Taubman in the *Times* praised her performance and praised the play, too, with reservations (in particular for the "generous helping of foolish jokes about homosexuality"). He thought it worked best as "a lampoon with an undercurrent of bitterness" about the place of "a shrewd Negro in white society.... At the end it achieves intensity of emotion."

In his different memoirs, White speaks of *Blue Boy* dismissively or not at all. But it must have been exhilarating for a twenty-three-year-old to see his first play get a full-scale New York production. He must've felt he had arrived. (There was even a small part for Redfern.) But *Blue Boy* never found an audience, and it closed after twenty-three performances. The only evidence that the experience may have stung more than White later admitted is that he does not remember exactly what year it happened.

During his first months in New York, he found work as a writer at Time-Life Books, in offices on the thirty-second floor of a skyscraper in Midtown Manhattan. He stayed there for the next seven years. He tried one new therapist, then another (both wanted him to give up men), but he continued to cruise the streets for sex (bars and baths were few and often raided). White in the 1960s and early '70s was a handsome fellow of medium height with dark hair and melancholy brown eyes. A man who met him at this time still remembers his charismatic bad-boy persona. "He made you think that having sex with him would be the greatest experience in the world." When he began to put on weight, he joined a gym, one of the first gay men to do so—Mart Crowley fondly described his pecs years later. He grew a mustache soon after the macho clone look came in, then shaved it off when everyone else shaved theirs. A younger writer, David Leavitt, would later say he envied White for having "such a representative life." And it's true: the zeitgeist blew through White more easily than it did through most people.

He spent much of his free time looking for sex, but he also continued with his own writing, not just plays but stories and novels. He was a sexual compulsive, but he was also a literary compulsive, with a strong need to string words together. In time he would become a brilliant prose stylist, yet writing did not come easily to him. Good prose is solitary work, and White disliked being alone. He eventually found a way around his difficulty: he wrote in longhand in bed in the morning before his inner critic awoke; after he amassed enough pages for a first draft, he met with a typist and dictated from his draft, revising as he went along. It was sociable yet productive.

One of his first typists was Patrick Merla. Originally a waiter at a small restaurant in the West Village, a long-haired boy from Brooklyn who had shown White his poetry, Merla was an expert typist. He later said, "I am probably his only typist who never had sex with Ed." He worked with him off and on for the next thirty-five years on a variety of books. The process often involved much give and take, with Merla asking questions and White clarifying phrases. Once when White was dictating one of his longer, more elaborate metaphors, Merla stopped typing and just sat there. White asked why he wasn't typing. Merla replied, "The metaphor stops here." When White took a job at the newly restructured *Saturday Review* magazine, he got Merla hired there as an editor.

Using this method of longhand and dictation, White was able to produce novels, plays, book reviews, and essays. He later used it to produce textbooks when he needed money, but he saved Merla for more literary projects. (Merla went on to become a writer himself, penning a book of fairy tales, as well as being the editor of several gay publications and putting together the important collection *Boys Like Us: Gay Writers Tell Their Coming Out Stories*.)

The end of the 1960s and first half of the 1970s was a strange time for fiction. There was much talk that the novel was dead (even more so than now). Most serious writers were too intellectually self-conscious to simply tell a story. Many novelists were so desperate to "make it new," in Ezra

Pound's words, that they only made it strange. The novels from those years that are still read include *Gravity's Rainbow* by Thomas Pynchon and *Sula* by Toni Morrison, but it's chiefly more old-fashioned titles like *Humboldt's Gift* by Saul Bellow, *Angle of Repose* by Wallace Stegner, and early Ann Tyler that remain popular. Most of the experimental books are forgotten. (To name a few: *Speedboat* by Renata Adler, *Sheeper* by Irving Rosenthal, *The Blood Oranges* by John Hawkes, *The Public Burning* by Robert Coover. Susan Sontag's novels—*The Benefactor* and *Death Kit*—are remembered only because they were written by a famous essayist.)

White explored different approaches. He began a realistic novel about his love affair with an unpredictable blond named Jim Ruddy. A chapter was later excerpted in Seymour Kleinberg's 1977 gay and lesbian anthology, *The Other Persuasion*, under the title, "The Beautiful Room Is Empty"—a line from Kafka that White would use as the title for an entirely different novel. The excerpt tells the story of two gay friends visiting Puerto Rico before one marries a woman. They pretend to be there only for sex, but the protagonist reveals that he's in love with his marrying friend. It's a strong piece of writing, clear and real. But White knew he couldn't publish such a book at the time and he put it aside.

He next tried something mysterious and experimental, a novel narrated by a man suffering from amnesia. The protagonist of *Forgetting Elena* wakes up in a house on the ocean and does not know who he is or where or what the rules are:

> I wonder what sort of an impression I might make if I should go to the bathroom now? Perhaps no one would notice or care that I was the first to use it; perhaps people here are "natural" about bodily functions and find them humorous or, alternately, too trivial to mention. On the other hand, a carefully regulated procedure may govern the whole matter, and the men of the house may take turns in the order of their height, popularity or seniority.

White sustains this deadpan semi-comic tone for almost two hundred pages, creating a French nouveau roman fairy tale out of what is probably just a weekend on Fire Island. We never learn for sure—White never drops the mask. But his make-it-strange strategy enables him to describe a gay world of parties and dances without writing a gay novel. The prose has a stiff,

English-as-a-second-language oddness that's perfect for the brain-damaged narrator; there are no metaphors. The book is a genuine curiosity, but it works in its own strange terms. It's not too long and it has a strong ending, reached with the help of suggestions from Merla and others. It's a fable, yet one can't help feeling a nervous autobiographical note in the young protagonist who doesn't know who he is or what he wants, who anxiously fakes his way through life while hoping nobody sees through his act.

White was befriended at this time by the poet and French translator, Richard Howard, an energetic, generous man fond of flamboyant gestures—he gave poetry readings wearing old-fashioned pince-nez glasses. Howard was well-connected, and he helped White sell *Elena*. It was published in 1973 and received good reviews, but was too strange to attract many readers, gay or straight. (The book achieved some delayed fame when Vladimir Nabokov praised it in an interview. White learned Nabokov's wife, Vera, had read *Elena* first and recommended it to her husband. When White later said his ideal reader was "a cultivated heterosexual woman in her sixties who knows English perfectly but is not an American," he was thinking of Mrs. Nabokov.)

For his next project, White returned to realistic fiction with what he thought would be a commercial novel. He called it first *Like People in History*, then *Woman Reading Pascal*. The most commercial thing about it was that the chief gay character was only secondary. The protagonist was a woman like a modern Isabel Archer from *Portrait of a Lady*. White finished the novel, but nobody liked it much and he was unable to sell it.

His big break came with a different kind of book, a nonfiction title that actually was commercial, surprisingly so: *The Joy of Gay Sex*. Alex Comfort's *The Joy of Sex* had been a huge best seller in 1972. A book packager decided he could have similar success by doing two follow-up titles, one for gay men and one for lesbians. Psychiatrist Charles Silverstein was chosen as one of two writers for the men's book. Silverstein had been a leader in the campaign to get homosexuality removed as a disorder from the *Diagnostic and Statistical Manual* of the American Psychiatric Association in 1973. He was also White's therapist, the first to tell him his problem wasn't that he was queer but elsewhere; his attempts to "cure" his homosexuality were only distracting him from his real problems. Silverstein dropped White as a patient when they became collaborators.

Joy was not just a how-to book, it was also an illustrated work of erotica. It functioned much like a cookbook, pretending to be practical but providing lots of fantasy. The paintings by Michael Leonard and sepia drawings by Julian Graddon are sexy but classy. (The period pastiches by Ian Beck are less successful.) The text, however, includes much valuable information about health, psychology and behavior. There are entries for "Loneliness," "Guilt," and "Growing Older," as well as entries on various sex acts. The book is full of good-humored sanity. The entry on "One-night Stands" advises: "Should one of your friends drop by don't shoo him out the door or bury your face in your hands and moan. Let them talk together, and if the evening should turn into something social and not sexual, accept it with grace." Unshockable yet courteous, it sounds a bit like Judith Martin's Miss Manners, who was also writing at the time. I don't know who wrote what, but I assume White wrote the detailed how-to descriptions that often become little short stories. The entry on "First Time," meaning one's first experience of anal sex, is highly detailed, taking the reader step-by-step to orgasm, then closing with: "At this point neither of you should succumb to sleep or dissolve in idle chatter, but rather he should look you in the eye and tell you how wonderful the experience was for him. You'll probably find you have all sorts of things you want to tell him."

It's a friendly, even sweet picture of gay life, a counterweight to the macho clone culture beginning to be popular. Seventies macho was both a look—mustache, jeans, leather jacket—and an attitude—cool, heartless, virile—that were reactions against the old-style homosexuality of too much art and too much emotion. Silverstein and White were not afraid of emotion.

The book still reads as wise and careful. Nowadays a reader will stumble only over the entry on "Promiscuity":

> It is a word that makes little sense in gay life and even straights are tiring of the concept and finding it irrelevant and misleading. . . . If a gay man is quite unattached, then there's no harm in his having as much sexual experience as he wants.

Statements like these would be used against the book a few years later. When *Joy* was published by Crown in 1977, however, White's only fear was what it would do to his reputation as a serious writer. But he was paid well, and the book sold more copies than anything else he wrote for years to come.

Meanwhile he had begun to write regularly for *Christopher Street* magazine, introduced to the editor by Patrick Merla. He reviewed art and poetry and brought in a few writers himself, including James Merrill. He was also working on a new novel.

A few years earlier he fell in love with his second actor, Keith McDermott. The boyish McDermott was handsome, smart, funny, self-aware, and serious about his career. He soon appeared on Broadway opposite Richard Burton in *Equus*. But he wanted White as a friend, not as a lover. White domesticated unrequited love first by sharing an apartment with McDermott, then by bringing his troubled teenage nephew, also named Keith, to New York. Sixteen-year-old Keith Fleming was an unhappy boy with divorced parents. His father sent him to a mental hospital after he ran away from home. His mother, White's sister, got him released and sent him to New York. Fleming would live with the two gay men for the next nine months until he moved in with a girlfriend.

White further sublimated his love for McDermott by writing a novel about him. His new novel was nothing like his Jim Ruddy book, but wildly experimental and full of hallucinogenic prose. All the metaphors he had repressed for *Elena* were released in the new work: *Nocturnes for the King of Naples*.

Nocturnes is a dream novel narrated by a highly fictional version of McDermott speaking to an unidentified "you," an older man like White, recounting a few gaudy scenes from his life. Some readers love *Nocturnes*. I don't. The novel is full of shapely sentences that are pretty enough individually but become absurd when strung together:

> No need to tell you that in the midst of my own adventures I would push back the body of the other man until I could see his face; for a moment I'd forgotten who he was. No need to tell you I argued with idiots about Verdi's place in the history of music. No need to tell you that one day I offered God the same prayer in eight churches.

There are no characters, only presences. There is no plot, only a few bits of story: "I" goes to Rome; he has a lover in the theater who shares his life of pure artifice; he remembers his childhood, which ended when his father left his mother and she committed suicide (gassing herself and the family dog in a car in the garage). He later meets up with his father, now a womanizer and heroin addict. In the last chapter, he learns that "you," who barely appears in the book, has died of pneumonia. He goes out on a foggy beach and shouts:

> "But I have no pity to offer, since I, too, am dying, and someone saw fit to play the same prank on me, imprisoning me within an antiquated tot's body, lacing me into a straitjacket that holds my arms folded in resignation before the maddening vision of a man or god who has died, gone away or never existed save in the tense opaque presences of those things and people who, by virtue of claiming attention but denying the understanding, of demanding love at the cost of rewarding sympathy, must be addressed as 'You.'"

It's prose on amphetamines, leaping from one pretty phrase to another until it becomes a knotted jumble.

White hid gay experience inside a Trojan horse of high art in order to smuggle it into the city of literature. As I said, it works for many readers, but for me *Nocturnes* now reads like a closet novel, its druggy, baroque style a gorgeous closed door. But it seems coy chiefly because of what else was published the year that it appeared.

Michael Denneny at St. Martin's picked up *Nocturnes* and scheduled it for publication in 1978. After the success of *Joy of Gay Sex*, it should have made its author king of the gay cats. But it was upstaged not by one novel but by two: *Faggots* by Larry Kramer and *Dancer from the Dance* by Andrew Holleran. And there was a fourth novel that year that would later outshine them all: *Tales of the City* by Armistead Maupin.

One hesitates to use the Latin phrase in this context, but 1978 really was the *annus mirabilis* of gay fiction.

Larry Kramer was forty-three when he published his first book, older than the other writers, but he already had a full career behind him. A native of Washington, D.C., and a graduate of Yale, he had worked in the film industry, starting in New York and ending at the Columbia offices in London. On his own he wrote and produced a movie of D. H. Lawrence's *Women in Love*, which was nominated for an Academy Award for Best Adapted Screenplay in 1970. (It lost to *M*A*S*H*.) The successful writer/producer was a pugnacious man with a square jaw, heavy brow, and full head of dark hair. He soon began to lose the hair. He moved to New York, discovered the world of bars and clubs, and wrote a play, *The Sissies' Scrapbook*, about four friends at Yale, one of whom is gay. It had a brief run off-Broadway. He next wrote a movie about two brothers going to a disco, one of whom is gay. He couldn't get it produced. He burned to write about the gay new world he was exploring and decided it'd be easier to do in a novel. He began the story of a year in gay New York; he eventually brought it down to a weekend. *Faggots* went through four drafts, two of them over a thousand pages each. He sold the book to Random House.

One day at the Midtown YMCA, Kramer ran into a younger friend, Eric Garber, a tall, shy thirty-four-year-old with the posture of an awkward adolescent. Garber had gone to Harvard and was drafted into the army afterward, but went to Germany instead of Vietnam. He started law school but dropped out to join the writing program at Iowa. He published a story, "The Holy Family," in the *New Yorker* in 1971 under his real name. Everything else he ever wrote would appear under his nom de plume: Andrew Holleran.

The two men were at the Y presumably to exercise and cruise, but they fell into a conversation about writing. Garber told Kramer that he'd just finished a novel about gay life in New York. Kramer confessed that he'd just finished a novel about the same subject. Kramer then generously suggested Garber send his book to his agents, Ron Bernstein and Pat Loud. (Loud had become famous a few years earlier when she and her family were the subject of the 1973 documentary *An American Family*. During the filming, she got a divorce and her son, Lance, came out, the first openly gay man on TV. Pat Loud teamed up with Bernstein and, with her reputation as a gay-friendly mother, they attracted several gay writers as clients.)

Bernstein and Loud liked Garber's novel and were able to place it with another woman named Pat—Pat Golbitz at William Morrow. At the last minute Garber decided to publish under a pseudonym. He was the only son of upper-middle-class parents who had recently retired to a small town in Florida. "I didn't care who knew I was gay, but I was afraid if certain people in the town my parents lived in found out that they would hold it over them in some way." He hadn't told his parents he was homosexual; he never would explicitly. (He didn't even tell his mother he was publishing a book.)

And so in the summer of 1978 two very different novels about the same world came out within weeks of each other. The authors not only remained friends, they did a book tour together.

So much has been said about *Faggots* over the years, especially by its author, that it's easy to forget what the book is really like. It's a party novel much as *The Boys in the Band* is a party play. But the party in *Faggots* lasts several days, sprawls across Manhattan and Fire Island, and includes hundreds of guests. The gay characters range from a sad schoolteacher to a sadistic movie producer to a manly Winston cigarette model to a giddy sixteen-year-old fresh off the bus from Maryland. At the center is Fred Lemish, a successful screenwriter who wants to make a movie about the wild gay life of the 1970s. He is also pursuing his beloved, Dinky Adams, a character-less beauty who does not believe in monogamy. Kramer weaves this plot and a dozen others into an elaborate Rube Goldberg sex machine. It's a deliberately cartoony novel that often suggests an animated porn movie full of giant penises and bulbous bottoms. But now and then Fred or another character makes a long speech about how empty and destructive all this sex without love can be.

Faggots is an erotic novel that denounces sex, which is kind of schizophrenic, but sex often turns people nuts. Kramer and his enemies would later claim the book is a uniform denunciation of gay promiscuity, but it actually revels in sexuality. It's very sexy, which is why gay men continue to read it despite the sermons, repetitions, and frequent bad writing. (Irving Howe once wrote that the cruelest thing one can do to *Portnoy's Complaint* is read it twice, a line I often remembered while rereading *Faggots*.)

But folded inside the clumsy, conflicted novel is a very good novel where the novelist acknowledges that there are no simple choices. Fred famously lectures Dinky on how he must choose love and monogamy, "Before you fuck yourself to death," a line that was later read as prophetic of AIDS. But Fred gives his speech while Dinky is dressing up in leather for an orgy; Fred is so turned on by the sight that he doubts his own pretty words about marriage. Later, Fred and a hundred other men watch while Dinky is hoisted in a sling and fisted by another resentful lover, Jack Humpstone. Both angry lovers want to see Dinky die. The reader holds his breath, afraid of what might happen. It's a grotesque but powerful scene, not least because it shows that love is benign only when it gets what it wants. Otherwise love can be far more destructive than mindless sex.

Dancer from the Dance is much quieter, restrained, and elegiac. It too is a party novel, but one where it's always *after* the party. *Dancer* is an oddly chaste book; there's constant talk about sex but no actual sex scenes. The title comes from William Butler Yeats, whose work inspired many gay writers. (Yeats was straight, but as Auden wrote in "In Memory of W. B. Yeats": "You were silly like us.") *Dancer* is soaked in literary voices: F. Scott Fitzgerald (so strong that readers have referred to it as *The Gay Gatsby*), Ronald Firbank, Marcel Proust, and a large dollop of Truman Capote. Holleran's word-painting evokes the New York of the 1970s as strongly as Capote evoked the city of the 1940s in *Breakfast at Tiffany's*.

It got very hot that summer—tremendous heat that made the East Village almost sensual for a spell....Peaches were ripe in the fruit stall on Second Avenue, the streets south of Astor Place were empty at dusk, and every figure you came upon walking south shimmered for a moment in the distance, then materialized into a group of boys playing ball in a lot littered with broken glass.

But Holleran's lyricism goes on to add something new:

Even Sutherland, when you ran into him on Fifth Avenue after the office workers had rushed home for a game of tennis before the light had failed, was ecstatic as he stopped to talk after an afternoon in the men's room at Grand Central, picking the pubic hair from his teeth: "Oh, my dear, there is no other time, no other time at all, but now, when the city is overripe, like a fruit about to drop into your lap, and all the young stockbrokers' underwear is damp! My dear!"

It's sensuous, funny, raunchy, sweet, and sad, all at once.

The story could not be simpler. A beautiful young man, Malone, comes to New York, comes out, leaves corporate life, lives with a lover, then leaves him to meet a hundred other men, often as a hustler, attending endless dances and parties before he disappears. Along the way he is advised by a witty older man, Sutherland, who has the best lines in the book. When Malone decides he's wasting his life and wants to go back to work, Sutherland asks what he will put on his résumé for the past ten years. Malone hesitates. "Looking for love," he finally says. Sutherland replies:

> "Looking for love...No, I don't think that would get very far with Union Carbide. Or Ogilvy and Mather. Or the Ford Motor people. Looking for love is not one of the standard entries on the resume. You see, *you* have been writing a journal for the past ten years, and everyone else has been composing a resume. Don't think you will be forgiven that...After all, the Empire State Building is nothing but a mass of sublimated love."

Dancer is about looking for love, living for love, but it's a love story with no love object, no beloved. It's all longing, all dreams and melancholy. *Dancer* is a scrapbook of mood pieces that shouldn't work as a novel, but it does: the moods are so perfectly rendered that they are enough.

Malone's story is told by a narrator whose exchange of letters with a friend opens and closes the book. They use a variety of camp pseudonyms ranging from the Duc de Saint Simon to Rima the Bird Girl. The framing device was inspired by the playful letters Holleran and another writer, Robert Ferro, wrote to each other after they met at Iowa University. Only at the end does the fictional author use his real name: Paul. With Andrew Holleran we find pseudonyms behind pseudonyms, masks behind masks. It gave him the anonymity he needed to protect a very delicate, finely tuned sensibility.

Christopher Street featured *Dancer* on its July 1978 cover and called it "the gay novel of the year." It began to sell immediately. Soon it was being cited in the gay press as the "good gay novel" against the "bad gay novel," *Faggots* by Larry Kramer. There were reviews of both books in the *Advocate*, *Fag Rag*, the *Body Politic* (by George Whitmore, who said *Faggots* should be burned), and *Gay Community News*.

Despite the attacks, *Faggots* sold very well: 40,000 in hardcover and 300,000 in paper. And why shouldn't it be successful? It gave gay readers the opportunity to feel morally superior to men who got laid more often than they did *and* to jerk off. But *Dancer* sold equally well. More interesting, both books succeeded with almost no help from the mainstream. It took several months for general reviewers to catch up. John Lahr reviewed the two books together in the *New York Times Book Review* in January 1979 under the title "Camp Tales." He loved *Dancer*, praising the language and calling Malone "a mercurial and strangely moral figure." He hated *Faggots*. "Here are characters like Randy Dildough, Blaze Sorority, Boo Boo Bronstein, Jack Humpstone, Nicolo Loosh presented in a jocular, baroque style which is, sentence by sentence, some of the worst writing I've encountered in a published manuscript.... Mr. Kramer wants the book to be a rambunctious farce, but his frivolity isn't earned and so it becomes an embarrassing fiasco."

Yet literary quality was only part of the problem for gay readers. It was Kramer's picture of liberated life that they rejected. But as Holleran himself later pointed out, his own picture in *Dancer* is as dark in its way as Kramer's: love between two men is beautiful but impossible. White's vision in *Nocturnes* is sad as well. If *Faggots* hadn't existed to serve as a lightning rod, Holleran and White might also have been attacked for being grim and negative.

The reviewer at *Harper's* hated all three books. It had been nine years since the GAA zap and Midge Decter was gone—she felt the magazine had become too liberal—but the publication remained unfriendly. Somebody named Jeffrey Burke tore apart a half dozen gay titles in a single sneering review: *Faggots*, *Dancer*, and *Nocturnes* were beaten up along with *Chamber Music* by Doris Grumbach, *Wild Man* by Tobias Schneebaum, and *Dress Grey*, a West Point murder mystery written by a straight man, Lucian Truscott (who had covered the Stonewall riots for the *Village Voice*). These are very different titles with only one thing in common: "Six books by, about, or for homosexuals appear in as many months. To the rattling sound of typewriters racing and presses rolling is added the ringing of the register. And more often than not, art is shortchanged." It was ten years after Stonewall, but in the eyes of *Harper's*, the new books were being written much too quickly. At least the magazine was paying enough attention, however, to notice a new development in contemporary literature.

The fourth novel to appear in 1978 received less press than the others, but *Tales of the City* didn't look important when it first came out. It was a paperback original from Harper and Row with a cover that suggested a book of comic strips—which in a way it was: a series of humor columns from the *San Francisco Chronicle* by an unknown writer named Armistead Maupin. There were few reviews and many returns. Yet *Tales* became a sleeper hit and ultimately the most successful novel of the four.

As his full name should indicate, Armistead Jones Maupin Jr. was from the South. He was born in 1944 in Washington, D.C., while his father was an officer in the navy. After the war, the family settled in Raleigh, North Carolina, where the father became a lawyer. A friend nicknamed the parents "John Wayne and Auntie Mame," yet Maupin's mother was a repressed Mame. Maupin lived an anxiously normal adolescence that included the Boy Scouts and Boys State, a political boot camp for honor students run by the American Legion. He attended the University of North Carolina at Chapel Hill and became more involved in politics—conservative politics—working for a local TV commentator named Jesse Helms. He started law school, intending to work in his father's firm; but he hated law and dropped out to join the navy, attending officer candidates school just as his father had.

Maupin had been attracted to men since he turned twelve but he denied the desire, kept it hidden. He did not have his first sexual experience until he was an ensign stationed in Charleston. He picked up a man at the Battery one evening while dressed in his civvies and took him back to his apartment. It was summer 1969, the summer of Stonewall, but Maupin didn't hear of the riots until years later. He began to cruise the Battery regularly and enjoyed himself, but when his superior officer was transferred to Vietnam, Maupin applied to go with him. The Vietnam War was the most important event in his world at the time; he didn't want to miss it. He spent an entire year over there, doing jobs that ranged from serving as a protocol officer in Saigon, where he took visiting dignitaries shopping, to being the navy liaison officer in a small army camp on the Cambodian border, supervising patrol boats like the one in *Apocalypse Now*.

He saw San Francisco briefly in 1970 when he was discharged from the navy, but he did not stay. He returned to Vietnam as a civilian working for the Nixon administration, building homes for Vietnamese soldiers in a campaign to win hearts and minds. When he came back to the States, he was invited to the White House to meet Richard Nixon. Maupin and his colleagues spent an uncomfortable half hour trying to make small talk with the beleaguered president. It was the week of Nixon's second inauguration and the Watergate scandal had not yet fully broken. Years later Maupin still owned a photo of his younger self shaking hands with Nixon, but he kept it in his bathroom.

A reporter who had met Maupin overseas recommended him for a job with the Associated Press. He accepted and the AP sent him to San Francisco. It was either that or Buffalo.

The city of *Howl* had gone through many changes since the days of Allen Ginsberg. The working-class bohemia of beatniks and poets continued into the Sixties, until the Summer of Love of 1967 flooded the rundown Haight-Ashbury district with would-be hippies. Most went back home, but many stayed and moved into other neighborhoods, including the Castro. People set up communes revolving around sex, drugs, and music; the city of poets became the city of the Grateful Dead, Jefferson Airplane, and the drag troupe, the Cockettes. Many of the newcomers were gay and lesbian. Harvey Milk came from New York at this time and began to run for public office. Alongside the new counterculture city existed older cities of working-class Irish, Latinos, Asians, and even old-money Anglos, a lively mix of cultures packed into a small peninsula.

San Francisco loosened Maupin's Republican beliefs. His friend, British novelist Patrick Gale, writes that Maupin's political philosophy "suffered a slow process of attrition in a city where no one approved of Nixon and where the counterculture held sway. Principally it was sex that brought him to transfer his allegiances. The orgy room at Dave's Baths was democracy made flesh; race and social standing were checked at the door along with clothes." Like many gay men who come out late to themselves, Maupin became very political about his sexuality. He came out locally in 1974 when *San Francisco* magazine wanted to include him as one of the ten sexiest men in the Bay area. He agreed, but insisted he be identified as a gay man.

He did not stay long with the Associated Press. He tried other jobs in San Francisco, including advertising, but he wanted to write. He began to do articles for local magazines and newspapers, including the *Pacific Sun*, a weekly based across the bay in Marin County. When the *Sun* started a San Francisco edition in 1974, they used Maupin more frequently and suggested he add recurring characters to his pieces about local places. A new column was created, "The Serial by Armistead Maupin." In the *Sun*'s Marin County edition, Cyra McFadden began a column also titled "The Serial," satirizing the well-heeled liberals over there. Five weeks after Maupin started, however, the *Sun* decided to shut down its San Francisco edition. Luckily, his column had caught the attention of editors at the daily newspaper, the *San Francisco Chronicle*, who were looking for ways to attract a younger readership. They hired Maupin at a standard reporter's salary and he started his column all over again, now retitled "Tales of the City."

He began with Mary Ann Singleton, a smart, curious girl from the Midwest, and set her loose among recognizable city landmarks and fads. Soon Mary Ann was meeting a host of transplants and natives, including gay men and, most famously, Anna Madrigal, her pot-smoking landlady. Maupin needed to produce daily eight-hundred-word installments five days a week for six months. "There were times when he was barely two days ahead of his readers," he wrote of the experience thirty years later, speaking of himself in the third person. "Like them, he was waiting breathlessly for what would happen next—but counting on his life to provide it." He tried not to plan too much in advance, but let his story and characters surprise him.

The column caught on and became very popular locally. After *Newsweek* wrote about it, Harper and Row approached Maupin about doing a book. A collection of Cyra McFadden's columns, *The Serial*, had been a best seller for Random House in 1977; Harper and Row hoped to have similar success with Maupin. He revised his columns, removing a subplot about a serial killer and adding a few dirty words. However, he kept the quick, elliptical approach to sex scenes that he had devised for a "family" newspaper. The droll ease with which he can allude to almost anything between the lines—impotence, oral sex, a rich wife fucking a delivery boy—is often quite funny in itself.

Tales works beautifully as a book. The prose is crisp, smart, and lively. It's dialogue driven, but it reads more cleanly and precisely than any play or screenplay. Here are Michael Tolliver, aka Mouse, and his friend Mona before Michael performs in the jockey shorts dance contest at a local gay bar:

> Michael groaned and readjusted his shorts. "What the fuck am I doing here, Mona? I used to be a Future Farmer of America."
>
> "You're paying the rent, remember?"
>
> "Right. I'm paying the rent, I'm paying the rent. *This* is a recording..."
>
> "Just take it easy."

"What if I lose? What if they laugh? Jesus! What if they don't even *notice* me?... I think I'm gonna throw up."

"Save it for the finale."

The best writing is usually in Maupin's dialogue, but there is no bad prose. The novel is built out of short, concise scenes because it was first written for serialization, yet those scenes snap along briskly in book form. People often compare Maupin to Charles Dickens, but only because Dickens is the world's most famous serial novelist. Maupin himself has said he read little Dickens (he was more familiar with E. F. Benson of the Mapp and Lucia novels). I think he's closer to a different Victorian serial storyteller, Anthony Trollope. Like Maupin, Trollope often used pure dialogue to tell his tales. He had a similar gift for improvisation, and the same ability to create characters who grow and deepen during the long haul of a novel created in installments. Both writers start with clear, simple outlines for their figures and let the developing story reveal new colors and dimensions. Both men's curiosity and imaginations are so rich that they could produce sustained series of lively books: Trollope wrote seven novels about the people of Barchestershire and six around the Palliser family; Maupin would eventually write eight novels about the circle of friends at 28 Barbary Lane.

That's the address of Anna Madrigal's house, a brown-shingled three-story mansion on Russian Hill divided into apartments. *Tales* is a boardinghouse novel, following in the footsteps of *Père Goriot* and *Goodbye to Berlin*—both of which also include gay characters. Sociologists say a neighborhood is perceived as gay if anywhere between 15 to 25 percent of the residents are homosexual. That was true of San Francisco, and it's true of the Barbary Lane novels. Three-quarters of the primary characters are straight, yet it's seen as a gay series. The chief gay character, Michael Tolliver, isn't introduced by name until page 70 of the first book. Michael plays a larger role as the novel progresses, and a much bigger role in the whole series. But the strongest plotline of the first *Tales* is the love story of a terminally ill, fifty-something, married businessman, Edgar Halcyon, and the fifty-something free spirit, Anna Madrigal. Madrigal is a transsexual, of course, but it's not fully revealed until the next book, *More Tales of the City*. The love story reads as straight until then, and maybe afterward, too. Anna Madrigal is so entirely herself that her sex change feels secondary. She is literature's first nonthreatening, nonsuffering, three-dimensional androgyne. Maupin told his editors at the *Chronicle* her secret before he began the series. They accepted her but asked that he not tell readers until the second year. It was inspired advice.

The *Chronicle* editors nervously kept count of the number of gay characters in the series, but they had no difficulty with the high percentage of characters who smoke grass. Well, it *was* California in the Seventies. Yet Maupin acknowledged this freedom might be only temporary. In one memorable scene, Michael gets stoned with his straight neighbor, Brian, a lawyer-turned-waiter, and they talk about the changing times. Brian croakily describes a stricter future: "We're gonna be...I mean people like you and me...we're gonna be fifty-year-old libertines in a world full of twenty-year-old Calvinists."

Despite its relative straightness, *Tales* found its first audience with gay readers. They were initially drawn to the book because it was set in the gay mecca of San Francisco, but they enjoyed visiting a world whose straight inhabitants were as goofy as its gay ones. Everybody is Other in Maupin. The free-and-easy attitude toward all sex, gay *and* straight, was a welcome relief from the guilty dramas of Kramer and Holleran, which weren't very different from the guilty erotics of Updike and Roth. Early readers were steered to *Tales* by word of mouth, and the most important mouths were the gay bookstores. Maupin himself contacted stores across the country and told them here was something that would interest their customers, even when his publisher stayed quiet about it. (Later, when his gay base was firmly established, he would have to press his publisher to pursue straight readers, too.)

Shortly before the book came out, Maupin met his hero, Christopher Isherwood, in Los Angeles at a 1978 Oscar night party for *Saturday Night Fever*. Isherwood already knew his column. "Oh, that marvelous funny thing." He told Maupin not to apologize for being entertaining. "It's possible to commit art *and* entertainment in the same moment." Maupin asked if he'd give the book a blurb, and Isherwood did—he compared Maupin to Dickens. Maupin also met Bachardy that night and later sat for a portrait, a beautiful drawing that brings out a casual sexiness that photos often miss.

He was still unattached, falling in and out of love and having an occasional affair, including one with the closeted Rock Hudson ("As much as I liked Rock, I was just part of his sexual sub-life"), but he had not yet met a significant other.

Maupin worked nonstop for six months on each new series of *Tales*, then took six months off. On November 27, 1978, during one of his breaks, city supervisor Harvey Milk and mayor George Moscone were murdered by city supervisor Dan White. Maupin never included the murders in the novels. Nor did he include the White Night riots of May 21, 1979, after a jury found Dan White guilty of nothing worse than manslaughter and gay people rioted in the streets. Such large public tragedies would have overwhelmed the private world of Barbary Lane. Yet politics found their way into the novels in a more intimate, personal manner. The feminist phrase "the personal is political" had already been picked up by gay men and women (Edmund White even wrote an essay with the title); Maupin's politics were deeply personal.

Anita Bryant's 1977 antigay Save Our Children campaign in Dade County, Florida, infuriated him. He gave his anger to his characters. Michael's mother writes Michael in praise of Anita Bryant; Michael is so furious that he finally comes out to her.

> I wouldn't have written, I guess, if you hadn't told me about your involvement in the Save Our Children campaign. That, more than anything, made it clear that my responsibility was to tell you the truth, that your own child is homosexual, and that I never needed saving from anything except the cruel and ignorant piety of people like Anita Bryant.
>
> I'm sorry, Mama. Not for what I am, but for how you must feel at this moment. I know what that feeling is, for I felt it most of my life. Revulsion, shame, disbelief—rejection through fear of something I knew, even as a child, was as basic to my nature as the color of my eyes...
>
> Being gay has taught me tolerance, compassion and humility. It has shown me the limitless possibilities of living. It has given me people whose passion and kindness and sensitivity have provided a constant source of strength.
>
> It has brought me into the family of man, Mama, and I like it here. I *like* it.

Michael's coming-out letter served as Maupin's coming-out to his own parents. They subscribed to the *San Francisco Chronicle*, and he knew they would read the column. His father responded with a drily indignant letter written at his office on yellow legal paper, accusing Maupin of hurting his mother, who was ill at the time—but she already knew. Maupin heard over the years from scores of gay men who clipped out this column and sent it to their own mothers with a note declaring, "me too."

Most straight people, and many gay people, especially those who came of age more recently, don't understand how momentous and difficult coming out was to men and women of this generation. It seems so obvious now, so banal. But the straight world made coming out important and dangerous. They despised homosexuals so much that the homosexuals responded with either total silence or the clever argument of Gore Vidal and others that there was no such thing as a homosexual—if only people understood that gay identity was a social fiction, then antigay feeling would go away. Yet it wasn't until huge numbers of men and women took the banal and embarrassing step of naming themselves and sharing the name with their families that not just culture but the whole body politic began to change, shifting forward a few inches.

14. White Noise

—✺—

Back in New York, the newly published writers were getting to know each other. Writers often begin their careers working in isolation, but afterward discover they have siblings.

There's an entertaining account of this time in the diaries of novelist Felice Picano, a useful picture of friendship and networking in the gay New York literary circuit of parties and book signings. The New York–born Picano had written a couple of popular thrillers, including a best seller, *Eyes*, and founded a small press for gay titles, Sea Horse Press. He met Andrew Holleran at a party on Fire Island in September 1978, after the publication of *Dancer*. He offered to advise Holleran on his career; Holleran asked to meet Picano's sexy friend, George Whitmore. A talented writer from Colorado, Whitmore was working on an autobiographical novel, *The Confessions of Danny Slocum*. He and Holleran met and briefly courted each other—there was a sexual charge to many of these friendships in their early stages. Back in the city, Whitmore introduced Picano to *his* new friend, Edmund White. White invited Picano to lecture his class at Johns Hopkins about suspense. They rode the train down to Baltimore and back, talking the whole time. Afterward Picano wrote in his diary, "Edmund White...is a charming man given to stringent self-analysis, but hiding it behind a lovely surface of shifting polish and childlike delight....I suspect he is unsure whether he wants pure love or respect more. I can love him more easily because I so much respect his work." Sometime that fall White met Holleran on his own. Everyone soon met Holleran's friend from Iowa, Robert Ferro, an Italian-American from New Jersey. Ferro's boyfriend, Michael Grumley, was another writer who'd studied at Iowa. The two had a close yet open marriage—friends called them the Ferro-Grumleys. White appeared with a new boyfriend, Christopher Cox, an actor (yet another actor) from

Alabama who wanted to be a writer but would end up becoming an editor. Floating in and out of the larger parties like an unwelcome older relative was Larry Kramer. He appeared less often after Whitmore published his scathing attack on *Faggots* in the *Body Politic*.

The core group of friends were almost all in their thirties in 1978, with White the oldest at thirty-eight and Cox the youngest at twenty-nine. They socialized for another year before they began to think of themselves as a club, first as the Lavender Quill, then the Violet Quill. A group reading at Three Lives Bookstore in Greenwich Village was such a success that Holleran and Ferro suggested they get together for private readings like the writer workshops in Iowa. The first official meeting was March 31, 1980 at the Ferro-Grumley apartment on West Ninety-fifth Street. The guests were Holleran, White, Cox, Picano, and Whitmore. Holleran read a story titled "Sleeping Soldiers" about his time in the army, Ferro the opening chapters of a new novel titled *Max Desir*, and Picano an internal monologue later published as "Spinning." They discussed specifics from the stories and larger literary issues, and Grumley served dessert.

The friends met four times in the spring of 1980 and twice in July out on Fire Island. There were no meetings that fall or winter, but, in October, Holleran, Picano, White, and Whitmore all appeared in a hardcover anthology of stories from *Christopher Street* magazine, *Aphrodisiac: Fiction from Christopher Street*. (The title story, featured only because it made a catchy title, was by a young writer who'd recently moved to New York from Virginia, Christopher Bram.) At the end of the winter, Whitmore irritably quit, angry over criticism from Ferro. There were two more meetings in March 1981, the second attended by film scholar Vito Russo, who read from his work-in-progress, *The Celluloid Closet*. That was the last meeting of the Violet Quill. Most of the writers remained friends and continued to share help and advice (and review and blurb each other's books), but they had met officially only eight times over the course of a year.

Back in November 1980, the *SoHo Weekly News* published a cover story, "Fag Lit's New Royalty." The article inside was titled, "A Movable Brunch—the Fag Lit Mafia" and was written by Australian gay writer Dennis Altman. This bitchery was the first bit of fame for the group. But people didn't talk about the Violet Quill again until after the AIDS epidemic killed over half its members.

It is sometimes claimed that the Violet Quill as a group created the new gay literature. I don't see that. The group was simply a brief bonding of like-minded friends—and they were hardly the only game in gay books at the time. Their most important members, White and Holleran, had voices and careers completely independent of the others. Holleran later wrote a fine essay about Robert Ferro after Ferro's death, where he downplayed the Violet Quill and called it a "dessert-and-short-story" club. White in his memoirs and autobiographical fiction never mentions the group at all.

More important, I'm not convinced their work marks a real break with what was written before Stonewall. The old novels offered mostly pictures of unhappy homosexuals: *The City and the Pillar, Other Voices, Giovanni's Room*, even *A Single Man*. And so did the first novels by the Violet Quill writers. And why shouldn't they? The scars were deep, and liberation could work its benefits only slowly. As was said earlier, *Nocturnes* and *Dancer* are as sad in their way as *Faggots*. It's not that literature needs to be sunny. How many heterosexual classics end happily? But in the old style—and Holleran would remain locked in the old style—homosexuals are always unhappier than heterosexuals, and they're unhappier *because* they're homosexual. In the new style, homosexuals and heterosexuals could be equally unhappy, equally happy, and equally screwed up.

Shortly before the first meeting of the Violet Quill, Edmund White published a new book that won him the wider audience he had missed with *Nocturnes*. It was, of all things, a travel book.

States of Desire: Travels in Gay America was the brainchild of Charles Ortleb at *Christopher Street*. He thought the time was right for a full-scale portrait of gay life, not just in New York and San Francisco, but the entire country. He felt White was the man to do it. He pitched the idea to the novelist, who pitched it to editor Bill Whitehead at Dutton. Whitehead could pay an advance of only $15,000. White needed another $5,000 to fund his travels. Ortleb paid the difference, in exchange for four chapters to be serialized in the magazine.

White needed to do the book quickly and cheaply. This meant making short, concentrated visits in different cities, where he saw old friends and made new ones. Many of his contacts were sexual—men met in bars or at the baths. In some ways the book is a continuation of *The Joy of Gay Sex*, but with White's mind roaming outside of beds to explore whole communities and cities. He downplays his sexual activities, but they inform his meetings and conversations with a friendly, frisky energy. The book might begin in sex, but it looks out at class, politics, race, and the many different ways that all Americans live their lives.

States is an exuberant, freewheeling book, the everything-but-the-kitchen-sink quality of travel writing freeing the author to change topics frequently, leaping from places to people to ideas. The book is full of miniature essays about hedonism, work, religion, friendship, art, socialism, and happiness. Years of theories and observations squirreled away while White made "art" were put to use. Reality worked wonders for his prose. Free to call a spade a spade (and a cock a cock), he no longer hid in baroque metaphor but returned to the clearer, more direct style of his unpublished fiction. The book is full of wonderful observations expressed in smart sentences:

> So few human contacts in Los Angeles go unmediated by glass (either a TV screen or automobile windshield) that direct confrontation renders the participants docile, stunned, sweet.

A dazzling two-page account of the semiotics of cars in Los Angeles builds to a damning joke:

> Jeeps—elaborately painted, crested by a golden eagle and lined with coordinated seats and wheel covers—also spell M-A-C-H-O, a condition that only gay men and a few suburban straights in Akron still aspire to.

The book includes a vast variety of men in different worlds: from publisher David Goodstein lounging naked in his heated swimming pool and holding forth on est; to a tall, shy, handsome businessman who's succeeded in the lumber industry in Portland, Oregon; to a pack of unhappy young queens trapped in Memphis. White visits the black gay community in Atlanta, the radical political community in Boston, and the many gay communities in Texas, including a bar full of gay cowboys:

When a city slicker has a jerk-off fantasy about cowboys, he usually forgets their true distinguishing marks—the air of detachment and the polite old-fashioned decorum. He ignores the fact that cowboys are low in perceived status, suspicious of outsiders, grave, insecure, a bit touching—and quite conventional about sex (they would be appalled by rough stuff, for instance).

The book returns to New York, where White analyzes ideas about gay sensibility, art, and media. He includes an extended, brilliant riff on the varieties of New York gay men as defined by the neighborhoods where they live:

Greenwich Village is the gay ghetto, though in a city where one out of every four men is homosexual the term doesn't mean much. The gay Villager can be a well-heeled executive who works midtown.... Or he can be an actor-waiter-singer-dancer-pusher-hustler in a dismal room in a tenement filled with Italian families; he was originally attracted to the Village when he arrived in New York ten years ago by its artistic associations; he stayed for the sex. This is the world of freelancers, those gay men who can arrange their hours to suit themselves, who piece together a day out of two hours of clerking at a boutique, three hours researching a history of magic and eleven hours of loafing.

It's very tongue-in-cheek and nobody should take it literally. Yet it's impressive how much truth White captures with his jokes. A playful satire, *States* makes fun of both straight and gay life. Like most satire, it exaggerates for effect. Yet a basic decency and sanity always shines through.

A travel book can be all voice and no story, a grab bag of data strung upon an itinerary. *States* belongs to a literary tradition that extends from Charles Dickens and Mark Twain to Paul Theroux and Bruce Chatwin. It remains for many people their favorite book by White. It still gives pleasure, and not simply as history. (Yet it's fascinating to see how much has changed in thirty years. Casual sex was more casual then, but over two-thirds of the men White meets require pseudonyms: "let's call him Bill." Even the appliances are different. White excitedly reports that wealthy David Goodstein owns a refrigerator with *an ice cube dispenser in the door!*)

States of Desire was published in January 1980 and dedicated to Patrick Merla. It received much attention from the mainstream, for good and ill. Two reviews, one by Paul Cowan in the *New York Times Book Review*, one by John Leonard in the daily *Times*, make an interesting study in contrasts. Leonard felt he was visiting a strange new world and he wasn't comfortable, but he *was* fascinated. He loved the prose. Cowan, on the other hand, despised everything about the book, including the writing. He called it dishonest and misleading because it wasn't a complete picture of gay America: it didn't include any nice homosexuals, only rich ones who wanted to have sex with each other. (He must have skipped the pages about community service in Los Angeles, prison work in Utah, and political activism in D.C. and Boston.) He and Leonard were both startled by the phrase "filthy breeders," said not by White but by an unhappy man stranded in the boondocks. Cowan and Leonard were two straight white guys who had never been treated as Other. But Leonard accepted the phrase as a bitter joke and enjoyed it, even played with it. Cowan was outraged that White could even quote it. Didn't he know that heterosexuals needed to breed so homosexuals could even exist?

States established White as the voice of the new gay generation. He was regularly invited to write articles on gay life for various publications—he did a fine essay on gay words for an anthology, *The State of the Language*—and to review and interview the older generation. He wrote about Christopher Isherwood and William Burroughs for the *Times*. He met and interviewed Truman Capote for *After Dark*.

It was a promising encounter, like the passing of a baton in a relay race, even if Capote and White ran in slightly different races. Capote had finally overcome the disaster of *Answered Prayers* and finished a new book in 1980, a collection of short pieces, *Music for Chameleons*. White visited him in his U.N. Plaza apartment, bringing photographer Robert Mapplethorpe to take pictures. White was surprised Capote showed no interest in the sexy Mapplethorpe or his sexy assistant. Capote was distracted and depressed throughout the interview, making repeated trips to the next room for sips or hits of something. He came to life only when White mentioned his nasty portrait of Tennessee Williams in "Unspoiled Monsters." Capote laughed loudly and said he and Williams had known each other a thousand years and were friends again. Mapplethorpe took a photo of the two writers together,

White looking happy and confident, Capote barefoot and weary. The picture represents a changing of the guard, the old giving way to the young, and it's not a pretty image. White reports that when he left, Capote "gave me a cheek to peck, a purely routine gesture, as though we were Gabor sisters air-kissing each other for the benefit of the camera. 'Well,' he told me, 'you'll write some wonderful books, I'm sure, but believe me...' He took off his glasses and stared at me. 'It's a *horrible* life.'"

Each time gay people made themselves more visible in print or public life, a social critic felt obligated to respond. In September 1980 the response came in an essay by Midge Decter, "The Boys on the Beach." It had been ten years since the GAA liberated her offices at *Harper's*. She was not happy with the new age and had already written extended criticisms of other groups: feminists, liberal parents, the radical young. She now took aim at a new target.

She opens by expressing surprise that homosexuals could claim they were discriminated against. After all, she knew homosexuals intimately from years ago when she and her husband, Norman Podhoretz, spent summers in the Pines on Fire Island. Homosexuals there weren't oppressed. In fact, *they* were the oppressors, making straight people feel bad with their well-kept bodies: "a never-ending spectacle, zealously and ruthlessly monitored, of tender adolescence...an insistent reminder of the ravages to [our] own persons wrought by an ordinary heterosexual existence." (This was before gym culture caught on for straight people, too, and they could blame fat on being moral and married.) Even worse than the bodies were the jokes: "I am referring here to the manner of speech, gesture, and home decoration known as 'camp'...entirely a homosexual creation, a brilliant expression of homosexual aggression against the heterosexual world."

Gay people couldn't possibly suffer from discrimination, she insists, since they went into fields dominated by other homosexuals, such as interior decorating and theater. She claims they rarely become lawyers or doctors. She admits that many school teachers are homosexual, but thinks their only restriction is that they must be discreet. She apparently didn't know that teachers were still regularly fired when arrested on gay misdemeanor charges well into the next decade. She apparently didn't ask or look around enough to see that there were millions of homosexuals outside the "soft professions." She never mentions that gay people existed outside New York and San Francisco.

Halfway through the essay (and it's a very long essay), Decter abruptly announces that she's been talking about the good old days and that these were the homosexuals she *liked*. Now she's going to talk about the new activist homosexuals, whom she can't stand. She unhappily recalls the zap at *Harper's*: "They arrived with the inevitable platoon of TV cameras and reporters and, having had their moment in the sun of media, settled down for a rather rude daylong visit." She complains about their clothes, "the drab and unprepossessing appearance of the demonstrators; no gathering of homosexuals I had ever seen had been so without dash or high taste." She doesn't like their politics, either, and she despises their new literature "devoted to photographic genuflection before the altar of Phallus...Homosexuality, like negritude and womanhood, had become a small 'market.'" (*Negritude*? It's the name of a literary movement of French African writers in the 1930s, but I don't think it's what Decter had in mind.) She finds one exception, however, in *States of Desire*, which she likes. She calls White "a gifted and cultivated writer, far more suitably and recognizably a representative of the kind of homosexuals who were my neighbors in the Pines."

I suspect *States* inspired her to write her own essay on gay culture, but it's hard to believe she read the book carefully: so much of it contradicts her arguments. However, she did notice White's mention of frequent sex, and she was appalled. She goes on at length about S&M, fisting, leather, the new movie *Cruising*, and transsexual surgery—all of which she believes are an expression of a homosexual death wish. She even argues that the high rate of gay suicide, which the GAA first told her about, is caused not by oppression but by this death wish. She goes on to blame everything—death wish, promiscuity, bad haircuts—on the gay rights movement. Before gay rights, homosexuals not only dressed better, they didn't think they were oppressed. According to Decter, they didn't even know homosexuality was an option.

This long, wild piece appeared in *Commentary*, which was edited by her husband. I discuss it at length only because it shows what some members of the so-called thinking class could still think about gay people in 1980—and because it irritated Gore Vidal into writing one of his most powerful essays, "Pink Triangle and Yellow Star."

* * *

Vidal had found a new career as a historical novelist. He followed *Burr* with another novel in 1976, *1876*, a counter-Bicentennial novel about the corruption and racism of a hundred years earlier and, by implication, the present. The book put him on the cover of *Time*. He next wrote a novel about religion, *Creation*, set in Persia in the fifth century B.C. He didn't write gay novels anymore, but he still had his principles and his temper. Ronald Reagan soundly defeated Jimmy Carter in 1980 and the Reagan Revolution began. The Christian conservatives were on the rise, supported by Jewish neoconservatives like the Podhoretzes. An editor at the *New York Review of Books* showed Vidal the Decter essay, thinking it would interest him. It moved him to scorn and fury.

"Pink Triangle and Yellow Star" displays Vidal at his most brutally comic. He has much fun at the expense of Decter's pseudosociological observations. After quoting her puzzlement over why Fire Island lesbians are always accompanied by "large and ferocious dogs," Vidal comments, "Well, if I were a dyke and a pair of Podhoretzes came waddling toward me on the beach, copies of Leviticus and Freud in hand, I'd get in touch with the nearest Alsatian dealer pronto." Vidal actually succeeds in making sense out of her cockamamie death wish theory: homosexuality is so "hateful"—her word—that homosexuals want to obliterate themselves, either literally or figuratively. But as Vidal points out, she also believes this is a life they've idly chosen. He describes her view as "a world of perfect illogic."

He counters Decter's catalog of types and stereotypes with a recent French memoir, *Tricks* by Renaud Camus, a matter-of-fact diary of one-night stands that dissolves all generalizations about the kinds of men who enjoy sex with other men. Vidal avoids identity names like "gay" and "homosexual" and uses his own: "homosexualists" and "same-sexers." But the boldest device in the essay, and what got Vidal into trouble with some readers, was his comparison of same-sexers with Jews. It's a running theme throughout the piece and he announces it early in a powerful paragraph. He believes they have much in common and should band together. After all, the Nazis sent both to concentration camps, where the Jews wore yellow stars and the "homosexualists" wore pink triangles.

I was present when Christopher Isherwood tried to make this point to a young Jewish movie producer. "After all," said Isherwood.

"Hitler killed six hundred thousand homosexuals." The young man was not impressed. "But Hitler killed six million Jews," he said sternly. "What are you?" asked Isherwood. "In real estate?"

The *New York Review of Books* insisted he cut this paragraph. Vidal refused. He gave the essay instead to the *Nation*, whose Jewish editor Victor Navasky was happy to run it as is. It appeared in November 1981 under the confrontational title "Some Jews and the Gays." The title was changed when the essay was reprinted in a book, the new title emphasizing the shared oppression of the two minorities. "Pink Triangle and Yellow Star" has been regularly quoted ever since it appeared, mostly its jokes but also its ideas.

In 1982, Vidal decided to run in the Democratic primary in California for a seat in the U.S. Senate. He had kept a home in Los Angeles as a legal residence while he spent most of the year in Italy. Running for public office was a strange decision, and Vidal himself didn't fully understand why he did it. "I am sauntering for the Senate," he wrote a friend. "Does one want to win? Ah, that's a question."

So why did he do it? He was now a highly successful novelist. Perhaps he was restless and wanted to try something new. Here was an opportunity to speak out against the new conservative movement that had put into power Reagan and other friends of his old enemy, William F. Buckley. But politics is a very expensive medium for speaking out, even at a time when corporate money had not yet bought up the store. Vidal assumed he would spend $30,000 of his own money on the primary. If he won, he expected to spend another million in November running against the Republican nominee. He had always had a political itch, but he hadn't scratched it since his congressional race in New York in 1960. Maybe he just needed to scratch it one last time.

The primary campaign lasted only ninety days. Vidal gave speeches up and down the state, in colleges and town halls, usually variations on the 1980 "State of the Union Revisited" essay he had written for *Esquire*. Planks in his platform included the reduction of the military, the legalization of drugs, the decriminalization of sex, the abolishment of the CIA, and the taxing of churches. There's a very entertaining documentary about the campaign, *Gore Vidal, the Man Who Said No*, that captures how exciting Vidal was as a speaker, and how drab other politicians were in comparison, especially his opponent, Governor Jerry Brown. Vidal offered to contribute $20,000 to the charity of Brown's choice if he would debate Vidal; Brown refused to rise to the bait. The only time they shared a stage was at a luncheon for journalists. Vidal warned Brown—in dulcet, pussycat tones—that he was growing stale; he needed a vacation from politics: "Take time off. Think about things. Maybe read a book."

Homosexuality was more visible and discussable in 1982 than it had been in 1960, yet nobody brought up Vidal's sex life—except for Armistead Maupin. He interviewed Vidal for *California* magazine and asked about Howard Austen. Vidal said it was a private matter and that they were simply "old friends.... He's lived various places, I've lived various places. We travel together, we travel separately."

When the primary was held on June 4, Vidal lost badly, getting only a third as many votes as Brown. But only party loyalists vote in primaries, and they tend to be loyal to conventional politicians. In November, Brown lost to the Republican candidate, Pete Wilson. After all, it was the age of Reagan. But by then Vidal had found another way to express himself politically: he was writing a novel about Abraham Lincoln.

That same year, 1982, Edmund White published his next novel, *A Boy's Own Story*. He had been working on it steadily since finishing *States of Desire*. The opening chapter had run as a cover story, "First Love," in *Christopher Street* in 1980. Fresh chapters were read aloud by White to the Violet Quill during the year they met. Gay readers knew the book was coming and eagerly awaited it.

With its ironically old-fashioned title, *A Boy's Own Story* is a first-person autobiographical novel that follows a gay boy from childhood into adolescence. It looks at first like a classic coming-of-age/coming-out tale—yet in a perverse, original twist, White's unnamed narrator *doesn't* come out. The novel ends in a dark, unfinished place.

The book isn't constructed as a continuous narrative, but offers scenes from a life out of chronological order, as if the life were broken. In the famous first chapter, the unnamed narrator is fifteen and meets a tough little twelve-year-old, Kevin, whose family is visiting the narrator's family. Each night the two boys take turns "cornholing" each other, but during the day they barely speak. The narrator thinks he's in love.

The second chapter steps back in time: the narrator is fourteen and has a summer job working for his father, which enables him to buy a hustler. The third chapter steps back further and we learn about the boy's life before and after his parents' divorce when he was seven.

The novel doesn't become dramatic until the halfway point, when the narrator starts high school and wins the friendship of the class jock, Tommy, and falls in love with him. The two boys have sleepovers where they sprawl on twin beds in their underpants and talk about Sartre and God and girls. We can't be sure where we are in time until the narrator reports that the following summer was the summer he hired his hustler, a blond like Tommy. When he returns to school, he and Tommy have a double date and the narrator decides he's in love with the girl. When she gently rebuffs him, the narrator decides he really is homosexual and must cure himself. He tries Buddhism, but it doesn't work. He decides he must escape his mother and sister and provide himself with male role models. He asks his parents to send him to an all-male prep school.

The broken chronology adds to the somnambulistic feeling of the book, a tale told by a sleepwalker—which is perfect for the story of any adolescent, gay or straight. The narrator is deliberately vague about time and place. Cities are left unnamed and dates obscure. White is still working with one foot in experimental narrative.

The real star of the book is its prose. *States of Desire* loosened White's style and enabled him to be both more direct and leisurely. The dense poetry of *Nocturnes* is leavened with mundane reality and essaylike observations. Here's his portrait of his gruff, antisocial, cigar-smoking, Brahms-loving father:

> I mention the constant music because, to my mind at least, it served as an invisible link between my father and me. He never discussed music beyond saying that the *German Requiem* was "damn nice" or that the violin and cello concerto was "one hell of a piece," and even these judgments he made with a trace of embarrassment; for him, music was emotion, and he did not believe in discussing feelings.

White celebrates sex with Kevin in this memorable passage:

> I didn't particularly like getting cornholed, but I was peaceful and happy because we loved each other. People say young love or love

of the moment isn't real, but I think the only love is the first. Later we hear its fleeting recapitulations throughout our lives, brief echoes of the original theme in a work that increasingly becomes all development, the mechanical elaboration of a crab canon with too many parts.

Many will ask if a few nights of sex between two boys who rarely talk during the day can really be called love. But for many gay men the first experience of good sex is so electric that it magnetizes the body and soul forever. When we catch up to the spot in the narrative, however, where this prelude of love takes place, the summer after the narrator's first semester at prep school, it's only mentioned briefly and then passed over, as if sealed in a separate dream.

The sixth and last chapter is the strongest in the novel. The narrator attends prep school, sees a psychiatrist (the vividly awful Dr. O'Reilly) and goes with friends to a brothel. Nothing helps him overcome his homosexuality.

By day I gave myself over to a covert yearning for men. I'd linger in the locker room and study the brawny back of a senior, a body builder, a German with blond hair greased into symmetrical waves, with a faint dusting of brown hair on his shoulders and (he's turning around, he drops his towel) with an almost pinkish red puff of seemingly rootless pubic hair somehow floating in a cloud around his penis, as though the big gun had just been fired.

He evokes a whole catalog of naked schoolmates, a sensuous portrait of the world seen from the closet:

Just as each shell held to the ear roars with a different ocean timbre, each of these bodies spoke to me with a different music, although all sounded to me unlike my own and only with the greatest effort could I remember I was longing after my own sex. Indeed, each of these beings seemed to possess his very own sex.

The boy obsesses over a French gym teacher. He babysits for a Latin teacher and his wife and becomes intimate with their unhappy marriage. They take him to bed, but only to watch while *they* make love. Then a jazz musician comes to the school to teach part-time, Mr. Beattie, a hipster out of Baldwin's *Another Country.* The fifteen-year-old narrator recognizes a man who enjoys sex with men. He sets up an assignation with Beattie, then goes to the headmaster to report that Beattie distributes marijuana to students. He meets with Beattie and goes down on him, happily knowing he will soon be fired.

> Sometimes I think I seduced and betrayed Mr. Beattie because neither one action nor the other alone but the complete cycle allowed me to have sex with a man and then to disown him and it; this sequence was my ideal formulation to love a man and not be a homosexual. Sometimes I think I liked bringing pleasure to a heterosexual man (for after all I'd dreamed of being my father's lover) at the same time I was able to punish him for not loving me.... Tommy had not loved me. My dad had not loved me.

A Boy's Own Story is a disturbing, tricky novel. In contrast to the sunny, more open world of *States of Desire*, the world of *Boy's Own Story* is dark and claustrophobic. Shut off from his real feelings by his fear, the young protagonist is forever trying out different emotions, unsure what's appropriate. The novelist does something similar years later, trying out different explanations. In the name of realism, White often leaves matters unfinished or uncertain. He has since made clear how autobiographical the book really is. The novelist is trying to make sense of episodes from his own life.

White presents his young self as a monster child who thought that love is power and the ultimate power is betrayal. It's a strong, brutal idea. It makes a powerful condemnation of closet life. And yet I find myself resisting the idea, in part because the story is told in chilly, essaylike fragments rather than as a fully involving drama. And also because the idea feels too strong, too brutal, too neat. I wonder if White isn't being too harsh on his younger self and something else was happening there. He isn't the first and he won't be the last gay writer who needs to think of himself as a villain.

The book received rave reviews from the gay and straight press alike when it appeared in September 1980. The feminist scholar Catharine R. Stimpson praised it in the *New York Times Book Review*, saying "White has crossed *Catcher in the Rye* with *De Profundis*, J. D. Salinger with Oscar Wilde to create an extraordinary novel. It is a clear and sinister pool in which goldfish and piranhas both swim.... The subject of *A Boy's Own Story* is less a particular boy than the bodies and souls of American men: the teachers and masters; the lovers, brothers, hustlers and friends; the flawed fathers who would be kings to the sons who should be princes." Christopher Lehmann-Haupt reviewed the book in the daily *Times* three months after it was published, but made up for tardiness by calling it "superior fiction.... It is any boy's story, to the degree that it evokes the inchoate longing of childhood and late adolescence.... For all I know it may be any girl's story as well." The *Washington Post* said American literature "is larger by one classic novel."

The mainstream had finally accepted a gay novel as a real work of literature. The high quality of White's prose certainly helped. And the sorrow of the story didn't hurt. But I also believe that culture had changed and critics were finally ready to treat gay fiction as the equal of straight fiction. This difficult yet beautiful book happened to come along at the right time.

A Boy's Own Story sold well, not only because of the reviews but because of its classy cover with a hand-tinted photo of a handsome boy on a beach. (Later there were complications: the boy was underage and the family had not given the photographer permission; there was talk of a lawsuit. The publisher put the photo of a professional model on future editions.)

Boy's sold a healthy 30,000 in cloth but sold even better in trade paperback. Trade paper opened up a whole new world for gay fiction. Avon Books had had some success with gay titles in mass market paperback, beginning with sexy potboilers like *The Lord Won't Mind* and *One for the Gods* by Gordon Merrick. They tried other gay books, ranging from murder mysteries to reissues of Christopher Isherwood, but the profit margin on mass market was so slim that they could make money only with big sellers. Dutton, on the other hand, found that trade paperbacks with their higher list price could turn a profit with lower sales figures. *Boy's Own Story* was so successful in trade paper that Dutton decided to do more gay books—all in trade in their Plume line, all with hand-tinted photos on the covers. Dutton, the home of Winnie the Pooh, would find a second identity as a home for gay fiction.

A Rick Fiala cartoon in *Christopher Street* at this time showed a gay bar with three or four men sitting at the counter, all busily writing or typing. Another man complains, "This used to be a fun place before everyone started writing a gay novel."

People worried that there were only so many gay plotlines, and authors would soon run out of stories. But then a virus appeared that gave both writers and readers a terrible new subject.

IV
The Eighties

15. Illness and Metaphor

The virus had been present for several years before it began to sicken and kill. Even then it only slowly came into focus. It was some time before it had a name. And in a cruel moral twist, it was spread sexually, which meant it could be interpreted as punishment for sex.

Sex was the most visible and exciting thing about gay life in the 1970s. Homosexuality was no longer about lies and guilt, secrets and suicide, but about fun and games, freedom and joy. Gay men had been having sex with strangers—many strangers—long before Stonewall. As the lives of these writers should make clear, gay liberation did not create gay promiscuity. There was sex before there were marches, politics, or books—it was the best reason for being homosexual, it and love. After the Sixties, however, the numbers of participants increased wildly. Bars, baths, and clubs opened in every major city. Anyone could be sexually active. You didn't need to be brave or beautiful or bohemian. You didn't need to be political or even to come out. The sexual liberation of everybody at the end of the 1960s set the scene for the gay sexual freedom of the 1970s.

Any sexually communicable disease introduced into this highly conductive circuit board was going to spread rapidly. It was analogous to the spread of bubonic plague by overland trade at the end of the Middle Ages or the spread of cholera by steamships in the nineteenth century: new avenues of communication opened new doors of infection. The old sexual diseases—gonorrhea, syphilis, herpes, and hepatitis—exploded in frequency, but it was believed they could be contained. Penicillin was as liberating for gay sex as the pill had been for straight sex—every city had a free clinic. But nobody had ever seen anything like this new disease.

The bad news first appeared as rumors among New York gay men in 1981 about a virulent strain of pneumonia. Lawrence Mass, a doctor and writer, investigated the story for the *New York Native*, a new gay newspaper that was a spin-off of *Christopher Street*. Chuck Ortleb had created the newspaper chiefly to generate revenue to support his magazine. Mass spoke to one doctor and several public health officials and cautiously reported in the *Native* in May 1981, "Disease Rumors Largely Unfounded."

Two months later, however, the *Morbidity and Mortality Weekly Report* of the Centers for Disease Control published startling figures on a different disease: Kaposi's sarcoma, a skin cancer that afflicted only the elderly and was rarely fatal, had been found in otherwise healthy gay men. The *New York Times* ran a brief piece in its inside pages on July 3, 1981: "Rare Cancer Seen in 41 Homosexual Men." Mass went back to the doctors and investigated further and wrote a more troubling article that appeared on the front page of the *Native* at the end of July: "Cancer in the Gay Community." A few days later he received an urgent phone call from novelist Larry Kramer. Kramer wanted to hear more about this "cancer."

The author of *Faggots* had been relatively silent since 1978. Kramer lived in Manhattan, in a large third-floor apartment in a high-rise building at the foot of Fifth Avenue; his balcony faced the Washington Square Arch. Money earned in movie work had been smartly invested by his brother, Arthur, and he was financially comfortable. Andrew Holleran remembers his apartment being full of books, "like a bookstore"; Kramer couldn't go for a walk without buying more. He seems to have been too restless to read carefully or deeply, however, judging by his later comments on other people's work. He was writing a new novel himself—about a Jewish widow in Palm Beach—but it wasn't going well. He was seeing his eleventh psychiatrist. (He was as familiar with shrinks as Edmund White.) And he continued to go to the baths regularly, despite his criticism of that life. He initiated a few romances, but they didn't take. Someone who had a brief affair with him at this time told acquaintances that the sex was great but they couldn't talk afterward without getting into an argument.

Kramer was disturbed when a couple of friends were struck by a mysterious illness. That was why the articles in the *Times* and *Native* got his attention and why he called Mass. Mass put him in touch with Dr. Alvin Friedman-Kien, who was working with the gay cases of Kaposi's sarcoma. Kramer invited Friedman-Kien to speak at his apartment on August 11, 1981, to a gathering of eighty men. Friedman-Kien told the crowded room what the doctors knew and what they feared. A few weeks later, on Labor Day weekend, Kramer and friends went out to Fire Island to distribute copies of Mass's *Native* article and to raise money.

Right from the start, it was feared that the new disease was connected to sex. The first diagnosed cases were all gay men with histories of high sexual activity. Nobody was sure how a cancer could be spread sexually—early hypotheses included poppers and fisting. Fears of illness were naturally tangled with guilt about sex. "After sex, all animals are sad," said the ancients, and sadness often leads to guilt, even in a sexual revolution.

Kramer's first piece in the *New York Native*, "A Personal Appeal," appeared in September 1981. It was short and carefully worded, unlike what he wrote later. The closest he came to blaming the disease on sex were two sentences: "The men who have been stricken don't appear to have done anything that many New York gay men haven't done at one time or another.... It's easy to become frightened that one of the many things we've done or taken over the past years may be all it takes for a cancer to grow from a tiny something-or-other that got in there who knows when from doing who knows what."

The following month, playwright Robert Chesley responded with a letter in the *Native*. Chesley was the thirty-seven-year-old author of *Stray Dog Story*, a play about a dog magically turned into a gay man who is then used and abused by other gay men. Chesley, too, was critical of gay life. He had been friends with Kramer and had even been to bed with him. He began his letter by saying he would contribute money to Kramer's fund. But he went on to warn, "I think the concealed meaning in Kramer's emotionalism is the triumph of guilt: that gay men *deserve* to die for their promiscuity.... Read anything by Larry Kramer closely, I think you'll find the subtext is always: the wages of gay sin are death.... I am not downplaying the seriousness of Kaposi's sarcoma. But something else is happening here, which is serious: gay homophobia and anti-eroticism."

There is nothing in Kramer's original statement to justify this attack. Chesley was reacting to things left unsaid in the article, or to things said by Kramer only in conversation. Yet Chesley's words must have hit a nerve or Kramer would've ignored them.

Kramer responded two months later (after speaking to his psychiatrist), in a long, bitter, rambling letter in the *Native*. He gave his history with the "gay cancer," describing the sickness of friends and his initial efforts at fund-raising. He went on at great length defending *Faggots*, as if that were his real injury, quoting from six different good reviews in the British and French press. Then he let loose at every target imaginable: the National Cancer Institute, the inept organizers of the annual gay march, the silence of the *New York Times*, the impurity of poppers, the awfulness of Mayor Ed Koch (he seemed to hate Koch even before Koch did anything wrong), and "the 'eroticism' that has made gay health such a concern in New York that every gay doctor in this city is, as Dr. Mass puts it, 'exhausted.'" Kramer had found the manic, high-octane, punching-in-all-directions voice he would use for all his polemical prose.

Imaginative writers often project their own monsters and meanings on basic facts. We cannot pretend that Kramer (or Chesley) was an objective observer here. In terms of what was known about the illness at the time, Kramer *was* overreacting. Yet he turned out to be right. His sexual anxiety enabled him to see things that others were not yet ready to recognize, just as a color-blind person can see patterns not immediately visible to the color sighted. And his injured pride and loose-cannon temper enabled him to say what others were slow to express. His anger was partly a rhetorical device, but one that put him in touch with real anger; his real anger did not always select its targets well.

Robert Chesley went on to write the first major play produced about AIDS, *Night Sweat*, in 1984. He followed it with an even more powerful AIDS play, *Jerker*, in 1986. He died of AIDS in 1990.

Shortly after Kramer's counterattack in the *Native*, he held another meeting in his living room off Washington Square, on January 4, 1982. Joining him were Dr. Mass, writer/editor Nathan Fain, publisher Paul Popham, investor Paul Rappaport, and novelist Edmund White. Kramer wanted to form an organization to fight the amorphous illness. When Rappaport said, "Gay men certainly have a health crisis," Kramer cried out, "That's our name!" The group was called Gay Men's Health Crisis, soon known as GMHC. The six founders immediately set about fund-raising, recruiting members, and arguing with each other.

The name of the disease was changing as its identity changed. The Centers for Disease Control first called it GRID (gay-related immune deficiency). Then, in the summer of 1982, it became known as Acquired Immune Deficiency Syndrome, soon shortened to AIDS. It was the failure of immunity that made bodies vulnerable to strange diseases like Kaposi's sarcoma, which produced purplish lesions on the skin, and *Pneumocystis carinii* pneumonia, which did not respond to the usual antibiotics. These were the chief markers and killers at the time; other opportunistic diseases followed. The cause was identified as a virus in 1984, but not until the French and American discoveries were reconciled in 1986 did it become known as HIV (human immunodeficiency virus). The first AIDS antibody test was not available until 1985. Complicating matters further, the virus could have an incubation period of three years or more. Nobody could be sure when they had been infected or if they would become sick.

Early in 1983, it was learned AIDS could be transmitted by blood transfusion. Only when doctors found the disease could affect heterosexuals did mainstream media begin to cover the story.

The number of cases was still remarkably low, especially when one considers how high they would rise in the years to come. The first volunteers at GMHC worked mostly out of imagination and fear. Feared possibility can be more slippery and exhausting than factual reality. Individuals often burned out. Mass left first, worn down by trying to mix activism with his journalism and medical practice. He continued to go to the baths, however, where he met his life partner, Arnie Kantrowitz (one of the zappers at *Harper's* in 1970). Edmund White moved to Paris in 1983 after he won a Guggenheim Fellowship. "I wanted to go on having industrial quantities of sex," he later claimed, "and I thought I could go on in Paris. New York was turning into a morgue." We shouldn't take him entirely at his word. White often attacked himself before other people could, making his own preemptive self-condemnations. Yet in France, philosopher Michel Foucault dismissed the disease as a puritanical illness imagined by antisex Christians; it couldn't possibly be real. Foucault would die of AIDS in 1984.

Kramer's next article in the *Native*, "1,112 and Counting," appeared on March 14, 1983, on the front page. It's probably his most famous single piece of journalism.

He begins with cold facts. There were now over a thousand reported cases of AIDS and 418 deaths. He talks about the kinds of gay men who get AIDS: "There are drug users and non-drug users. There are the truly promiscuous and the almost monogamous. There are reported cases of single-contact infection. All it seems to take is one wrong fuck. That's not promiscuity—that's bad luck." He talks about the hospitals, the forms of treatment, and the poor response by the federal government's National Institutes of Health. All very strong and clear. He then lurches into two pages attacking Mayor Koch for his silence, not only in the city but for failing to confront President Reagan and demanding a stronger response from the federal government. He did not call the baldheaded, nasal-voiced, three-term bachelor mayor a closeted homosexual—not yet, anyway. But Kramer believed that was the real reason for Koch's silence: he was a closet case who didn't want to be identified with homosexuals. (The closet for Kramer was the sin of sins. But as others pointed out, many undeniably straight public figures were as aloof and silent about AIDS as Koch.) Kramer then lambastes a long list of enemies, ranging from closeted gay doctors, to the *New York Times*, to the gay press that (with the exception of the *Native*) said little about the epidemic, to gay men who can't bear the idea of giving up sex until it's learned what spreads the illness. He concludes with a call for protests and asks for volunteers for future civil disobedience.

GMHC had insisted Kramer include a disclaimer that he was speaking only for himself and not for GMHC. He did. Yet his attack on Koch would be the catalyst for his break with the organization.

Two weeks later, on Sunday, April 10, Kramer and twenty protesters with placards stood outside Lenox Hill Hospital in the rain during an AIDS conference attended by Koch. The protest made the evening news. The next day Koch agreed to meet with representatives from the gay community, including two from GMHC. Kramer assumed he'd be one, especially since his protest had helped bring about the meeting. The board said no. They knew how much he despised Koch and feared he'd lose his temper. Director Paul Popham would attend with the young executive director. Another AIDS group, the AIDS Network, said Kramer could go as their representative, but Kramer said no. He must go as part of GMHC or he would quit the organization he had founded. Popham refused to back down. So Kramer quit. He was like a jilted lover who feels he can best prove his love by shooting himself in the foot.

The gay groups had their meeting with Koch, nobody lost his or her temper, and GMHC made connections that helped them to become the most important AIDS organization in the country.

Feeling betrayed and angry, Kramer kept away from the group and resumed work on his novel. But it was no good. He couldn't write. He realized he'd lost his platform by quitting GMHC, and he asked to be reinstated on the board. They refused to take him back. They had found that work was easier and less stressful without him. At a GMHC dance, Kramer entered the DJ booth, took over a microphone and pleaded with the volunteers to make the board let him back in. Again, nothing. That June he spoke at the gay pride rally in Central Park. He denounced the *Times*, President Reagan, and Mayor Koch, but he also tried to make peace with GMHC.

> I want to apologize to any of the people dear to me whose feelings I may have bruised these past two years. I have been very much an angry man. It seems that in my frustration at seeing AIDS ignored so long I just couldn't shut up.... I am by nature an impatient man.

He left for England that very night, determined to put it all behind him.

He hoped to visit old friends in London and have a good time. He went to the theater and saw several plays, including *Map of the World* by David Hare. Hare's drama about infighting among U.N. bureaucrats battling poverty could not help but make Kramer think of his own experience. He decided to write a play himself in an attempt to understand what he'd been through. Before he returned to the U.S., he went to Germany and visited Dachau outside Munich. He was struck by parallels between the Holocaust and the AIDS epidemic, two huge crimes that were initially ignored by the world. The echoes gave his new project a larger purpose.

He rented a place on Cape Cod and wrote the first draft of a long, autobiographical play that was not just about GMHC but about his entire life, with flashbacks to his parents and his brother. He finished the first draft at the end of August and began a second draft. He found his title in W. H. Auden's poem, "September 1, 1939," from a different stanza than the stanza that includes the famous line, "We must love one another or die," one where Auden declares that "the normal heart" wants what it cannot have, "to be loved alone."

Kramer began to send the play around. People were respectful but not interested. Some confessed they were afraid of the subject. Also, the play was incredibly long at this point, over seven hours. He wanted it read by Joe Papp at the Public Theater, the downtown arts theater housed in the old Astor Library off Cooper Square; he sent it to Papp through a GMHC volunteer, Emmett Foster, who was Papp's administrative assistant. When Kramer didn't hear back, he wrote a furious letter for Foster to give to Papp.

Foster remembered it saying in effect, "Your own son is gay and you don't want to do this play because you're homophobic." Foster told Kramer that if Papp saw the letter he would never touch his play. Kramer backed off.

The play was eventually read by Papp's wife, Gail Merrifield, head of the Public's development office. She received a seven-pound manuscript, more like a novel than a play. She later described reading it as "tough sledding." It felt like two different plays, one a family drama about two brothers, the other a political play about AIDS. "Characters spouted pages of medical facts that were unactable. It had no shape. When I finished it, however, I was moved." She met with Kramer and told him what she thought. To her surprise, he immediately began to take notes; he was willing to rewrite the play.

He visited Merrifield's office repeatedly over the next eight months, discussing the story and using her questions to find its heart. He cut back heavily on the family; he reduced the medical details. When Merrifield decided the script was good enough to show her husband, she still had to force him to read it. Papp didn't like plays about any kind of illness. He put it down after twenty pages, saying it was much too overblown. But he resumed reading. "Finally I get through the whole thing and say, 'This is one of the worst things I've ever read'—and I'm crying. I was crying!" He agreed to produce the play but said it needed more work. He teamed Kramer with the Public's literary manager, Bill Hart, and rewriting continued. The play went through another ten drafts. Kramer ignored most of Hart's suggestions, but pushing and prodding from Hart got him to produce the most memorable scene in the play, when the protagonist, Ned Weeks, loses his temper with his sick lover and hurls groceries and milk against the floor.

Michael Lindsey-Hogg was brought in to direct, and he worked with Kramer on further cutting and sharpening. This is one of those cases where many cooks actually *improved* the broth. Theater is always collaborative, but input from other minds helped Kramer strip away the fat and find the bones of his story—the bones are always his real strength. *The Normal Heart* is infinitely superior as a play to what *Faggots* was as a novel.

Throughout the process Kramer remained unpredictable. Often warm and generous, he could also be mean and childish. The casting director found him condescending and distrustful. The production designer barred him from his office after Kramer called a pair of costume shoes ugly and threw them out a third-story window. But his only serious quarrel with Papp was over the attacks in the play on Mayor Koch. The city was the Public Theater's landlord, and Papp did not want to alienate the mayor. Nevertheless, he gave in to Kramer and let his protagonist repeatedly badmouth Koch.

The part of Ned Weeks was cast with Brad Davis, an intense, handsome actor who had starred in the movie *Midnight Express*. He was Lindsey-Hogg's idea, not Kramer's. Kramer thought he was too young. But Kramer knew it wouldn't hurt to have himself played by a movie star.

It's fascinating to reread the play now knowing the actual history it covers. Kramer drew a clear, coherent, fictional story out of a mess of facts, but remained true to the spirit of the facts. A handful of doctors, mostly male, are combined into one female doctor, Emma Brookner, the only woman in the cast. But Ned Weeks isn't just based on Kramer—he *is* Kramer, without being overly idealized. All criticisms one could make about the author are made in the play about Ned, from being a megalomaniac to hating sex to the idea that he became political only because he found writing too hard.

The dialogue is sharp and quick; scenes are well-chosen and well-paced. Ned is present in Dr. Brookner's office when cases of the mysterious illness first appear. He and his friends quickly organize to get the word out. When Ned visits the *Times* to get them to cover the story, he meets Felix, a fashion writer who will become his lover. Everything moves rapidly. There is no waste. Dr. Brookner is given most of the balder, clunkier lines, but they hurry the story along.

A major achievement in the play is its full-scale portrait of life at the unnamed, GMHC-like organization. Office politics is difficult to dramatize without becoming boring, but the battles here are involving and revealing. At one time or another Kramer shows sympathy for *all* the participants. These men are overworked and exhausted, worn out by their campaigning and organizing and by looking after sick friends and lovers. Accusations from Kramer's articles appear almost verbatim in the play, but he lets the other side answer. One of the most powerful scenes is when Mickey Marcus, a health officer loosely based on Lawrence Mass, returns exhausted from a truncated trip to Rio and flips out when Ned blames the epidemic on sex yet again.

Mickey: (to Ned) And you think I'm killing people?

Ned: Mickey, that's not what I—

Mickey: Yes, you do! You know you do! I've spent fifteen years of my life fighting for our right to be free and make love whenever, wherever…And you're telling me that all those years of what being gay stood for is wrong…and I'm a murderer. We have been so oppressed! Don't you remember how it was? Can't you see how important it is for us to love openly, without hiding and without guilt? We were a bunch of funny-looking fellows who grew up in sheer misery and one day we fell into the orgy rooms and we thought we'd found heaven. And we would teach the world how wonderful heaven can be. We would lead the way. We would be good for something new. Can't you see that?

The Normal Heart is, in part, a documentary play, akin to 1930s social dramas like Waiting for Lefty by Clifford Odets or the Federal Theatre Project's Living Newspapers. The latter was actually evoked at the Public Theater by covering the whitewashed walls with facts and figures from the epidemic—the theater itself became a scrambled newspaper. Despite the documentary foundation, however, there were two major fictional changes, one large but justified, the other a bit stickier.

The justified change was giving Ned a lover, Felix. The two men's relationship is a major engine of the play, a sweet subplot in Act One that builds to the powerful moment when Felix shows Ned the purple lesion on his foot. Felix's illness and death are the heart of Act Two. Not even such awkward touches as a deathbed wedding or the dying Felix telling Ned, "Don't lose that anger," can spoil the emotional power of this love story. With so much of the play based on reality, many people needed to believe Felix was real, too. Kramer became prickly when asked about Felix's identity. He insisted Felix had existed but that he didn't want to talk about him. Maybe there was a Felix, but, as one friend observes, it's out of character for Kramer not to talk about something. More striking, the play isn't dedicated to the memory of a lost love, but to Norman J. Levy, Kramer's psychiatrist. This does not take anything away from the play. Felix is an inspired invention. He humanizes Ned and makes the play more accessible and involving. And why shouldn't a writer imagine for himself the boyfriend he has not yet found?

The sticky change is smaller yet connects to bigger issues. In Ned's ouster from the board, he doesn't quit as Kramer did, but is abruptly voted out for being antisex. It simplifies a very tangled story, but it's not only untrue, it also reduces Ned to a righteous victim. Ned responds with Kramer's own preachy words: "The only way we'll have real pride is when we demand recognition of a culture that isn't just sexual....Being defined by our cocks is literally killing us. Must we all be reduced to becoming our own murderers?" Then he abruptly backtracks and pleads, "Bruce, I know I'm an asshole. But please, I beg you, don't shut me out."

People often talk about *The Normal Heart* as if it weren't art but raw news. Yet by using himself as the central character, Kramer created a tragic hero of sorts, one whose tragic flaw is that he *is* an asshole. The man who is tough and difficult and crazy enough to bring the world a terrible truth is too tough and difficult and crazy to organize the proper response to it. *The Normal Heart* is frequently compared to Henrik Ibsen's *The Enemy of the People*, and for good reason. Not only is there much talk about the baths in the two plays (in Ibsen the waters of a spa are infected), but both offer challenging portraits of the asshole as hero. We're happier when the assholes are villains. But Ibsen's Dr. Stockman is an arrogant, unlikable, unpopular man who happens to be right. Ned Weeks is a righteous, irritable, short-tempered man who also happens to be right. Yet the real Kramer was more of an asshole, and more interesting, than Ned. He was a highly emotional man with a gift for shooting himself in the foot. Those exasperating, human qualities are present in the play if you look, but they're softened by rewriting his break with GMHC. Kramer would fix that when he adapted the play for film, making his fictional self more difficult and more interesting when he produced multiple drafts of a screenplay for a movie that Barbra Streisand promised to make.

The play opened at the Public Theater on April 21, 1985, to reviews that weren't just mixed but complicated. Critics were reviewing not only a play but a minority group in an epidemic. Respect and unease were mixed with literary judgments. Frank Rich in the *New York Times* began with praise: "The blood that's coursing through *The Normal Heart*, the new play by Larry Kramer at the Public Theater, is boiling hot." Then the criticisms started—"Although Mr. Kramer's theatrical talents are not always as highly developed as his conscience"—and increased, with complaints about petty politics, a shrill protagonist, and "galloping egocentricity," until Rich concluded, "One wishes the play's outrage had been channeled into drama as fully compelling as its cause." Michael Feingold, who was gay himself, *began* with criticism in his review in the *Village Voice*, but closed with praise: "The aesthetic failings of Larry Kramer's *The Normal Heart*—as plentiful as bacteria in a human mouth—are balanced by the truth of what Kramer has to say: historically, politically, epidemiologically."

One of the better reviews came from, of all people, John Simon in *New York* magazine. The tall, haughty, womanizing Simon was notorious that spring for hating homosexuals. He had been overheard loudly declaring in a lobby after a bad production of *Anatol* by Arthur Schnitzler, "Don't you sometimes wish that all the faggots in the theater...would get AIDS and die and we'd be rid of them, and we could go on from there." The following week he wrote in a review that a show about middle-aged women was "faggot nonsense." His gay friend, composer Ned Rorem, took him to see *The Normal Heart* as preparation for an interview in the *New York Native*. Simon cried at the end of the Kramer play, but in the interview he was unapologetic about his earlier remarks. His good review of Kramer may have been an act of penance, but he was not a penitent man. He wrote, "What could have been a mere staged tract—and, in its lesser moments, is just that—transcends often enough into a fleshed-out, generously dramatized struggle, in which warring ideologies do not fail to breathe, sweat, weep, bleed—be human."

Reviewers and audiences were more comfortable with another AIDS play which opened only a week before Kramer's, *As Is* by William Hoffman. The *Times* review of *Normal Heart* ran with a note from the editor defending the newspaper against Kramer's charges, and a sly quote from a spokesman for Mayor Koch saying the mayor hadn't seen the play and he couldn't comment on its attacks on him, but he hoped it was as good as *As Is*. The Hoffman play *is* better written and better crafted, telling the simpler story of a gay man looking after an ex-lover who becomes sick and dies. It offers snapshots of life in the epidemic: gentle, human glimpses. Nevertheless, *it* is the play that has become dated, that now looks like old news. *The Normal Heart*, with its bureaucratic quarrels and impossible hero, has a story that stays relevant and involving.

It ran for over a year at the Public, longer than any other production there, with Papp's strong support. It would be performed all over the country during the next years, a message show like a new incarnation of the Living Newspaper, but a powerful drama in its own right.

GMHC continued to grow, becoming an important and necessary service organization. As the numbers of sick increased, it provided help and care that federal and local governments didn't. Kramer remained barred from the board, but he became the lover of the next executive director, Rodger McFarlane. This might explain his praise of GMHC at the time for its counseling and home support services. Then he broke up with McFarlane and the attacks resumed. He criticized GMHC for being nothing but caregivers, for not being political, for not providing experimental drugs, for not condemning sex, then for promoting safe sex, then for not knowing how to promote itself. He is often compared to a Jewish mother, always complaining, never satisfied, but Catholic and Protestant mothers (and fathers) can be just as bad. "You and your huge assortment of caretakers perform miraculous feats helping the dying to die," Kramer jeered. Yet there are times when the world sorely needs caretakers. GMHC accomplished much that needed to be done.

Kramer believed in the politics of anger. And he was good at anger, both real anger and playacted anger. However, anger can get you started, but it can accomplish only so much by itself before entropy sets in and you run out of gas or, worse, you self-destruct. Which can be a private disaster for an artist, but would be a public catastrophe in a political leader. Luckily Kramer wasn't a leader with obligations but an artist, a free agent. He could drop out whenever he wanted, and he did.

16. Dead Poets Society

—〰—

Death is almost never timely, even for the old.

On February 24, 1983, alone in his room in the Hotel Elysée in New York, seventy-one-year-old Tennessee Williams died after choking on the cap of his eyedrop bottle. He often held the cap in his teeth while applying his eyedrops; he must have inhaled the cap with his head tilted back. Williams would have laughed in delight over such an absurd death—if it had happened to someone else. More than one obituary quoted Blanche's line from *Streetcar*: "You know what I shall die of? I shall die of eating an unwashed grape one day out on the ocean."

A year and a half later, in August 1984, while visiting his friend Joanne Carson in Palm Springs, Truman Capote died in his sleep from "a multiple drug intoxication" complicated by liver disease. He was fifty-nine. A year earlier Gore Vidal had dropped his libel suit after Capote wrote a public letter of apology. Asked to comment on his death, Vidal shrugged and cited what had been said about the death of Elvis Presley: it was "a good career move."

The deaths of Williams and Capote were oddly anticlimactic. They had both died as writers years ago and, in this sense, their deaths were almost posthumous. Williams had continued to write, yet his later plays are more manner than matter and never emotionally engaged. Capote had stopped writing altogether, but nobody knew that until his executors went through the desks and closets of his different homes, hunting for the rest of *Answered Prayers*. Nothing existed except the chapters published in *Esquire*.

The two men died just as the plague years began. The deaths of gay artists had not yet become commonplace.

"2,339 and Counting" was the title of Kramer's October 1983 article, published as an ad in the *Village Voice* when the *Voice* refused to run it as an article. (Kramer wanted to reach a larger audience than he was reaching with the *Native*.) The numbers had doubled since the last article six months earlier. Of the sick, 945 were dead. In addition to the gay men, there were IV drug users, hemophiliacs, and a few Haitians. A nasty joke of the time went: What's the hardest thing about being diagnosed with AIDS? Convincing your parents that you're Haitian.

Famous people began to die of AIDS, yet they didn't want the world to know what killed them. AIDS was like the dye on a biologist's tissue sample identifying who was homosexual. The obituaries in the *New York Times* were routinely vague or said simply "heart failure"—but the heart always stops when a person expires. When Roy Cohn, the fiercely anti-Communist, fiercely closeted lawyer became sick in 1986, he did everything he could to keep his diagnosis a secret. Liberace died of AIDS in 1987 after claiming he was wasting away because of a watermelon diet. But one famous figure chose to be honest. Movie star Rock Hudson was visibly ill when he appeared with his former costar Doris Day on a television talk show in July 1985. He said he had the flu. But after ten days of attention and speculation by the press (and a quote from Armistead Maupin in the *San Francisco Chronicle* saying, yes, Hudson was gay), the actor told his spokesperson to tell the public what he had and who he was. For most of straight America, Rock Hudson was the first actual person they knew with AIDS. He died that October.

How does one write about an epidemic that is so public yet experienced so privately, almost secretly? The first major work appeared in the most public literary art, the theater. There were timely plays by Robert Chesley, Victor Bumbalo (*Adam and the Experts*) and others as well as those by Kramer and William Hoffman. But this highly public art was soon joined by the most private art, poetry.

Poetry offers a more personal and immediate response to experience than any other literary form. It does not require the machinery of plot and character, but can directly address intensely felt moments. The great poets of the First World War, Wilfred Owen, Robert Graves, and Siegfried Sassoon, responded directly to the slaughterhouse of the trenches, writing about the war in the middle of the war, sometimes composing passages in the front lines. The cool, dry, bitter, matter-of-factness of *"Dulce et Decorum Est"* by Owen would find its counterpart in poems written by young Americans seventy years later. Take, for example, this passage:

> If you could hear, at every jolt, the blood
> Come gargling from the froth-corrupted lungs,
> Obscene as cancer, bitter as the cud
> Of vile, incurable sores on bitter tongues...

Only the old-fashioned cadence indicates to most readers that this man is dying from poison gas and not from *Pneumocystis carinii* pneumonia.

Men and women immediately began to write poems about their friends, their lovers, and themselves, what they saw, what they feared, what they lost. Some of the writers were already famous, others on their way to fame, others barely outlived their first books. The work was published in little magazines, chapbooks, handmade brochures, and hardcover anthologies. Some poems make one think of Randall Jarrell's description of bad poetry: "It is as if the writers had sent you their ripped-out arms and legs, with 'This is a poem' scrawled on them in lipstick." Yet the best work describes these raw experiences so precisely and clearly that any reader can come away with a better understanding of the world.

Some of the strongest poems were little more than sharply observed snapshots of feeling. They did what journalism is supposed to do but rarely does, making alien experiences accessible. Has anyone ever written a better description of what it's like to be sick with AIDS-related pneumonia than Melvin Dixon's poem, "Heartbeats"? It's a brutally simple poem, composed in double beats like a fist knocking at a door.

> No air. Breathe in.
> Breathe in. No air.
>
> Black out. White rooms.
> Head hot. Feet cold.
>
> No work. Eat right.
> CAT scan. Chin up.

Breathe in. Breathe out.
No air. No air.

Thin blood. Sore lungs.
Mouth dry. Mind gone.

Six months? Three weeks?
Can't eat. No air.

Today? Tonight?
It waits. For me.

Sweet heart. Don't stop.
Breathe in. Breathe out.

Dixon was a teacher, poet and novelist, author of *Trouble the Water*, a promising first novel about growing up gay and black. He died of AIDS in 1992 at the age of forty-two.

Other poets wrote poems about the fear of AIDS. There were also poems about sex in the shadow of death and poems about survivor's guilt. And there were elegies, many elegies.

James Merrill had finished *The Changing Light at Sandover*, his ambitious epic about life after death, in 1982, before the epidemic made itself fully felt. Yet the mammoth poem now took on new meaning for readers. As Edmund White said of the fictionalized Merrill character in his 1997 novel, *The Farewell Symphony*, "Now I understand why [he] had invented his dress-up party version of the afterlife.... It was a normal way of keeping the dead alive."

Merrill wrote a memorial tribute in prose for his scholarly friend, David Kalstone, who died in 1986, describing how he scattered his remains in Long Island Sound: "In the sunlit current the white gravel of our friend fanned out, revolving once as if part of a dance, and was gone." He followed with two elegies for Kalstone, including one that elaborates on the scattering of the ashes.

You are gone. You caught like a cold their airy
lust for essence. Now, in the furnace parched to

ten or twelve light handfuls, a mortal gravel
sifted through fingers...

In his cool, calm, quietly tender poems, Merrill never indicated that he himself had tested positive for the virus in 1986. He had his reasons for keeping it secret, including the fact his mother was still alive. (She was not happy when he talked frankly about being gay in his 1993 memoir, *A Different Person*.) The closest he came to making it public is a strangely intense, hallucinogenic poem, "Vol. XLIV, No. 3" where details under the microscope become electric fantasies.

Chains of gold tinsel, baubles of green fire
For the arterial branches—
Here at *Microcosmics Illustrated*, why,
Christmas goes on all year!

The poem then turns more serious.

Defenseless, the patrician cells await
Invasion by barbaric viruses,
Another sack of Rome.
A new age. Everything we dread.

When it was published, Merrill seemed to be talking only about the vague, generalized fear all gay men were feeling at the time, no matter what their health was.

His life with David Jackson had changed. They no longer shared their nights at the Ouija board; they were both seeing other men. They remained in touch, yet they didn't always live together in their different homes in Stonington, Key West, and Athens.

Some of the strongest poems about AIDS were written by Thom Gunn, the English poet who had met Christopher Isherwood back in 1954. Another Brit who decided he was happier living in America, he followed his American boyfriend, Mike Kitay, to San Francisco, settling first on Russian Hill, where he was neighbors with Armistead Maupin, then buying a house in the Haight-Ashbury, where he lived with Kitay and various mutual friends for the next thirty-three years.

Cambridge-educated like his peer Ted Hughes Gunn enjoyed being in the city of the Beat poets, but their poetics never rubbed off on him. His life could be as anarchic as theirs—he stopped teaching for a few years so he could experiment with LSD—yet he loved old-fashioned form and meter. "Later I realized what I was doing," he told an interviewer. "I was filtering the experiences of the infinite through the grid of the finite." A lean, handsome man who wore leather jackets like Marlon Brando in *The Wild One* and was photographed by Robert Mapplethorpe, he also edited scholarly editions of Elizabethan verse. His own work grew more matter-of-factly gay, the Auden-like "you" of beloveds becoming actual male bedmates, the urban landscapes including an occasional gay bar or drag queen. He lost his fans, who feared he was writing too much "hippy silliness and self-regarding camp." Then he wrote *The Man with Night Sweats*.

The book came out in 1992, but the poems were written between 1982 and 1988. The volume includes work that has nothing to do with AIDS, evocations of adolescence, flowers, and neighbors, but it was the AIDS poems, all in Part 4, that seized the attention of readers, gay and straight. They cover the whole gamut of the epidemic, addressing dying friends, personal fear, tainted desire, and grief. The title poem is about a man waking up from a fever dream covered in sweat, the night sweat that's a symptom of either AIDS or fear—or both. (Gunn himself was HIV negative.) Just the titles of other poems speak volumes: "In Time of Plague," "To a Dead Gym Owner," "To a Dead Graduate Student," "Terminal," "Death's Door." Yet it is not a depressing book. Gunn remains calm and clear-eyed throughout, and his people remain complex and human even in the midst of illness.

Look, for example, at "Lament," written about Gunn's friend Allan Noseworthy. In four pages of rhyming or half-rhyming couplets, we follow a man into a hospital and stay with him until he dies. The Auden-like "you" is no longer coy.

A gust of morphine hid you. Back in sight
You breathed through a segmented tube, fat, white,
Jammed down your throat so that you could not speak...

A man struggles to keep his identity, his wit and curiosity, even with a breathing tube filling his mouth.

The clinical details of hospital life block out easy Victorian sentimentality. There is no death of Little Nell in this book. These are lean, tough poems, with no emotional fat. There is no straining for meaning either, although larger meanings sometimes come through. In "The Missing," Gunn uses the loss of friends to talk about his circle and how friendship (and sex) opened into a larger community, "an unlimited embrace." Walt Whitman's "city of comrades" is updated to the 1980s and made more real and poignant by the fact that death is chipping away at it.

Critics who had grown lukewarm about Gunn rediscovered him and admired what he accomplished in *The Man with Night Sweats*. It really is an amazing book, each poem shining a fresh light on actual experience, the sum larger than the parts. As one straight critic wrote, "Gunn restores poetry to a centrality it has often seemed close to losing, by dealing in the context of a specific human catastrophe with the great themes of life and death, coherently, intelligently, memorably."

Meanwhile the novelist Andrew Holleran was writing prose poems like little elegies. *Dancer from the Dance* had been a kind of elegy for impossible love. He feared there was nothing more to say about gay life, which may have been true for him—his second novel, *Nights in Aruba*, feels like eloquent leftovers from *Dancer*. Now, however, there was real cause for elegy. Holleran explored loss in a remarkable series of essays written for a monthly column in *Christopher Street* magazine, "New York Notebook." He wrote his first column in 1983. A selection, *Ground Zero*, was published in 1988.

Each essay is beautifully written, constructed with recurring motifs and metaphors. They are learned and personal, mixing allusions to Proust and Greek mythology with medical facts and sexual grit. Holleran explored a broad range of topics: friendship, bathhouses, celibacy, porn theaters, George Santayana. His dazzling celebration of the comic playwright/actor Charles Ludlam, who died of AIDS in 1987, includes some of the best descriptions of camp drama ever written: "like a child running through the contents of his bedroom closet, putting on fake noses, mustaches, pulling out toy airplanes, little plastic gladiators, goldfish bowls, ray-guns, Cleopatra wigs, he always gave the impression of having assembled the particular play from a magic storeroom in which he kept, like some obsessed bag lady, every prop and character that two thousand years of Western history had washed up on the shores of a Long Island childhood." Then Holleran ends the piece with a blanket declaration: "Not only is Charles Ludlam gone, it seems, so is humor. One can no longer make jokes about death. One can no longer make jokes at all—the curtain is down."

AIDS crowded his mind and it brought down the curtain on everything. Even essays that aren't about AIDS become essays about AIDS. An appreciation of Henry James includes Holleran imagining that the gay men filling the hospitals had all listened to Lambert Strether's heartfelt speech from *The Ambassadors*, "Live, live all you can, it's a mistake not to!"—as if James had brought on the disease.

Holleran moved to Gainesville, Florida, partly to look after his aging parents but also to flee the epidemic. Many people in the 1980s thought AIDS was a New York/San Francisco disease and they could escape it. But once out of New York, Holleran's fears and accusations grew even darker and heavier:

> AIDS destroys trust.... AIDS is a form of pollution; in this case, polluted blood and semen. We've spoiled even that. AIDS is a form of terrorism—sex becomes Paris the summer the bombs went off. Nobody goes. Like Central Park—empty at night because everyone's afraid of muggers—homosexual life becomes a vast empty space from which everyone has withdrawn.

Holleran had always been melancholy, yet his chronic depression now served as a magnifying glass for the depression and fear that affected many gay men at this time. He was far from alone in feeling devastated, confused, and more than a little crazy.

But in addition to the elegies, a kind of counterelegy appeared, an appreciation of love and sex more tender than what had been written before the epidemic. A young poet, Mark Doty, would eventually write elegies, too, but his strongest early poems include warm, witty appreciations of the body written in defiance of the disease. Doty was born in 1953, grew up in Tennessee and Arizona, went to school in Iowa and Vermont, and spent most of his twenties married to a woman. They divorced, and he came out and moved to New York. His second collection, *Bethlehem in Broad Daylight*, includes a gorgeous tribute to a dirty movie house, "The Adonis Theater," and a sweetly tender poem, "63rd Street Y," where he compares the view of men from across the street to "a voyeur's advent calendar":

> And on the twelfth floor
>
> just the perfect feet and ankles
> of the boy in the red-flushed room
> are visible. I think he must be disappointed,
> stirring a little, alone, and then
> two other legs enter the rectangle of view,
>
> moving toward his and twining with them,
> one instep bending to stroke
> the other's calf. They make me happy,
> these four limbs in effortless conversation...

AIDS remains offstage for most of his poems, but is acknowledged now and then. In "Tiara" ("Peter died in a paper tiara/cut from a book of princess paper dolls"), Doty answers the mourners who say their promiscuous friend had "asked for it."

> Asked for it—
> when all he did was go down
>
> into the salt tide
> of wanting as much as he wanted,
> giving himself over so drunk
>
> or stoned it didn't matter who,
> though they were beautiful,
> stampeding him into the simple,
>
> ravishing music of their hurry.
> I think heaven is perfect stasis
> poised over realms of desire,

where dreaming and waking men lie
on the grass while wet horses
roam among them, huge fragments

of the music we die into
in the body's paradise.

It's a highly romantic celebration of sex, something that was badly needed at a time when so many people talked about promiscuity as a selfish, evil activity. Doty was not writing out of ignorance. His own partner, Wally Roberts, had recently tested positive for HIV.

The older writers didn't always understand what was happening. In an interview in *Playboy*, Gore Vidal said he thought people were overreacting to AIDS. After all, he had grown up with syphilis in the years before penicillin; he was used to sexual diseases. Allen Ginsberg startled the audience at OutWrite, the gay literary conference, when he confessed he didn't worry about AIDS since his sex life consisted chiefly of giving blowjobs to straight college boys.

But Christopher Isherwood understood. More accurately, he understood how little he knew. "I don't feel I know nearly enough about the AIDS situation," he told Armistead Maupin in 1985, when Maupin interviewed him and Don Bachardy for the *Village Voice*. "But these younger men who find they have it—some absolutely awful pressures begin to assert themselves. They're told by their relatives that it's a sort of punishment, that it's dreadful and it's God's will and all that sort of thing. And I think they have to be very tough with themselves and decide which side they're on." Then he added, "You know, fuck God's will. God's will must be circumvented, if that's what it is."

Maupin interviewed Isherwood and Bachardy as a couple and they talked mostly about their life together. They no longer fought about outside boyfriends but fought instead about Bachardy's driving—he was a terrible driver. They said they still slept tangled together in the same bed.

This was the last interview Isherwood would give. He had been diagnosed with prostate cancer, which he didn't tell Maupin. Approaching death himself, he firmly rejected the glib judgments that people often make about illness and mortality.

Bachardy had been drawing pictures of Isherwood ever since he first studied art as a teenager. Beginning in August 1985, as his lover grew more ill, Bachardy drew him more steadily, constantly, obsessively. The pictures were in black acrylic on paper, the paint diluted to the consistency of ink and applied with different brushes. The images have the stark simplicity of Japanese ideograms fleshed out with washes of gray. The drawing sessions were intense and intimate—Bachardy drew his eighty-one-year-old lover both clothed and nude. Later published in a book with selections from Bachardy's diary, *Christopher Isherwood: Last Drawings*, the pictures suggest a storyboard of dying, a comic strip of death. Stephen Spender called them "merciless and loving," and Bachardy agreed. "The thought occurs to me," Bachardy wrote in his diary, "am I so insistent about these sittings with Chris as a means of extending the time I have left with him...?" Isherwood would sign and date each picture.

He went into the hospital in October and the pictures stopped for three weeks. When he returned to their house in Santa Monica and the sessions resumed, his face was more gaunt and angular. More disturbing was his indifference to the artwork, he who had always been Bachardy's biggest enthusiast. "Oh, the pain, the pain," he grumbled whenever he moved. He stopped signing the pictures.

That December, Thom Gunn wrote a poem about his friend, "To Isherwood Dying," where he compared Death to the young men whistling for girls outside Isherwood's apartment in the opening pages of *Goodbye to Berlin*.

Isherwood died at home late in the morning on January 4, 1986. Bachardy had made six drawings of him the night before. After he expired, however, Bachardy continued to draw, unwilling to stop. He drew only the head now, from different angles, the sheet drawn up to his chin, a harrowing abstraction of sharp chin, big nostrils, and open eyes. "I started drawing Chris's corpse at two o'clock and worked more or less steadily until [the doctor] came around nine.... Chris's body spooks me because it already has so little to do with him." The body was taken away to a medical school where it was dissected by students.

On the last page of *A Single Man*, Isherwood writes that the body is only trash after individual consciousness floats off to rejoin the ocean of consciousness. Christopher Isherwood was now part of that vast metaphysical ocean—and of a smaller ocean of books and readers.

17. Tales of Two or Three Cities

—ɱ—

During the first thirteen years after Stonewall, gay life and culture
had finally begun to achieve some acceptance. With the coming of
AIDS, however, homosexuality was demonized all over again. Antigay politicians now used the disease to resist campaigns for tolerance and equality.
Homosexuality was not just a moral hazard, it was a health hazard. Gore
Vidal's old enemy, William F. Buckley, went so far as proposing that people
who tested positive for the virus be tattooed—on a private spot, such as the
back or buttocks. He insisted he was only being practical even after it was
pointed out that the Nazis tattooed people in concentration camps.

A window had been opened, but it could be closed again. The age of
AIDS was also the age of Reagan. Nevertheless, the old silence of the 1950s
and 1960s did not return. TV resumed its old timidity about homosexuality
now that it was synonymous with illness, but the plays and books continued
to appear, actually increasing in number, especially the books.

After the success of *A Boy's Own Story*, Dutton decided to publish more
gay fiction. In 1984 the publishing house issued *The Family of Max Desir* by
Robert Ferro, Edmund White's colleague from the Violet Quill. *Max Desir*
features painful, realistic episodes about an unhappy family with a dying
mother juxtaposed with sweet chapters about the son's gay romance in
Italy. Also in 1984, Knopf put out a first book of short stories, *Family Dancing*, by twenty-three-year-old David Leavitt. Leavitt had made a splash as an
undergraduate at Yale when he published a story in the *New Yorker* about a
divorced mother and her gay son. His stories were quiet slices of day-to-day
life, the gay characters young and still in college, good sons who are just
coming out and not promiscuous or wild. Mainstream readers felt safe with
these nice young men in the darkening shadows of AIDS. The book was
remarkably successful for a short story collection and was reprinted again

and again. Ferro and Leavitt both showed that there was more to gay life than sex, and that families were an important part of that life.

Leavitt followed two years later with his first novel, *The Lost Language of Cranes*, which took these themes into more dangerous territory: a young man comes out to his family and forces his father to acknowledge his own homosexuality. It's a double coming-out story, but the mother/wife is the real protagonist. Her situation is the most interesting since she is both victim and willfully blind enabler. Reviews in the mainstream press were more mixed—Leavitt was hitting straight readers closer to home—but *Lost Language* sold even better than his stories.

Dutton put out an anthology of gay short stories in 1986, *Men on Men*, edited by George Stambolian, showcasing a wide variety of writers. Additional *Men on Men* collections followed, a total of eight volumes over the next fifteen years with 152 stories by 139 different writers. Meanwhile Dutton published more gay novels and a few lesbian novels, too. The titles were reprinted in their trade paperback line, Plume. Michael Denneny at St. Martin's Press continued to publish gay novels in hardcover, although his biggest success was the 1987 history of the AIDS epidemic, *And the Band Played On*, by Randy Shilts. St. Martin's initiated its own gay paperback imprint, Stonewall Inn Editions, in 1988.

The publishing industry had discovered niche marketing, taking a concept from ecology (each species finds a niche in an ecosystem) and applying it to a species of reader. Thanks to the existence of the gay press and gay bookstores, gay-themed titles virtually sold themselves—with an approximate 7,500 copy ceiling in hardcover. They didn't need to be reviewed by the *New York Times Book Review* to find a readership—and they rarely were. It was the age of the gay midlist novel. Publishers could count on a small but solid profit while hoping an occasional novel would cross over into bigger sales. By 1992, 10 percent of Plume's titles would be gay. The new literary presence was so strong that *Esquire* made a joke about it in their August 1987 overview, "Who's Who in the Literary Power Game." A list of absences ("Lost in Space") included "Young heterosexual male authors."

But *Esquire* was ahead of other publications in their awareness that the culture was changing. In November 1987 they ran a long article by Frank Rich, chief drama critic of the *New York Times*, "The Gay Decades," a smart, friendly, openly curious exploration by a straight man of how gay life had changed since 1960 and how it affected the world at large. Rich's point of view was different from a gay man's, which made the piece even more interesting. For example, he admitted he found the giant Calvin Klein underwear ad towering over Times Square intimidating: "I couldn't decide whether the image was more threatening as a homoerotic come-on or as an unrealizable heterosexual physical ideal that women would now expect me and all men to match. But the billboard quickly became part of the landscape." His honesty was a breath of fresh air.

Out in San Francisco, Armistead Maupin continued to follow the tangled lives of the circle of friends at 28 Barbary Lane. Harper and Row continued to issue the books as paperback originals and the audience continued to grow. The *San Francisco Chronicle* serial was so popular that other newspapers and magazines tried their own serialized novels, the most memorable being *Leap Year* by the gifted short story writer Peter Cameron, published in the New York weekly, *Seven Days*, in 1988. Cameron, too, mixed straight and gay characters, but this time in Manhattan.

The Barbary Lane novels were comedies, but Maupin was not afraid to include harsh realities. He brought a lesbian couple back from Guyana in time to miss the Jonestown massacre. When AIDS hit, he was the first established novelist to write directly about the epidemic. He had an advantage over other writers in that his fictional world was already up and running, with characters who were in harm's way. But how does one introduce a murderous plague into a comic pastorale without destroying its mood or scaring off readers?

Maupin did it deftly in his fourth novel, *Babycakes*, which came out as a book in 1984. People go on with their lives, especially straight people. Mary Ann Singleton, the ingenue from the Midwest, is now a TV journalist married to Brian Hawkins, the former libertine. They are struggling to have a baby. Mrs. Madrigal continues to dispense wisdom and joints. And Michael Tolliver now works for an AIDS hotline. He is quieter and sadder, but still himself. He can make jokes about the disease, then drop the comic mask and acknowledge how much it hurts. As the novel progresses, however, we realize a major character is missing: Jon Fielding, the immensely likable doctor who was involved off and on with Michael during the first three novels. Michael has a dream about him early on, but we're not told he died of AIDS until a third of the way in, when Michael discusses his death with

Mrs. Madrigal. Then Michael visits his friend Mona in England and tells her the full, excrutiating story. It's an ingenious storytelling device, subtle and true to life, but quietly devastating.

And life still went on. The next novel, *Significant Others*, appeared three years later in 1987. Mary Ann is a highly successful TV personality and she and Brian have adopted a daughter and moved into a high-rise overlooking 28 Barbary Lane, where Michael still lives. Michael is now HIV positive; he carefully monitors his health as he goes on with *his* life.

When Brian learns that an old girlfriend is sick, he panics that he too has AIDS. The novel takes place during the ten days he waits for the results of his HIV test. He doesn't dare tell his wife. He and Michael and many other characters leave town for the Russian River, where the wealthy "boys only" Bohemian Grove is meeting just down the road from the lesbian "girls only" Wimminwood music festival. More tightly constructed than its predecessors, the book is like a bedroom farce set in the forest, Maupin's own *As You Like It*. Much of it is pure slapstick, but the last twenty pages, as everyone comes to terms with his or her demons, are full of complex emotions. Among those demons is the fact that Michael has fallen in love.

Because a happy real-life event had affected the series: Maupin himself had found love. He met him in 1985 when he was invited to speak at the Gay Students Alliance at Georgia State University in Atlanta. The visit was arranged by Terry Anderson, a cute, boyish, twenty-five-year-old blond who had not read Maupin's novels but admired his rules for gay men recently published in the *Advocate*. ("1. Stop begging for acceptance.... 3. Refuse to cooperate in the lie....5. Don't sell your soul to the gay commercial culture.") He met Maupin at the airport and the two immediately hit it off, talking endlessly on the ride into town. "We were finding instant points of agreement," Maupin recalled, "largely about the closet and movies, which are the two things that are most important to me." At the hotel they tumbled into bed together, then proceeded with the weekend's scheduled events, ending up back in bed each night. Maupin returned to San Francisco but the relationship continued over the phone. He invited Anderson to come out for a month. Anderson came and stayed.

Accelerating the progress of love, making it both urgent and dangerous, was the fact that, six weeks after moving to San Francisco, Anderson took the antibody test and found he was seropositive. Maupin was still seronegative. They knew how difficult life could be in a serodiscordant couple, yet they decided to risk it. They assumed Anderson had only so much time and they must make it count.

Much of this went into *Significant Others* but with changes. The fictional lovers connect more gradually than the real lovers did, each pretending to be cool and aloof. And the new fictional love, Thack (short for Thackeray) Sweeney, is negative while Michael is positive. But then Maupin has as much in common with Thack as he does with Michael. Thack is Southern, but comes from the upper-class South of Maupin. Michael comes from the public-school South of Terry Anderson. Yet Anderson was far more confident and brash than Michael can be.

Anderson got involved in local gay activism and eventually became manager of the city's Different Light Bookstore. He managed Maupin, too, forming a business around him called Literary Bent. He was fiercely protective of his partner and very demanding of people in the book trade; they missed dealing with the laid-back author alone. Maupin later acknowledged that business affected their life together: It was good to work with someone he trusted, but it "increases the intimacy and it increases the dangers of fights, because you're professionally *and* romantically entwined." But Anderson helped his partner's career immensely, getting him better contracts and more public attention.

They became a highly public gay couple—they appeared together on TV in Britain and in the "Couples" column of *People.* They were very sociable. Among their new friends was British actor Ian McKellen, who first visited San Francisco while filming in New Mexico. One night Maupin and Anderson began to complain about famous people who stayed in the closet. McKellen listened quietly, then asked, "Do you think I should come out?" They told him yes and spent the rest of the evening telling him why. They thought nothing would come of it. But several months later, in an interview on Radio Four in Britain, McKellen told the world that he was gay. Maupin's next novel would be dedicated to McKellen.

When *Sure of You* was published in 1989, Maupin announced it would be his last Barbary Lane novel. He'd been considering ending the series for a while. He did not want it to go on like a TV show that overstays its welcome. He yearned to write something new and decided that *Sure of You* would be a good place to stop.

The novel begins quietly. Michael and Thack now live together. Their scenes of domestic life, the daily exchanges of talk, affection, aggravation, and apology, are expertly done—a convincing happiness. AIDS remains present in the chorus of beepers regularly going off to tell Michael and others to take their AZT. Brian works with Michael in a landscaping business and is still married to Mary Ann—he dotes on their daughter. An old boyfriend of Mary Ann's comes to town, Burke, who suffered from amnesia three novels back. Now a TV producer, he offers Mary Ann her own national talk show in New York. She not only wants the job, she intends to use it to leave Brian.

It's a surprisingly simple crisis for the climax of the entire series, yet it's enough. Michael and Thack are caught in the middle. Mrs. Madrigal and Mona are visiting Lesbos—the literal Greek island—in a subplot that's a pleasant break from the heavy drama back home. The drama becomes even heavier when Michael fears his HIV has turned into full-blown AIDS.

Maupin's prose was always good, but it's even better here. Scenes have the precision and pacing of good comedy, yet Maupin folds real emotions and serious ideas into his characters' thoughts. Here is Michael sitting on a bench after a nurse tells him that the purple blotch on his leg might be a Kaposi's sarcoma lesion:

> Three years of daily fretting had left him overrehearsed for this moment, but it still seemed completely unreal. He had vowed not to rail against the universe when his time came. Too many people had died, too many he had loved, for "Why me?" to be a reasonable response. "Why not?" was more to the point.

Michael imagines all the pornographic details of illness, growing more upset. Then he remembers he has Thack and friends to help him and he recovers a little.

> He tilted his head and let the sun dry his tears. The air smelled of new-mown grass, while what he could see of the sky seemed ridiculously blue. The birds in the trees were as fat and chirpy as the ones in cartoons.

The emotions leading up to this are so strong that the last image isn't really sweet, but slightly bitter, even angry.

The book and the series end not in a deathbed scene or an operatic confrontation, but in a handful of very real, well-observed encounters. Mary Ann acts simply, but badly. I won't give away the ending completely, but say only that what she does is human and plausible. Yet it is shocking in the world of Barbary Lane. Readers were appalled. Some blamed Maupin, as if he'd *made* her behave badly. But I believe Mary Ann is only being true to herself; I admire Maupin for letting her do what she does. She is his boldest creation: a character we like and even identify with but who changes over the years, achieving what she wanted but being changed by success. Maupin gave her emotions and needs that he must have feared in himself. He even implies that we, his gentle readers, could behave just as badly. Readers don't like being told such things.

Mary Ann is the dark note in the novel, the good person who fails and is expelled from Arcadia. More accurately, she leaves freely. Yet there was another dark note for readers who paused to think about it: What will happen to Michael? He might be fine for now, but there was no treatment for AIDS in 1989. Maupin left the question hanging, though there was only one answer at this time. That might be another reason for Maupin ending the series here: he did not want to see Michael die.

In a highly involving, deceptively entertaining relay race of tales and stories, Maupin explores some very profound subjects. He asks important questions about love and loyalty. He shows a circle of disconnected people inventing an alternative family that's more flexible than any natural family yet not without its problems. He demonstrates how gay and straight people can bond, using each other to define and redefine themselves. And he discovers a different kind of morality, a newer, truer set of values more real and right than the petrified, secondhand rules that too easily turn into hypocrisy. He found a middle way between the libertines and the Calvinists.

Sure of You was not serialized in a newspaper but came out as a finished book. The last novel in the series was the first to get a full review in the *New York Times Book Review*, written by gay novelist David Feinberg, who'd just published a first novel, the angrily comic *Eighty-Sixed*. Feinberg was known for his scathing wit and cynicism, yet he adored Barbary Lane. He called the series a love letter to San Francisco, found it as valuable as social history as John Updike's Rabbit novels, and concluded, "Mr. Maupin writes for everyone: gay, straight, single, married, square or hip. His most subversive act is to write in such a matter-of-fact manner about his gay characters. There is nothing exceptional or lurid about them: acceptance is a given."

Yet Maupin had found success without the *Times*. His books sold 700,000 copies by the end of the decade and his readers didn't just buy them, but read and reread them, longing to enter his world. When he appeared at A Different Light Bookstore in New York in 1989, the store was mobbed and Maupin was besieged by fans—one man wanted his picture taken sitting in his lap, as if Maupin were Santa Claus. He was so popular that, like Shakespeare, there were rumors he was actually somebody else. An obsessed reader figured out that "Armistead Maupin" was an anagram for "is a man I dreamt up."

Nevertheless, Maupin now walked away from Barbary Lane, much as Conan Doyle tried to walk away from Sherlock Holmes or Frank Baum tried to shut down the Land of Oz. He needed to try something new; he wanted to explore something besides gay lives.

Oddly enough, the man whose novel had done more than any other to trigger the recent wave of gay fiction did not immediately ride it himself. Edmund White was off in Paris, working on a different kind of book. He not only left New York after *A Boy's Own Story*, he left gay literature, too, for the time being.

His next work, *Caracole*, was a highly literary novel set in an alternate reality like Nabokov's *Ada*, a return to the experimental mode of *Forgetting Elena*. But this time White replaced sexual ambiguity with overt heterosexuality. A young teenager, Gabriel, is sent from a run-down provincial estate to a decayed city of palaces and canals to live with his uncle—much as White's nephew, Keith Fleming, had lived in New York with White. Gabriel has love affairs with two older women while his true love, a wild girl of the forests, fourteen-year-old Angelica, comes to the city and becomes Uncle Mateo's mistress. After some complications, the young lovers escape their corrupt elders and happily reunite to lead a revolution.

Caracole is part adult fairy tale, part dream novel, part satirical allegory, and a complete dud. It's understandable that White would want to take a vacation from both gay fiction and AIDS at this time, but his new novel was all lobster shell and no lobster. It fails not because it's straight but because it's dry and uninvolving. The only interesting element is its fantasy autobiography. Uncle Mateo is a hetero White. The "nasty little blond" actress, Edwige, is another version of his unrequited love, Keith McDermott. (McDermott later told White's nephew, "Well, at least you got to stay your own gender.") And the imperious bluestocking, Mathilda, is none other than Susan Sontag. Gabriel becomes her unlikely lover. "You've given me the gift of your completely innocent trust," she tells him. "I'll give you fame and power—and my love, too, if you want it." There's a heavy whiff of 1950s costume drama in the novel—it might be more entertaining if there were more. There's a perverse joke in a gay man writing a heterosexual love story where he imagines his skinny nephew breaking the heart of a famous closeted lesbian, yet *Caracole* is too sluggish to be much fun. Not even the finale at a masked ball where Mathilda guns down Edwige is half as enjoyable as it sounds.

The novel received mostly bad reviews when it appeared in 1985. The gay press and British press sometimes praised it (although one wonders if novelist Peter Ackroyd meant White mischief when he called it the "most accomplished of his novels") yet the book attracted few readers, gay or straight. It ended Sontag's friendship with White. She had blurbed *A Boy's Own Story* and recommended him for his Guggenheim. She not only dropped him, she insisted her blurb be removed from all future editions of *Boy's Own Story*, foreign and domestic. It's hard to understand how White could think Sontag would be amused by his mocking portrait of her. Later he blamed his unconscious, repeating his claim that he couldn't help betraying people who got close to him. I suspect it was a return of the repressed: his unconscious was tired of being nice to someone important. Or maybe his unconscious just wanted to burn his American bridges so he could stay in Europe.

White thoroughly enjoyed living in Paris. He had a little two-room apartment on the Île Saint-Louis, an island in the Seine east of Notre Dame full of seventeenth-century mansions and hotels. He lived off his Guggenheim money, book advances, and occasional articles he wrote for *Vogue*. He had a new boyfriend, John Purcell (the dedicatee of *Caracole*), but they were more friends than lovers, and both saw other men. He shaved off his mustache and stopped drinking. He wrote for an hour each morning, in longhand while sprawled on his bed, and was free for the rest of the day. He told an interviewer, "In Paris people cultivate social life as an art form; in New York people cultivate it as a form of self-advancement." He may have been referring chiefly to himself: he did not need to play courtier in Paris the way he had in New York. Through his French translator, Gilles Barbedette, he met other French gay writers, including Michel Foucault and Hervé Guibert, future author of *To the Friend Who Could Not Save My Life*. He tricked with men he picked up each night in a nearby park on the Seine and explored an early version of phone sex.

In 1985 he met Matthias Brunner, the Swiss-German owner of a chain of movie theaters. Brunner was close to White in age, handsome, wealthy, and urbane. They saw each other regularly and often traveled together. White became more serious. Then Brunner suggested they take the HIV test. White agreed. Brunner tested negative but White tested positive, as he thought he would. Visiting Vienna with Brunner shortly afterward, White found himself constantly crying. Brunner insisted that their different HIV statuses were not important, but the two men began to drift apart.

White visited a friend in Greece whose partner had recently died. He returned to Paris thinking about illness and death. He wrote a long short story, "An Oracle," the quiet tale of an AIDS widower trying to come to terms with the death of his lover of twelve years.

"An Oracle" is a great work of fiction, perhaps White's best up to this point. The prose is plain and direct, with a new kind of urgency.

> Even though George had been a baby, he'd fought death with a winner's determination but had lost anyway. Ray thought that he himself wouldn't resist it so long. If and when the disease surfaced (for it seemed to him like a kid who's holding his nose underwater for an eerily long time but is bound to come up gasping for air), when the disease surfaced he wouldn't much mind. In a way dying would be easier than figuring out a new way of living.

White concisely captures the pampered life of this New York/Fire Island couple in the first half of the forty-page story. George, an advertising executive, is the more successful and dominant of the two. Ray selflessly looks after him when he's ill. Before he dies, George tells him, "You must look out for yourself." In the second half, numb and drifting, Ray visits a friend in Crete. He regularly has sex there with a teenage hustler, Marco, who speaks no English. Projecting his own thoughts and emotions on the boy, Ray falls in love. Before Ray leaves, he gets a friend to translate a love letter into Greek, one that says he will return to Crete and wants Marco to live with him. He gives the letter to Marco on his last night. The boy reads the letter; he gently says no; he actually speaks English. "You must look out for yourself," he tells Ray. Afterward, Ray finds himself smiling and crying, "as he'd never allowed himself to cry over George, who'd just spoken to him once again through the least likely oracle."

White published the story in *Christopher Street* in 1986. Two more stories about AIDS followed, including "Palace Days," about his friend, David Kalstone, who also died that year. These were collected with four stories by British writer Adam Mars-Jones in *The Darker Proof* in 1988, still one of the best books, fiction or nonfiction, about the epidemic.

But White could think more clearly about AIDS in fiction than when he wrote nonfiction about it. He followed his fine short story with a manifesto on art and AIDS, "Esthetics and Loss," in *Artforum* in 1987. It's a notorious essay, cold and haughty, full of rules and judgments. White speaks dismissively of *The Normal Heart, As Is*, and the 1985 TV movie *An Early Frost*, before he lays down the law: "If art is to confront AIDS more honestly than the media have done, it must begin in tact, avoid humor, and end in anger. . . . Humor domesticates terror. . . . Humor, like melodrama, is an assertion of bourgeois values." It sounds like a parody of bad French criticism. Many gay readers and writers hated the essay for being not only condescending but just plain wrong. Ed Sikov, media columnist of the *New York Native*, usually a supporter of White, angrily pitched into the essay at length, calling his admonition against humor "pure twaddle."

The truth of the matter is White didn't know what the right response to the epidemic was. Nobody did. Everyone was badly shaken and nervously grabbing at contradictory ideas about the role of art. But trust the tale, not the teller. When White himself wrote fiction about AIDS, he was not afraid to use humor *or* melodrama.

He now resumed work on a new novel, a sequel to *A Boy's Own Story* tentatively titled *The Beautiful Room Is Empty*. He decided to explore his life in a series of autobiographical novels, as Marcel Proust, Doris Lessing, and others had done. He mapped out a tetralogy, four novels, which meant he needed to write three more. He was unsure if he would live long enough to finish them.

The deaths of both the young and the old continued. AIDS jumbled together the chronologies of different generations so that newcomers died at the same time as the old guard. On December 1, 1987, in the south of France, James Baldwin died.

He had lived a curious life since the civil rights movement and the attacks by Eldridge Cleaver. After years in Istanbul, he moved back to France, dividing his time between Paris and the village of St. Paul-de-Vence in Provence. He visited the United States for teaching engagements and public speaking. He still drank heavily and his appearances were often unpredictable.

In 1979, he published *Just Above My Head*, his novel about a gay gospel singer, Arthur Montana, as told by his straight brother, Hall. Baldwin mixed pieces of himself with pieces of his own brother David. He imagined his family talking about him after he was gone. "Whatever the fuck your uncle was, and he was a whole lot of things, he was nobody's faggot," Hall tells his son. The book is full of promising stories, such as a love affair between two teenage boys in a gospel quartet touring the postwar South. ("They walked in the light of each other's eyes...they were called 'lovebirds' and 'Romeo and Romeo' because they were alone, they were far from other people, they were in danger.") But the narrative keeps sliding around without building to anything. The book badly needed another draft, but Baldwin no longer knew how to revise. It would be his last novel.

He continued to write essays, including a book-length set of riffs on his obsession with movies, *The Devil Finds Work*, that's also a mess but full of fine things. He published an essay in *Playboy* in 1985, "Freaks and the Ideal of American Masculinity," later reprinted as "Here Be Dragons," that's his only nonfiction account of his own sexuality. The essay is full of free association about sex and androgyny, American imperialism and the Industrial Revolution, Boy George and Michael Jackson, but it also includes indelible snapshots of Baldwin's sex life in the 1940s in Times Square ("There were no X-rated movies then, but there were, so to speak, X-rated audiences") and Greenwich Village ("I quickly learned that my existence was the punchline of a dirty joke"). It's a painful but powerful piece.

Baldwin's health was bad, his body weakened by chain-smoking and drinking. He was diagnosed with cancer of the esophagus in the spring of 1987. Surgery was performed but the results were not good. He was taken to St. Paul-de-Vence, where he spent his last months surrounded by friends, including his brother David; his biographer, David Leeming; and his loyal ex-lover, Lucien Happersberger, who had finished his third marriage.

Baldwin died at home. His body was flown to New York and a memorial service was held on December 8 at St. John the Divine, the mammoth unfinished cathedral on the border of Harlem and the Upper West Side. Among the speakers were Toni Morrison, Maya Angelou, and Amiri Baraka. Their eulogies were reprinted in the *New York Times Book Review*, but they celebrated him solely as a black writer, not a gay one. The *Times* obituary mentioned homosexuality only as something Baldwin was criticized for discussing too frankly in his fiction. His best novels, *Giovanni's Room* and *Another Country*, were cited only in passing, while he was celebrated primarily as an essayist. The degayification of James Baldwin had begun.

Robert Ferro wrote a letter to the *Times* challenging their silence about Baldwin's sexuality: "[T]oo little has been made of his important contribution in this area. Perhaps this is not surprising; perhaps it is for gay people to claim him as our champion, as blacks have done. For as a man and writer, Baldwin was both black and gay, and in this combination he found his voice, his strength and his crown."

Nevertheless, in the years ahead, the literary mainstream continued to downplay or ignore Baldwin's sexuality. It was too complicated to address both minority sides of him, so they sacrificed the side that made them uncomfortable. But this left Baldwin incomplete, a writer who had promised much but delivered little; he was remembered chiefly as a beautiful talker and another sad American failure—instead of the great novelist he often was.

Robert Ferro was sick with AIDS when he wrote his letter about Baldwin. He and his partner, Michael Grumley, died that summer—within ten weeks of each other.

18. Laughter in the Dark

—w—

Laugh and you are free.
—Charles Ludlam

Edmund White might call humor bourgeois and Andrew Holleran could claim that AIDS had killed comedy. Nevertheless, humor not only remained a part of gay life, it flourished during the epidemic, sometimes as an escape, but also as a counterattack.

Charles Ludlam was a comic magician, a short, balding, often ordinary-looking young man from Long Island who used makeup and imagination to transform himself into an astonishing array of stage divas and villains. He studied drama at Hofstra and moved to New York's Lower East Side in 1965 to work in the downtown theater scene with Ronald Tavel and other avant-garde performers. He then formed his own troupe, the Ridiculous Theatrical Company, helped by his best friend from high school, Christopher Scott. (Scott was the lover of the well-connected Henry Geldzahler—they can be seen together in a famous painting by David Hockney—and the couple helped Ludlam financially as well as artistically.) The company, also known as the Theater of the Ridiculous, eventually found a home on Sheridan Square in Greenwich Village, in a large basement that had been a magic theater called the Shrine of the Orient in the 1920s, and in the 1930s Cafe Society, the integrated nightclub where Billie Holiday sang "Strange Fruit." ("It's got great ghosts," said Ludlam. "I feel they're there.") Here Ludlam staged a startling series of plays, from *Conquest of the Universe, or When Queens Collide* and *Der Ring Gott Farblonjet*, his Yiddish-flavored parody of Wagner's Ring Cycle, to his own versions of *Bluebeard* and *Camille*. ("I think that I am the Camille of our era.")

Ludlam loved theater in all its forms: high, low, grand, trashy, children's plays, and sex shows. His parody celebrations of theater and movies were grounded in gay sensibility and included gay jokes (when Ludlam as the dying Marguerite in *Camille* is told there are no faggots of wood for the fire, she turns to the audience and plaintively asks, "No faggots in the house?") yet his wit and invention could be enjoyed by anyone with a taste for absurdity. When film critic Pauline Kael wanted to describe the joy of movie parody in 1978, "that golden hysteria of taking the situations in old movies to a logical extreme...the true happy dirty madness," she cited TV comedian Carol Burnett *and* Charles Ludlam.

It was an art-for-art's-sake comedy in a world of its own, yet Ludlam also lived in the larger world. When he created a sword-and-sandal parody, *Salammbo*, in 1985, he said the show was his response to AIDS. Not only did he consider the cast of half-clad bodybuilders his gift to his gay audience ("We decided we gays have been through enough in the last couple of years. We are going to give them a little something"), but a play about ancient Carthage couldn't help being about fascism and religion. It began previews midway between the opening nights of *As Is* and *The Normal Heart*.

"Loosely based" on the Gustave Flaubert book that may be the most absurd novel ever written by a major novelist, a weird mix of solemn prose and purple drama, Ludlam's *Salammbo* was a mad extravaganza with a huge cast, elaborate decor, live doves, and a gigantic naked fat lady playing a man. The publicity stills feature Ludlam as Salammbo sprawled on a divan like a chubby Elizabeth Taylor surrounded by well-oiled beefcake. Gay audiences loved it, but straight audiences stayed away, fearing it was *too* gay. An expensive show to produce, Ludlam kept it running by reviving his amazing two-man send-up of Victorian melodrama, *The Mystery of Irma Vep*, with his lover, Everett Quinton. The two men raced on- and offstage, each playing four different characters, an exhausting workout, but Ludlam continued to perform *Salammbo* on alternate nights. (*Irma Vep* contained the funniest piece of comic business I've ever seen on stage: On a dark and stormy night, Ludlam in a nightgown and blond sausage curls settles in front of a fireplace with a book. Behind her, a great clawed hand begins to tap on a window. She doesn't hear it. The claw keeps tapping. The audience laughs. Ludlam remains engrossed in her book. The claw taps louder.

Ludlam pauses, takes a deep breath—then licks her finger and turns the page. The audience laughs even harder. Moments pass, an eternity. Just when you think the joke cannot last another second, Ludlam hears the noise and looks up, her eyes wide in horror. The audience goes wild. It's pure schtick, but schtick of genius.)

Ludlam and Quinton continued to do *Irma Vep* after *Salammbo* closed and Ludlam's next play, *The Artificial Jungle*, opened. He was also acting for film and television; he even found time to direct an opera in Santa Fe.

In the middle of all this, in November 1986, Ludlam was diagnosed with AIDS. He told only Quinton and remained active so nobody would guess he was ill. He began preparations on a summer production of *Titus Andronicus* for Shakespeare in the Park. He shut himself away with "the flu" for a month in March. Then in April he was rushed to St. Vincent's Hospital, unable to breathe. He died there on May 28, 1987. His obituary ran on the front page of the *New York Times*, celebrating his achievements and declaring he had died of AIDS. Such honesty was rare at the time. He was only forty-four.

When Andrew Holleran claimed in his essay on the death of Ludlam that AIDS marked the end of comic drag and camp, he could not have been more wrongheaded. Other artists followed Ludlam. Actor/actress/playwright Charles Busch had already written and starred in his first hit, *Vampire Lesbians of Sodom*, in 1984. He followed it in 1987 with *Psycho Beach Party* (he wanted to call it *Gidget Goes Psychotic*, but the girl's name was trademarked) and a noir parody, *The Lady in Question*, in 1989. His work is more pop-driven than Ludlam's, yet there is the same transformative love of bad theater and bad movies, a keen appreciation for the poetry of camp.

The same can be said of John Epperson, who created the Kabuki-like drag queen, Lypsinka, a thin, unearthly figure who has no voice of her own but speaks in recorded songs and sound bites from old movies. Epperson was so thin that when he did a striptease in *I Could Go on Lypsinking*, many in the audience couldn't help but think of emaciated friends in the hospital, only here the skeletal figure was happily singing *against* death.

Humor remained a strong presence in fiction, too. Armistead Maupin had begun with comedy yet successfully incorporated everyday sorrow into his work. David Feinberg began with comic anger in his 1988 first novel, *Eighty-Sixed*, juxtaposing the life of his smartass narrator, B. J. Rosenthal, in

1980 before AIDS, with his life in 1986 after the epidemic has cut his world wide open.

Comedy was not sugarcoating but an additional weapon, an extension of vocabulary. Yet there were also talented writers who used comedy to get away from AIDS. They were not mindless escapes but intelligent, clear-minded diversions that acknowledged the fact that gay life went on despite disease. The strongest and most successful was *The Object of My Affection* by Stephen McCauley.

McCauley grew up outside Boston, attended the University of Vermont, moved to New York, and worked as a travel agent before he studied writing at Columbia University. There he began work on a novel which he finished after returning to Boston. Published in 1987, *The Object of My Affection* is the first-person account of a gay man in Brooklyn, George, whose friends include gay men, straight men, women, and one best friend, Nina. Their friendship has an excellent literary pedigree, going back to *Breakfast at Tiffany's*, but McCauley did not need to be coy or mysterious about George's life. He avoided the subject of AIDS, yet he did not avoid serious emotion. George and Nina are two equally neurotic, nervous souls who use their friendship as a foxhole to hide from serious romantic involvements. They must learn to let go of each other before they can move on with their lives.

There are dark sides to McCauley's artistry (best shown in his startling short memoir about his family, "Let's Say," published in *Boys Like Us*), but the surface is smart, sane, and truly funny. *Object of My Affection* was one of the few genuine crossover successes in gay fiction. When people talk about gay crossover, it's often assumed that a book has found straight readers. But many editors and critics suspect that increased sales figures only mean a book is finding a wider gay readership, attracting gay men who don't want to read anything "too gay." However, McCauley's tale of friendship between a gay man and straight woman found a huge audience among straight women: single, young females who longed for a gay best friend, even an imaginary one. Armistead Maupin found a crossover audience, too, although he had to press his publisher to build on it—they were happy with their success in the gay market. A few smart people in movies and television recognized early the story possibilities in both Maupin and McCauley. *Tales of the City* was optioned for film in 1979 shortly after it was published. Years passed before it was developed as a series for PBS. The series was finally aired in 1993 but, despite its enormous popularity, PBS was afraid to continue for fear they'd lose federal funding. Four more years went by before *More Tales of the City* was filmed by the cable channel Showtime.

The Object of My Affection was optioned as soon as it came out, but didn't reach the screen until 1998. The screenplay by Wendy Wasserstein is very different from the book, telling the story of an unhappy straight woman in love with a perfect gay man—the novel is more complex and balanced. But novel and movie both proved the existence of an audience for the straight woman/gay friend plotline. Max Mutchnick, cocreator of the TV series *Will and Grace*, has never mentioned *Object* in any of his interviews, but it's hard to believe the book or movie were unknown to him and that they weren't brought up at development meetings with the network. The movie opened in March 1998; *Will and Grace* premiered six months later. The highly popular situation comedy ran for eight seasons and was seen by far more people than have read any of the books discussed here.

One gay novelist got out of books and into television as soon as he could. After two ingenious lighter-than-air comic novels, *Blue Heaven* in 1988 and *Putting on the Ritz* in 1992, Joe Keenan left New York for Los Angeles to work on the TV series *Frasier*. He did first-rate work in television, and his jokes about gay life—with special emphasis on the closet and gay/straight differences—were always surprising and slippery.

Several playwrights addressed the epidemic directly with comedy. *Adam and the Experts* by Victor Bumbalo used the blackest comedy imaginable to tell the absurdist tale of a gay man and his doctors. Bumbalo used gentler comedy to humanize his very real account of a year in the waiting room of an AIDS clinic, *What Are Tuesdays Like?* Paul Rudnick boldly incorporated broad, revue-style comedy in *Jeffrey* to capture a screwy modern world of sex addict support groups and cheerful AIDS fund-raisers. Even Larry Kramer tried his hand at stage comedy. But first he returned to politics.

After the success of *The Normal Heart*, he worked on a few plays and even went back to his novel. But art is long and life is short. The AIDS crisis continued to eat at him. He was not alone in his frustration over how little was being done. There were now 37,000 cases of AIDS in the United States and over 16,000 deaths. The FDA was slow in approving new drugs; the one drug available, AZT, was considered both overpriced and toxic. A new activist group, the Lavender Hill Mob, held 1960s-style zaps in New York and Atlanta to call attention to these problems.

When a speaker canceled at the Lesbian and Gay Community Center in New York on March 10, 1987, Kramer was invited to talk instead. He eagerly accepted.

The Center was housed in an old high school on West Thirteenth Street (opposite the building where Anaïs Nin introduced Gore Vidal to Truman Capote). The ground-floor meeting room was big and shabby. Kramer stood in front of a crowd of three hundred sitting in folding chairs. He began by asking the people on the lefthand side of the room to stand. "At the rate we are going, you could be dead in less than five years. Two-thirds of this room could be dead in less than five years. Sit down now." He spoke quickly and to the point. Time was running out, he said, and GMHC and other AIDS organizations were not political enough. Gay people needed to get more political. He praised the Lavender Hill Mob for what they had done in Atlanta.

Michael Petrelis of Lavender Hill was in the audience that night. At the end of the speech he jumped up and proposed they do a public action in New York. Kramer agreed. "We have to go after the FDA—fast. That means coordinated protests, pickets, arrests. Are you ashamed of being arrested? Well, until we do, I don't have to tell you what's going to happen."

Two nights later another meeting was held at the Center. More people attended and they formed the AIDS Coalition to Unleash Power, better known as ACT UP. Their immediate goal was to press the government to release new drugs more quickly. It was a highly ad hoc, totally democratic group, avoiding the bureaucracy that many felt had hobbled GMHC. Their first action was a demonstration on Wall Street, a few blocks from the stock exchange. The Public Theater provided a dummy of the FDA director to hang in effigy. Traffic was blocked and seventeen people were arrested, including Kramer, Petrelis, and a few GMHC board members.

ACT UP grew quickly. It energized the AIDS wars, attracting thousands of young men and women, including people with media savvy and a gift for graphic design. Their posters and slogan, "Silence = Death," became ubiquitous. They organized major protests against federal health agencies and the major drug companies, including Bristol-Myers and Burroughs Wellcome. Their weekly Monday night meetings became so large that they needed to move across town to the Great Hall of Cooper Union, where Abraham Lincoln once spoke.

However, a year after the Wall Street action, Kramer left ACT UP, just as he had left GMHC. He decided ACT UP was *too* ad hoc, *too* democratic. He wanted more structure. Later, when Kramer said the organization was his child, his creation, several members argued that his speech had been a catalyst but other people were more important as founders. The details remain confusing. David Feinberg joked about Kramer's tendency to turn against his offspring in a satirical fantasy where he imagined news items in a time after AIDS: "Larry Kramer forms an organization dealing with our most pressing health concern since the AIDS epidemic: DSBU (Deadly Sperm Build-Up). Three months later he will be forcibly removed from the board of directors, at his own request."

Whatever the reason for his departure, Kramer returned to playwriting, going back to an unfinished script, an out-and-out comedy, *Just Say No: A Play about a Farce*, set in Washington, D.C. A gay protagonist, Foppy Schwartz, a Capote-like confidant of famous women, serves as ringmaster for a parade of thinly disguised public figures, including a Koch-like closeted mayor, a Nancy Reagan–like First Lady, and her Ron Reagan Jr.–like dancer son. The story has something to do with the stolen videotape of a White House orgy; a call girl is murdered; the First Son falls in love with a man. A black maid regularly addresses the audience with asides like "White Jew Georgetown Faggot Strangles Loyal Schvartzah for Talking Cheap." On the page it reads as energetic, noisy, obvious, and not very funny. Friends who saw the 1988 production, however, report that it was highly entertaining.

Just Say No opened off-Broadway in October on the eve of the 1988 presidential election. The first-rate cast included the expertly droll Kathleen Chalfant as Mrs. Potentate, the Nancy Reagan character. The show had a successful run, in part because Reagan's vice president, the first George Bush, defeated the Democrat, Michael Dukakis, and people needed to purge their grief. But the reviews were almost all bad. Mel Gussow in the *Times* compared Kramer unfavorably to Charles Ludlam and added that "having written the script and articulated his hostilities, perhaps Mr. Kramer should have put the play in his bottom desk drawer."

The consensus was that Kramer was better at politics than theater. Nevertheless, there is a lot of theater in his politics. This became clear the following year when St. Martin's published *Reports from the Holocaust: The Making of an AIDS Activist*, a collection of his polemical pieces. Kramer framed each piece with remarks on how it came to be written and its effectiveness. This made his tirades and attacks seem less wild and more controlled, more like dramatic monologues performed by a character named Larry Kramer. The book showed him trying different voices, including sermons in the style of Martin Luther King. It humanized him, at least for people who weren't worn out by Kramer or hadn't been personally attacked by him.

Ed Koch was no longer mayor, but he still lived in New York. He remained in the public eye—he was named Honorary Chair of GMHC, which infuriated many. Then he moved into 2 Fifth Avenue, the same big apartment building where Kramer lived. There's a story that Kramer regularly confronted Koch in the lobby until Koch took out a peace order prohibiting Kramer from speaking to him. Kramer found a way around the restriction by talking to his dog whenever the ex-mayor was in earshot: "Molly, that's the man who murdered so many of Daddy's friends."

Kramer resumed work on his novel, now expanded and titled *The American People*, a mix of autobiographical fiction, history, and historical fiction. But he missed theater and returned to another unfinished play, a companion piece to *The Normal Heart* about the past and future of Ned Weeks. It was called first *The Furniture of Home*, then *The Tyranny of Blood*, and finally *The Destiny of Me*. (The title is from Walt Whitman's "Song of Myself.")

Staying in a hospital for an experimental procedure to cure AIDS, Ned Weeks enters a long fantasy conversation with his younger self. Kramer was able to incorporate material cut from *Normal Heart* as well as explore what had happened since he left GMHC. The scenes with his father, mother, and brother are very strong, their endless exchanges of blame and guilt achieving real power. The present-day story is less effective: demonstrators chant outside the hospital; the experimental treatment fails; Ned and the doctor scream at each other; and Ned throws bags of blood against the floor, just as he threw a carton of milk at the end of *Heart*. He can't be saved by medicine, politics, or the love of other people. The play ends with Ned and his younger self singing a love song to each other: "Make Believe" from *Showboat*.

The play opened in October 1992 at the Lucille Lortel Theatre on Christopher Street in a first-rate production with an excellent cast. Piper Laurie was the mother, Peter Frechette the brother, Jonathan Hadary was Ned, and the amazing John Cameron Mitchell (years before he wrote and performed *Hedwig and the Angry Inch*) was young Ned. It received good reviews and had a successful run.

Shortly before *The Destiny of Me* opened, Kramer met Gore Vidal. He was ostensibly interviewing Vidal for a new gay weekly, *QW*, over dinner at the Plaza Hotel. Vidal was back in the States to promote *Live from Golgotha*, his uneven satire about ancient Christianity and modern media. But an encounter between these two world-class monologuists could not help being problematical.

"He is very fat," Kramer declares in his introductory remarks. He nags Vidal for ordering a steak, then tells us, "He is one of my heroes and, like me, he's obviously very tired....I identify with him completely. Who has listened to him? What has his wrath made right?" Kramer seems to think he is interviewing himself. But that doesn't stop him from hectoring Vidal for not talking about AIDS, for not calling himself gay, and for not making Lincoln gay in his 1984 best-selling novel.

LK: There has been talk in gay historical circles that maybe Lincoln had some sort of gay relationship.

GV: I'm fairly convinced of it, yeah.

LK: Well, isn't it important that this be written about?

GV: Yeah, but you see, I wasn't covering that period of his life...

LK: But who better to tell the world than you?

GV: If I'd been writing about the young Lincoln I would've done it, but I'm writing about the Presidency during the Civil War.

LK: But I want you to write about the young Lincoln! Who better to tell the world than Gore Vidal? It would be ten times more useful than attacking the Constitution, to tell this fucking country that its most beloved President was gay, or had a gay period in his life.

Worn down by Kramer, the suavely articulate creator of *Myra Breckinridge* grows gruff and irritable. It is one of those rare occasions where the reader actually feels sorry for Gore Vidal.

V

The Nineties and After

19. Angels

A t first the new decade did not look so different from the old one. The Republicans still occupied the White House. The AIDS epidemic deepened and hardened, growing more familiar and less shocking even as it killed larger numbers of Americans.

More gay books and plays continued to be written, but nothing so strong that it broke through to a wider public. Then a brilliant new playwright arrived, someone with remarkable verbal and imaginative powers, and the desire to include *everything* in his work: gay life, straight life, politics, anger, comedy, fantasy, and religion. He won the attention of the culture at large and, stranger still, he did it on Broadway in a single play that appeared in two parts and was seven hours long.

Tony Kushner was an excitable, fast-talking, wire-haired man in his thirties with lively eyes framed in various glasses and a tall body that waxed and waned depending on where he was in the writing process—he tended to binge during first drafts and diet afterward. He was born in New York in 1956, the son of two classical musicians, a clarinetist father and bassoonist mother; he had a younger brother who became a horn player and a deaf older sister who became a painter. The family moved to Lake Charles, Louisiana, a small city of sixty thousand with a Jewish community of one hundred families, so the father could work in the family lumber business. It was not a happy household. The parents missed their musical careers; the mother tried other arts, including acting—her son saw her in local productions of *Death of a Salesman* and *The Diary of Anne Frank*—before she was stricken with cancer in 1969. She was successfully treated, but the treatments left her exhausted and unable to return to acting or music.

The father recognized early that his middle child might be gay and sent him to a therapist at sixteen hoping to make him straight. "I wouldn't want to be the father of Tchaikovsky," he said. The boy would find psychoanalysis useful for the rest of his life.

Kushner came to New York to attend Columbia University and majored in, of all things, medieval studies, a realm of religion, allegory, plagues, and prophets. He wanted to write but was afraid he wasn't good enough—his father taught him there was no point in doing art if you were going to be second-rate. He fell in love with theater in New York, seeing a wide variety of work, including Richard Foreman's production of *The Threepenny Opera* by Bertolt Brecht and Kurt Weill, which he saw many times. He entered NYU's graduate program in directing in 1984, thinking directing would be easier than writing. He began to write chiefly to give himself plays to direct.

Like several other writers here, he was a late bloomer sexually: he did not go to bed with a man until he was twenty-one. His first boyfriend was Mark Bronnenberg, a classmate and actor in his theater troupe. (He would dedicate the first part of his most famous work to Bronnenberg, "my former lover, my forever friend, my safe haven and my favorite homosexual.") Kushner also came late to gay literature in his reading. He would eventually write smart, generous introductions to *The Boys in the Band*, *The Normal Heart*, and the plays of Charles Ludlam, but, in a long list of favorite writers he put together for Baltimore's Center Stage in 1994, the only modern gay authors he included were Tennessee Williams and the poets Adrienne Rich and Thom Gunn.

Poetry was always important to Kushner: it electrified his imagination and fed his playwriting. He wrote an occasional poem himself, including "The Second Month of Mourning," a powerful poem about his mother, who suffered a relapse of cancer and died in 1991.

> You, or
> the loss of you.

> Now what kind of choice
> is that?

> You, or
> the loss of you.

And what if the rock can't be budged?
And what if never again the free flow of air?

And now you are the loss of you.

Different as they are, one can't help thinking of "Kaddish," the poem that Allen Ginsberg wrote about the death of *his* mother.

One of Kushner's most important relationships during this period was with another theater colleague, a woman, Kimberly Flynn. They shared books and plays and endless conversations about art and politics. They even lived together for a time. Kushner has said *Angels* can be read as an intellectual history of their friendship, but it also includes some buried emotional history. An accident in a New York taxi left Flynn crippled for an extended period; Kushner feared he was abandoning her when he took a directing job in St. Louis. He was able to imagine the worst with those fears a few years later in his portrait of a gay man abandoning a sick lover.

His first success was with a very free adaptation of a play by seventeenth-century French playwright Pierre Corneille, *The Illusion*. A father goes to a magician to learn what's happened to his estranged son. The magician shows him scenes of the son's life, episodes of adventure and romance that end in the son's murder. The father is heartbroken. Then he learns the son is an actor and the scenes are all make-believe. In a bitter, realistic twist, the father decides that since his son is well, he doesn't need to visit him after all. (By this time Kushner and his father had not yet made peace with each other.)

Kushner's first original work was a wildly ambitious play, *A Bright Room Called Day*, set in Berlin both during the rise of Hitler *and* after the fall of the Berlin Wall. A Jewish-American woman, Zillah, stays in an apartment in 1990 that was the home of a circle of anti-Nazi friends in 1933: their ghosts still haunt the place. *Bright Room* is, among other things, a corrective to *Cabaret*. The musical and the movie (but not Isherwood's stories) imply that Hitler came to power because all the good folks were too busy going to nightclubs to notice what was happening. Kushner shows something very different: a handful of theater people fighting Hitler by working for the left. A series of slides with Brecht-like titles, historical notes, and election results show how the rise of the left frightened the middle class into the arms of the Nazis. It was a no-win situation for German anti-Fascists—the Devil himself appears at the end of Act One. Yet this bleak but sophisticated history lesson was missed by many when the play opened in January 1991, on the eve of the First Iraq War. All they heard was one of the breathless monologues delivered to the audience by Zillah.

> The problem is we have a standard of what evil is, Hitler, the Holocaust—THE standard of absolute evil....But then everyone gets frantic as soon as you try to use the standard, nothing compares, nothing resembles—and the standard becomes unusable and nothing qualifies as Evil with a capital E....I mean like a certain ex-actor-turned-president who shall go nameless sat idly and I do mean idly by and watched tens of thousands die of a plague and he couldn't even bother to say he felt bad about it, much less try to help... I mean do you have to pile up some magic number of bodies before you hit the jackpot and rate a comparison with you-know-who?

It's a brilliant, damning observation: when Hitler is the ultimate measure of evil, then most bad guys look good. But that wasn't how Frank Rich, theater critic for the *Times*, heard the speech. "Perhaps if the world were not actually on the brink of war," his review began, "*A Bright Room Called Day*, a fatuous new drama about a world on the brink of war, would not be an early frontrunner for the most infuriating play of 1991. But then again, is the time ever right for a political work in which the National Socialism of the Third Reich is trivialized by being equated with the 'national senility' of the Reagan era?" People change—even theater critics—and by the time of the Second Iraq War in 2002 Rich was no longer a drama critic but a political columnist and as skeptical of war presidents as Kushner had been.

Kushner included one gay character in *Bright Room*: Baz, a depressed young man who works for the Institute of Human Sexuality, which Isherwood himself frequently visited. Baz is accepted by his friends and his sexuality is a matter of small importance. But Kushner's next play would be full of homosexuals. The author was placing gay life squarely at the center of things.

The new play was commissioned in 1988 by Oskar Eustis at the Eureka Theatre in San Francisco. It began as a two-hour work about five gay men, including a married Mormon and the infamous Roy Cohn, who had just died of AIDS. A few years earlier Kushner had had a dream about a sick friend where an angel crashed through the friend's ceiling. Kushner wrote a poem about it called "Angels in America." He never looked at the poem again, but used the title for the new play. He didn't know what would happen in it. At one point he thought it might be a musical.

It grew as he wrote and continued growing. Soon it had a subtitle, *A Gay Fantasia on National Themes*, echoing the subtitle of George Bernard Shaw's *Heartbreak House: A Fantasia in the Russian Manner on English Themes*. Kushner loves ideas as much as Shaw did, but he drew upon a wide range of other sources: Bertolt Brecht again, the Book of Mormon, Karl Marx, and *The Wizard of Oz*. As Mike Nichols later said, "For the first-rate artist, there's a moment when he's really getting revved up, and the time just flows into him. It only happens once. It happens without his awareness at all. He planned nothing. He was just going ahead doing his next thing."

One cannot really describe the dense weave of plots in *Angels* in a single paragraph, but here goes nothing: When a gay man, Prior, is diagnosed with AIDS, his bookish lefty lover, Louis, panics and abandons him. Guilty Louis becomes involved with Joe, a closeted gay Mormon lawyer with an unhappy, pill-popping wife, Harper. Joe is being courted for political work by Roy Cohn—Cohn, too, is sick with AIDS. Joe's Mormon mother, Hannah, comes to New York to save his marriage. Prior's friend Belize, a black male nurse, does what he can to save Prior. As if this weren't rich and complicated enough, many of the characters have dreams and visions. Cohn dreams of Ethel Rosenberg, whom he sent to the electric chair. Harper dreams of Prior, whom she's never met. And Prior has visions: first of ghosts and then of an angel—an angel who crashes through his ceiling and promises to tell him Everything.

The scope of the play is enormous: a panorama of different individuals all striving to repair their moral failures with politics and religion. Their world is stricken by AIDS, which releases still more demons. It resembles the millennial landscape of *The Seventh Seal*, also set during a plague—Kushner's time in medieval studies paid off—yet the play could not be more American. Mark Twain called the Book of Mormon "chloroform in print," but it's also our own homegrown visionary religion, William Blake and Revelations translated to a world of cowboys and Indians. Kushner brings together *two* Chosen People, Mormons and Jews; both migrant nations prove to be equally, fiercely American.

This unwieldy epic is kept airborne with short, rapid-fire scenes, aria-like monologues, cockeyed poetry, and surprising comedy. Kushner had a liberating love of camp, which had been fed by his discovery of the Theater of the Ridiculous when he first came to New York. (Kushner wrote of Charles Ludlam: "He sees how ridiculous the world is...and look out! He sees through you, he's learned your secret, he knows what you hope no one has noticed, that you too are ridiculous.") His use of comedy is always serious. His jokes spring naturally out of the situation, catch the audience off guard, and always add to the discussion. Here's Prior and Harper meeting for the first time in *his* dream and *her* drug hallucination.

> Harper: I *never* drink. And I *never* take drugs.
> Prior: Well, smell *you*, Nancy Drew.
> Harper: Except Valium.
> Prior: Except Valium; in wee handfuls.
> Harper: It's terrible. Mormons are not supposed to be addicted to anything. I'm a Mormon.
> Prior: I'm a homosexual.
> Harper: Oh! In my church we don't believe in homosexuals.
> Prior: In my church we don't believe in Mormons.

In addition to comedy, the play is carried by Kushner's gift for fantasy. This is not a naturalistic play, but one of dreams and visions. It frequently breaks free of box-set realism—it builds, in fact, to a visit to heaven. Like James Merrill in his Ephraim poems, Kushner uses the spirit world to expand his storytelling vocabulary; the two writers use similar grammars of poetic escape. Each fantasy comes out of a particular character's pain and need; there's always a psychological truth to what they imagine. Yet the episodes do not remain simply dreams but have broader, more mysterious resonances. As with Merrill, we often suffer the poignant wish that Kushner's fantasies were true.

Kushner also has a real talent for creating character. All the roles are good, but one in particular is so strong that it wins over even people who resist the rest of the play.

Roy Cohn is the villain of *Angels*, a Shakespearean dynamo of words and ideas, one of those grand monsters who are a gift to actors and audiences. He talks nonstop and is always thinking, arguing, conniving; he has a wonderfully foul mouth. He is a human monster of selfishness who unembarrassedly eats off other people's plates in restaurants. He thinks as badly of himself as he does of others—he doesn't trust Belize until Belize calls him "a greedy kike." Kushner gives him good arguments for everything he does, including his denials. He famously tells his doctor why he can't be called a homosexual:

> Homosexuals are not men who sleep with other men. Homosexuals are men who in fifteen years of trying cannot get a pissant antidiscrimination bill through City Council. Homosexuals are men who know nobody and nobody knows. Who have zero clout. Does this sound like me, Henry?

He turns the poststructuralist arguments of Michel Foucault and others into an airtight case for lying.

Cohn is offset by a kind of countervillain, a figure who's more antivillain than antihero: Louis. The man who leaves his sick boyfriend is smart and self-aware, weak and conflicted. Kushner has said that Louis is the character most like himself. We shouldn't take him literally. The playwright is harsher on Louis than he is on any other character, including Cohn, in much the same way that Mart Crowley is harshest with *his* alter ego, Michael, in *Boys in the Band,* and Edmund White merciless with *his* in *A Boy's Own Story.* Gay authors are often more self-critical than straight male authors—as hard on their fictional counterparts as many women writers are. I often wish they showed themselves more mercy, but bitter self-doubt can also be transformed into useful self-knowledge. (I've heard several gay men dismiss the whole idea of Louis abandoning Prior; they say they know of nobody doing such a terrible thing during the epidemic. One good friend, however, with a sick partner whom he took care of to the end, said he was glad to see abandonment depicted onstage—the play recognized how very hard it was to stay with a dying loved one.)

After Cohn dies, Belize insists that Louis say kaddish over him before they steal his cache of AZT. The Hebrew prayer is an invocation to God that builds to a plea for peace. ("May He who makes peace in His high places, grant peace for us and all Israel. And say amen.") It's one of the strongest scenes in the play. Louis, the very secular Jew, delivers the prayer in Hebrew, prompted by, of all people, the ghost of Ethel Rosenberg. In the eyes of God, even the worst of us must be—not forgiven, exactly, but noticed, attended to, acknowledged. Ethel Rosenberg closes the prayer with a bit of English, "You sonofabitch," which Louis instantly repeats.

News of the play began to go out in the world even before Kushner finished writing it. My own first encounter was in May 1990 when the first part was presented in a workshop at the Mark Taper Forum in Los Angeles. Oskar Eustis had left San Francisco but he took the play with him to his new theater. My boyfriend knew an actress who was appearing in it. When she heard we were coming to town, she said we should come see this new show. "You might find it interesting." We didn't know what to expect. When we arrived and saw the title *and* elaborate subtitle *and* the fact it was only part one of a two-part play, our hearts sank. *Angels in America: A Gay Fantasia on National Themes; Part One: Millennium Approaches.* Out of our friendships with actors we'd seen a lot of bad theater.

By the time we stepped outside at the first intermission, however, we were dumbstruck, intoxicated. We'd never experienced anything like this play. We were even more excited at the end. We couldn't wait for it to come to New York, nor could we wait for *Part Two* and find out how the story ended. We had to wait a long time.

Part One had its world premiere in 1991 at the Mark Taper. It opened in January 1992 in London. Word continued to spread that something very exciting was on its way, like the angel itself. *Part One* didn't reach New York until May 1993, directed by George Wolfe and with a cast that included Stephen Spinella as Prior, future director Joe Mantello as Louis, Ron Leibman as Roy Cohn, and Kathleen Chalfant (the Nancy Reagan of *Just Say No*), playing Hannah Pitt and Ethel Rosenberg. It opened at the Walter Kerr Theatre on West Forty-eighth Street—not off-Broadway like so many other gay plays, but in an actual Broadway house, one named after the critic who'd revised his rave of *Who's Afraid of Virginia Woolf?* after he learned its author was a homosexual.

Frank Rich was still lead critic for the *Times*. He saw the play repeatedly, the first part in London, then with *Part Two: Perestroika*, at the Mark Taper in November 1992, a week after Bill Clinton was elected president. Rich saw the play often enough to understand and appreciate it. When *Part One* opened on Broadway, he gave it a complete rave, calling it "the most thrilling American play in years." More praise followed, from all the major newspapers and magazines. "The most ambitious American play of our time," wrote Jack Kroll in *Newsweek*. "A victory for theater," wrote John Lahr in the *New Yorker*, "for the transformative power of the imagination to turn devastation into beauty." *Part One* won both the Pulitzer Prize and the Tony Award. (During the Tony broadcast, Kushner's thank-you speech inevitably ran over the time limit; the orchestra tried to cut him off. "This is one scary orchestra," he said with a giddy laugh and kept going.) *Part Two* opened simultaneously in New York and London that November. There was still more praise—*Variety* called it "a monumental achievement," and *New York Newsday* said it was "playful and profound, extravagantly theatrical and deeply spiritual, witty and compassionate"—yet with occasional notes of uncertainty.

Angels was genuinely exciting theater, but people weren't always sure what it meant. It is full of characters but even more full of ideas. Kushner juggles ideas the way a symphonic composer juggles musical phrases, adding even more ideas as the play progresses. It's an idea-driven drama as much as it is one driven by character or plot. No wonder he had trouble finishing *Part Two*. At one point he considered putting all his characters on top of the Empire State Building and setting off a nuclear bomb.

Angels is so full of ideas that not only do different readers have different readings, but the same reader can have different readings at different times. Here is how I understand the play—this year, anyway:

There are two significant thematic strands. First, there is the more earthbound theme built around a simple moral question: what does an individual owe to others?

The question affects not just one plotline but all: What does Louis owe Prior? What does Joe owe his wife, Harper? What does Joe owe the Mormon church? And so on. It's a question that transcends positions of left and right, gay and straight, believer and agnostic. We all perform balancing acts between self and family, individual and community, private desire and group expectation. Gay people in particular must break with the groupthink of church and society in order to live their own lives. (It's why you still see half-read copies of *Atlas Shrugged* on the night tables of otherwise intelligent gay men.) But the freedom that enables a man to be gay can also enable him to abandon his sick lover. It can help a Mormon leave his church and at the same time put him on the same political page as Roy Cohn. Even the angel goes, "I I I I!" Roy Cohn is the gold standard of self-empowerment here, and it's not a pretty ideal. Kushner swings back and forth between the extremes of self and selflessness; he gives no final, simple answer—there *is* no final answer. He offers instead what he elsewhere calls "a dialectically shaped truth." We must all spend our lives moving back and forth between these two absolutes.

The second theme is the more famous one, the theme of prophecy. It is bigger, stranger, more original and more elusive. It drives the first play, *Millennium Approaches*, like an engine. At the end Prior and the audience are promised a revelation that will explain *everything*.

Angel: Greetings, Prophet;
The Great Work begins:
The Messenger has arrived.
(*Blackout.*)

It's one of the great curtain speeches of all time.

The second play, *Perestroika* (Russian for "rebuilding"), opens with a long speech from Aleksii Antedilluvianovich Prelapsarianov, the world's oldest living Bolshevik, who complains that people no longer have any "*Theeeery*" (in Kathleen Chalfant's unforgettable mad Russian accent) and they are like a snake with no skin without "the next Beautiful *Theeeery*." The audience assumes the angel will give Prior a new theory.

But in the next act, after much angel talk ("Open me Prophet. I I I I am/The Book") and an ecstatic celestial orgasm, the angel offers only a shockingly blunt message: "STOP MOVING!" Change is bad, stasis is good. Motion is the enemy—activities like immigration only get us in trouble. The world must remain the same. When Prior describes his vision to Belize, his friend immediately understands that it's a fantasy built around Louis, the man who got away. Prior only wants life to go back to what it was. We see where the message comes from and patiently wait to see where it will take us.

Three acts later, Prior climbs up to Heaven. He finds no God there— God has fled—only little gods, ineffectual angels who don't know how to operate the world. Not even their radio works. The angels offer Prior the gift of eternal sameness. But Prior recognizes that without change there is only paralysis, and paralysis is death. Change is life. He tells them:

I want more life. I can't help myself. I do.

I've lived through such terrible times, and there are people who live through much worse, but...I want more life.

He wakes up from his dream, like Dorothy Gale in Kansas surrounded by friends. "I had the most remarkable dream. And you were there, and you... And you...And some of it was terrible, and some of it was wonderful, but all the same I kept saying I want to go home."

The first time I saw *Part Two*, the *Wizard of Oz* echoes produced laughter of relief from the audience. Heaven had been so confusing, and people were pleased to be on familiar ground again, even if they didn't know what it meant.

So what does this thematic plotline mean? I think it's primarily a shaggy dog story or, more appropriately, a shaggy God story. There is no "beautiful theory," which might be for the best since we know from the Soviet Union where beautiful theories can lead. It's a deliberate letdown, a carefully crafted anticlimax.

The answer that there is no answer disappoints many people. Yet it works for me. It provides a home chord where this polyphonic drama of characters, ideas, and history can stop—for now, anyway. And it connects up with the "dialectically shaped truth" I mentioned earlier. There are no final, simple answers. But a work of art doesn't need to provide complete answers in order to succeed. It needs only to excite us into asking questions and give us a place to think about them while we become involved in other people's lives.

Angels in America was phenomenally successful, not only winning prizes and audiences in New York but touring the entire country. Later it was staged by colleges and universities, with religious conservatives protesting school productions in North Carolina and elsewhere. It was performed in translation as well, with major productions in Germany, Spain, Japan, and even Poland. From the start there was talk of turning this highly cinematic play into a movie. After several near misses, including a deal with Robert Altman, it finally became a two-part TV movie on HBO in 2003, directed by Mike Nichols with a cast that included Al Pacino as Roy Cohn and Meryl Streep in the Kathleen Chalfant parts.

One would like to think the critical success of *Angels* showed that the literary world had finally outgrown its old bigotry. But a few hobgoblins survived. Roger Shattuck, a professor in French literature, seemed to hate homosexuality so much he couldn't see what was actually onstage. He believed "the play advocates the extinction of moral restraints" and that the angel at the end of *Part One* was there to bless everyone for behaving so badly. He never saw *Part Two*. Lee Siegel, reviewing the TV movie in the *New Republic*, said *Angels* was "a second-rate play written by a second-rate playwright who happens to be gay, and because he has written a play about being gay, and about AIDS, no one—and I mean no one—is going to call *Angels in America* the overwrought, coarse, posturing, formulaic mess that it is." He must not have read Shattuck or the play's gay critics. The only real specific Siegel offers on *why* the play is bad is that the characters always talk about their feelings, analyzing and describing them like a director working with actors, rather than simply expressing them—but that's how people talk in modern life.

A few gay writers criticized the play, but with their own curious agendas. Leo Bersani, yet another professor of French literature, author of the provocative essay, "Is the Rectum a Grave?" claimed, "The enormous success of this muddled and pretentious play is a sign...of how ready and anxious America is to see and hear about gays—provided we reassure America how familiar, how morally sincere, and particularly in the case of Kushner's work, how innocuously full of significance we can be." It's odd hearing anyone complain about the moral sincerity of gay people, but odder still when it's a tenured professor in his sixties, hardly a model of anarchic nihilism. But I believe he's right about one of the reasons for the success of *Angels*: it showed that gay people *were* morally serious, which the general population—at least those who went to the theater—was finally ready to hear.

The strangest enemy of the play was Andrew Sullivan, the young, openly gay, British-born editor of the *New Republic*. Sullivan had never shown much interest in theater but he became fixated with *Angels*. "Gay life—and gay death—surely awaits something grander and subtler than this." His criticisms were incoherent. First he complained the play was too funny, that it "never ascended...above a West Village version of Neil Simon." Then he complained that it was nothing but "political agitprop," appealing only to "the hard left, which is partly why it won a Pulitzer." I don't know which is more comical, the idea of a Communist Neil Simon play or the picture of the Pulitzer Prize committee as a hotbed of Marxists.

Kushner responded in passing to Sullivan's attack on *Angels* when he wrote an essay on gay liberation for the *Nation* on the twenty-fifth anniversary of the Stonewall riots, "A Socialism of the Skin (Liberation, Honey!)" This smart, well-considered, often funny, ultimately serious piece was written partly in response to an article by Sullivan published a year earlier, "The Politics of Homosexuality." Kushner adds a playful nelliness to his repertoire of voices. He admits, "I used to have a crush on Andrew, neo-con or neo-liberal (or whatever the hell they're called these days) though he be. I would never have married him, but he's cute! Then he called me a 'West Village Neil Simon,' *in print*, and I retired the crush. This by way of background for what follows, to prove that I am, despite my wounded affections, capable of the 'restraint and reason' he calls for at the opening of his article." Kushner proceeds to examine the article seriously and respectfully. Sullivan argued that gay activists were wrong to connect gay issues with issues of race, class, and gender; gay issues should be kept separate in order to gain broader support. Kushner disagrees, believing a narrower focus won't win additional voters and, more important, that minority groups are all in the same boat. "Our suffering teaches us solidarity; or it should." Kushner was totally dismissive of a recent essay by gay conservative Bruce Bawer, author of *A Place at the Table* ("Bruce doesn't like it when gay men get dishy and bitchy and talk sissy about boys.... He's also, and I mean this politely, a little slow. It took him five years to figure out that maybe a gay man shouldn't be writing movie reviews for the viciously homophobic *American Spectator*"). But he addressed Sullivan as an equal, respecting his motives and some of his points, even as he argued that gay rights must be part of a bigger picture. It's a very strong—and persuasive—piece of prose.

Sullivan was able to respond soon afterward, face-to-face, when he and Kushner met on TV on *Charlie Rose*.

The old days when novelists and playwrights were occasional guests on late-night talk shows were long gone. Gore Vidal and Truman Capote had been replaced first by the likes of Burt Reynolds and Charo, then by lesser celebrities. PBS took up some of the slack, but they rarely featured gay or lesbian figures. Bill Moyers, a good liberal who could talk to philosophers and physicists, never interviewed anyone about gay issues on any of his major TV series. Charlie Rose, however, who had five hours to fill every week, now and then included a gay man or woman. He first invited Kushner on his show after *Angels* broke the record for Tony nominations for a nonmusical play. A year later he invited Kushner back when, on the night of June 24, 1994, in commemoration of the twenty-fifth anniversary of Stonewall, Rose devoted his entire hour to gay talking heads.

The show began with historian Martin Duberman, activist Jim Fouratt, and publisher Barbara Smith talking about the riots. They were followed by Kushner, *Village Voice* journalist Donna Minkowitz, and the two men whom Kushner had just criticized in the *Nation*: Sullivan and Bawer. It was one of those controversial combinations that sounds lively on paper but is usually only messy in fact.

Rose began the segment by admitting that heated words had already been exchanged before the cameras were turned on. What followed must've made most viewers feel they had walked in on the middle of a family quarrel. There was much talk of single-issue gay rights versus broad-issue human rights, politics versus culture, and the left versus the right. Rose never mentioned Kushner's recent *Nation* piece, but much of what Sullivan said was in response to it. Bawer, in a coat and tie that brought out his unfortunate resemblance to young Roy Cohn, complained steadily about "a certain left politics," "the Left-leaning agenda," and "a handful of leftists." Sullivan maintained a boyish grin as he interrupted again and again, refusing to let anyone else finish. Kushner often winced in pain over what was said—he had no room to be playful or funny. Minkowitz held her own in the debate, making good points about the myth of gay wealth and the differences between lesbian identity and gay male identity. More than once, all four spoke simultaneously, sounding like a pack of birds. Rose was overwhelmed. Famous for interrupting guests, he spent much of the segment with his chin in his hand, just listening. He was in calmer waters in the last segment, a one-on-one conversation with actor Ian McKellen, who was in town to perform his one-man show, *A Knight Out*, and to march in the international Stonewall 25 parade.

All in all, it was a lively hour of television. One would think that Rose or another talk show host would be eager to repeat it. But nobody ever did, not to my knowledge. It was the exception that proved the rule. Anyone who wanted to hear discussions of gay issues remained dependent on books and magazines.

Minkowitz continued to write smart journalism for the *Voice* and a new monthly magazine, *Out*. Bawer left the United States to live in northern Europe, attracted by the culture and finding a whole new career attacking liberal Europeans for being too tolerant of Muslim immigrants. Sullivan left the *New Republic* after announcing he had AIDS, but he continued to write about politics and gay issues in books and magazines. A ceaseless pump of opinions, he became a pioneer in the new field of blogging. In the months leading up to the broadcast of *Angels* on HBO, he resumed his war against the play. He blogged about it often, calling it "a pretentious left-wing screed," gloating over its ratings ("only" 4.2 million viewers), quoting any negative review he could find, yet still never making clear exactly why he hated it so much.

Kushner enjoyed his success even though it made his life more frantic. His father finally came around, admitting he was proud to have Tchaikovsky for a son. He continued to write. *Angels* was a hard act to follow and Kushner knew it. He did a follow-up in 1994, *Slavs*, about the collapse of the Soviet Union, using ideas developed for *Perestroika*. He began another epic drama, *Henry Box Brown or The Mirror of Slavery*, about an African-American theater troupe touring England during the American Civil War, but he put it aside after a workshop production in London. In 2000 he began work on a semiautobiographical novel of ideas, *The Intelligent Homosexual's Guide to Capitalism and Socialism with a Key to the Scriptures*—the title is another riff on Shaw: his book *The Intelligent Woman's Guide to Socialism and Capitalism*. Kushner never finished the novel but ten years later gave the title to a new play about a dysfunctional political family in Brooklyn, a sort of *Heartbreak House* of the American left. (The play has been produced but is still a work in progress, and it's too soon to say if it succeeds or not.) He produced nothing gay between *Angels* and *Guide*. I may be wrong, but I feel his writing has suffered as a result. His play *Homebody/Kabul* and his opera *Caroline, or Change* have their pleasures, but they don't electrify and illuminate the way that *Angels* does.

Kushner is a luftmensch, a man of air and ideas, an abstract thinker who does his strongest dramatic work when he uses gay bodies. He writes about all bodies, of course, but gay bodies best enable him to divide his mind into conversing components. They also move him to poetry, feed his sense of humor, and bring out his sensual side. When he taps into his sexuality, he is like Antaeas touching the earth and gaining strength. Without it, he is all mind like a watch, as his hero Herman Melville said of God.

By writing about gay men he ultimately writes about everyone. Sometimes silence is good for a gay artist (Albee, perhaps), but I don't think it is for Kushner. When he suppresses his gay self, he can't help but suppress other selves. Releasing it releases the others. A wonderful example of this is the epilogue of *Angels.*

Prior returns from his dream of heaven ready to die, but then he lives. Four years after his dream, in 1990, he joins his friends at the Bethesda Fountain in Central Park. (His survival seems more plausible now than it did when the play first opened.) He talks to the audience about his friends and their lives. He closes by addressing the audience first as a gay man:

> We won't die secret deaths anymore. The world only spins forward.
> We will be citizens. The time has come.

Then he addresses them in a more inclusive voice:

> Bye now.
> You are fabulous creatures, each and every one.
> And I bless you: More Life.
> The Great Work Begins.

Releasing the gay self releases other selves, including an all-encompassing, universal self. But as Prior says, there is no final, simple answer. The work can only continue.

20. Rising Tide

—∽∽—

In the world of books, gay novels continued to appear in record numbers. They were not always reviewed or recognized by the literary mainstream (Joe Keenan joked that "the mainstream" sounded like "something Republicans pee in"), but queer literature had developed its own support system.

A new magazine, *Lambda Rising Book Report*, was founded in 1987 by Lambda Rising Bookstore in Washington, D.C. Almost entirely book reviews, it began as a quarterly, became a bimonthly, then a monthly—there were now so many books that editor Jim Marks had no trouble filling its pages. In 1989, the magazine initiated a set of annual literary prizes, the Lambda Book Awards.

In New York, a group of editors and writers started a new organization, the Publishing Triangle, to promote gay and lesbian books. They held their first meetings in a conference room at St. Martin's Press in the Flatiron Building. The Triangle not only provided publicity and networking, they administered additional awards. The Ferro-Grumley Prize for gay and lesbian fiction was created in the name of Robert Ferro and Michael Grumley with money left in their wills for that purpose. There was the Robert Chesley Award for Playwriting. The Bill Whitehead Award for Lifetime Achievement was established in the name of the editor, who died of AIDS in 1987. The award alternated between men and women: the first was given in 1989 to Edmund White, who had worked with Whitehead; the second, the following year, was given to poet/essayist Audre Lorde.

During its first decade, the Triangle presented its awards at the Lambda Book Award dinners, which were held during the annual American Booksellers Association convention. Whatever city was the site of the ABA each year—Los Angeles, Chicago, even Las Vegas—found itself inundated with openly gay and lesbian authors and editors. Their presence was undeniable.

Another important public event was the annual OutWrite literary conference, begun in 1990 by *Out/look* magazine. Intended initially as an occasion for writer workshops, these weekend festivals became celebrations of gay and lesbian literature. The first two OutWrites were in San Francisco; the next six were held in Boston. In Boston, young men and women would take over the old Park Plaza Hotel for the weekend, filling the shabby, genteel lobby with Doc Marten boots, ACT UP T-shirts, and Tenaxed hair. Over a thousand participants attended nearly a hundred different panels and readings. There was always a dance on Saturday night.

The chief events at each conference were the opening and closing addresses by literary elders. It was here that Allen Ginsberg admitted he didn't worry about AIDS, since his sex life was limited to giving blowjobs to straight college boys. The following year Edward Albee told the audience, "I don't think being gay is a subject any more than being straight is a subject.... With some writers there's a bit of opportunism involved there. Writing on gay themes has become big business and some of the lesser ones are cashing in." People began to boo. "Boo away," he said. "I don't care." (Albee had been kicked in the teeth twenty-five years earlier not for writing anything gay but simply for *being* gay. He and the people at the conference spoke very different languages.)

In the Park Plaza ballroom in 1992, Allan Gurganus, author of the literary best seller *Oldest Living Confederate Widow Tells All*, stood onstage in a flamboyant white suit worthy of Mark Twain and gave a speech like an evangelical sermon—"Brothers and sisters! And brothers who are sisters and sisters who are brothers!"—celebrating the value of gay experience to literature. The following year, Samuel Delany, the black science-fiction pioneer, author of *Dhalgren* and *The Motion of Light in Water*, spoke at length about the amorphousness of sex, using episodes from his own amorphic life—he was once married to lesbian poet Marilyn Hacker—and his visits to the old porn theaters of Forty-second Street. (He later incorporated this material into a fascinating book, *Times Square Red, Times Square Blue*.)

And at the 1995 conference, Tony Kushner gave a long, brilliant talk in praise of excess, "On Pretentiousness," a breathless monologue that tossed together Melville, de Tocqueville, his fears about the new Republican Congress, his response to Leo Bersani's attack on *Angels* ("I still don't know if the rectum is a grave, but now I think I have an answer to the question: Is Leo Bersani an asshole?"), a defense of political art, *and* his recipe for lasagna:

Baking lasagna has long been my own personal paradigm for writing a play....A good play, like a good lasagna, should be overstuffed: It has a pomposity and an overreach: Its ambitions extend in the direction of not-missing-a-trick, it has a bursting omnipotence up its sleeve, or rather, under its noodles: It is pretentious food.

Kushner had won the Pulitzer for theater in 1993, but similar recognition was slow in coming to gay novels. Readers tend to be more conservative than playgoers. As late as 1995, when Edmund White was considered for inclusion in the prestigious if invisible American Academy of Arts, committee member Ned Rorem needed to be cagy in presenting him. He wrote in his diary: "Oral support of Edmund White at the Academy Meeting. It is important to stress the unimportance of homosexuality in his fiction, given that 95 percent of his characters are gay. Their problems are never those of polemical activists, but simply those of more or less intelligent citizens living and loving in the same world we all inhabit." As if the only good gay people are those who don't care about politics. Nevertheless, Rorem succeeded in getting White in.

The epidemic continued to take its toll on literature as well as on the larger world. New writers appeared every year, published one or two books, then became ill and died. Allen Barnett won several prizes for his collection of short stories, *The Body and Its Dangers*, including a citation from PEN, and died a year later in 1991. David Feinberg died in 1994 after publishing one novel and a book of essays. Poet and essayist Essex Hemphill died in 1995. Many, many more died without the chance to make any kind of mark.

In Tucson, Arizona, on February 6, 1995, James Merrill passed away. "We won't die secret deaths anymore," says Prior at the end of *Angels*. But it was kept a secret that Merrill died of AIDS until 2002, when his literary executor, J. D. McClatchy, wrote about it in a fine essay, "Two Deaths, Two Lives," comparing his secretive death to the angrily honest death of novelist and memoirist Paul Monette.

A new writer made a big splash in 1990 with his second novel, *A Home at the End of the World*. Michael Cunningham was a craggily handsome thirty-nine-year-old who grew up in Pasadena, California, studied writing at Stanford and Iowa, then came east and divided his time between Provincetown and New York. He became the boyfriend of psychologist Ken Corbett.

Cunningham had published a first novel back in 1984, *Golden States*, a coming-of-age story about a twelve-year-old boy in southern California who's discovering his sexuality. His half sister disappears and he hunts for her, hitchhiking to San Francisco, where he's befriended by a gay man in his early twenties; things end well. It's somewhat conventional, but full of good prose and keen observations. Nevertheless, Cunningham later dismissed it as "not good enough" and has refused to let it be reprinted. I suspect he had high hopes for the novel, felt burned when it didn't get more attention, and then blamed the book. It was six years before he published his next novel. "I had my head in the oven, on and off, during those six years—not literally," he later said. "You know, it's hard to do something like write a novel....I probably have a little less self-confidence than a lot of writers."

But he eventually began a new novel, which he sold to Farrar, Straus, and Giroux. A major chapter, "White Angel," was published in the *New Yorker* a year before the book came out. There was much advance buzz, and *A Home at the End of the World* was a big success. It's an excellent book but, as with *A Boy's Own Story*, one can't help suspecting it succeeded not only because of its quality but because it was what readers needed at the time: in this case, a serious, accessible novel about gay men in the age of AIDS.

Four first-person narrators tell the story of Bobby, a tramautized straight boy befriended in school in the 1960s by a gay kid, Jonathan. Bobby grows up to be a cook. He moves to New York and rejoins Jonathan, and they set up house with a female friend, Clare, who becomes pregnant with Bobby's child. (The fourth narrator is Jonathan's mother.) The shadow of death appears in the form of Jonathan's friend, Erich, who is sick with AIDS. It's a gentle story about trying to recover lost paradises of youth and high school, with the Woodstock festival as a symbolic Eden. Bobby, Jonathan, and Clare actually move to Woodstock and open a restaurant. For me, the freshest element is the friendship between a gay man and a straight man, where the sissy helps the wounded hetero pull his life together, instead of the other way around.

People who resist the novel complain that the chapters about adolescence are stronger than the adult chapters, and that the four first-person narrators sound too much alike. I disagree with both charges. The death of Bobby's brother and loss of his mother are hard acts to follow, but Bobby and Jonathan are more interesting as grown-ups than they are as kids. And the four narrators actually do have their own voices. However, they all have a weakness for pretty-sounding metaphors which pop up now and then like cake frosting roses. (For example, Bobby remembers his mother: "She looked at me as if she were standing on a platform in a flat, dry country and I was pulling away on a train *that traveled high into an alpine world*." I have italicized the frosting rose.) They can be mildly distracting, but they don't hurt the novel.

The increased numbers of gay books was enough by itself to improve the chances of good work getting published. Many so-so books appeared, but the amount of first-rate work remains impressive. It didn't always get the attention it deserved. I'm thinking in particular of the novels of Paul Russell. His third book, *Sea of Tranquillity* (1995), juxtaposes the lives of an astronaut and his wife trapped in a bad marriage with the wild life of their gay son, who strives to experience everything physical *and* spiritual. AIDS lifts him and the book into a higher sphere. Russell's other novels are equally ambitious and startling; he has a devoted readership, but his books never got many reviews in the general press.

He was not alone in this. Mark Merlis followed an impressive first novel about academic life in the 1940s, *American Studies* (1994), with an even finer second novel, *An Arrow's Flight* (1998), where the Philoctetes story is transposed from ancient Greece to the gay urban scene of the 1990s. It sounds pretentious or silly, but it's genuinely witty and ultimately wise. Michael Nava, a lawyer in Los Angeles, wrote a remarkable series of mysteries about a gay defense attorney, Henry Rios: *The Little Death* (1986), *Goldenboy* (1988), *How Town* (1990), *The Hidden Law* (1992), *The Death of Friends* (1996), *The Burning Plain* (1997), and *Rag and Bone* (2001). Each book functions as an individual murder mystery, but the series forms the sustained fictional biography of a gay Hispanic American dealing with issues of career, family, and love over a span of twenty years. Nava had a huge following among gay readers and won the Lambda Book Award for Mystery six times. However, caught in the double bind of being both a gay writer and a mystery writer, Nava did not get his full due from mainstream critics.

AIDS played an important role in this literary ferment, yet one that's hard to define. It's not irrelevant that two of the literary prizes—the Ferro-Grumley and the Whitehead—were named after men who died of AIDS. Death can feed creativity. Times of trouble often coexist with intense artistic productivity, so long as the trouble leaves one room to breathe. The

AIDS epidemic was not a sudden cataclysm but a slow-motion disaster, a creeping fire that left people with time to brood and worry. Writers used this time to write, fighting off their fears with prose and poetry. AIDS gave a new urgency to the work, and it gave gay writing a new importance in the culture at large. For many straight people, the epidemic provided gay men with a respectability they didn't have before: they were tragic heroes now. A few lesbian journalists even complained that the plague gave men an unfair advantage over the women in the cultural marketplace.

During these years, Edmund White remained in Paris and continued with the series of autobiographical novels he had begun with *A Boy's Own Story*. They were his most popular books and they promised to be his master-work, his own *In Search of Lost Time*. Yet he kept being distracted.

After *Caracole*, his straight novel, he returned to the project with a new book bearing an old title, *The Beautiful Room Is Empty*. It comes from a gno-mic passage in a letter from Franz Kafka to his neglected fiancée, Milena Jesenska, comparing them to two people at opposite ends of a room with facing doors: sometimes both are in the room, sometimes only one, and sometimes "the beautiful room is empty."

The novel picks up where *A Boy's Own Story* left off, with the unnamed narrator still a teenager at prep school. But the world now has names (Detroit, Chicago, Cincinnati) and the narrator gets a real friend, some-one who can tell him the truth about himself. It's a woman, not a man, a painting student named Maria who's seven years older than the hero and attends the art school across the street. Based on White's friend Marilyn Schaeffer, she is one of his best characters, a sometime Stalinist and some-time lesbian who loves abstract expressionism, grand opera, and the Everly Brothers.

She is the first of several characters in a book built not so much out of narrative as out of character sketches. White is a gifted portrait painter, able to conjure a man or woman in a handful of words. Other vivid fig-ures include Annie, an unhappy anorexic; Tex, an old-style queen who runs a bookstore; and Lou, a lean, handsomely ugly, self-educated advertising executive who is also a heroin addict. This portrait gallery takes the narra-tor first to college, then to New York. He is still the anxious courtier trying to understand each royal court he stumbles into, the amnesiac from *Forget-ting Elena* faking it until he learns the rules. Although he describes himself as an amoral monster out of Gide or Genet ("My own immorality didn't trouble me"), he's basically a nice middle-class boy from the Midwest. He's no longer the chronic betrayer of *A Boy's Own Story*. The worst thing we see him do in this volume is make *himself* miserable.

Unfolding chronologically, *Beautiful Room* does not have the broken, somnambulistic feel of the earlier book. The prose is tighter, with urgency and momentum. Best of all, the narrator changes. He unhappily cruises the toilets in college, but then gets a room off campus, where he happily beds men and also begins to write. We hear for the first time of his ambition to be an author. The sex grows less guilty. One of the most famous scenes in the book is a highly democratic orgy in a New York subway restroom around a young man who looks like a farm boy:

> Now everyone is at work on him at once, breath in his ear, lips on his lips, mouths on his balls, cock and ass, that arm around his waist, as though he really is a bride and this the last minute flurry of seamstresses fitting him into his gown.

When it's over, there's none of the old guilt and shame. The narrator uses the second person to make the reader a participant:

> In two seconds you've buttoned up, wrapped your raincoat around you, and rushed out into the flood of passengers flowing up the stairs and rivuleting into the night. Your hair is rumpled, your face flushed, and your hand still smells of the country boy. At the subway entrance you catch sight of the businessman just behind you. Without thinking, you glance at his trousers...he looks at your wet knees at the same moment, and you and he exchange the tiniest smile of wintry complicity.

White does not include anything like *The Blue Boy in Black*, the college play that first brought him to New York. He also leaves out his first lover, acting student Stanley Redfern. (The book, however, is dedicated to Redfern.) The great love of this novel is a vague, elusive blond named Sean, based on Jim Ruddy. Sean is even more divided over his sexuality than the narrator. He decides to go straight and, in a puzzling development, the narrator follows him into group therapy. Not until the last pages, when he is a witness at the Stonewall riots—as White was himself—is the narrator finally blasted out of his maze-like closet.

> "Gay is good." We were all chanting it, knowing how ridiculous we were being in this parody of a real demonstration, but feeling giddily confident anyway. Now someone said, "We're the Pink Panthers," and that made us laugh again. Then I caught myself foolishly imagining that gays might someday constitute a community rather than a diagnosis.

That last sentence is a surprise coming from Edmund White, sounding more like propaganda than literature. Yet it makes clear how necessary politics is to his protagonist's liberation.

The Beautiful Room Is Empty was published in 1988 by Knopf. White's editor at Dutton, Bill Whitehead, had just died, and his agent moved him to the more prestigious house. The novel received excellent reviews in the gay press and admiring if uncomfortable ones in the straight press; the sales figures were good. Yet it was never as popular as *A Boy's Own Story*. I suspect many readers simply prefer adolescence, no matter how miserable, to later periods of life. Gay wits who hadn't read the novel took to calling it "The Beautiful Book Is Empty," but I find it superior to its predecessor, with better characters, stronger narrative, and an exciting change in the protagonist. One looks forward to what will happen to him.

White intended to write two more novels, one about the Seventies and another about the Eighties and AIDS. He outlined his plans in an interview in the *Paris Review* in 1988. But instead of writing the next novel, he took another detour, this time to produce a fat biography of French novelist Jean Genet. He received a good advance for the project and it gave him a good reason to stay in Paris. He thought he could do it quickly, but it took five years. *Genet: A Biography* won White praise and attention when it finally appeared in 1993, including a review on the front page of the *New York Times Book Review* and an award from the National Book Critics Circle; in France he was made a Chevalier de l'Ordre des Arts et des Lettres. The literary world prefers biographies of dead writers to novels by live ones. Among my well-read friends I know of only two people who have read it. Yet the book established White's talent for literary biography, which he later continued with his excellent short lives of Proust and Rimbaud.

White now had a new boyfriend, a young French architect, Hubert Sorin. Sorin was married, but even his wife knew he was gay. He claimed his family was minor French nobility, but White later learned his mother was a hairdresser. Shortly after he moved in with White in 1989, Sorin tested positive for HIV. The two men came to the States together in 1990 when White taught for a year at Brown University. They bought a dog there, a basset hound named Fred, whom they took back with them to Paris.

Sorin grew more ill. Unable to do architectural work, he began to draw cartoons and illustrations, working in a style that suggests Aubrey Beardsley crossed with the animated Beatles movie *Yellow Submarine*. He collaborated with White on a humorous sketchbook about their life in Paris. His health continued to deteriorate.

Sorin loved the desert—he had studied architecture in North Africa— and he wanted to visit one last time while he was well enough to travel. White reluctantly agreed. They flew to Morocco in March 1994. The first days went well. While visiting a small town in the mountains, however, Sorin's body suddenly gave out. In a nightmare journey that lasted several days, White rushed Sorin by ambulance to a hospital in Marrakesh. Exhausted, he fell asleep beside Sorin in his hospital bed. He woke up the next morning to find his partner had died alongside him an hour earlier.

White knew of only one way to deal with grief, which was to write about it. That morning he found a private corner and wrote an introduction to their sketchbook.

> Hubert Sorin, my lover, who just died two hours ago in the Polytechnique du Sud in Marrakesh, was an architect who turned himself into an illustrator with a remarkable patience and diligence and above all with a flair for capitalizing on his talents and pictorial discoveries....
>
> I'm writing this page with his beautiful Art Pen, which he always forbade me to touch; today I couldn't find anything else to write with, and I wanted to—needed to—give a form to my grief that he would approve of. That's why I'm daring to use your pen, Hubert.

The book was published in Britain as *Sketches from Memory* with the pages about Sorin's death as the introduction. In the United States the book appeared as *Our Paris*, with the introduction moved to the back.

White had briefly resumed work on his tetralogy the summer before Sorin's death. He returned to it now and made an important decision: he would combine the last two novels into one. He later said he did this because he feared a novel about just the orgy years would be "intolerable to read in this post-AIDS period, just as a fourth volume which would be nothing but people dying would be equally intolerable." But White was HIV positive himself. After Sorin died, he may have feared he didn't have enough time to write *two* books. He has never said this outright, but admitted in an interview that he felt haunted by death. "First I had to finish the Genet book, and now I have to finish this novel. I think when I finish that, then I'll die.... It's like some fairy tale; when the princess finally finishes weaving the cloth, then she must die."

The Farewell Symphony consists of the third novel, the novel about the Seventies, wrapped in a few notes for the fourth novel, the novel about AIDS. The narrator begins at the grave of his French lover, here named Brice. He warns us that he might not have the courage to tell us about Brice's death when he comes to it in the narrative. The reader assumes he's saying this only for suspense.

This is a long book, longer than both *Boy's Own Story* and *Beautiful Room* combined, yet its prose is the best White has ever written. The tight sentences of *Room* have relaxed and lengthened; they are full of metaphors that surprise without ever being gaudy or silly. The language is tough rather than flowery, literary but gritty with facts. The novel is full of wonderful things—maybe too many wonderful things.

The chief drama in the Seventies portion is the story of a young man breaking into the literary world, a gay New York version of *Lost Illusions* by Balzac. As in *Beautiful Room*, White works chiefly in portraits, exploring the scribbling class in lively character studies: the poet/teacher Max Richards (based on Richard Howard); the critic/teacher Joshua (based on David Kalstone); and a famous poet, Eddie. Eddie is James Merrill, and White offers a full-length portrait of the actual artist and his work.

In Eddie the man I detected a perversity and snobbishness that he radiated in spite of himself, qualities he'd entirely transformed in his writing into impishness and humor. In life he had an age...a maddening drawl; on the page he was eternally youthful, a charged field of particles, a polyphony of voices.

White evokes a congenial life of art and friendship in a circle of gay men. He also captures, in his anxious narrator, the hunger and self-doubt of the writer who's still unpublished, who fears he's deluding himself, who questions his own sanity.

There's also a lot of sex. It's presented more matter-of-factly than in the previous books, treated as a human necessity almost as natural as eating. White weaves it in and out of the rest of life so sex is never just sex. A threeway with a couple in Capri fills the narrator with admiration for the love the other two men share. A visit with his mother in Chicago is purged afterward in an orgy with a large, friendly man called the Doofus. A snotty speech in praise of secrecy by an older gay writer (based on Glenway Westcott) is answered a few pages later with a compressed account of an encounter in a warehouse that involves beer and piss. "I supposed Ridgefield [Westcott] would assign us both to Brunetto Latini's [Dante's] ring in hell, but I thought eternal damnation seemed an excessive punishment for a game babies in a playpen would have found wonderfully sociable."

Yet the sex is important for darker reasons. White is setting us up for the epidemic to come, for the deaths alluded to in the brief flashforwards and the inspired title. Joseph Haydn's Symphony No. 45 in F sharp minor is known as "The Farewell Symphony" for its simple but chilling final movement, an adagio where, one by one, the musicians stand up and depart, until only two violinists remain.

There is also love, but, as before, it's unrequited. The vague, elusive Sean is replaced with the vivid, funny Kevin, a boyish actor like a gay Huck Finn. He is modeled on Keith McDermott and, like McDermott, ends up in a play like *Equus*. (The visiting boy in the opening chapter of *A Boy's Own Story* was also named Kevin; White told us there "the only love is the first. Later we hear its fleeting recapitulations throughout our lives...." The only trait the two Kevins share is that they don't love the narrator, but maybe that's enough.) There is also family love, represented by the narrator saving his nephew from a mental hospital. Keith Fleming is called Gabriel here, the same name White used for him in *Caracole*.

The narrator finally publishes a first novel, Gabriel goes back to the Midwest, and Kevin leaves New York. This span of narrative bridge reaches a satisfying conclusion. We expect the novel to jump ahead to Brice and Paris. After all, only ninety pages remain.

Instead, the novel starts all over again. New friends and lovers are introduced, along with new developments in the author's life. The prose remains excellent and there are some fine episodes, such as last visits with the father and the mother, and the sad account of the bookish Joshua ill with AIDS. But for this reader, the novel falls apart, turning into loose, overly inclusive autobiography. When we finally do get to Brice, three pages before the end, it becomes a powerful novel again. The narrator describes his life with Brice and Brice's death in Morocco in two startling pages, then closes with a beautiful page on the deaths of Joshua and Eddie—White could give his fictional Merrill an AIDS death when the real world was still secretive. He hopes their spirits will continue to live on in his book.

It's a frustrating finish to a sometimes great novel. The death of Brice is similar to the shaggy dog story of prophecy in *Angels in America*, yet it doesn't have its own meaning; it only feels like fatigue. One reviewer, the usually hypercritical Dale Peck, the future author of *Hatchet Jobs*, actually praised White for his silence, claiming this was the most honest way to write about AIDS. One could even argue that *Symphony*'s shapeless finish makes it a good bookend for *A Boy's Own Story*: White's trilogy begins with a broken novel and ends with a broken novel. But I am not alone in wishing he had given us the sustained story he promised. White must've felt it, too, because his next book, *The Married Man*, published three years later, told the very tale left out of *Symphony*: how he loved and lost a young Frenchman. He told it in third person with a slightly different protagonist (a historian of eighteenth-century furniture, of all things) and a grayer voice. The prose is plainer, looser, even flabby—White needs his artistic lobster shell. But his life with Sorin is a good story and the last days in Morocco are very powerful, even after the shorthand version in *Symphony*.

Despite its problems, there are great things in White's trilogy—or maybe we should call it his trilogy and a half. It's full of fine prose, excellent portraits, and fresh observations. Several strong narratives run through the three novels. There is the social history of American life, gay and straight, from the 1950s to the 1990s, including manners and morals, food and travel. There's the portrait of the artist as a young gay man. There's the classic coming-out story: the narrator is buried so deep in a closet of many rooms that it takes him two whole novels to get out. Gay people regularly dismiss coming-out stories, as if embarrassed that we all have one to tell. Yet it's a great plot in its own right—"When we dead awaken" or "I once was blind but now I see"—and it overlaps with White's other major narrative: the bildungsroman, the story of spiritual education. As noted before, *spiritual* is not a word one associates with White, yet such a plot is visible in these books. A cold, heartless, wounded boy escapes to the big city, where he remains a neurotic man of poses. He falls in and out of love, growing less neurotic, until he falls in love with a young man who becomes ill and dies. The hero breaks his heart and gains a soul. This plotline is broken up in the three novels, like a horizon viewed in a broken mirror. It might not be entirely true for the real Edmund White, but that doesn't mean it's untrue for his fictional protagonist.

I think it was a mistake for him to combine the last two books. He needed more space to work out the development of ideas and character. He shoveled too much into the end of *Farewell Symphony,* as if afraid he might die with these stories untold. But all art involves chance and accident. Sometimes circumstance can enable an artist to find something better than what he or she intended. Sometimes it can cause a writer to take the cake from the oven too soon—or leave it in too long. We never know in advance what will work for the best. The trilogy is White's *Jean Santeuil,* the unfinished novel Proust wrote on the way to *In Search of Lost Time.* White published his own work in progress without revising it. But he remained in good health and continued to write. He is now working on his third nonfiction memoir, as if trying to make up for the book he didn't quite finish.

Meanwhile, Larry Kramer had been working on his own novel. Now called *The American People,* it was up to one thousand pages with no end in sight. He was also trying to get a movie made of *The Normal Heart.* He continued to revise the screenplay for Barbra Streisand, but she decided to do another movie instead and her studio let the option lapse. On the plus side, he finally had a boyfriend, David Webster, the very man who was the model for Dinky Adams in *Faggots*—the beloved who's told to commit to love before "you fuck yourself to death." Webster hadn't fucked himself to death. Like Hubert Sorin, he was an architect; he designed a house for himself and Kramer in Connecticut, a large, postmodern box of wood and glass. (Kramer has said his wealth comes from money made in movies and theater and invested by his brother, but one can't help suspecting there is also family money.)

Kramer had criticized White a few years earlier for writing about Genet when he felt all gay writers should be writing about AIDS. White had now written a novel that did just that. Kramer asked to see the advance galleys of the new novel. White sent them, thinking his old friend might give him a quote.

Instead Kramer wrote a vicious attack. "Sex and Sensibility" ran in the *Advocate* in May 1997, three months before *The Farewell Symphony* was published and anyone else had a chance to read the book. Kramer accused White of doing little more than turning his sex diary into a novel:

> [H]e parades before the reader what seems to be every trick he's ever sucked, fucked, rimmed, tied up, pissed on, or been sucked by, fucked by, rimmed by, tied up by....Surely life was more than this, even for—especially for—Edmund White. He did not spend thirty years with a nonstop erection and an asshole busier than his toilet.

He says nothing about the prose, the portraits of friends or family, the accounts of literary life or the deaths from AIDS; all Kramer can talk about is the sex. He goes on to trash *all* gay men's fiction, saying it was all sex, nothing but sex, but that his own novel would set things right, when he finally finished it. (Thirteen years later, he announced it was done, all four thousand pages, but as of fall 2011 none of it has been published.)

It is an ugly piece of writing. To my mind, it's unforgivable Kramer wrote it. It's more unforgivable the *Advocate* printed it. But the Los Angeles–based magazine seemed to be losing interest in books. They gave more space to movies and television, even when little was available. A catfight, however, was something they could appreciate. And so, many years after Gore Vidal and Truman Capote, another generation of gay men were quarreling. One can't help but think of the Charles Ludlam subtitle, "When Queens Collide." Literary history is full of feuds, of course, from the age of Alexander Pope to the time of Lillian Hellman. Membership in a minority only turns up the volume and makes such attacks a little crazier.

One can speculate that Kramer was angry because White had finished a novel while he still struggled with his own. Or that he was afraid White's look at the 1970s would displace *Faggots*, which really is about nothing but sex. A generous reader might even argue that Kramer was sincerely worried White's novel would reignite the old sexual frenzy. In fact, this article was the first shot in Kramer's strange new war against gay promiscuity, one he would wage over the following year in a number of places, including the op-ed page of the *New York Times*. The sixty-two-year-old author was suddenly obsessed with the idea that gay men in their twenties were once again having too much sex now that AIDS appeared to be less dangerous.

Because, in a surprising development, the epidemic seemed to be subsiding.

21. High Tide

—ɯɯ—

The change had begun a few years earlier when the safe-sex campaigns began to show results: the infection rates for HIV were dropping. Annual deaths from AIDS peaked in the United States in 1995 at 50,000. Then in 1996 protease inhibitors were introduced. Andrew Sullivan wrote a cover story on the new treatments in the Sunday *New York Times Magazine*, declaring that the epidemic was over. Well, it was over for him, but it took time for the expensive drugs to help people without money or access to better care. Even so, AIDS deaths dropped to 37,000 in 1996, 21,000 in 1997, and 18,000 in 1998. The rate of new infections decreased, too, although not as rapidly.

This was good news, but it was not the dramatic conclusion that people had hoped for, the discovery or cure that would change everything overnight. Instead there was only a slow shift, like the return of daylight on the morning of a cold rainy day. AIDS became a manageable, chronic condition, but there was still no cure. It didn't feel real, but what would feel real after so much death? By 2000, over half a million Americans had died in the epidemic. It's estimated that anywhere between three-quarters to three-fifths of those deaths were gay or bisexual men. Homosexuality was still such a shameful secret that there is no clear statistical record.

In a curious bit of timing, soon after protease inhibitors were introduced, the movie of *Object of My Affection* finally got made and the sitcom *Will and Grace* premiered on network television. Maybe it's only coincidental, but it was as if the zeitgeist decided that being gay was no longer synonymous with death and our stories were safe for popular entertainment.

There were soon more gay movies, almost all of which were independently produced—the rise of low-budget independent filmmaking energized American cinema for everyone, gay and straight, white and black, male and female. Some of these films were quite good: *Longtime Companion*, with a script by playwright Craig Lucas; *Gods and Monsters*, from my own novel *Father of Frankenstein*; and *Mysterious Skin*, from the novel by Scott Heim. On the other hand, any partnership between big-money studios and gay lit remained difficult. Lucas and another gay playwright, Douglas Carter Beane, were brought out to Los Angeles after their successes on the New York stage. Both men apparently had bad experiences there, at least based on the plays each wrote afterward about gay artists in Hollywood. *The Dying Gaul* by Lucas is a bitter, angry piece about a gay writer who is tricked into betraying his principles and becomes so furious that he inadvertently causes the death of a woman and two children. The accident doesn't entirely make sense (it involves a killer salad), but the anger is utterly plausible. Beane was angry, too, but he expressed it in a joyfully nihilistic, excoriating comedy, *The Little Dog Laughed*, where everyone sells out: an actor, his agent, even a hustler who falls in love with him—all of them preferring conventional success to real happiness.

But books and plays were not the only game in town anymore. There were now movies and even TV shows to compete against. A few years later, in 2002, when Edmund White wrote an introduction for a reissue of *A Boy's Own Story*, he wrote it as an elegy for gay fiction, which he claimed had been killed off by *Will and Grace*.

Michael Cunningham kept his distance from the literary battles of White, Kramer, and others. He was involved with AIDS groups, especially ACT UP, but he stayed out of gay literary politics. He did not like public speaking, anyway. He spent a lot of time at the gym, maintaining a muscular build well into his fifties. Success was good for him. He was frequently seen strolling on the streets in New York or Provincetown, a model-handsome man with the blissful serenity of a satisfied lion.

He published a third novel in 1995, *Flesh and Blood*, a family saga that includes a mother who becomes friends with a drag queen. The book received good reviews, but also critical ones in the *Washington Post* and *New York Times* from reviewers who were indignant that a gay novelist thought he had the right to make moral judgments about straight people. Cunningham kept his old readers but did not gain any new ones. Then in 1998, a year after *The Farewell Symphony*, he published the novel that made him famous: *The Hours*, his homage to *Mrs. Dalloway* by Virginia Woolf.

Mrs. Dalloway is a difficult book, a headlong prose poem that darts in and out of the minds of a dozen different characters during a single day in London after the First World War. The prose is dense, the psychology complicated, the range of characters—from the fragile title character to her society friends to a veteran of the trenches who goes insane—daunting. I have always admired the novel but confess that it wasn't until my third reading that it finally unlocked and fully came to life for me. *The Hours*, however, is instantly accessible, like a guidebook to Woolf with a plot— or rather, three plots. Cunningham tells three different stories about *Mrs. Dalloway*: one about Woolf writing it ("The Hours" was her working title) and two about American women who read it in different decades and use it to give shape to their own lives. All three stories are haunted by madness and suicide. The American stories connect together in a surprising, satisfying way.

The Hours is smart and well-written with serious literary credentials. It succeeded with both critics and readers, winning the Pulitzer Prize, the PEN/Faulkner Award, the Ferro-Grumley, and the American Library Association's Stonewall Award. (The Lambda Book Award, however, went that year to *An Arrow's Flight*.) It was briefly a best seller in hardcover and became a perennial seller in trade paper. But I have to say that I prefer *A Home at the End of the World*, which told a brand-new story. Bear in mind that I had unlocked *Mrs. Dalloway* for myself and did not need a substitute. People who love *Mrs. Dalloway* often think less highly of *The Hours*.

The book's huge success was also helped by the fact that the three protagonists were all female, and because Cunningham had learned to downplay gay sex. Unlike Edmund White, he left his private life out of his fiction. Cunningham himself said in an interview in *Poz* that he couldn't help noticing that as soon as he wrote a novel without a blowjob, they gave him the Pulitzer Prize. Yet we cannot ignore the significance of a book by an openly gay writer with major gay characters winning a bundle of mainstream awards. It would've been unthinkable ten years earlier.

A more direct, less overtly literary yet equally important novel appeared two years later in 2000, another story about the value of storytelling: *The Night Listener* by Armistead Maupin.

After leaving Barbary Lane, Maupin, like other writers here, tried his hand at more mainstream material. *Maybe the Moon* (1992) is about a woman, an actress, Cadence Roth, who is also a dwarf and bisexual. Okay, the subject is not really mainstream, but this is not quite a gay novel, either. Cadence was based on Maupin's friend, Tammy De Treux, whose acting career included working inside the costume of the title character in Steven Spielberg's *E.T.* Cadence narrates her own story, Maupin writing for the first time in first person, but as a woman. One can't help thinking of an earlier act of transvestite ventriloquism, *Myra Breckinridge*, although Maupin brings us so close to Cadence that there's nothing freakish about her. As always, he humanizes everyone he touches.

Maybe the Moon is good, but his next novel is amazing. *The Night Listener* is Maupin's best single book; it's also his most autobiographical.

It, too, is written in first person; here Maupin turns himself into a late-night radio storyteller, Gabriel Noone. Like Maupin, Noone is a San Francisco–based local and national celebrity from the South. And he is breaking up with his partner, Jess, much as Maupin had recently broken with Terry Anderson.

After years of living with AIDS, Anderson started the new cocktail of protease inhibitors and antivirals and regained much of his health. The two men had been able to overlook difficulties in their life together when they thought time was limited. When time opened up again, Anderson wanted to be on his own. "Learning you're going to live can cause as many upheavals as learning you're going to die," Maupin has said. Such separations were so common among gay couples that they had a name: cocktail divorces. Maupin and Anderson remained friends, like Noone and his ex.

The new novel includes other pieces of autobiography: Maupin's relationship with his father, his memories of his late mother, his private thoughts about writing, sex, politics, marijuana, and getting old. But the most important piece of autobiography is at the center of the book, a stranger-than-fiction, true-life story that was already public.

Back in 1991, a teenager wrote a fan letter to novelist Paul Monette, author of a highly successful memoir about living with AIDS, *Borrowed Time*. Tony Johnson was thirteen and he, too, was living with AIDS— contracted when he was sexually abused by a pedophile ring led by his mother and father. He had escaped his parents and now lived with his adopted mother, a social worker named Vicki Johnson, in Union City, New Jersey. Monette lived in Los Angeles, but the two talked every night by telephone.

Everyone who ever spoke to Tony was impressed by how smart and upbeat the boy was despite all he had suffered. He had also had syphilis, suffered a stroke, and lost a testicle *and* a leg. Monette encouraged him to write his story, which Tony did. Monette sent the manuscript to his editor at Crown, David Groff, one of the founders of Publishing Triangle. Groff loved the book and bought it, paying a moderate advance of five thousand dollars. When he sent the galleys to Armistead Maupin for a quote, Maupin was so taken with the tale that he wanted to get in touch with Tony. They too began to talk regularly on the phone.

A Rock and a Hard Place: One Boy's Triumphant Story by Anthony Godby Johnson appeared in the spring of 1993. It received a lot of attention, and Tony was treated as the Anne Frank of AIDS. But when TV newsmagazines asked to interview him, Vicki Johnson said no, insisting she needed to protect him from the pedophile ring.

Maupin and Tony never met face-to-face—nobody ever met Tony Johnson face-to-face. Years later, after *The Night Listener,* Tad Friend wrote a remarkable article for the *New Yorker,* "Virtual Love," where he tried to discover the truth about the boy. Reading it is like falling down a rabbit hole of secret identities and multiple personalities. Tony appears to have been the persona of Vicki Johnson, whose real name was Joanne Fraginals, but we can't even be sure who *she* is.

Tony had been very busy by mail and telephone, winning over not only Monette, Maupin, and Groff, but many others, including Fred Rogers of *Mr. Rogers' Neighborhood,* baseball star Mickey Mantle, and Keith Olbermann, then still a sports commentator. Doubts sometimes set in, but they were guiltily willed away. When Monette died in 1995, he was less certain that Tony existed. Maupin didn't begin to doubt until the night Anderson spoke on the phone to both the boy *and* Vicki Johnson. They sounded so much alike, he said afterward, that they must be the same person. Maupin resisted, but then asked Groff if he'd met Tony. Groff admitted he hadn't but insisted, "Tony's like God. He's someone you just have to believe in." Maupin signed a contract for a novel about a long-distance friendship with a boy with AIDS, but found himself blocked, unsure if Johnson were real or not, for the next three years. Then he decided *that* was the story.

A different man would've been ashamed of being so gullible. But Maupin understood this was a great story and it was not just about him. It opened into public realms of fact and fantasy and the solace of storytelling.

He tells this tale beautifully in *The Night Listener*. His prose has a new, quiet authority announced in the first paragraph:

> I know how it sounds when I call him my son. There's something a little precious about it, a little too wishful to be taken seriously. I've noticed the looks on people's faces, those dim, indulgent smiles that vanish in a heartbeat. It's easy enough to see how they've pegged me: an unfulfilled man on the shady side of fifty, making a last grasp at fatherhood with somebody else's child.

Maupin changes a few details of place and chronology—and he gives the story a different outcome—but he remains true to the soul of what happened. He deftly lays it out, starting with his narrator's daily reality: Gabriel is depressed over losing Jess, blocked with his writing, and full of family issues, especially about his father. Then another reality breaks into his world in the form of phone calls. The boy, called Pete here, is described as sounding like the "Artful Dodger by way of Bart Simpson." He is a foul-mouthed kid who talks to Gabriel every night. He discusses his past, reports the ups and downs of his health, wishes he had a girlfriend, but mostly asks Gabriel about himself—the boy is the real night listener of the title. He tries to get Gabriel to explain his break-up with Jess.

> "Do you know why he left?"
> "No," I said. "Not completely."
> "What *do* you know?"
> I couldn't let him take me there. "Peter, look…this is sweet but—"
> "Fuck you, I'm not sweet! Talk to me, man."
> I hesitated a moment. "I'm just not comfortable with that, Pete."
> "Why?"
> "I just…"
> "Because I'm not a dicksmoker?"
> I startled myself with a noise that resembled laughter. "No, it's just that it's kind of personal and…you know, sexual. I don't think it's really appropriate, considering."
> "Considering what?"
> I didn't have an answer ready.

"Are you calling me a kid or something?"

"No. Well, yeah, I guess I am."

"You think I don't know about that shit?"

"Pete..."

"I bet I know more than you do."

Maupin lets the reader's imagination provide the book's physical reality. Pete and his adopted mother, Donna, are only voices on the telephone for most of the novel—as voices they are as slippery and porous as ghosts. Best of all, Maupin makes us understand how people could be won over by a child who's nothing but audio.

Doubt isn't introduced until a third of the way in. It's Jess, the man with AIDS, who first questions Pete's medical history (which is less horrific than Tony Johnson's). He then talks with both Pete and Donna and hears how similar their voices are. Explanations are offered—Maupin answers every objection a reader might raise—yet once the idea is introduced that Pete might only be Donna in disguise, it won't go away; the book becomes very exciting. Pete remains convincing even when we think he's Donna's second persona. Readers are usually impressed by an author's powers of invention; here we're impressed by Donna's powers. She might be a con artist or a sociopath, but she's also a storytelling genius, knowing how to play both Gabriel and us. After doubt sets in, Gabriel's conversations with Donna/Pete become exchanges between dueling storytellers, each trying to out-guess and outplay the other.

People like to say, "Nobody could make up a story like that" as proof a story must be true. Yet novelists make up wild stories all the time. Pablo Picasso famously said that art is a lie that tells the truth. He might have added that bad art is a lie that only tells more lies. Maupin juxtaposes the sensational, invented life of Pete with the quiet, daily life of Gabriel. That's one reason why he uses so much actual autobiography: he wants to weigh fact and fiction—good lies and bad lies—against each other. Gabriel's arguments with Jess, his ex, have genuine emotional weight—I don't think anyone has written a better quarrel between ex-lovers who remain friends. Maupin also wants to show the emotions that left Gabriel (and himself) hungry for a son, even a fictional one.

Determined to meet Pete and prove he exists, Gabriel travels to north-ern Wisconsin, a prosaic, snowbound place of truck stops, gas stations, and small-town streets that feels grimly real in a book that otherwise happens in the unreal ether of the telephone. But the novel doesn't end there. The final chapters mix realism, melodrama, and metafiction in a dizzying, satisfying way. Maupin makes us complicit in Gabriel's wishing: Pete is such an amazing boy we don't want to see him exposed as fiction. Maupin later said, "I wrote the ending of the book the way I'd like it to be in life, because I'd have great trouble killing that child in my head." I won't completely give away the ending, but say only that Maupin closes the story in a subjunctive tense of possibility, leaving the door ajar.

Maupin understood what a dark, magic story he had been given. After decades of secrets about sexuality followed by years of lies about an epidemic, a mystery woman took advantage of all the silence, fear, and naïveté. We still don't know why she did it, if it were for profit or out of craziness or simply for the fun of the game. But her tale is not just about gullibility. G. K. Chesterton once wrote (in his book about Dickens, appropriately enough) that people are often being "taken in," but that isn't always a bad thing. "To be taken in everywhere is to see the inside of everything. It is the hospitality of circumstance.... And the skeptic is cast out by it."

Stories have the ability to take us *inside* all kinds of life.

It's significant, and appropriate, that we close with two different novels, *The Hours* and *The Night Listener*, about the uses (and dangers) of storytelling. Almost all the works discussed in this history have been stories—I include poems, too, since a poem often suggests a story even when it doesn't tell one.

Stories are wonderfully slippery things. They are not sermons or editorials that noisily declare yea or nay. They are more silent, almost secretive. They matter-of-factly describe an action or a drama or an individual life in a way that can suggest approval for one reader, disapproval for another, and complete indifference for a third. They can slip past public censors (in some countries, anyway), and our own private censors (guilt and fear and shame). Most important, they can put us into other skins, enabling us to experience things we might not feel otherwise: sorrow, joy, lust, and love; but also how it feels to be oppressed, and even how it feels to be the oppressor. There are good stories and bad stories—true lies and false lies—but the best stories are those that take us someplace new and real; we don't need to revisit old assumptions and stale prejudices.

This book has offered a history of the different kinds of stories that gay men have told each other and their friends and, ultimately, the world at large. It began with what they were allowed to tell: cautionary tales of doom and destruction, like *The City and the Pillar* and *Giovanni's Room*. But doom is often sexy, and readers frequently found their own hopeful meanings here. Already there was the liberation plot, the explosion of freedom first seen in "Howl" and developed further in the often maligned coming-out story. As said before, it's surprising how few novels use this powerful plot directly, a narrative as strong as religious conversion. Yet we find it embedded in the denser worlds of Edmund White's trilogy, Maupin's chronicle, even *Angels in America*. There were also stories of romantic friendship, sometimes between gay men and straight women, such as *Breakfast at Tiffany's*, and sometimes between gay men, as in *Down There on a Visit*. Most important of all were the cooler, unapologetic, here-is-how-we-live stories that strive to escape both judgment and sensationalism. There were early glimmers in the poems of Frank O'Hara, but the new honesty didn't fully come into its own until *A Single Man*. Gay writers have been building on it ever since: White, Stephen McCauley, Mark Doty, Paul Russell, myself, and many, many others. AIDS introduced a terrible new set of plots that brought gay literature into the older literary traditions built around death, the elegies and tragedies that confront both fear and grief. The stories in *The Hours* and *The Night Listener* show the power of story to deceive, but also its power to contain and even drive out melancholy.

Changing times meant a wider variety of stories could be told, yet the earlier plots remained potent and never went away. All of these stories were part of the change, altering the ways that gay readers thought about themselves and the world.

We should not be surprised that so much of the gay revolution was accomplished through storytelling. It played a larger role for us than it did for the civil rights movement or even the women's movement. And why not? A disproportionate number of stories are love stories—and what is homosexuality but a special narrative of love?

Epilogue

Rewriting America

G ore Vidal came home to the United States with Howard Austen early in 2003 to live in the Hollywood Hills. Austen was ill and needed better medical care than what they could get in Italy. Also the stairways and paths of La Rondinaia in Ravello were now too steep for the two aging men.

Our narrative began with Gore Vidal and it feels appropriate to end with him. He was the last surviving elder from the years after World War II. Allen Ginsberg had died in 1997, spending his final years as a surprisingly placid, clean-shaven, public man. He continued to write new poems but usually performed only the famous old ones. His readings were enormously popular; he remained a political example and a moral touchstone. His lover, Peter Orlovsky, was in and out of mental hospitals because of his drinking, but Ginsberg stayed serene through it all, concerned yet never overwhelmed. He was seventy-one when he died.

Vidal was anything but serene. He remained fiercely productive, writing new historical novels to fill the gaps for what he called his "Narrative of Empire," a continuous series from *Burr* to *Washington, D.C.*, with a postscript, *The Golden Age.* The new volumes are well-crafted and informative but not as exciting as the first ones. In between he wrote odd experiments like *Duluth* and a free-associative memoir, *Palimpsest*, meant as a preemptive strike against biographers. He quarreled with his "official" biographer, Fred Kaplan, when Kaplan refused to show him the manuscript before publication; he later denounced the book while insisting he hadn't read it. In his own contentious, controlling way, Vidal was preparing for death.

But Howard Austen died first, in November 2003. Vidal had spent the past fifty-three years insisting Austen was only a friend, not a lover. Yet he was devastated. He wrote about it in his next memoir. *Point to Point Navigation* is occupied chiefly with settling scores, but in the middle of the grumbling is a surprisingly intimate chapter about Austen's final illnesses: peritonitis, lung cancer, a brain tumor, and pneumonia. As Austen was being wheeled one more time into an operating room, he told Vidal, "Kiss me," and Vidal did. "On the lips, something we'd not done for fifty years." After he died, Vidal went to look at the naked body on the gurney and regretted that he couldn't cry. The two men were deeply, inextricably knitted together. There are intimacies that have nothing to do with sex.

Vidal sold La Rondinaia and moved to California for good. At the beginning of *Point to Point*, he declares, "As I now move, graciously, I hope, toward the door marked Exit..." But he wasn't gracious. He grew more truculent and short-tempered. He had always been critical: it powered his intelligence and fed his wit. As he grew older, however, he suffered a hardening of intellectual arteries. He repeated fewer ideas over and over; his wit seemed to disappear. When he joined a BBC panel via satellite on election night 2008, reprising his time at the 1968 Democratic convention, he was only testy and snappish when asked about Barack Obama, treating his colleagues as idiots.

He cannot have been happy with the posthumous revival of Truman Capote. He had been more right than he knew when he called Capote's death "a good career move." Now that Capote's later, disastrous public self was out of sight, critics and readers could rediscover his best work and see he was often a great writer.

Vidal was loudly unhappy when Edmund White produced a play, *Terre Haute*, about Vidal's pen-pal friendship with Timothy McVeigh, the Oklahoma City bomber. White, too, had moved back to the United States (to teach at Princeton) and he had a new boyfriend, a young American writer, Michael Carroll. When White took up playwriting again, for the first time in thirty years, Vidal gave him his permission to write about himself and McVeigh. The simple, two-character piece doesn't really work (it would take Dostoyevsky to understand either McVeigh or Vidal's angry fascination with the mass murderer), but Vidal hated it for other reasons. "That play implies that I am madly in love with McVeigh," he declared, then denounced White for everything he'd ever done. "I look at his writing and all he writes about is being a fag and how it's the greatest thing on Earth. He thinks I'm another queen and I'm not." It's like a blast of gay invective from the 1950s, a startling throwback to another era. But Vidal was in a wheelchair now and often in pain. The arthritis that first afflicted his legs in the Aleutians during the war had returned. And Howard Austen was no longer in his life to provide an anchor and an ear and remind him of his wiser, more rational angels.

Vidal was a godfather of gay literature, in spite of himself—a fairy godfather. He would cringe at this description. He continued to insist there is no such thing as a homosexual person, only homosexual acts. Yet generations of younger gay-identified men read and admired him: for *The City and the Pillar*, for *Myra Breckinridge*, and especially for his eloquent essays. He had spoken out about sexuality when few writers were able or willing to speak out. He had praised Tennessee Williams and Christopher Isherwood at a time when the literary world was finished with the first and not yet ready for the second. He was smooth, articulate, witty, and necessary. He pointed us in a new direction, but he could not go there himself. The arguments and defenses he once needed for protection had rusted around him like an old suit of armor. The world had changed more than he could have anticipated, and in ways he couldn't appreciate.

When you stop to think about it, the transformation is nothing short of amazing. And the process was reflected in the written word.

In just over fifty years, between 1948 and 2000, a tiny literary species, a handful of books and plays that appeared only now and then to abuse or silence, grew into a lively ecology of many animals, hundreds of titles that came out every year and sometimes won national praise and prizes. The world changed, too, but the literature itself was an agent of that change, feeding it and reporting it, serving as both cause and effect. During a half century when books and plays lost much of their importance in American culture at large, they played a major role in the growth of gay life.

But where else could gay people tell their stories? They couldn't tell them in movies or on television in the 1950s and 1960s. For the longest time, it was hard enough to tell them in print or onstage. We can only guess at the numbers of gay men and women who read or saw this work. The sales figures tell one story: *The City and the Pillar* was a best seller with 30,000 copies in 1948; *The Night Listener* was not quite a best seller in 2000 when it sold 100,000 copies (with dozens of other gay titles, old and new, to compete against). But the social impact of the literature goes beyond the size of its immediate audience, especially in the beginning. Books and plays gave journalists an opportunity to discuss a forbidden topic with a wide reader-ship. Initially they could discuss homosexuals only negatively, yet any kind of talk was preferable to silence for people who needed simply to be told, "You are not alone." The attacks were often as valuable as the defenses—in the long run.

The personal cost to the writers, however, was high, and remained high for decades. We've seen how Gore Vidal and Truman Capote were bru-tally slammed at the start of their careers; how James Baldwin was attacked for writing about his sexuality instead of his race, first by white liberals, then by black activists; how Christopher Isherwood was dismissed when he started filling in the blanks about his life in Berlin. Abuse made these men unhappy, difficult, and sometimes crazy. It's a wonder they functioned as well as they did. Their careers would've been so much easier, and more profitable, if they'd written about things outside their experience—which they all tried at one time or another with varying degrees of success. (And it didn't protect Tennessee Williams and Edward Albee from insult and criti-cal dismissal.) But making art is difficult enough without needing to pre-tend to be someone else. A writer who can't use his firsthand experience must turn to secondhand experience, which can lead to thirdhand clichés. Writers as talented as Vidal, Isherwood, and Edmund White floundered when they tried to tell more conventional love stories. A gay man who writes nothing but straight stories works with his heart only half connected. The gap can sometimes produce interesting sparks, but it's not good for the work or the writer in the long run. More important, literature can grow and change only when new experience is introduced—not just new techniques, but unexamined emotions and fresh identities.

These novels, plays, and poems spoke first to gay readers, giving them a place to explore and understand their own feelings. They enabled isolated individuals to imagine themselves in couples and even communities. The stories changed over five decades, becoming less coded and more frank, even graphic. Yet their role remained much the same as when they spoke in whispers. They have always said in effect: "You are different, but you are not alone." There were sometimes additional twists and variations: "You are not normal, but nobody is. There is no such thing as normal."

Later this work spoke to the culture at large, the so-called mainstream, but that's harder to describe. In the world of novels, we can only guess at how many, or how few, straight readers visited this country. Straight novelists, however, soon recognized that there were great stories here and began to include gay characters in their work: Charles Baxter in *Feast of Love*, Bharati Mukherjee in *Desirable Daughters*, and, most famously, Annie Proulx in "Brokeback Mountain." These writers saw homosexuality as just one more culture in a lively, multicultural America. In the world of poetry, gay work was less of a problem, chiefly because poets and poetry readers are happy to find each other no matter who they are. But in the world of theater, the change was clear and visible. Gay story lines became an accepted mainstay on and off Broadway. Richard Greenberg won the Tony in 2003 for *Take Me Out*, his play about baseball and homosexuality. In 2004 *I Am My Own Wife* by Doug Wright, a dazzling monologue by an East German transvestite who survives both Hitler and Communism, won the Tony *and* the Pulitzer. Theater has always been more progressive than books, but the gay presence in American theater offers a promising model of equality.

And then, a few years into the new millennium, the book business began to change. Around the time that Hollywood decided to concentrate on blockbusters and lost interest in independent movies, publishing lost interest in midlist novels—and gay fiction is nothing if not midlist. The number of new gay books declined. The recession of 2008 then took a heavy toll on the entire industry, hurting publishers and killing bookstores. Chain and independent stores began to close, including many gay bookstores. The Oscar Wilde Memorial Bookshop shut its doors in 2009. The coming of the e-book added to the confusion: nobody knew what would sell or how to sell it anymore.

First-rate work by established gay writers continued to be printed by mainstream houses. Armistead Maupin returned to Barbary Lane with *Michael Tolliver Lives* and *Mary Ann in Autumn*. Peter Cameron put out his best novel yet, *Someday This Pain Will Be Useful to You*, a worldly meditation disguised as a young adult novel. Mark Doty issued *Fire to Fire: New and Selected Poems*, which won the National Book Award. But life became very difficult for other gay writers. New voices continued to be heard, but they now depended on small presses and blogs, in the same way that gay writers in the Fifties had depended on pulp houses and little magazines. Blair Mastbaum published a wonderful first novel about a gay skateboarder, *Clay's Way*, with Alyson. Vestal McIntyre did his first book of short stories, *You Are Not the One*, with Carroll and Graf. James Hannaham put out a surprising first novel about a closeted African-American born-again Christian, *God Says No*, with McSweeney's. And Rakesh Satyal did a remarkable first novel, *Blue Boy*, with Kensington, about a precocious gay Hindu boy in Cincinnati who believes he's Krishna.

In an ironic twist, this time of reduction in the book trade was a time of enormous gains in the real world. Gay people were being treated less like outlaws and more like fellow citizens. In April 2003, the *New York Times* ran their first wedding announcement for a same-sex couple: playwright Tony Kushner married magazine editor Mark Harris. It was a symbolic marriage, not a legal one, but more announcements followed, including those for legal marriages—first in Massachusetts, then in Vermont, Connecticut, and most recently New York. Even more amazing, at the end of 2010, Congress overturned the law known as "Don't Ask, Don't Tell," which prevented openly gay people from serving in the military. Nobody could have imagined such a thing in the years after World War II.

One might claim that gay people have won their rights but lost their literature. It has a nice dramatic sound, but I don't see things so harshly. As I said, good work continues to be produced. However, we *are* going through a transitional period, in both the medium for storytelling and the kinds of stories people want. We don't know yet what the next phase will be.

Gay life today is highly visible in music, television, stand-up comedy, the Internet and YouTube. But it got its first foothold in the public consciousness in novels, plays, and poems. The influence of that work is now everywhere, ranging from the trivial to the profound. The kinky sex acts featured in *Sex and the City* or a Margaret Cho monologue were first described in books by Gore Vidal, Edmund White, and Larry Kramer. The gender-role clowning of Sacha Baron Cohen, *Glee*, and Lady Gaga was pioneered by Vidal and Charles Ludlam. And the inclusive mixing of gay and straight characters in TV shows like *Six Feet Under* and *Ugly Betty* was first seen in the novels of James Baldwin, Christopher Isherwood, and Armistead Maupin—our initial glimpse of a plausible Eden.

Before gay experience crossed over into other media, it energized American literature—in much the same way Jewish experience energized it in the 1950s and 1960s, and feminism energized it in the 1970s, introducing new subjects and fresh points of view. The best work discussed in this history remains alive and relevant. It was most valuable when it first appeared, but good art has a way of staying fresh, of living in the past, present, *and* future.

During the two years I wrote this book, a movie was adapted from *A Single Man*, another movie was made about the writing of "Howl," and a musical based on *Tales of the City* opened in San Francisco; there were New York revivals of *Boys in the Band*, *The Normal Heart*, and *Angels in America*, as well as new editions of essays by James Baldwin and letters by Allen Ginsberg.

These men continue to speak to us through their poems, plays, novels, and lives. Directly and indirectly, this loose conspiracy of writers opened doors in the imaginations of both gay people and straight people. These eminent outlaws succeeded in rewriting America.

Acknowledgments

Without being aware of it, I spent much of my life preparing to write this book. I came of age during a remarkable period of American history—the Sixties and Seventies—reading many of the novels, poems, and plays discussed here when they first came out. And I spoke steadily over the years with a circle of friends about literature and politics, developing the ideas that inform this narrative. I continued to talk with these friends while I wrote this book, bouncing ideas off them and picking their brains. My extended literary family includes: Schuyler Bishop, playwright and editor; Kim Brinster, bookstore manager; Michael Bronski, critic and teacher; Victor Bumbalo, playwright; Philip Clark, critic and librarian; David Fratkin, painter; Mary Gentile, consultant and writer; Michael Goodwin, painter; Damien Jack, writer and reader; Mary Jacobsen, novelist and therapist; Richard Kassner, psychiatrist and writer; Michael Matarese, family physician and history reader; Patrick Merla, editor and writer; Mark Murtagh, investor, reader, and education expert; Mark Owen, chef and writer; Richard Reitsma, teacher and writer; Paul Russell, novelist and teacher; Ed Sikov, biographer; Neil Theise, liver pathologist and reader; Sarah Van Arsdale, novelist and teacher; Brenda Wineapple, biographer; and Draper Shreeve, filmmaker, reader, and partner.

I owe a special thank you to Ed Sikov and Sam Wasson for a happy accident. When Sam began research on *Fifth Avenue, 5 A.M.*, his book about the movie of *Breakfast at Tiffany's*, Ed suggested he talk to me about Truman Capote. We had a good, long conversation on the phone while I gave Sam a quick overview of gay literary history. Afterward he said, "This is great stuff. Where can I read it?" And I realized no such book existed. So I began work on this one.

Many writers took the time to talk with me, either face-to-face or by telephone or e-mail. In particular I want to thank: Mart Crowley, Armistead Maupin, Edmund White, Arnie Kantrowitz, Lawrence Mass, Rakesh Satyal, and J. D. McClatchy.

My print sources are all cited in the notes, but I must thank the biographers and historians whose heavy labor proved invaluable to me. *Gore Vidal* by Fred Kaplan and *Isherwood* by Peter Parker were especially useful. I'd also like to mention a few books that gave me real pleasure as a reader. *Lost Friendships* by Donald Windham is a neglected gem, a fine memoir that brings Truman Capote and Tennessee Williams fully to life with their charms as well as their vices. Also wonderful on Williams is *Gentlemen Callers* by Michael Paller, a sympathetic exploration of the playwright as a gay writer—not always the self-hating one of reputation. *Digressions on Some Poems by Frank O'Hara* by Joe LeSueur is an intimate account of the poet and his friends. *Something Inside: Conversations with Gay Fiction Writers* by Philip Gambone, and *Gay Fiction Speaks: Conversations with Gay Novelists* and *Hear Us Out: Conversations with Gay Novelists*, both by Richard Canning, are full of gold. And *Armistead Maupin* by Patrick Gale is a short bio so deftly done that I want to forgive Gale for the bad review he gave to my first novel.

At Twelve Books I owe deep thanks to Jonathan Karp, who initially took on this project. I owe further gratitude to Colin Shepherd, who took over after Jon left and provided close, detailed readings and constant support. Colin has been a joy to work with, full of smart ideas and good conversation. Susan Lehman and Cary Goldstein also gave much helpful advice and support. My production editors, Leah Tracosas and Dorothea Halliday, and my copy editor, Mark Steven Long, were invaluable. And as always, my agent, Edward Hibbert, has been a wise adviser and an excellent friend.

Notes

INTRODUCTION

p. x *"Gay people are just like straight people. But straight people lie about who they really are."* Michael Bronski, "The Future of Gay Politics," forum at the Kennedy School of Government, 1994. Verified by Bronski in conversation with the author, June 2009.

p. x *"what you really felt, rather than what you were supposed to feel,..."* Ernest Hemingway, *Death in the Afternoon* (New York: Scribner's Sons, 1932), 2.

p. x *The names are only approximations, anyway.* I do not want to get too deep into the "essentialist vs. constructionist" debate about sexual identity. Gore Vidal famously argued that there are no homosexual people, only homosexual acts. It was a good strategy, a smart way to outmaneuver prejudice. Academics later picked up the idea when Michel Foucault proposed that there was no such thing as a homosexual before 1869, when the word was first coined. Queer theorists imagined a wonderful arcadian past where men and women simply did what they did and only their actions were judged, not their souls.

Graham Robb points out in his very fine book *Strangers* that Foucault proposed this idea only as a possibility and never explored it. And it's a pretty idea, but I don't buy it, simply because I've read too much Victorian fiction. People in the nineteenth century *were* their acts. Men who embezzled were embezzlers, even if they were clergymen. Women who committed adultery were adulteresses, no matter what saintly deeds they performed later. Novelists like Anthony Trollope and Nathaniel Hawthorne attempted to separate action from identity, but they were fighting against an established custom of thinking. You *were* your sin, whether it was the jilting of a fiancée or an adulterous affair or an unspeakable act of sodomy.

PART I: INTO THE FIFTIES

p. 1 *"America when will you be angelic?"* Allen Ginsberg, "America," *Howl and Other Poems* (San Francisco: City Lights Books, 1956), 39.

Chapter 1. Innocence

p. 4 *Vidal and Merrill wrote letters to the editor...* Deirdre Bair, *Anaïs Nin* (London: Bloomsbury Publishing, 1995), 318.

p. 5 *"I think you are everything, man, woman, and child..."* Gore Vidal, *The City and the Pillar* (New York: Dutton, 1948 edition), 165.

p. 6 *"'You're a queer,' he said..."* Vidal, *The City and the Pillar*, 306.

p. 7 *"He listened content and untroubled..."* Truman Capote, *Other Voices, Other Rooms* (New York: Modern Library, 2004), 26.

p. 8 *"Honey...you stay away from him"* John Malcolm Brinnin, *Truman Capote: Dear Heart, Old Buddy* (New York: Delacourt Press, 1986), 34.

p. 8 *"the faggots'* Huckleberry Finn." *The Grand Surprise: The Journals of Leo Lehrman*, ed. Stephen Pascal (New York: Knopf, 2007), 63.

p. 8 *"A short novel which is as dazzling a phenomenon..."* Quotes from *Chicago Tribune* and *Time*; from Gerald Clarke, *Capote* (New York: Simon & Schuster, 1988), 155–156.

p. 8 *"The story of Joel Knox did not need to be told..."* Carlos Baker, "Deep South Guignol," *New York Times Book Review*, January 18, 1948. http://www.nytimes.com/books/97/12/28/home/capote-guignol.html.

p. 8 *"Is no member of society, then, to be held accountable for himself, not even Hitler?"* Diana Trilling, *Reviewing the Forties* (New York: Harcourt Brace Jovanovich, 1978), 232.

p. 8 *"Presented as the case history of a standard homosexual..."* C. V. Terry, "The City and the Pillar," *New York Times Book Review*, January 11, 1948. http://www.nytimes.com/books/98/03/01/home/vidal-pillar.html?scp=2&sq=City%20and%20the%20Pillar%20by%20Gore%20Vidal&st=cse.

p. 8 *"Essentially it's an attempt to clarify the inner stresses of our time..."* Charles Rolo, "Reader's Choice," *Atlantic Monthly*, January 1948, 110.

p. 9 *"Aside from its sociological demonstrations, Mr. Vidal's book is undistinguished..."* J. S. Shrike, "Recent Phenomena," *Hudson Review*, Spring 1948, 136. (I suspect Shrike is film critic Vernon Young, but only because Young was a regular contributor to the quarterly and cited Kinsey in another review.)

p. 9 *"Many a first novel is sounder, better balanced..."* Orville Prescott, *New York Times*, January 21, 1948. http://www.nytimes.com/books/97/12/28/home/capote-voices.html?_r=1&scp=1&sq=orville%20prescott,%20%22other%20voices,%20other%20rooms%22&st=cse.

p. 10 *not bad for the hardcover book slump of the early Fifties...* Fred Kaplan mentions this slump in passing in *Gore Vidal*, but the best account I've found is in *Heavy Traffic and High Culture* by Thomas L. Bonn, a detailed history of New American Library from 1945 to 1982. Bonn reports that in 1952 sales figures were down for hardcover, and it was rumored that big houses were kept in the black only by the sale of reprint rights (32). This was followed in 1954 by huge paperback returns— 44 percent (before, the returns had been 25 percent). Bennett Cerf in *At Random* says the returns were so high that people joked books were now landfill. The earnings for authors for paperbacks were shockingly low. Getting one cent on a twenty-five cent book, an author could sell 100,000 copies but see only five hundred dollars (after dividing the money with his publisher). Only as the decade progressed and paperback prices rose to thirty-five and fifty cents did the market level out.

p. 10 *"Most people seem to be born knowing their way through literature..."* Quoted in Fred Kaplan, *Gore Vidal: A Biography* (New York: Doubleday, 1999), 329.

p. 10 *"I am back amongst my people..."* Quoted in Kaplan, *Gore Vidal*, 287.

Chapter 2. The Kindness of Strangers

p. 14 *"He did something I longed to do..."* Donald Windham, *Lost Friendships* (New York: Morrow, 1987), 113. Windham was an excellent novelist himself, writing several first-rate books, including *Two People* (1965), a novel about the love affair between a married American businessman and a hustler in Rome.

p. 15 *"The richness of words in Tennessee's stories and plays..."* Windham, *Lost Friendships*, 179.

p. 15 *[a] poetry-reciting waiter at the Beggar's Bar in Greenwich Village...* The bar's owner, Valeska Gert, was a brilliant character actress in German cinema, appearing in *Joyless Street* and *The Threepenny Opera*, but Williams never knew that.

p. 17 *"What you have done is removed my style..."* Vidal, introduction to *Collected Stories*, by Tennessee Williams (New York: New Directions, 1985), xx.

p. 17 *"You know, you spoiled it with that ending..."* Vidal, "Some Memories of the Glorious Bird and an Earlier Self," in *Matters of Fact and Fiction: Essays 1973–1976* (New York: Random House, 1977), 137.

p. 17 *"I liked him..."* *Tennesse Williams' Letters to Donald Windham*, ed. Donald Windham (New York: Penguin Books, 1980), 216.

p. 17 *"Between Tennessee's solemn analyses of the play and Cocteau's rhetoric..."* Vidal, "Some Memories of the Glorious Bird and an Earlier Self," 143.

p. 18 *"full of fantasies and mischief."* Quoted in Vidal, ibid., 142.

p. 19 *Section 1140-A of New York City's Criminal Code, known as the Wales Padlock Law...* There's an excellent account of this in the pioneering study of gay and lesbian theater, *We Can Always Call Them Bulgarians,* by Kaier Curtin.

p. 21 *Walter Kerr compared the accusation in* Cat... Michael Paller, *Gentlemen Callers* (New York: Palgrave Macmillan, 2005), 102. (Paller's account of the writing of *Cat* and its reception is invaluable.)

p. 22 *"He said I wrote cheap melodramas..."* Quoted in Paller, *Gentlemen Callers,* 130.

p. 22 *"He said I was overworked..."* Williams to Elia Kazan, June 4, 1958, in Tennessee Williams, *Notebooks,* ed. by Margaret Bradham Thornton (New Haven: Yale University Press, 2006), 711.

p. 23 *"How could you give up* The Novel?*..."* Quoted in Vidal, "Dawn Powell: The American Writer," in *At Home: Essays 1982–1988,* (New York: Random House, 1988), 242.

CHAPTER 3. HOWL

p. 25 *"Wrapped in Ashes' arms I glide. / (It's heaven!)..."* Frank O'Hara, "At the Old Place," in *Selected Poems* (New York: Knopf, 2008), 85.

p. 25 *including Lionel Trilling...* Trilling wrote about a student like Ginsberg, a mentally ill boy wonder named Tertan, in a short story, "Of This Time, Of That Place." But the story was published a couple of months *before* Trilling first met Ginsberg. Ginsberg seemed to fit the type, and many assumed he was as fragile as Tertan, especially when they heard about his mother. Yet Ginsberg was remarkably resilient.

p. 27 *"At 26, I am shy, go out with girls..."* Allen Ginsberg, *Journals: Early Fifties Early Sixties,* ed. Gordon Ball (New York: Grove Press, 1977), 17.

p. 28 *"If you ever catch me talking the way Chester did tonight..."* Joe LeSueur, *Digressions on Some Poems by Frank O'Hara* (New York: Farrar, Straus, and Giroux, 2003), 39.

p. 30 *"Oh, you're a nice person... There's always people who will like you."* Quoted in Barry Miles, *Ginsberg* (London: Virgin Publishing, 2001), 180.

p. 31 *"I saw the best minds of my generation..."* Allen Ginsberg, *Howl and Other Poems* (San Francisco: City Lights Books, 1956), 9.

p. 31 *"who let themselves be fucked in the ass..."* Ginsberg, *Howl and Other Poems,* 13.

p. 32 *"I'm with you in Rockland..."* Ginsberg, *Howl and Other Poems,* 26.

p. 32 *"America I am putting my queer shoulder to the wheel."* Ginsberg, *Howl and Other Poems,* 43.

p. 33 *"My expression, at first blush..."* Quoted in *Family Business: Selected Letters Between a Father and Son, Allen and Louis Ginsberg,* ed. Michael Schumacher (New York: Bloomsbury USA, 2002), 46.

p. 33 *"Don't go in for ridiculous things."* Naomi Ginsberg to Allen Ginsberg, June 1956, quoted in Michael Schumacher, *Dharma Lion* (New York: St. Martin's Press, 1992), 234.

p. 33 *"Its positive force and energy come from a redemptive quality..."* Richard Eberhart, *New York Times Book Review,* September 2, 1956, BR4.

p. 33 *"a dreadful little volume..."* John Hollander as well as quotes from James Dickey and Ezra Pound, quoted in Michael Schumacher, *Dharma Lion,* 239.

p. 35 *"like any work of literature, attempts and intends to make a significant comment..."* Mark Schorer, quoted in *Howl on Trial,* ed. Bill Morgan and Nancy J. Peters (San Francisco: City Lights Books, 2006), 135.

p. 35 *"the work of a thoroughly honest poet"* Walter Van Tilburg Clark, quoted in *Howl on Trial,* 154.

p. 35 *"is probably the most remarkable single poem, published by a young man..."* Kenneth Rexroth, quoted in *Howl on Trial,* 166.

p. 36 *"Therefore, I conclude the book* Howl and Other Poems *does have some redeeming social importance..."* Quoted in *Howl on Trial,* 199.

p. 36 *"I quoted the first line of Whitman..."* Ginsberg to Louis Ginsberg, August 1, 1957, quoted in *Family Business: Selected Letters,* 69–70.

p. 37 *"Natch was glad and thankful..."* Ginsberg to Lawrence Ferlinghetti, October 10, 1957, quoted in *Howl on Trial,* 78.

CHAPTER 4. SOUL KISS

p. 39 *"You must've thought to yourself, 'Gee, how disadvantaged can I get?'"* James Baldwin: The Price of the Ticket, documentary, produced and directed by Karen Thoren, Nobody Knows Productions and Maysles Films, 1991, distributed on video by California Newsreels.

p. 39 *"I have not written about being a Negro..."* James Baldwin, "Autobiographical Notes," in *Collected Essays* (New York: Library of America, 1998), 8.

p. 40 *"As they were born..."* James Baldwin, "Autobiographical Notes," 5.

p. 40 *"a cross between Brer Rabbit and St. Francis..."* David Leeming, *James Baldwin* (New York: Random House, 1994), 270.

p. 41 *"There were very few black people in the Village..."* James Baldwin, "Freaks and the American Ideal of Manhood" (later retitled "Here Be Dragons"), in *Collected Essays*, 823.

p. 41 *"I was far too terrified..."* Ibid., 822.

p. 43 *"all these strangers called Jimmy Baldwin."* Quoted in James Campbell, *Talking at the Gates: A Life of James Baldwin* (New York: Viking, 1991), 56.

p. 47 *"My agent told me to burn it."* Fern Maja Eckmann, *The Furious Passage of James Baldwin* (New York: M. Evans, 1966), 137.

p. 49 *"The thought becomes poetry and the poetry illuminates the thought..."* Langston Hughes, "Notes of a Native Son," *New York Times Book Review*, February 26, 1956.

p. 49 *"Every time I read Langston Hughes I am amazed all over again by his genuine gifts..."* James Baldwin, in "Sermons and Blues," *Collected Essays* (Library of America), 614.

p. 49 *"as grotesque and repulsive as any that can be found in Proust's* Cities of the Plain*..."* Granville Hicks, "Tormented Triangle," *New York Times Book Review*, October 14, 1956. http://www.nytimes.com/books/98/03/29/specials/baldwin-giovanni .html?scp=1&sq=granville%20hicks%20on%20james%20baldwin&st=cse.

p. 50 *Giovanni murdered the boss.* Years later, in his *Paris Review* interview, Baldwin said the murder was inspired by the 1944 killing of David Kammerer by Lucian Carr, Allen Ginsberg's friend. It would make a nice link between Baldwin and Ginsberg, only the two killings have nothing in common. The situations are completely different, as are the murder weapons. I suspect Baldwin confused his use of the Carr murder in an earlier, unfinished novel, *Ignorant Armies*, with the invented murder by Giovanni. An author's imaginings can become more real than his facts.

p. 51 *"an unpleasant attempt..."* Otto Friedrich, *The Grave of Alice B. Toklas* (New York: Holt, 1989), 372.

p. 51 *"marred by a portentous tone that at times feels cheaply secondhand..."* Claudia Roth Pierpont, "Another Country," *New Yorker*, February 9, 2009. http://www.new yorker.com/arts/critics/books/2009/02/09/090209crbo_books_pierpont.

p. 51 *"James Baldwin is too charming a writer to be major..."* Norman Mailer, *Advertisements for Myself* (New York: Putnam, 1959), 407.

p. 52 *"They thought he was a real sweet ofay cat..."* James Baldwin, "The Black Boy Looks at the White Boy," in *Collected Essays*, 272.

p. 52 *"His work, after all, is all that will be left..."* Ibid., 284–285.

Chapter 5. Going Hollywood

p. 55 *"Oh, I'm a genius, too?"* *Views from a Window: Conversations with Gore Vidal*, ed. Robert V. Stanton and Gore Vidal (Secaucus: Lyle Stuart, 1980), 219 (quoting an interview in *Newsweek*, "Gore Vidal on…Gore Vidal" by Arthur Cooper, November 18, 1974).

p. 55 *"'Don't,' he said with great intensity,…"* Gore Vidal, "Christopher Isherwood's Kind," *The Second American Revolution and Other Essays*, 37.

p. 58 *"I'll try to be absolutely honest about this…."* Isherwood, *Diaries: Volume One 1939–1960*, ed. Katherine Bucknell (New York: Harper Collins, 1996), 83–84.

p. 59 *"Dramatically and psychologically, I find it entirely plausible…."* Quoted in Peter Parker, *Isherwood: A Life* (London: Picador, 2004), 572–573.

p. 60 *"He is a big husky boy…"* Isherwood, *Diaries: Volume One*, 401.

p. 60 *"He's a strange boy…"* Ibid., 290.

p. 60 *"We are the dreaded fog queens…"* Christopher Isherwood, *The Lost Years*, 145.

p. 61 *"Christopher has with him the youngest boy ever…"* Leo Lehrman, *The Grand Surprise: The Journals of Leo Lehrman*, 150.

p. 61 *"much too hearty…"* Parker, *Isherwood*, 630.

p. 61 *"I have received lots and lots of fan-mail…"* Ibid.

p. 62 *"He has pockmarks and a vertically lined face…"* Isherwood, *Diaries: Volume One*, 506.

p. 62 *"He was tanned and youthful-looking…"* Thom Gunn, "Getting Things Right," in *Shelf Life* (Ann Arbor: University of Michigan Press, 1993), 173.

p. 62 *"Perhaps I'll never write another novel…"* Ibid., 456.

p. 63 *"I believe he really thinks about 'posterity'…"* Isherwood, *Diaries: Volume One*, 521.

p. 63 *"Two days ago, for example, I was quite blue…"* Ibid., 533.

p. 64 *Abbey "was very funny…"* Ibid., 588.

p. 64 *"There was one wonderful thing about Truman…"* John Gregory Dunne, quoted in George Plimpton, *Truman Capote* (New York: Nan A. Talese/Doubleday, 1997), 432.

p. 66 *Donald Windham… had hoped to use the title himself…* Windham, *Lost Friendships*, 57.

p. 68 *"As boys they were lovers…"* Vidal, *The Second American Revolution and Other Essays*, 144.

p. 69 *"but for God's sake don't tell Ralph."* Charlton Heston, *In the Arena* (New York: Simon & Schuster, 1995), 187.

p. 69 *"Gore is running for Congress…"* Isherwood, *Diaries: Volume One*, 859.

CHAPTER 6. THE GREAT HOMOSEXUAL THEATER SCARE

p. 73 *"Get that ass!"* Gore Vidal, "Tennessee Williams: Someone to Laugh at the Squares With," *At Home*, 50.

p. 74 *"Poison…"* Windham, *Lost Friendships*, 212.

p. 74 *Merlo's Italian nickname for Williams's grandfather…* Donald Spoto, *Kindness of Strangers* (Boston: Little, Brown, 1985), 245.

p. 75 *"It is time to speak openly and candidly about the increasing incidence and influence of homosexuality…"* Howard Taubman, "Not What It Seems," *New York Times*, November 5, 1961, Art X1. (This article was brought to my attention by Michael Paller in *Gentlemen Callers*. His chapter on the homosexual theater scare is excellent.)

p. 75 *"I took to it, as they say, as a duck to water."* Gussow, 49.

p. 76 *the Sisters Grimm…* Ned Rorem, quoted in Mel Gussow, *Edward Albee: A Singular Journey* (New York: Simon & Schuster, 1999), 80.

p. 76 *"Why do homosexuals always write rotten love poetry…?"* Ibid., 85.

p. 77 *"That's the best fucking one-act play…"* Quoted in Gussow, 120.

p. 78 *Richard Howard could hear echoes…* Ibid., 158.

p. 78 *"Martha: Hey, put some more ice in my drink…"* Edward Albee, *Who's Afraid of Virginia Woolf?* (New York: New American Library, 2006), 15.

p. 79 *"Like Strindberg, Mr. Albee treats his women remorselessly…"* Howard Taubman, *New York Times*, October 15, 1962. http://theater.nytimes.com/mem/theater/treview. html?res=FC77E7DF1730E062BC4D52DFB6678389679EDE&scp=2&sq=H oward%20Taubman/Edward%20Albee&st=cse.

p. 81 *"a homosexual daydream…"* Philip Roth, "The Play That Dare Not Speak Its Name," *New York Review of Books*, February 25, 1965. ://www.nybooks.com/ articles/archives/1965/feb/25/the-play-that-dare-not-speak-its-name/. (But enlightenment can come at a slant. Critic Michael Bronski reports that in his early teens in the 1960s in New Jersey, his parents were afraid he might become gay. His father spoke to a psychiatrist who suggested that he bond with his son. He should find some activity they both enjoyed. They both liked theater, so the father regularly took Michael into New York to see new plays. As Bronski points out, he still became gay, but he and his father saw some good shows and they now have a pretty good relationship.Among the plays they saw was *Tiny Alice*, which puzzled both of them.)

p. 81 *Wilfrid Sheed...in* Commentary... Quoted in Michael Sherry, *Gay Artists in Modern American Culture: An Imaginary Conspiracy* (Chapel Hill: University of North Carolina Press, 2007), 130. (Sherry concentrates on American music, but his book is a gold mine of material and ideas about theater, too.)

p. 81 *Martin Gottfried in* Women's Wear Daily... Quoted in Paller, *Gentlemen Callers*, 179.

p. 82 *"The principal charge against homosexual dramatists is well known..."* Stanley Kauffmann, "Homosexual Drama and Its Disguises," *New York Times*, January 23, 1966, Arts and Leisure, 93.

p. 83 *"[T]he great artists so often cited as evidence of the homosexual's creativity..."* "The Homosexual in America," *Time*, January 21, 1966, 40. (Michael Sherry's book brought this essay to my attention.)

p. 84 *"The two pioneering forces of modern sensibility..."* Susan Sontag, "Notes on Camp," *A Susan Sontag Reader* (New York: Farrar, Straus, and Giroux, 1982), 118.

p. 85 *"brilliant" became "admirable."* Gussow, 179.

p. 85 *"There's not that much difference between straight and gay couples in their fights."* Ibid., 159.

p. 85 *"I know I did not write the play about two male couples..."* Ibid.

p. 85 *"If I am writing a female character, goddamnit, I'm going to write a female character..."* Quoted in Paller, *Gentlemen Callers*, 190.

p. 86 *"Yes, those first two acts of* Virginia Woolf *are marvelous bitch dialogue..."* William Goldman, *The Season* (Harcourt, Brace & World, 1969), 411. (This book is recommended for anyone who wants to see just how ugly and unrelenting fag-baiting could get in the 1960s.)

p. 87 *"With Frank ill, Tennessee just couldn't cope for himself..."* Spoto, *Kindness of Strangers*, 257.

p. 87 *"Frankie was the only one who really understood him..."* Ibid., 258.

p. 87 *"I've grown used to you..."* Williams, *Memoirs* (Garden City: Doubleday, 1975), 194.

p. 87 *"They say he just gasped..."* Tennessee Williams, *Five O'Clock Angel: Letters of Tennessee Williams to Maria St. Just* (New York: Knopf, 1990), 185.

CHAPTER 7. THE MEDIUM IS THE MESSAGE

p. 88 *"Never pass up the opportunity to have sex..."* This is frequently attributed to Gore Vidal, but not even he can remember exactly when he said it. Vidal, *Point to Point Navigation* (New York: Doubleday, 2006), 251.

p. 91 *"Capote did not look small on the show..."* Norman Mailer, *Pieces and Pontifications* (Boston: Little, Brown, 1982), 41.

p. 92 *"The village of Holcomb stands on the high wheat plains..."* Truman Capote, *In Cold Blood: A True Account of a Multiple Murder and its Consequences* (New York: Modern Library, 1992), 3.

p. 93 Capote *and* Infamous... The first movie is a grim slog that treats the author as an autistic robot whose exploitation of Smith and Hickock is a worse crime than the murder of the Clutters. Philip Seymour Hoffman works hard to overcome the fact that he is miscast as Capote, and for this he won an Academy Award. The second movie, *Infamous*, is livelier, funnier, smarter, and more emotionally complex; its Capote, Toby Jones, is so effortless that he doesn't seem to be acting at all. The movie is a neglected masterpiece.

p. 93 *"Steps, noose, mask..."* Capote, *In Cold Blood*, 340–341.

p. 94 *"Are we so bankrupt, so avid for novelty..."* Stanley Kauffmann, *New Republic,* January 22, 1966; quoted in Gerald Clarke, *Capote.*

p. 95 *"For the first time an influential writer in the front rank..."* Kenneth Tynan, "The Coldest of Blood," *The Observer*, March 13, 1966, reprinted in *Tynan Left and Right* (New York: Atheneum, 1968), 445.

p. 95 *"For although the word 'friends' should be put into quotation marks..."* Windham, *Lost Friendships*, 74. Windham also writes intelligently about the liberties Capote took with facts, which he knew about since his boyfriend, Sandy Campbell, spent time with Capote in Kansas as a fact-checker for the *New Yorker*. "His triumph is the accuracy of his imaginative invention, the instinctive truths he found in himself, which enabled him to create convincingly and movingly within the confines of the known facts the inner workings of his major characters, especially of the killer Perry Smith" (78).

p. 96 *"A hotel's enormous neon name..."* James Baldwin, *Early Novels and Stories* (New York: Library of America, 1998), 368.

p. 97 *"they do not matter..."* Randall Jarrell, *Poetry and the Age* (New York: Knopf, 1953), 112.

p. 98 *"incessant homosexuality"* Quoted in Magdalena Zaborowska, *James Baldwin's Turkish Decade: Erotics of Exile* (Durham: Duke University Press, 2009), 49. A weird, fascinating book that asks all the right questions but rarely gives direct answers.

p. 99 *"I read late last night...* Another Country..." Donald Vining, *A Gay Diary*, vol. 3, *1954–1967* (New York: Pepys Press, 1981), 308.

p. 100 *"If we do not now dare everything..."* Baldwin, "Letter from a Region in My Mind," in *Collected Essays* (Library of America), 347.

p. 100 *"Bobby Kennedy's assurance..."* Ibid., 340.

p. 100 *"Ask any Negro...."* Ibid., 345.

p. 101 *a conversation that can be seen on YouTube* (www.youtube.com/watch?v=Xy3ounR w9Q&playnext=1&list=PLE7353AF1FDA22441).

p. 101 *"the only hope this country has..."* Taylor Branch, *Parting the Waters* (New York: Simon & Schuster, 1988), 895.

p. 102 *"love of his people in his writing..."* Quoted in James Campbell, *Talking at the Gates* (New York: Viking, 1991), 205.

p. 102 *"If there is ever a Black Muslim nation..."* Philip Roth, "Channel X: Two Plays on Race Conflict," *New York Review of Books*, May 28, 1964. http://www.nybooks .com/articles/archives/1964/may/28/channel-x-two-plays-on-the-race-conflict/.

p. 102 *"One cannot let one's name be associated with shits..."* Richard Davenport-Hines, *Auden* (New York: Pantheon, 1996), 319.

p. 102 *"By the time you are thirty..."* "James Baldwin Debates William F. Buckley," You-Tube: www.youtube.com/watch?v+nbkObXxSUus. (Baldwin later reworked his remarks for a strong article in the *New York Times Magazine*, "The American Dream and the American Negro," reprinted in *Collected Essays*, 714.)

p. 103 *did not want to live like a Henry James character.* Leeming, *James Baldwin*, 258. Leeming can only paraphrase this important letter... see "Notes on a Native Son" by James Campbell, *The Guardian*, February 12, 2005. (Campbell originally quoted from Baldwin's correspondence but had to go back and paraphrase. Sol Stein was able to include letters in his book, but nobody else was able to do likewise. Hilton Als has argued that Baldwin's letters are his unpublished masterpiece.)

CHAPTER 8. LOVE AND SEX AND *A SINGLE MAN*

p. 106 *"as brutal as* Pal Joey*"* Quoted in Parker, *Isherwood: A Life*, 664.

p. 106 *"At last!"* quoted in Parker, 667.

p. 107 *"There were businessmen with flesh-roll necks..."* Christopher Isherwood, *Down There on a Visit* (New York: Simon & Schuster, 1962), 340.

p. 107 *"I see my twenty-three-year-old face..."* Ibid., 29.

p. 107 *"You know, you really are a tourist, to your bones..."* Ibid., 349.

p. 108 *"World Is Just One Big Sodom to Him..."* Reviews from *Miami News, Detroit Free Press,* and *Oxford Times,* quoted in Parker, 695.

p. 108 *"It's saying a great deal about Isherwood's ability as a novelist..."* Herbert Mitgang, *New York Times,* March 23, 1962, 31. Gerald Sykes in the *New York Times Book Review,* in one of the rare good reviews, saw *Down There* as a gay novel: "Even readers who feel they have had more than enough in recent years of the modern Sodom and Gomorrah will be surprised, I believe, to find how freshly and movingly these men are presented." "Compulsively Detached," March 18, 1962, *Times Book Review,* 288. (It's hard to guess what this overdose of Sodom and Gomorrah refers to: *Another Country* was not published until June and *Virginia Woolf* didn't open until the end of the year.)

p. 108 Welcome to Berlin, *to star Julie Andrews...* Keith Garebian, *The Making of Cabaret* (Oakville, Ontario: Mosaic Press, 1999), 3.

p. 109 *"Right now he is nerve-strung almost to screaming point..."* Quoted in Parker, 702. (One of several odd things about the Parker bio is how in most of the book he takes the side of almost anyone except Isherwood, but in the last third he takes Isherwood's side against Bachardy.)

p. 110 *"When I suffer, I suffer like a dumb animal..."* Quoted in Parker, 709.

p. 110 *"And in no time at all the blindingly simple truth was revealed..."* Christopher Isherwood, diary, September 19, 1962; quoted in Parker, 706.

p. 111 *"And I'll tell you something else..."* Isherwood, *A Single Man* (New York: Simon & Schuster, 1964), 72.

p. 112 *"As long as one precious drop of hate remained..."* Ibid., 102.

p. 113 *"George smiles to himself, with entire self-satisfaction..."* Ibid., 180.

p. 113 *"Then one by one the lights go out..."* Ibid., 186.

p. 113 *"Let us even go so far as to say..."* Ibid., 28.

p. 114 *"While I can believe this novel, I don't find it particularly interesting..."* Roger Angell, quoted in Parker, 715.

p. 114 *"a small masterpiece..."* as well as reviews in the *Los Angeles Times, Catholic Standard, The Daily Worker* the *Catholic Herald,* and the *Nashville Tennessean,* quoted in Parker, 727.

p. 114 *"Poor Corydon is now in California…"* Elizabeth Hardwick, "Sex and the Single Man," *New York Review of Books*, August 20, 1964. Other Hardwick quotes: "His is a fairly modest anal disposition, respectable enough, with a finicky, faggoty interest in the look of things—far from the corruption and splendor of his type in French fiction." One cannot win in the eyes of straight intellectuals. You're either a flaming criminal in a Jean Genet novel or you're nobody. http://www.nybooks .com/articles/archives/1964/aug/20/sex-and-the-single-man/.

p. 115 *"The most honest book ever written about a homosexual…"* Quoted by David Garnes, "A Single Man, Then and Now" in *The Isherwood Century*, ed. by James J. Berg and Chris Freeman (Madison: University of Wisconsin Press, 2000), 199.

p. 115 *"As long as I quite unashamedly get drunk…"* Isherwood, *My Guru and His Disciple* (New York: Farrar, Straus, and Giroux, 1980), 271.

p. 115 *"When Don isn't here…"* Isherwood, diary, November 2, 1964; quoted in Parker, 721.

CHAPTER 9. THE WHOLE WORLD IS WATCHING

p. 117 *"I decided to examine the homosexual underworld…"* Gore Vidal, *The City and the Pillar*, rev. ed. (New York: Dutton, 1965), 245. (Michel Foucault said something similar fifteen years later in *History of Sexuality*, but he read it back into history, proposing that an innocence existed before doctors named "the illness" at the end of the nineteenth century.)

p. 118 *"had too much ego to be a writer of fiction…"* Jason Epstein, quoted in Fred Kaplan, *Gore Vidal*, 771.

p. 118 *"Then Enid was right. You do love Clay. And you are mad."* Gore Vidal, *Washington, D.C.* (Boston: Little, Brown, 1967), 374.

p. 119 *"My entire life is now devoted to appearing on television…"* Quoted in Kaplan, *Gore Vidal*, 593.

p. 119 *"things tending toward the final erosion of our cultural values…"* *CBS Reports: The Homosexuals*, CBS, March 7, 1967; available at http://www.akawilliam.com/watch-cbs -reports-the-homosexuals-from-1967.

p. 120 *"I am Myra Breckinridge…"* Gore Vidal, *Myra Breckinridge* (Boston: Little, Brown, 1968), 1.

p. 120 *"The novel being dead…"* Vidal, *Myra Breckinridge*, 4.

p. 120 *"I AM HONORED AND DELIGHTED…"* Christopher Isherwood to Gore Vidal, August 12, 1967, quoted in Kaplan, *Gore Vidal*, 584.

p. 120 *"A funny novel, but it requires an iron stomach..."* Eliot Fremont-Smith, "Like Fay Wray If the Light Is Right," *New York Times*, February 3, 1968. http://www.nytimes.com/books/98/03/01/home/vidal-myra.html?scp=1&sq=myra%20breckinridge&st=cse.

p. 120 *"the pokerfaced jacket art..."* James McBridge, "What Did Myra Want?" *New York Times Book Review*, February 18, 1968. http://www.nytimes.com/books/97/06/22/reviews/hollywood-myra.html?scp=4&sq=myra%20breckinridge&st=cse.

p. 123 *Ginsberg calmed a group of protesters...* Mailer, *Miami*, 167. One year later, on the witness stand at the trial of the Chicago Seven, Ginsberg would OM in an attempt to make peace between defense attorney William Kunstler and angry judge Julius Hoffman.

p. 124 *"And some people were pro-Nazi..."* *ABC News*, August 28, 1968. The famous exchange can be watched on YouTube (http://www.youtube.com/watch?v=uajX661byMw&NR=1). People have accused Vidal of making the crypto-Nazi charge out of nowhere, but the pro-Nazi line was introduced by Buckley. Presumably he was referring to George Lincoln Rockwell, whom he discussed later, but he didn't explain himself yet. (Incidentally, Buckley *was* in the army during World War II and attended Officer Candidates School, but never went overseas.)

p. 125 *That should have been the end of it...* Buckley supporters pretend that Buckley did not instigate the articles. The details here are drawn almost entirely from Kaplan, *Gore Vidal*, pp. 603–612, who backs up his account of the order of events with many sources, most importantly an unpublished manuscript by Harold Hayes, editor of *Esquire*.

p. 126 *"almost obsession with homosexuality..."* William F. Buckley, "On Experiencing Gore Vidal," *Esquire*, August 1969, 110.

p. 126 *"faggotry is countenanced..."* Ibid., 128.

p. 126 *"Can there be any justification in calling a man a pro crypto Nazi...?"* Gore Vidal, "A Distasteful Encounter with William F. Buckley, Jr.," *Esquire*, September 1969, 140.

p. 128 *"They were younger than they thought they were..."* James Baldwin, *Tell Me How Long the Train's Been Gone* (New York: Dial Press, 1968), 454.

p. 128 *"the most grueling, agonizing, total hatred of the blacks..."* Cleaver, "Notes on a Native Son," in *Soul on Ice* (New York: McGraw Hill, 1968), 124.

p. 129 *"It seems that many Negro homosexuals..."* Ibid., 127.

p. 129 *"I, for one, do not think that homosexuality..."* Ibid., 136.

p. 129 *He closes by quoting Murray Kempton out of context…* Ibid. Cleaver's full quote from Kempton reads, "When I was a boy Stepin Fetchit was the only Negro actor who worked regularly in the movies…. The fashion changes, but I sometimes think that Malcolm X and, to a degree even James Baldwin, are *our* Stepin Fetchits." Kempton appears to say that black militants, including Baldwin, are the only blacks one hears about anymore, but that's not how Cleaver uses the quote.

p. 129 *"the silent ally, indirectly but effectively…"* Cleaver, "The Allegory of the Black Eunuchs," *Soul on Ice*, 162. There's a smart defense of Baldwin by Michele Wallace in *Black Macho and the Myth of the Superwoman*, where she argues that Cleaver was put off not only by Baldwin's inclusion of gay men in his fiction but also by his inclusion of tough, sympathetic black women.

p. 129 *"All that toy soldier has done is call me gay…"* W. J. Weatherby, *James Baldwin: Artist on Fire* (New York: D. I. Fine, 1989), 292.

p. 129 *"I thought I could see why he felt impelled…"* James Baldwin, *No Name in the Street*, in *Collected Essays*, 459.

p. 130 *"Since Martin's death in Memphis…"* Ibid., 357.

p. 131 *"I think both sides, Hanoi and Washington, are terribly, tragically…"* Eric Norden, "Playboy Interview: Truman Capote," *Playboy*, March 1968; reprinted in *Truman Capote: Conversations*, ed. M. Thomas Inge (Jackson: University Press of Mississippi, 1987), 146.

p. 131 *"a roman à clef, drawn from life…"* Ibid., 161.

p. 132 *"a bloody mary before lunch…"* Windham, *Lost Friendships*, 87.

p. 132 *"looking suspiciously like a fat and aged version of tough Truman Capote on ugly pills…"* Mailer, *Miami*, 223.

p. 132 *"[He] began to talk to me as though I knew no more about him…"* Windham, 87.

CHAPTER 10. RIOTS

p. 134 *"Oh, my God, it's Lily Law!"* Mart Crowley, *The Boys in the Band* (New York: Alyson, 2008), 32.

p. 135 *"habitués of the place were reported to embrace each other…"* Chas. K. Robinson, "The Raid," *ONE*, July 1960; excerpted in Neil Miller, *Out of the Past* (New York: Vintage, 1995), 323.

p. 135 *The most famous case is that of Newton Arvin…* The fullest account of Arvin's arrest is Barry Werth, *The Scarlet Professor* (New York: Nan Talese/Doubleday, 2001), 193–280.

p. 135 *"It's happened to many others—"* Truman Capote, *Too Brief a Treat: Letters of Truman Capote*, ed. Gerald Clarke (New York: Random House, 2004), 293.

p. 135 *"Bill of Rights for Homosexuals!"* Martin Duberman, *Stonewall* (New York: Dutton, 1993), 113.

p. 136 *"Book reviews? Who reads books these days?"* ONE, July–December 1967.

p. 136 *a new male magazine,* DRUM…Diarist Donald Vining bought an early issue of *DRUM*: "I wouldn't waste my money on it soon again but at least it has some dignity as it tells of efforts to amend the law and reviews some of the books on the subject, giving the back of the hand to trashy ones." *Gay Diary*, vol. 3, 471 (entry dated March 4, 1967).

p. 137 *He first came to New York in 1957…* Mart Crowley, conversation with the author, November 16, 2009.

p. 138 *Every Sunday, Crowley liked to buy the* New York Times, *go to the Swiss Cafe…* Ibid.

p. 138 *"The homosexual dramatist must be free…"* Stanley Kauffmann, "Homosexual Drama and Its Disguises," *New York Times,* January 23, 1966.

p. 138 *He was surprised at how quickly the writing went…* Mart Crowley, conversation with the author, November 16, 2009.

p. 139 *"sphinx-like and inscrutable…"* Mart Crowley, conversation with the author, November 30, 2009.

p. 140 *"a forties-movie bomber-crew cast…"* Pauline Kael, *Deeper into Movies* (Boston: Little, Brown, 1973), 137.

p. 140 *memorable one-liners…* Mart Crowley, *The Boys in the Band* (New York: Alyson, 2008); "Connie Casserole," and "Who do you have to fuck to get a drink around here?" (23), "You look like you been rimming a snow man" (54), "Life is a goddamn laff-riot" (53).

p. 140 *"The one on the floor is vicuna."* Ibid., 56.

p. 140 *"thirty-two-year-old, ugly, pockmarked Jew fairy…"* Ibid., 53.

p. 140 *"You are a sad and pathetic man…"* Ibid., 108.

p. 141 *"Crowley's most original creation…"* Tony Kushner, introduction to *Boys in the Band*, xiv.

p. 141 *As playwright Charles Busch later said…* Charles Busch, conversation with the author, December 2009.

p. 141 *"If we…if we could just…not hate ourselves…"* Crowley, *Boys in the Band*, 111.

p. 141 *"Oh Michael... thanks for the laughs..."* Ibid., 109.

p. 142 *"In the first act we screamed with laughter..."* Vining, *Gay Diary*, vol. 4, 37 (entry dated April 20, 1968). Vining goes on to say that he and his partner quoted favorite lines on the way home. "Ken rather acted as tho we had never been part of that world, which amused me since he fitted into it better than I did."

p. 142 *One friend of mine, now in his seventies...* Scott Fuchs, conversation with the author, October 2009; Schuyler Bishop, conversation with the author, October 2009.

p. 142 *"A bunch of gay friends hang out..."* Joe Keenan, conversation with the author, July 1997.

p. 142 *"one of the best acted plays of the season..."* Clive Barnes, "'The Boys in the Band' Opens Off Broadway," *New York Times*, April 15, 1968, 48.

p. 143 *"the best American play for some few seasons..."* Clive Barnes, "'The Boys in the Band' Is Still a Sad Gay Romp," *New York Times*, February 18, 1969, 36. People wrote differently back then, and Barnes could feel free to say, "Michael, a slightly aging Roman Catholic fag, is giving a birthday party for Harold, a slightly aging Jewish fag."

p. 143 *"in their amused, quick-minded, diminishing address..."* Walter Kerr, "To Laugh at Oneself—Or Cry," *New York Times*, April 28, 1969, Arts and Leisure, D1. Twenty years later Kerr said similar obtuse things about *Torch Song Trilogy*. He was another smart writer whose brain shut down as soon as homosexuality was mentioned.

p. 143 *"sounds too often as if it had been written by someone at the party..."* Vincent Canby, "The Boys in the Band," *New York Times*, March 18, 1970. http://movies .nytimes.com/movie/review?res=9E00E6D8173EE034BC4052DFB566838 B669EDE&scp=1&sq=vincent%20canby%20%22boys%20in%20the%20 band%22&st=cse.

p. 143 *"Realizing that the author's attempt..."* Donn Teal, "How Anguished Are Homosexuals?" *New York Times*, June 1, 1969, Arts and Leisure, D23. Compare this turgid prose with the annoying prose of Katie Kelly, who wrote about the movie two weeks after Stonewall: "There's Emory, the Tinker Bell of Third Avenue, flying in armed with his lisp and his lasagna recipe; Harold, the 'Before' of an acne medication testimonial, who spreads his spleen like a communicable disease." Katie Kelly, "The 'Boys' Are Having a Bit of a Party Again," *New York Times*, Arts and Leisure, D15, July 13, 1969.

p. 143 *a young straight director, William Friedkin...* During filming, Friedkin showed Crowley a novel he wanted to make into a movie, *Cruising* by Gerald Walker. Crowley disliked the story of a cop who goes undercover in the gay S&M scene to discover a gay serial killer. Crowley told Friedkin what he thought and assumed that nothing would come of the project. Ten years later, however, Friedkin made *Cruising*, which starred Al Pacino, and triggered a string of protests. Mart Crowley, conversation with the author, December 13, 2009.

p. 144 *"The story is about self-destruction...."* Katie Kelly, "The 'Boys' Are Having...," *New York Times*.

p. 144 *"What's more boring than a queen doing a Judy Garland imitation?..."* Crowley, *Boys in the Band*, 8. There's a rumor that the title came from a line of dialogue in *A Star Is Born*, but Crowley says he was thinking only of a standard line from the Big Band era: "Let's all have a round of applause for the boys in the band." Mart Crowley, commentary, *The Boys in the Band*, directed by William Friedkin (1970; Hollywood: Paramount Home Entertainment, 2008), DVD.

p. 144 *"Is this supposed to be funny?"* Edmund White, *City Boy* (New York: Bloomsbury U.S.A., 2009), 20.

p. 144 *"[A] mammoth paddy wagon as big as a school bus, pulled up to the Wall...."* Edmund White, "Letter to Ann and Alfred Corn, July 8, 1969," *The Violet Quill Reader*, ed. David Bergman (New York: St. Martin's Press, 1994), 1–2.

p. 145 *"We're one of the largest minorities in the country..."* Quoted in Martin Duberman, *Stonewall*, 208.

p. 146 *"Who knows what will happen..."* Edmund White, "Letter," 3.

p. 146 *More people heard about* Boys *than heard about Stonewall that first year.* Crowley followed *Boys* with *A Breeze from the Gulf* in 1973, an autobiographical play about two alcoholic parents and their gay son. All three protagonists love each other deeply, but love only leaves them more vulnerable to one another. It's a wonderful play and it received excellent reviews, but it never found an audience. Perhaps nobody wanted to hear a story where straight people are the wounded ones watched over by a gay son who is sane and grounded.

Thirty years after *Boys in the Band*, Crowley wrote a sequel, *The Men from the Boys*. The old friends are still friends and they get together for a funeral. Larry has died, though not from AIDS. Three new characters, a trio of younger gay men, are present to show how gay life has and hasn't changed. It's a quiet, ruminative play with much talk about love and death, like Plato's *Symposium* set in an East Side duplex.

CHAPTER 11. OLD AND YOUNG

p. 151 *"Does it date?"* Christopher Isherwood, *Christopher and His Kind* (Farrar, Straus, and Giroux, 1976), 126.

p. 151 *"Maurice, bad as it is,..."* Marvin Mudrick, *Books Are Not Life, But Then What Is?* (New York: Oxford University Press, 1979), 278.

p. 152 *"Elliott, the hairdresser of a lady friend of mine…"* Joseph Epstein, "Homo/Hetero: The Struggle for Sexual Identity," *Harper's*, September 1970, 49.

p. 152 *"If I had the power to do so, I would wish homosexuality off the face of this earth…"* Ibid., 51.

p. 152 *"Nothing they could ever do would make me sadder…"* Ibid.

p. 152 *They gave the staff coffee and doughnuts…* Arnie Kantrowitz, e-mail message to the author, January 15, 2010. Kantrowitz described the staff, with the exception of Decter, as "bemused but not unfriendly. They seemed to enjoy the break in the routine." There's also a very funny account in *Dancing the Gay Lib Blues* by Arthur Bell (New York: Simon & Schuster, 1971) 131–135.

p. 152 *"The homosexual influence in Forster's other novels…"* Joseph Epstein, *New York Times Book Review*, October 10, 1971, 24.

p. 152 *"homosexual high jinks"* Ibid., 25.

p. 153 *"I slept through the Sixties…"* Tennessee Williams, *Memoirs*; quoted in Gore Vidal, *Matters of Fact and Fiction*, 135.

p. 154 *"Who really gives a damn that Tennessee Williams has finally admitted…"* Lee Barton, *New York Times*, January 23, 1972; quoted in Paller, *Gentlemen Callers*, 192. (Most quotes in this section about Williams were brought to my attention by Paller.)

p. 154 *"I feel sorry for the author…"* Arthur Bell, *Village Voice*, February 24, 1972; quoted in Paller, 192.

p. 154 *"You helped me free myself but I can see that you are not free."* Michael Silverstein, "An Open Letter to Tennessee Williams," *Gay Sunshine*, October 1971; reprinted in *Out of the Closets: Voices of Gay Liberation*, ed. Karla Jay and Allen Young (New York: New York University Press, 1992), 69.

p. 156 *"a ridiculous weakness…like bedwetting."* "Christopher Isherwood Interview" by Winston Leyland from *Gay Sunshine Interviews*, reprinted in *Conversations with Christopher Isherwood*, ed. James Berg and Chris Freeman (Jackson: University of Mississippi Press, 2001), 103.

p. 156 *"I never do see much point in fag-mags—"* Quoted in Kaplan, *Gore Vidal*, 667.

p. 157 *"Fortunately our people have always preferred legend to reality…"* Gore Vidal, *Burr* (New York: Modern Library, 1998), 158.

p. 157 *"Gore has written a hilarious review of Memoirs…"* *Five O'Clock Angel*, 338.

p. 158 *"a chunky, paunchy, booze-puffed runt…"* Truman Capote, *Answered Prayers: The Unfinished Novel* (New York: Random House, 1986), 58.

p. 159 *Donald Windham was housesitting in Capote's UN Plaza apartment in 1970...*Windham, *Lost Friendships*, 96.

p. 159 *"just picked Gore up and carried him to the door..." Playgirl*, September 1975, quoted in Kaplan, *Gore Vidal*, 71. The story is false but not completely absurd. Arthur Schlesinger wrote about the night in his journals at the time of the lawsuit. He remembered how he and George Plimpton escorted a very drunk Vidal from the party before he got into a fistfight over politics with lawyer Lem Billings, also drunk. They hailed a cab and rode with Vidal back to his hotel, said good-bye to him in the lobby, and returned to the White House. Schlesinger thought it wrong for Vidal to sue Capote when Capote's career was in such a bad place. Arthur Schlesinger, *Journals 1952–2000* (New York: Penguin Press, 2007), 407–408.

p. 159 *ranted at length about the Jewish critics...*Victor Bumbalo, conversation with the author, February 2010.

p. 160 *its annual circulation had risen to 60,000...*This and all circulation figures come from Rodger Streitmatter, *Unspeakable: The Rise of the Gay and Lesbian Press in America* (Boston: Faber & Faber, 1995), 185.

p. 160 *Patricia Nell Warren, an editor at* Reader's Digest *who had divorced her husband and come out as a lesbian...*Jay Parini, ed., *American Writers, Supplement XX* (Detroit: Charles Scribner's Son, 2010), 259–260.

p. 161 *Giovanni's Room...named after the Baldwin novel...*Ed Hermance, conversation with the author, October 2009.

p. 161 *"For Christopher, Berlin meant Boys."* Christopher Isherwood, *Christopher and His Kind*, 2.

p. 162 *"At first I didn't think about Heinz at all..."* Ibid., 282.

p. 162 *"He is already living in the city where you will settle..."* Ibid., 339.

p. 162 *"There is no excess in an Isherwood sentence..."* Gore Vidal, "Christopher Isherwood's Kind," *The Second American Revolution*, 47. Earlier on the same page, Vidal talks about Isherwood's beliefs: "Lately he has become a militant spokesman of Gay Liberation. If his defense of Christopher's kind is sometimes shrill...well, there is a good deal to be shrill about in a society so deeply and so mindlessly homophobic."

p. 163 *"Suppose, Christopher now said to himself,..."* Isherwood, *Christopher and His Kind*, 335. Isherwood wrote an earlier version of this argument with himself in *Down There on a Visit*, with the fictional Waldemar standing in for Heinz. The argument is more personal, and poignant, when we know it's a lover and not just a friend.

p. 163 *"What had actually begun to surface in his muddled mind..."* Ibid., 336.

p. 164 *"My tits are on fire"* Quoted in Parker, *Isherwood*, 798.

p. 164 *"They're beginning to believe that Christopher Street is named after you."* Ibid., 797.

CHAPTER 12. LOVE SONGS

p. 165 *"Perhaps it is not possible to fit into American Life..."* Harold Rosenberg, "Death in the Wilderness, in *The Tradition of the New* (New York: Horizon Press, 1960), 258. The quote continues: "In America everything is a possibility or it is a sham. You cannot fit into American life except as a 'camp.' If American intellectuals accepted [Daniel] Bell's endism and agreed that possibility is an illusion and reality 'the routines of living,' their choice would be either the "camp" unto death or their traditional solution: expatriation." It's a slippery set of ideas, but the interesting point here is that "camp" was already being discussed in 1961, three years before Susan Sontag publicized it.

p. 165 *"his roommate of the past thirteen years."* Jane Kramer, *Allen Ginsberg in America* (New York: Random House, 1969), 22.

p. 166 *"Why do you eat..."* Allen Ginsberg, *Selected Poems 1947–1995* (New York: HarperCollins, 1996), 305.

p. 167 *"I stare into my head..."* Ibid., 190.

p. 167 *"I want to be there in your garden party..."* Ibid.

p. 168 *"To live in fear of matriarchal disapproval, all you have to be is gay and not necessarily young..."* Joe LeSueur, *Digressions on Some Poems by Frank O'Hara*, 226.

p. 168 *"Having a Coke with You..."* Frank O'Hara, "Having a Coke with You," *Selected Poems*, 194.

p. 169 *"It was founded by me after lunch with LeRoi Jones..."* Frank O'Hara, "Personism: A Manifesto," *Yugen*, 1961; reprinted in *Selected Poems*, 248.

p. 170 *"I never doubted that almost any poem I wrote..."* James Merrill, *A Different Person* (New York: Knopf, 1993), 141.

p. 171 *"Oh, God, I left out the human feeling!"* Quoted in White, *City Boy*, 130.

p. 171 *"The Book of a Thousand and One Evenings Spent..."* James Merrill, *Divine Comedies* (New York: Atheneum, 1976), 48.

p. 172 *"(Any reflecting surface worked for him..."* Ibid., 50.

p. 172 *"LONG B4 THE FORTUNATE CONJUNCTION,"* Ibid., 59.

p. 173 *"There's a phrase..."* Ibid., 74.

p. 173 *She reports how Merrill set his left hand on the teacup...* Alison Lurie, *Familiar Spirits* (New York: Viking, 2001), 90–92.

p. 174 *"It is the lesbian in every woman who is compelled..."* Adrienne Rich, "It Is the Lesbian in Us," *On Lies, Secrets, and Silence: Selected Prose 1966–1978* (New York: Norton, 1979), 200–201.

p. 174 *"The more I live the more I think..."* Adrienne Rich, "Twenty-one Love Poems," *The Dream of a Common Language* (New York: Norton, 1978), 34.

p. 174 *poem by poem, reader by reader.* A special Poetry and Art issue of *Christopher Street* in October 1977 celebrated the gay presence in poetry, with several major poets publishing in a gay magazine for the first time: James Merrill, Richard Howard, Thom Gunn, James Schuyler, and a new writer, Paul Monette.

CHAPTER 13. ANNUS MIRABILIS

p. 175 *both are fond of hustlers.* Years later, when White won the first Bill Whitehead Award for Lifetime Achievement, the rumor went out that he spent the prize money the night of the award by hiring hustlers for himself and his friends. "That's a complete lie," an acquaintance said. "Ed White has never shared a hustler in his life."

p. 176 *"generous helping of foolish jokes about homosexuality..."* Howard Taubman, *New York Times*, May 1, 1963.

p. 176 *"He made you think that having sex with him..."* Victor Bumbalo, conversation with the author, February 2010.

p. 177 *"such a representative life..."* Richard Canning, *Gay Fiction Speaks: Conversations with Gay Novelists* (New York: Columbia University Press, 2001), 369.

p. 177 *"I am probably his only typist who never had sex with Ed."* Patrick Merla, conversation with the author, January 2010.

p. 178 *"I wonder what sort of an impression I might make..."* Edmund White, *Forgetting Elena* (New York: Penguin Books, 1981), 4.

p. 179 *"a cultivated heterosexual woman in her sixties..."* Quoted in Stacy Schiff, *Véra: Mrs. Vladimir Nabokov* (New York: Random House, 1999), 316.

p. 180 *"Should one of your friends drop by..."* Charles Silverstein and Edmund White, *The Joy of Gay Sex* (New York: Crown Publishers, 1977), 170.

p. 180 *"At this point neither of you should succumb to sleep..."* Ibid., 102.

p. 180 *"It is a word that makes little sense in gay life..."* Ibid., 178.

p. 181 *"No need to tell you that in the midst of my own..."* Edmund White, *Nocturnes for the King of Naples* (New York: St. Martin's Press, 1978), 39.

p. 182 *"But I have no pity to offer..."* Ibid., 147.

p. 183 *"I didn't care who knew I was gay..."* Philip Gambone, *Something Inside: Conversations with Gay Writers* (Madison: University of Wisconsin Press, 1999), 187. Holleran remained in the closet of his double identity. When he was interviewed by *Publishers Weekly* for *Nights in Aruba* in 1983, he admitted "Holleran" was a pseudonym but did not give his real name. Meanwhile his mother found out he was a published writer when a neighbor read *Aruba* and recognized the parents. (So what did Holleran tell her?) He later said he loved "the little envelope of anonymity and a little envelope of distance...There's something very embarrassing about writing" (187).

p. 184 *"Before you fuck yourself to death..."* Larry Kramer, *Faggots* (New York: Random House, 1978), 316.

p. 185 *"It got very hot that summer..."* Andrew Holleran, *Dancer from the Dance* (New York: William Morrow, 1978), 194–195.

p. 186 *"Looking for love..."* Ibid., 142–143.

p. 186 Faggots *sold very well: 40,000 in hardcover and 300,000 in paper.* Stephen Holden, "Larry Kramer's Update on the War at Home," *New York Times*, October 9, 1988. http://query.nytimes.com/search/alternate/query?query=stephen+holden+%22faggots%22&st=fromcse.

p. 187 *"a mercurial and strangely moral figure..."* John Lahr, "Camp Tales," *New York Times Book Review*, January 14, 1979, 15.

p. 187 *"Here are characters like Randy Dildough..."* Ibid., 40. (Lahr's review is not available in the *Times* online archive. I had to read it on microfilm. I don't know if the absence is because of a request by Lahr or maybe by Kramer, or if it's purely accidental?)
The *Times* wasn't kind to *Nocturnes* either. It praised the prose before saying, "But this is narcissistic prose and *Nocturnes* is a narcissistic novel—which is not to deny the rareness of its beauty, only the breadth of its appeal." *Narcissistic* was and still is a code word for "gay." (John Yohalem, "Apostrophes to a Dead Lover," *New York Times Book Review*, December 10, 1978, BR6.)

p. 187 *"Six books by, about, or for homosexuals appear in as many months..."* Jeffrey Burke, "Of a Certain Persuasion," *Harper's*, March 1979, 122. He also writes: "Both Kramer (intentionally) and Holleran (artlessly) present a gay world worthy of little more than disdain. They do nothing for the cause of literature and less for the cause of gay rights." Which makes me wonder if Burke were gay. It wouldn't be the first or last time a gay critic is used by the mainstream to trash gay writers. Several gay men went on to build literary careers out of their willingness to attack their peers. (I won't name names.)

p. 188 *"John Wayne and Auntie Mame..."* Patrick Gale, *Armistead Maupin* (Bath, England: Absolute, 1999), 14.

p. 189 *"suffered a slow process of attrition in a city where no one approved of Nixon..."* Ibid., 39.

p. 190 *"There were times when he was barely two days ahead..."* Maupin, *Tales of the City* (New York: HarperCollins, 1996), P.S. section, "A Pleasing Shock of Recognition," 5.

p. 190 *"Michael groaned and readjusted his shorts..."* Ibid., 226.

p. 192 *"We're gonna be...fifty-year-old libertines in a world full of twenty-year-old Calvinists."* Ibid., 311.

p. 192 *"Oh, that marvelous funny thing..."* Quoted by Maupin in conversation with the author, September 27, 2010.

p. 192 *"As much as I liked Rock..."* Quoted in Gale, *Armistead Maupin*, 66.

p. 193 *"I wouldn't have written, I guess,..."* Armistead Maupin, *More Tales of the City*, 221–223.

p. 194 *"me too."* Gale, *Armistead Maupin*, 59.

CHAPTER 14. WHITE NOISE

p. 195 *"Edmund White...is a charming man given to stringent self-analysis..."* Felice Picano, "Rough Cuts from a Journal," *The Violet Quill Reader*, ed. David Bergman, 36–37.

p. 197 *"dessert-and-short-story"* Andrew Holleran, "A Place of Their Own," *The Violet Quill Reader*, ed. David Bergman, 402.

p. 197 States of Desire: Travels in Gay America *was the brainchild of Charles Ortleb...* Patrick Merla, conversation with the author, December 2009. (Merla was editor of *Christopher Street* at the time.)

p. 198 *"So few human contacts in Los Angeles go unmediated..."* Edmund White, *States of Desire* (New York: Dutton, 1980), 1.

p. 198 *"Jeeps—elaborately painted..."* Ibid., 11.

p. 199 *"When a city slicker has a jerk-off fantasy..."* Ibid., 132.

p. 199 *"Greenwich Village is the gay ghetto..."* Ibid., 265.

p. 201 *"gave me a cheek to peck, a purely routine gesture..."* Edmund White, *After Dark*; reprinted in *The Burning Library: Essays*, ed. David Bergman (New York: Knopf, 1994), 105–106.

p. 201 *"a never-ending spectacle..."* Midge Decter, "The Boys on the Beach," *Commentary*, September 1980. (www.commentarymagazine.com/article/the-boys-on-the -beach/).

p. 203 *"Well, if I were a dyke and a pair of Podhoretzes came waddling toward me..."* Gore Vidal, "Pink Triangle and Yellow Star," *Second American Revolution*, 171.

p. 203 *"a world of perfect illogic..."* Ibid., 180.

p. 203 *"I was present when Christopher Isherwood..."* Ibid., 169–170. Readers can't help but notice that a disproportionate number of antigay critics were Jewish: Stanley Kauffmann, Philip Roth, Joseph Epstein, Midge Decter. One reason for this is that postwar Jewish intellectuals were more fearless and outspoken than the gentiles. Writers with Catholic or Protestant backgrounds were just as intolerant, but did not like talking about sex of any kind. However, I suspect there was also another factor: turf. Jewish writers had broken into American intellectual life after the war. They were not ready to share their importance with the next rising minority group.

p. 204 *"Pink Triangle and Yellow Star" has been regularly quoted ever since...* The strain between Vidal and the Podhoretzes continued. Five years later, it erupted into all-out war. In January 1986, Vidal published another essay in the *Nation*, "The Day the American Empire Ran Out of Gas," where he declared that the American empire had died under Reagan, and good riddance. Podhoretz responded in the *New York Post* that political critics like Vidal and Norman Mailer had never liked America anyway. Decter added her own two cents in *Contentions* magazine, defending American imperialism. Vidal responded with "The Empire Lovers Strike Back," later retitled "A Cheerful Response." He called Podhoretz "a silly billy" and accused the couple of being bad Americans who didn't know their history and who cared more about Israel. Podhoretz furiously responded with an essay accusing Vidal of anti-Semitism, cleverly titled "The Hate That Dare Not Speak Its Name"—as if anti-Semitism were the moral equivalent of "the love that dare not speak its name." Before then, however, according to a story heard around town at the time, the indignant couple ran into Victor Navasky on the street. Podhoretz angrily told Navasky, "You are a son of a bitch," for printing such a piece in the *Nation*. Navasky only laughed and said, "And *you* are a silly billy."

p. 204 *"I am sauntering for the Senate..."* Quoted in Kaplan, *Gore Vidal*, 732–733.

p. 205 *"Take time off. Think about things..."* From *Gore Vidal, the Man Who Said No*, produced and directed by Gary Conklin (Gary Conklin Films, 1983). Available from Gary Conklin Films.

p. 205 *"old friends.... He's lived various places, I've lived various places..."* Quoted in Kaplan, *Gore Vidal*, 735.

p. 206 *"I mention the constant music..."* Edmund White, *A Boy's Own Story* (New York: Dutton, 1982), 22.

p. 206 *"I didn't particularly like getting cornholed..."* Ibid., 19.

p. 207 *"By day I gave myself over to a covert yearning for men..."* Ibid., 153.

p. 208 *"Sometimes I think I seduced and betrayed Mr. Beattie..."* Ibid., 218.

p. 209 *"White has crossed* Catcher in the Rye *with* De Profundis*..."* Catharine R. Stimpson, "The Bodies and Souls of American Men," *New York Times Book Review*, October 10, 1982, 15.

p. 209 *"It is any boy's story..."* Christopher Lehmann-Haupt, "Edmund White's Tale of a Gay Youth," *New York Times*, December 17, 1982. http://www .nytimes.com/1988/03/17/books/books-of-the-times-edmund-white-s-tale -of-a-gay-youth.html?scp=1&sq=christopher%20lehmann-haupt%20on%20 edmund%20white&st=cse. In other cases, one sometimes wonders how closely mainstream reviewers read gay books, even when they praise them. John Banville talking about White's work in the *New York Review of Books* years later cited "the unrelenting descriptions of gay shenanigans that so startled early readers of *A Boy's Own Story*" ("Coupling," August 10, 2000). But the only sex scenes are at the beginning and the end. Likewise Malcolm Bradbury, in his overview of postwar fiction, *The Modern American Novel*, described *The Beautiful Room Is Empty* as a novel about AIDS, assuming that was what the title meant.

CHAPTER 15. ILLNESS AND METAPHOR

p. 214 *"like a bookstore"* Andrew Holleran, "Larry Kramer and the Wall of Books," in *We Must Love One Another or Die*, ed. Lawrence Mass (New York: St. Martin's Press, 1997), 119.

p. 214 *Someone who had a brief affair with him...* Anonymous, conversation with the author, March 10, 2010.

p. 215 *"I think the concealed meaning in Kramer's emotionalism..."* Quoted in Larry Kramer, "The First Defense," *New York Native*, December 21, 1981–January 3, 1982; reprinted in Kramer, *Reports from the Holocaust* (New York: St. Martin's Press, 1989), 16. (In later editions, Kramer used a lower-case h for *holocaust* to differentiate the AIDS epidemic from the Nazi murder of the Jews. But we are referring here to the first edition and have left it as it stood to avoid confusion.)

p. 216 *"the 'eroticism' that has made gay health such a concern..."* Ibid., 21.

p. 216 *"Gay men certainly have a health crisis..."* Quoted in Patrick Merla, "A Normal Heart," in *We Must Love One Another or Die*, 38.

p. 217 *"I wanted to go on having industrial quantities of sex..."* White, *City Boy*, 288.

p. 217 *"There are drug users and non-drug users..."* Kramer, "1,112 and Counting," *Reports from the Holocaust*, 35.

p. 218 *But Kramer believed that was the real reason for Koch's silence: he was a closet case...* For the longest time, at least in print, Kramer only implied this or said it indirectly. Then he made the accusation through characters in *The Normal Heart* and included a Koch-like closeted mayor in *Just Say No*. Finally he began to say it directly, telling *New York* magazine, for example, that Koch was "a closeted gay man" (Maer Roshan, "Larry Kramer: Queer Conscience," *New York*, April 6, 1998). Kramer and others spoke in more depth about the charge in the 2009 documentary *Outrage*. Journalist David Rothenberg says on camera that Koch as a congressman had a boyfriend, Richard Nathan. He says Koch insisted Nathan leave New York after he became mayor. Nathan died of AIDS in Los Angeles in 1996. On the other hand, others have said Koch was not just asexual but asocial. His friend Bess Myerson said, "You have to remember something. Ed Koch has never lived with a woman. Ed Koch has never lived with a man. Ed Koch has never lived with a dog. That's why he's like that." (quoted in Michael Goodwin, *New York Comes Back*, 40). It should also be pointed out that Koch had no difficulty signing New York's gay rights ordinance in 1986, and he backed his health department's closing of the baths in 1985, which Kramer campaigned for. Kramer later attacked Koch for not providing money to GMHC in the city budget, but Koch was famously stingy with public funds. He had brought the city back from bankruptcy by cutting back on city services; he continued to cut services even with the epidemic of homelessness during the Reagan years.

p. 219 *"I want to apologize to any of the people dear to me..."* Kramer, "The Mark of Courage," *Reports from the Holocaust*, 64.

p. 220 *"Your own son is gay..."* Quoted in Gail Merrifield Papp, "Larry Kramer at the Public," in *We Must Love One Another or Die*, 257.

p. 220 *"tough sledding..."* Ibid., 259.

p. 222 *"And you think I'm killing people?"* Larry Kramer, *The Normal Heart and The Destiny of Me: Two Plays* (New York: Grove Press, 2000), 97–98.

p. 222 *"Don't lose that anger..."* Ibid., 117.

p. 223 *"The only way we'll have real pride..."* Ibid., 110.

p. 223 *making his fictional self more difficult and more interesting when he produced multiple drafts of a screenplay...* Author's reading of a later draft of the screenplay in November 1992.

p. 223 *"The blood that's coursing through* The Normal Heart *... is boiling hot..."* Frank Rich, *New York Times*, April 22, 1985. http://www.nytimes.com/1985/04/22/theater/ theater-the-normal-heart-by-larry-kramer.html?scp=1&sq=frank+rich+%22the +normal+heart%22&st=nyt.

p. 224 *"The aesthetic failings of Larry Kramer's* The Normal Heart*..."* Michael Feingold, *Village Voice*, April 19, 1985.

p. 224 *"Don't you sometimes wish that all the faggots..."* Quoted in Ned Rorem, "The Real John Simon," *New York Native*, 1985; reprinted in Ned Rorem, *Other Entertainments* (New York: Simon & Schuster, 1996), 136. That was how Simon himself remembered it. Liz Smith quoted a cleaner, more succinct version in her column in the *Daily News*: "Homosexuals in the theater! My God, I can't wait until AIDS gets all of them!"

p. 224 *"What could have been a mere staged tract..."* John Simon, *New York*, May 6, 1985.

p. 225 *"You and your huge assortment of caretakers..."* Larry Kramer, "An Open Letter to Richard Dunne," *Reports from the Holocaust*, 102.

CHAPTER 16. DEAD POETS SOCIETY

p. 226 *"a good career move."* Quoted in Kaplan, *Gore Vidal*, 707. Capote had settled with Vidal a year earlier in Vidal's million-dollar libel suit. Capote didn't have a million dollars—he didn't even have the money to pay Vidal's legal costs—but he did write a public letter of apology for what he'd said in *Playgirl*.

p. 228 *"If you could hear, at every jolt, the blood..."* Wilfred Owen, *"Dulce et Decorum Est."* from *The Poems of Wilfred Owen* (New York: Viking, 1931), 66. The poem was written between 1917 and 1918 and first published in 1920.

p. 228 *"It is as if the writers had sent you their ripped-out arms..."* Randall Jarrell, "A Verse Chronicle," in *Poetry and the Age*, 176.

p. 228 *"No air. Breathe in..."* Melvin Dixon, "Heartbeats," in *Love's Instruments* (New York: Tia Cucha Press, 1995), reprinted in *Persistent Voices*, ed. Philip Clark and David Groff (New York: Alyson Books, 2009), 87-88.

p. 229 *"Now I understand why [he] had invented his dress-up party..."* Edmund White, *The Farewell Symphony* (New York: Knopf, 1997), 414.

p. 229 *"In the sunlit current the white gravel of our friend..."* James Merrill, "Memorial Tribute to David Kalstone," reprinted in *Collected Prose* (New York: Knopf, 2004), 365.

p. 229 *"You are gone...."* James Merrill, "Farewell Performance," *Selected Poems*, 220.

p. 230 *Merrill never indicated that he himself had tested positive for the virus in 1986....* This was first revealed by J. D. McClatchy in his excellent essay, "Two Deaths, Two Lives" published in Edmund White, ed., *Loss within Loss: Artists in the Age of AIDS* (Madison: University of Wisconsin Press, 2001).

p. 230 *"Chains of gold tinsel, baubles of green fire..."* James Merrill, "Vol. XLIV, No. 3," *Selected Poems*, 239. The title, which sounds like an issue of a medical journal, has not been identified by J. D. McClatchy, Merrill scholar Stephen Yenser, or Merrill biographer Lanny Hammer. "I've always assumed the title was made up....It would be like JM to concoct a title whose numerals had some hidden meaning." J. D. McClatchy e-mail message to the author, September 2010.

p. 231 *"Later I realized what I was doing..."* James Campbell, *Thom Gunn in Conversation with James Campbell* (London: BTL, 2000), 40.

p. 231 *"hippy silliness and self-regarding camp."* John Mole, "Two-Gun Gunn," review of *Selected Poems* in *Poetry Review*, September 1980; quoted in *Thom Gunn in Conversation*, 108.

p. 231 *"A gust of morphine..."* Thom Gunn, "Lament," in *Collected Poems* (New York: Farrar, Straus, and Giroux, 1994), 466.

p. 232 *"an unlimited embrace..."* Thom Gunn, "The Missing," in *Collected Poems*, 483.

p. 232 *"Gunn restores poetry to a centrality..."* Neil Powell, "The Dangerous Edge of Things," *PN Review*, May–June 1992; quoted in *Thom Gunn in Conversation*, 111.

p. 232 *"like a child running through the contents of his bedroom closet..."* Andrew Holleran, *Ground Zero* (New York: Morrow, 1988), 94.

p. 233 *"Not only is Charles Ludlam gone..."* Ibid., 99.

p. 233 *"AIDS destroys trust...."* Ibid., 189.

p. 234 *"And on the twelfth floor..."* Mark Doty, "63rd Street Y," in *Turtle, Swan & Bethlehem in Broad Daylight* (Urbana: University of Illinois Press, 2000), 90.

p. 234 *"Peter died in a paper tiara..."* Mark Doty, "Tiara," ibid, 96.

p. 235 *"I don't feel I know nearly enough about the AIDS situation..."* from Armistead Maupin, "The First Couple: Don Bachardy and Christopher Isherwood," *Village Voice*, July 2, 1985; reprinted in *Conversations with Christopher Isherwood*, 191.

p. 236 *"merciless and loving..."* Don Bachardy, *Christopher Isherwood: Last Drawings* (London; Boston: Faber & Faber, 1990), x.

p. 236 *"The thought occurs to me..."* Ibid., xiii.

p. 236 *"Oh, the pain, the pain…"* Ibid.

p. 236 *"I started drawing Chris's corpse at two o'clock…"* Ibid., xvii.

CHAPTER 17. TALES OF TWO OR THREE CITIES

p. 238 *By 1992, 10 percent of Plume's titles would be gay.* Esther B. Fein, "The Media Business: Big Publishers Profit as Gay Literature Thrives," *New York Times*, July 6, 1992. http://www.nytimes.com/1992/07/06/business/the-media-business-big-publishers-profit-as-gay-literature-thrives.html?scp=1&sq=gay%20publishing%201992&st=cse.

p. 238 *"Young heterosexual male authors…"* "Who's Who in the Literary Power Game," *Esquire*, August 1987, 56.

p. 239 *"I couldn't decide whether the image was more threatening as a homoerotic come-on…"* Frank Rich, "The Gay Decades," *Esquire*, November 1987, 97.

p. 240 *"1. Stop begging for acceptance…."* Armistead Maupin, "Design for Living" *Advocate*, 1985; reprinted in Gale, *Armistead Maupin*, 149–151.

p. 240 *"We were finding instant points of agreement…"* Quoted in Gale, *Armistead Maupin*, 71.

p. 241 *"increases the intimacy and it increases the dangers of fights…"* Ibid., 75–76.

p. 241 *"Do you think I should come out?"* Ibid., 131.

p. 242 *"Three years of daily fretting…"* Armistead Maupin, *Sure of You*, (New York: HarperPerennial, 1994), 225–226.

p. 242 *"He tilted his head and let the sun dry his tears…"* Ibid., 226.

p. 243 *"Mr. Maupin writes for everyone: gay, straight, single, married,…"* David Feinberg, "Goodnight, Mrs. Madrigal," *New York Times Book Review*, October 22, 1989. http://www.nytimes.com/1989/10/22/books/goodnight-mrs-madrigal.html?scp=1&sq=david%20feinberg%20on%20armistead%20maupin&st=cse.

p. 245 *"Well, at least you got to stay your own gender."* Quoted in Melanie Rehnak, "The Way We Live Now: ShopTalk; Family Affair, *New York Times Sunday Magazine*, April 30, 2000. http://www.nytimes.com/2000/04/30/magazine/the-way-we-live-now-4-30-00-shoptalk-family-affair.html?scp=2&sq=keith%20fleming/edmund%20white&st=cse.

p. 245 *none other than Susan Sontag…*Mathilda argues like Sontag; she has the same strange relationship with a grown son that Sontag had with hers; she even irritably picks at her teeth at parties like Sontag (as White reports in his memoir, *City Boy*).

p. 245 *"You've given me the gift of your completely innocent trust..."* White, *Caracole* (New York: Dutton, 1985), 138.

p. 245 *"In Paris people cultivate social life as an art form..."* Edmund White, "The *Paris Review* Interview," *Paris Review*, Fall 1988; reprinted in Bergman, ed., *The Burning Library*, 264.

p. 246 *"Even though George had been a baby..."* Edmund White, "An Oracle," in *The Darker Proof* (New York: New American Library, 1988), 180.

p. 247 *"If art is to confront AIDS more honestly..."* Edmund White, "Esthetics and Loss," *Artforum*, January 1987; reprinted in Bergman, ed., *The Burning Library*, 216. White compares the surprisingly tough *An Early Frost* to *Love Story*. Did he ever see *Love Story*? For that matter, did he ever see *Frost*?

p. 247 *"pure twaddle"* Ed Sikov, *New York Native*, March 2, 1987, 14. Sikov had a lot of fun at the expense of White's pomposity. When White cryptically says the prevailing mood in the gay community is one of "evanescence...just like the Middle Ages," Sikov imagines a scene outside the Chelsea gym: "How ya doin', Butch?" "I'm feeling evanescent today, Larry—you know, kinda like Chartres in 1348."

p. 248 *his appearances were often unpredictable.* Patrick Merla, interview with the author, October 2009. Baldwin was represented by the Jay Acton agency, where Merla worked. Merla tells a story about going down to Washington, D.C., in 1979 or 1980 with a contract for Baldwin to sign so they could pay him. Merla had to ambush Baldwin at a black church where Baldwin was speaking. There, too, Baldwin was late.

p. 248 *"Whatever the fuck your uncle was..."* James Baldwin, *Just Above My Head* (New York: Dial, 1979), 27.

p. 248 *"They walked in the light of each other's eyes..."* Ibid., 183.

p. 248 *"There were no X-rated movies then..."* James Baldwin, "Freaks and the Ideal of American Masculinity," in *Collected Essays*, 819.

p. 248 *"I quickly learned that my existence was the punchline..."* Ibid., 819.

CHAPTER 18. LAUGHTER IN THE DARK

p. 250 *"Laugh and you are free."* Charles Ludlam, "Confessions of a Farceur," *Ridiculous Theater: Scourge of Human Folly*, ed. Steven Samuels (New York: Theatre Communications Group, 1992), 50.

p. 250 *"It's got great ghosts..."* Ibid., 89.

p. 251 *"I think that I am the Camille of our era..."* Ibid., 43.

p. 251 *"No faggots in the house?"* Charles Ludlam, *Camille*, in *The Complete Plays of Charles Ludlam* (New York: Harper & Row, 1989), 246. The speech continues: "Open the window, Nanine. See if there are any in the street."

p. 251 *"that golden hysteria of taking the situations in old movies to a logical extreme..."* Pauline Kael, *When the Lights Go Down* (New York: Holt, Rinehart and Winston, 1980), 504–505.

p. 251 *"We decided we gays have been through enough..."* Quoted in David Kaufman, *Ridiculous! The Theatrical Life and Times of Charles Ludlam* (New York: Applause Books, 2002), 405.

p. 253 *McCauley's tale of friendship between a gay man and straight woman found a huge audience among straight women...* I witnessed this firsthand when another novelist, Jesse Green, and I read with McCauley at Scribner's Bookstore in New York in 1988. After we all read, the audience was told to line up in front of each author for his autograph. Green and I got short lines of four or five readers apiece. McCauley's line ran the length of the store all the way to the street and was almost entirely female—with a scattering of gay men. Green and I were more amused than envious.

p. 254 *37,000 cases of AIDS in the United States...* Patrick Merla, "A Normal Heart," in *We Must Love One Another or Die*, 50.

p. 255 *"At the rate we are going, you could be dead in less than five years..."* Larry Kramer, *Reports from the Holocaust*, 128.

p. 255 *Michael Petrelis of Lavender Hill was in the audience that night...* Michael Petrelis, interview by Sarah Schulman, "Interview #020," *ACT UP Oral History Project*, http://www.actuporalhistory.org/interviews/index.html.

p. 255 *"We have to go after the FDA—fast..."* Merla, "A Normal Heart," 50.

p. 256 *He decided ACT UP was too ad hoc, too democratic. He wanted more structure...* Larry Kramer, interview by Sarah Schulman, "Interview #035," *ACT UP Oral History Project*. (The *Oral History Project* is an invaluable resource.)

p. 256 *"Larry Kramer forms an organization..."* David Feinberg, *Spontaneous Combustion* (New York: Viking, 1991), 225.

p. 256 *"White Jew Georgetown Faggot..."* Larry Kramer, *Just Say No: A Play about a Farce* (New York: St. Martin's Press, 1989), 10.

p. 256 *"having written the script and articulated his hostilities..."* Mel Gussow, "Skewers for the Political in Kramer's 'Just Say No,'" *New York Times*, October 21, 1988. http://www.nytimes.com/1988/10/21/theater/reviews-theater-skewers-for -the-political-in-kramer-s-just-say-no.html?scp=1&sq=just%20say%20no%20 by%20larry%20kramer&st=cse.

p. 257 *"Molly, that's the man…"* Quoted by Calvin Trillin, "Three Friends," in *We Must Love One Another or Die*, 310.

p. 258 *"He is very fat…"* Larry Kramer, "Interview with Gore Vidal," *QW* magazine, 1992; reprinted in *Conversations with Gore Vidal* (Jackson: University Press of Mississippi, 2005), 156.

p. 258 *"There has been talk in gay historical circles…"* Ibid., 167. One could write a book on gay Lincoln, and people have. The facts are simple: Lincoln shared a room and a bed in his twenties with another man, Joshua Speed, for four years when he was starting out as a lawyer in Springfield, Illinois. Shared beds were not uncommon in the nineteenth century (and well into the twentieth century, before affluence, sexual awareness, and central heating changed people's sleeping arrangements). There were sometimes other men sleeping in the same room as Lincoln and Speed. Lincoln often shared beds with still other men when he traveled the rural court circuit. He and Speed each married women and they drifted apart until Lincoln became president and they resumed their correspondence. The later letters are mostly about slavery, which Speed supported. (He appears not to have voted for his former bedmate in the 1860 election.) Speed's older brother became a member of Lincoln's cabinet.

Neither Lincoln nor Speed was secretive about their friendship or the shared bed. In fact, our prime source is Speed himself, who saved Lincoln's letters and wrote an account of their friendship for Lincoln's law partner and early biographer, William Herndon. There's an intelligent telling of the tale by Jonathan Ned Katz in his book, *Love Stories* (which is more ambiguous than Kramer claims), and a silly one in *The Intimate Abraham Lincoln* by C. A. Tripp (which argues, among other things, that Lincoln was not just bisexual but predominantly gay and clearly a "top," and that Speed must've been impotent with his wife since he includes fine descriptions of clouds and landscapes in a letter to her).

Kramer seems to believe two men can't share a bed without having sex, and they can't have sex without falling in love. I think he's wrong on both counts, but especially the second. Nothing I've read by or about Lincoln convinces me that he fell in love with men. Politicians are wired differently than other people—and Lincoln lived for politics—but I find no place in his biographical puzzle to put this missing piece. It does not give me new understanding of him. Nor do I see what gay people gain from claiming him as a secret brother. What do we win with an Honest Abe who spent his life lying to himself and to others? It's hardly a home run for our team.

A gay-related sidenote: Joshua Speed's younger brother, Philip, married Emma Keats, the niece of poet John Keats. Keats's brother George had emigrated to Louisville; many of the poet's famous letters were written to him there. Years later, in 1882, when Oscar Wilde toured America, Emma Keats Speed heard him speak in Louisville. Wilde praised Keats in his talk—the doomed boy poet was an early gay icon—and the niece, who was in her sixties, invited Wilde home and showed him her uncle's letters and manuscripts. Wilde was so appreciative that she later sent him one of the manuscripts. (Richard Ellmann, *Oscar Wilde*, 203; Ellmann knows nothing about Emma's brother-in-law or the Lincoln connection.)

CHAPTER 19. ANGELS

p. 261 *He was born in New York in 1956...* Most of the biographical material is from John Lahr, "Tony Kushner: After Angels," in *Honky Tonk Parade: New Yorker Profiles of Show People* (Woodstock: Overlook Press, 2005). This is easily the single best portrait of Kushner as both an artist and a man.

p. 262 *"I wouldn't want to be the father of Tchaikovsky..."* William Kushner, quoted in *Wrestling With Angels: Playwright Tony Kushner*, documentary, directed by Frieda Lee Mock (2006). Produced by American Film Foundation, available on DVD from Balcony Releasing.

p. 262 *He wanted to write but was afraid he wasn't good enough...* Tony Kushner, videotaped conversation, Dallas Museum, Dallas, TX, June 10, 2009. http://www.bing.com/ videos/search?q=Tony+Kushner&view=detail&mid=3D6628A98D1F6B1A96 203D6628A98D1F6B1A9620&first=0&FORM=LKVR.

p. 262 *"my former lover, my forever friend..."* Tony Kushner, *Angels in America: A Gay Fantasia on National Themes; Part One: Millennium Approaches* (New York: Theatre Communications Group, 1993), x.

p. 262 *a long list of favorite writers...* Charlotte Stroudt, "The Proust Questionnaire" originally published in a study guide for the 1995 Baltimore Center production of *Slavs!*; reprinted in Robert Vorlicky, ed., *Tony Kushner in Conversation*, 126.

p. 262 *"You, or/the loss of you..."* Tony Kushner, "The Second Month of Mourning," in *Thinking about the Longstanding Problems of Virtue and Happiness* (New York: Theatre Communications Group, 1995), 213.

p. 264 *"The problem is we have a standard of what evil is..."* Tony Kushner, *A Bright Room Called Day*; reprinted in *Plays by Tony Kushner* (New York: Theatre Communications Group, 1992), 50–51.

p. 264 *"Perhaps if the world were not actually on the brink of war..."* Frank Rich, "Making History Repeat, Even Against Its Will," *New York Times*, January 8, 1991. http:// theater.nytimes.com/mem/theater/treview.html?res=9D0CE0DB103AF93BA 35752C0A967958260&scp=3&sq=bright%20room%20called%20day&st=cse.

p. 265 *A few years earlier Kushner had had a dream about a sick friend...* Boris Kachka, "How I Made It: Tony Kushner on 'Angels in America,'" *New York*, April 7, 2008. http://nymag.com/anniversary/40th/culture/45774/.

p. 265 *"For the first-rate artist, there's a moment..."* Quoted in Lahr, "Tony Kushner: After Angels," 284.

p. 266 *"He sees how ridiculous the world is..."* Tony Kushner, "A Fan's Forward," in Charles Ludlam, *The Mystery of Irma Vep and Other Plays* (New York: Theatre Communications Group, 2001), vii.

p. 266 *"I never drink. And I never take drugs...."* Kushner, *Angels in America; Part One*, 32.

p. 267 *"Homosexuals are not men who sleep with other men..."* Ibid., 45.

p. 267 *Kushner has said that Louis is the character most like himself.* Lahr, "Tony Kushner: After Angels," 285.

p. 268 *"You sonofabitch..."* Kushner, *Angels in America: A Gay Fantasia on National Themes; Part Two: Perestroika* (New York: Theatre Communications Group, 1994), 126.

p. 268 *"the most thrilling American play in years..."* Frank Rich, "Embracing All Possibilities in Art and Life," *New York Times*, May 5, 1993. http://theater.nytimes.com/mem/theater/treview.html?res=9f0ce2dc1431f936a35756c0a965958260&scp=1&sq=angels%20in%20america&st=cse. The review of the Mark Taper production, also full of praise, was titled "Marching Out of the Closet, Into History." The *Times* never tired of the closet metaphor.

p. 270 *"a dialectically shaped truth."* Quoted in Lahr, "Tony Kushner: After Angels," 274.

p. 270 *"Greetings, Prophet;..."* Kushner, *Angels in America; Part One*, 119.

p. 270 *"Open me Prophet. I I I I am/The Book..."* Tony Kushner, *Angls in America; Part Two*, 47.

p. 271 *"I want more life. I can't help myself..."* Ibid., 135–136.

p. 271 *"I had the most remarkable dream..."* Ibid., 140.

p. 272 *"the play advocates the extinction of moral restraints..."* Roger Shattuck, "Scandal and Stereotypes on Broadway," in *Salmagundi*, Spring–Summer 1995; reprinted in *Candor and Perversion*, 388. Shattuck can't even get the subtitle right, calling it "A Gay Fantasy on American Themes."

p. 272 *"a second-rate play written by a second-rate playwright..."* Lee Siegel, *New Republic*, December 29, 2003. http://www.tnr.com/article/angles-america. He claims "the device of the angel is wonderfully campy, akin to the wild farces of Charles Lud-lam." No, it's not. "The angel is also a woman—with eight vaginas, we are told: the vagina dialogues!—who, in some sense, is tempting Prior to reject his love of men and live a 'normal' life...." But she also has eight penises and the future she offers is hardly normal. And so on. One suspects that if Siegel hadn't been bash-ing a popular gay writer the *New Republic* wouldn't have run such an incoherent essay. But they also ran his equally incoherent essay praising Stanley Kubrick's last movie, *Eyes Wide Shut*, as a masterpiece that was hated by Americans because we are all so stupid and corrupt.

p. 272 *"The enormous success of this muddled and pretentious play is a sign..."* Leo Bersani, *Homos* (Cambridge: Harvard University Press, 1995), 69.

p. 272 *"Gay life—and gay death—surely awaits something grander and subtler than this....never ascended...above a West Village version of Neil Simon..."* Andrew Sullivan, "Washington Diarist," *The New Republic*, June 21, 1993, 46. A curious note: John Simon quoted Sullivan in his generally positive review of *Angels* in *New York* magazine. Identifying the naysayer as "the homosexual editor of the *New Republic*," Simon could criticize a gay play without being accused *again* of being homophobic. (His chief criticism of the play was that despite it being well-written and full of good parts for actors, none of its characters come through its seven hours with their beliefs changed. But one could make the same complaint about the characters of two other American clas-sics, *A Long Day's Journey Into Night* and *A Streetcar Named Desire*.)

p. 273 *"I used to have a crush on Andrew..."* Tony Kushner, "A Socialism of the Skin (Liberation, Honey!)," *Nation*, July 4, 1994; reprinted in *Thinking about the Long-standing Problems*, 20.

p. 273 *"Bruce doesn't like it when gay men get dishy..."* Ibid., 21–22.

p. 274 *All in all, it was a lively hour of television. Charlie Rose*, PBS, June 24, 1994. The show can be seen on Google Video (http://video.google.com/videoplay?do cid=1121662526008590137); the transcript can be read in Vorlicky, ed., *Tony Kush-ner in Conversation*, 93–104.

p. 275 *"a pretentious left-wing screed..."* Quoted, with many other *Angel*-related entries, in another man's blog: The Sacred Moment, by Arthur Silber, January 3, 2004. http://thesacredmoment.blogspot.com/2004/01/angels-in-america-hymn-to -life.html. (These are no longer available on Sullivan's own blog site, The Daily Dish, which does not include an archive.)

Kushner always strove to give Sullivan his due. He acknowledged the real pain in Sullivan's essay, both in his own essay and on *Charlie Rose*. Later, in an interview in *Salon*, he said of Sullivan, "His homosexuality gave him a streak of decency." To my knowledge, Sullivan has never had a word of praise for Kushner.

p. 275 The Intelligent Homosexual's Guide...A chapter of the novel is published in Vorlicky, ed., *Tony Kushner in Conversation.*

p. 276 *"We won't die secret deaths anymore..."* Kushner, *Angels in America; Part Two,* 148.

CHAPTER 20. RISING TIDE

p. 277 *a group of editors and writers...*The first organizers of the Publishing Triangle were Michael Denneny of St. Martin's Press, David Groff of Crown, Trent Duffy of Dutton, and Robert Riger of the Book of the Month Club. They were soon joined by others, including editor Carol DeSantis of Dutton and publicist Michelle Karlsberg.

p. 278 *The first two OutWrites...*The panels and readings in San Francisco were organized by Jeffrey Escoffier, those in Boston by Michael Bronski.

p. 278 *"I don't think being gay is a subject any more than being straight is a subject...."* Quoted in Mel Gussow, *Edward Albee: A Singular Journey,* 350.

p. 278 *"Boo away..."* Quoted by Michael Bronski in conversation with the author, June 2010.

p. 278 *"Brothers and sisters!"* From the author's notes, April 1, 1992.

p. 278 *"I still don't know if the rectum is a grave..."* Tony Kushner, "On Pretentiousness"; reprinted in *Thinking about the Longstanding Problems,* 73.

p. 279 *"Baking lasagna has long been my own personal paradigm..."* Ibid., 61–62.

p. 279 *"Oral support of Edmund White at the Academy Meeting..."* Ned Rorem, *Lies: A Diary 1986–1999* (Washington: Counterpoint, 2000), 307–308.

p. 279 *"Two Deaths, Two Lives"* This essay by J. D. McClatchy appears in Edmund White, ed., *Loss within Loss* (Madison: University of Wisconsin Press, 2000). McClatchy gives some of Merrill's reasons for secrecy, and they aren't pretty: "He didn't want to become a spokesman, a hero, a case study. He didn't want to run away with the AIDS circus, in the company of a menagerie of less than minor talents hoisting a banner" (225).

p. 280 *"not good enough..."* "Michael Cunningham," in Richard Canning, *Hear Us Out: Conversations with Gay Novelists* (New York: Columbia University Press, 2003), 91.

p. 280 *"I had my head in the oven..."* "Michael Cunningham," in Philip Gambone, *Something Inside: Conversations with Gay Fiction Writers,* 143.

p. 281 *"She looked at me as if she were standing on a platform..."* Michael Cunningham, *A Home at the End of the World* (New York: Farrar, Straus, and Giroux, 1990), 76.

p. 282 *A few lesbian journalists even complained...* One occasionally heard this in conversation, but critic Victoria Brownworth also made the charge in an article, "Someone Has to Say No," in *Lambda Book Report* 2, no. 7 (November 1990).

There is no denying that gay male books did better than lesbian books, but other factors were involved. First there was the economics: anecdotally, gay men bought more hardcover books than lesbians did. Whether this was because gay men had more money or because lesbians were more frugal or because gay men outnumbered gay women is a topic for a different history. Whatever the cause, lesbian books were slower to turn a profit. Then there were the choices made by the editors. There were plenty of gay men and gay women in editorial staffs, but the men were in a better position—and were more willing—to stick their necks out for their own books. Carol DeSantis at Dutton took huge risks when she published novelist Sarah Schulman. Few of her peers at other mainstream houses did likewise. Finally, as several lesbian writers have pointed out, the women had fewer "out" elders. No major lesbian novelist spoke about her sexuality in the way that Christopher Isherwood or even Gore Vidal spoke about theirs. Adrienne Rich might talk of it in her poems and essays, but Susan Sontag remained coy about her sex life until she died. Gertrude Stein spent most of her life writing in modernist code. Alice Walker came out only late in her career.

p. 283 *"My own immorality didn't trouble me..."* Edmund White, *The Beautiful Room Is Empty* (New York: Knopf, 1988), 50–51.

p. 283 *Now everyone is at work on him at once..."* Ibid., 78.

p. 284 *" 'Gay is good.' We were all chanting it,..."* Ibid., 226.

p. 285 *"Hubert Sorin, my lover, who just died two hours ago..."* Edmund White, *Our Paris*, 131–133.

p. 286 *"intolerable to read in this post-AIDS period..."* Quoted in Richard Canning, *Gay Fiction Speaks: Conversations with Gay Novelists*, 84. White expanded on these reasons in his essay "Writing Gay," which was reprinted in *Arts and Letters*.

p. 286 *"First I had to finish the Genet book,..."* Quoted in Stephen Barber, *Edmund White: The Burning World* (New York: St. Martin's Press, 1999), 285.

p. 287 *"In Eddie the man I detected a perversity..."* Edmund White, *The Farewell Symphony*, 241. I have removed the phrase "a pear-shaped body," which is a fictional disguise. Merrill was always lean and unearthly.

p. 287 *"I supposed Ridgefield [Westcott] would assign us both to Brunetto Latini's [Dante's] ring in hell..."* Ibid., 191.

p. 288 *One reviewer, the usually hypercritical Dale Peck...* Dale Peck, "True Lies," *Voice Literary Supplement*, Fall 1997, 14. Christopher Benfey seemed to praise this gap, too, when he said, "This is an excruciating absence...around which the book, like scar tissue, is constructed." ("The Dead," *New York Times Book Review*, September 14, 1997. http://www.nytimes.com/books/97/09/14/reviews/970914.14benfeyt.html?scp=1&sq=farewell%20symphony%20by%20edmund%20white&st=cse.)

p. 289 *He continued to revise the screenplay for Barbra Streisand...* Patrick Merla, "A Normal Heart," *We Must Love One Another*, 67.

p. 290 *Kramer asked to see the advance galleys...* Edmund White, e-mail message to the author, October 3, 2010.

p. 290 *"[H]e parades before the reader what seems to be every trick..."* Larry Kramer, "Sex and Sensibility," *Advocate*, May 27, 1997, 59–60. For the record, the narrator of *The Farewell Symphony* never reports anyone being rimmed or tied up. There is only one reference to watersports, already quoted.

p. 291 *including the op-ed page of the* New York Times.... Larry Kramer, "Gay Culture, Redefined," *New York Times*, December 12, 1997. http://partners.nytimes.com/library/national/science/aids/121297sci-aids.html?scp=2&sq=larry%20kramer%20%22gay%20culture,%20redefined%22&st=cse. This was couched as an attack on a small, ad hoc group, Sex Panic, which he said "advocates unconditional, unlimited promiscuity." They didn't. They only wanted to stop the recent demonization of sex and wave of arrests in public places. But the mere mention of sex seemed to make Kramer irrational.

And he can still appear irrational. Recently, in 2010, Kramer admitted in an interview that he was visiting hook-up sites online, with his partner's permission. "There must be an awful lot of older men like me who are hungry for another sexual chapter before they die." He did not think he was being a hypocrite, but said his old denunciation of sex was necessary for the times. (Tony Adams, "The Fresh Bile and Sex Life of Larry Kramer," *South Florida Gay News*, May 2, 2010. http://www.southfloridagaynews.com/sfgn-columnists/columnists/tony-adams-column/1297-the-fresh-bile-and-sex-life-of-larry-kramer.html.)

CHAPTER 21. HIGH TIDE

p. 292 *Annual deaths from AIDS peaked in the United States in 1995 at 50,000....* Figures from University of California San Francisco *HIV InSite*. http://hivinsite.ucsf.edu/InSite?page=kb-01-03.

p. 294 *Cunningham himself said in an interview in* Poz... Joy Episalla, "Dances with Woolf," *Poz* magazine, February 2000. http://www.poz.com/articles/198_10543.shtml.

p. 295 *"Learning you're going to live..."* Quoted in Gale, *Armistead Maupin*, 76.

p. 296 *"Tony's like God..."* Tad Friend, "Virtual Love," *New Yorker*, November 26, 2001, 88. The story gets even weirder and more complicated after the period covered in *The Night Listener*. Friend reports how a TV producer, Lesley Karstein, became involved, and there was talk of an HBO movie. Tony appeared in a documentary—but it was only an actor playing Tony. Vicki Johnson continued to insist she must protect Tony, since the pedophile ring—which she claimed included Ed Koch and Sammy Davis Jr.—could still be after him. Then Vicki met a psychologist named Dr. Zackheim, moved to Chicago, and left Tony with Ms. Karstein back in New York.

It was Tad Friend who identified Vicki Johnson as Joanne Vicki Fraginals. By the time Friend started writing his article, Tony had disappeared. But in a chilling twist, Friend received a flurry of e-mails from Tony. Then Tony fell silent again. Friend closes his article with the first letter Maupin received from Tony, a Christmas card that included Francis P. Church's famous quote from the September 21, 1897, *New York Sun*: "Yes, Virginia, there is a Santa Claus. He exists as certainly as love and generosity and devotion exist.... The most real things in the world are those that neither children nor men can see."

p. 297 *"I know how it sounds when I call him my son...."* Armistead Maupin, *The Night Listener* (New York: HarperCollins, 2000), 1.

p. 297 *"Artful Dodger by way of Bart Simpson..."* Ibid., 28.

p. 297 *"Do you know why he left?..."* Ibid., 46.

p. 299 *"I wrote the ending of the book the way I'd like it to be in life..."* Quoted in Friend, "Virtual Love."

p. 299 *"To be taken in everywhere is to see the inside..."* G. K. Chesterton, *Charles Dickens* (London: Methuen & Co., 1906), 70–71.

EPILOGUE: REWRITING AMERICA

p. 302 *"Kiss me..."* Gore Vidal, *Point to Point Navigation*, 82.

p. 302 *"As I now move, graciously, I hope,..."* Ibid., 1.

p. 302 *"That play implies that I am madly in love with McVeigh..."* Tim Teeman, "Gore Vidal: 'We'll Have a Dictatorship Soon in the US,'" *Times* (London), September 30, 2009. http://women.timesonline.co.uk/tol/life_and_style/women/the_way_we_live/article6854221.ece.

p. 303 *The sales figures tell one story...* The figures for *City and the Pillar* are only hardcover—a paperback wasn't issued until five years later. *Night Listener* sold 58,000 in hardcover and 42,000 in trade paper during its first year. (Figures from Rakesh Satyal at HarperCollins.)

Selected Bibliography

Primary Works

Albee, Edward. *Collected Plays of Edward Albee, Vol. 1 (1958–1965)*. Woodstock, NY: Overlook, 2004.

———. *Who's Afraid of Virginia Woolf?* New York: New American Library, 2006.

Baldwin, James. *Another Country*. New York: Dial Press, 1962.

———. *Collected Essays*. New York: Library of America, 1998.

———. *Giovanni's Room*. New York: Dial Press, 1956.

———. *Go Tell It on the Mountain*. New York: Knopf, 1953.

Bumbalo, Victor. *What Are Tuesdays Like?* New York: Broadway Play Publishing, 2010.

Cameron, Peter. *Someday This Pain Will Be Useful to You*. New York: Farrar, Straus, and Giroux, 2007.

Capote, Truman. *Answered Prayers: The Unfinished Novel*. New York: Random House, 1987.

———. *Breakfast at Tiffany's*. New York: Modern Library, 1994.

———. *In Cold Blood*. New York: Random House, 1966.

———. *Other Voices, Other Rooms*. New York: Modern Library, 2004.

Crowley, Mart. *The Boys in the Band*. New York: Alyson, 2008.

———. *The Collected Plays of Mart Crowley*. New York: Alyson, 2009.

Cunningham, Michael. *A Home at the End of the World*. New York: Farrar, Straus, and Giroux, 1990.

———. *The Hours*. New York: Farrar, Straus, and Giroux, 1999.

Dixon, Melvin. *Love's Instruments*. New York: Tia Chucha, 1995.

Doty, Mark. *Turtle, Swan & Bethlehem in Broad Daylight*. Urbana: University of Illinois Press, 2000.

———. *Fire to Fire: New and Collected Poems*. New York: HarperCollins, 2008.

Ginsberg, Allen. *Collected Poems, 1947–1997*. New York: HarperCollins, 2007.

———. *Howl and Other Poems*. San Francisco: City Lights Books, 1956.

Gunn, Thom. *Collected Poems*. New York: Farrar, Straus, and Giroux, 1994.

Holleran, Andrew. *Dancer from the Dance*. New York: Morrow, 1978.

————. *Ground Zero*. New York: Morrow, 1988.

Isherwood, Christopher. *The Berlin Stories*. New York: New Directions, 1954.

————. *Christopher and His Kind*. New York: Farrar, Straus, and Giroux, 1976.

————. *Diaries, Vol. 1(1939–1960)*. ed. Katherine Bucknell. New York: Harper Collins, 1996.

————. *Down There on a Visit*. New York: Simon and Schuster, 1962.

————. *A Single Man*. New York: Simon and Schuster, 1964.

————. *The World in the Evening*. New York: Random House, 1954.

Kramer, Larry. *Faggots*. New York: Random House, 1978.

————. *The Normal Heart and The Destiny of Me*. New York: Grove, 2000.

————. *Reports from the Holocaust*. New York: St. Martin's Press, 1989.

Kushner, Tony. *Angels in America: Part 1*. New York: Theatre Communications Group, 1993.

————. *Angels in America: Part 2*. New York: Theatre Communications Group, 1994.

————. *Plays by Tony Kushner*. (*A Bright Room Called Day* and *The Illusionist*.) New York: Theatre Communications Group, 1992.

————. *Thinking about the Longstanding Problems of Virtue and Happiness*. New York: Theatre Communications Group, 1995.

Ludlam, Charles. *The Complete Plays of Charles Ludlam*. New York: Harper and Row, 1989.

————. *Ridiculous Theater: Scourge of Human Folly*, ed. Steven Samuels. New York: Theatre Communications Group, 1992.

Maupin, Armistead. *Babycakes*. New York: Harper and Row, 1984.

————. *More Tales of the City*. New York: Harper and Row, 1979.

————. *The Night Listener*. New York: HarperCollins, 2000.

————. *Significant Others*. New York: Harper and Row, 1987.

————. *Sure of You*. New York: HarperCollins, 1989.

————. *Tales of the City*. New York: Harper and Row, 1978.

McCauley, Stephen. *The Object of My Affection*. New York: Simon and Schuster, 1987.

Merlis, Mark. *An Arrow's Flight*. New York, St. Martin's Press, 1998.

Merrill, James. *The Changing Light at Sandover*. New York, Atheneum, 1982.

————. *A Different Person*. New York: Knopf, 1993.

————. *Divine Comedies*. New York: Atheneum, 1976.

————. *Selected Poems*. New York: Knopf, 2008.

Nava, Michael. *Howtown*. New York: HarperCollins, 1990.

O'Hara, Frank. *Selected Poems*. New York: Knopf, 2008.

Russell, Paul. *Sea of Tranquillity*. New York: Dutton, 1994.

Saytal, Rakesh. *Blue Boy*. New York: Kensington, 2009.

Vidal, Gore. *Burr*. New York: Random House, 1973.

————. *The City and the Pillar*. New York: Dutton, 1948. (Revised 1965.)

————. *Matters of Fact and Fiction: Essays 1973–1976*. New York: Random House, 1977.

————. *Myra Breckinridge*. Boston: Little, Brown, 1968.

————. *The Second American Revolution and Other Essays (1976–1982)*. New York: Random House, 1982.

White, Edmund. *The Beautiful Room Is Empty*. New York: Knopf, 1988.

————. *A Boy's Own Story*. New York: Dutton, 1982.

————. *Caracole*. New York: Dutton, 1985.

————. *The Farewell Symphony*. New York: Knopf: 1997.

————. *The Married Man*. New York: Knopf, 2000.

————. *Nocturnes for the King of Naples*. New York: St. Martin's Press, 1978.

————. *States of Desire*. New York: Dutton, 1980.

Williams, Tennessee. *Collected Stories*. New York: New Directions, 1985.

————. *Memoirs*. Garden City: Doubleday, 1975.

————. *Plays, 1937–1955*. New York: Library of America, 2000.

Biography, Criticism, and History

Bachardy, Don. *Christopher Isherwood: Last Drawings*. London, Boston: Faber and Faber, 1990.

Bergman, David, ed. *The Violet Quill Reader*. New York: St. Martin's Press, 1994.

Berube, Allan. *Coming Out Under Fire*. New York: Free Press, 1990.

Bronski, Michael. *Pulp Friction*. New York: St. Martin's Press, 2003.

Campbell, James. *Thom Gunn in Conversation with James Campbell*. London: BTL, 2000.

————. *Talking at the Gates: A Life of James Baldwin*. New York: Viking, 1991.

Canning, Richard. *Gay Fiction Speaks: Conversations with Gay Novelists*. New York: Columbia University Press, 2001.

————. *Hear Us Out: Conversations with Gay Novelists*. New York: Columbia University Press, 2004.

Clark, Philip, and David Groff, eds. *Persistent Voices: Poetry by Writers Lost to AIDS*. New York: Alyson, 2010.

Clarke, Gerald. *Capote*. New York: Simon and Schuster, 1988.

Cleaver, Eldridge. *Soul on Ice*. New York: Dell, 1968.

Curtin, Kaier. *We Can Always Call Them Bulgarians*. Boston: Alyson, 1988.

Davenport-Hines, Richard. *Auden*. New York: Pantheon, 1996.

Duberman, Martin. *Stonewall*. New York: Dutton, 1993.

Gale, Patrick. *Armistead Maupin*. Bath, England: Absolute, 1999.

Gussow, Mel. *Edward Albee: A Singular Journey*. New York: Simon and Schuster, 1989.

Gambone, Philip. *Something Inside: Conversations with Gay Writers*. Madison: University of Wisconsin Press, 1999.

Kaplan, Fred. *Gore Vidal.* New York: Doubleday, 1999.

Kaufman, David. *Ridiculous! The Theatrical Life and Times of Charles Ludlam.* New York: Applause, 2002.

Lahr, John. *Honky Tonk Parade.* Woodstock, NY: Overlook, 2005.

LeSueur, Joe. *Digressions on Some Poems by Frank O'Hara.* New York: Farrar, Straus, and Giroux, 2003.

Mailer, Norman. *Advertisements for Myself.* New York: Putnam, 1959.

———. *Pieces and Pontifications.* Boston: Little, Brown, 1982.

Mass, Lawrence, ed. *We Must Love One Another or Die.* New York: St. Martin's, 1997.

Merla, Patrick, ed. *Boys Like Us: Gay Writers Tell Their Coming Out Stories.* New York: Avon, 1996.

Miles, Barry. *Ginsberg.* London: Virgin, 2001.

Paller, Michael. *Gentlemen Callers.* New York: Palgrave Macmillan, 2005.

Parker, Peter. *Isherwood: A Life.* London: Picador, 2005.

Rich, Adrienne. *On Lies, Secrets, and Silence: Selected Prose, 1966–1978.* New York: Norton, 1979.

Rorem, Ned. *Other Entertainments.* New York: Simon and Schuster, 1996.

Schumacher, Michael, ed. *Family Business: Selected Letters Between a Father and a Son, Allen and Louis Ginsberg.* New York: Bloomsbury USA, 2002.

Sherry, Michael. *Gay Artists in Modern American Culture.* Chapel Hill: University of North Carolina Press, 2007.

Sontag, Susan. *A Susan Sontag Reader.* New York: Farrar, Straus, and Giroux, 1982.

Trilling, Diana. *Reviewing the Forties.* New York: Harcourt Brace Jovanovich, 1978.

Weatherby, W. J. *James Baldwin: Artist on Fire.* New York: Donald I. Fine: 1989.

White, Edmund, ed. *Loss within Loss: Artists in the Age of AIDS.* Madison: University of Wisconsin Press, 2001.

Windham, Donald. *Lost Friendships.* New York: Morrow, 1987.

Permissions

Index

About the Author

Christopher Bram is the author of nine novels, including *The Father of Frankenstein* (which was made into the Academy-Award-winning movie *Gods And Monsters*), *Lives of the Circus Animals*, and *Exiles in America*. He also writes book reviews, movie reviews, screenplays, and essays. He was a 2001 Guggenheim Fellow and received the 2003 Bill Whitehead Award for Lifetime Achievement. He grew up in Virginia, attended the College of William and Mary, and currently teaches at Gallatin College at New York University. He lives in New York City.